Saint Thomas More

SAINT THOMAS MORE

A Great Man in Hard Times

by
E. E. REYNOLDS

Reproduced faithfully from the original by:

MEDIATRIX PRESS

www.mediatrixpress.com

St. Thomas More
Reprinted from the Image Books edition of 1958.

ISBN: 978-1-953746-45-0

NIHIL OBSTAT:
P. MORRIS, S.T.D., L.S.S.
CENSOR DEPVTATVS

IMPRIMATVR: E. MORROGH BERNARD
VICARIVS GENERALIS
Westmonasterii:
die XV Maii MCMLIII

© Mediatrix Press, 2017
607 E. 6th St., Ste 230
Post Falls, ID 83854
www.mediatrixpress.com

This work may not be reproduced in electronic or physical format for commercial purposes.

TABLE OF CONTENTS

PREFACE XI

CHAPTER I
    THE HOUSEHOLD OF SIR THOMAS MORE 1

CHAPTER II
    BOYHOOD AND YOUTH 9

CHAPTER III
    THE YOUNG LAWYER 21

CHAPTER VI
    THE RISING LAWYER 59

CHAPTER VII
    RICHARD III 69

CHAPTER VIII
    SIGNS OF THE TIMES 83

CHAPTER IX
    EMBASSY TO FLANDERS 91

CHAPTER X
    UTOPIA 109

CHAPTER XI
    COUNCILLOR 125

CHAPTER XII
    THE SCHOOL 143

CHAPTER XIII
 'THE FOUR LAST THINGS'........................ 155

CHAPTER XIV
 THE PARLIAMENT OF 1523 175

CHAPTER XV
 CHELSEA...................................... 189

CHAPTER XVI
 CHANCELLOR OF THE DUCHY OF LANCASTER 207

CHAPTER XVII
 HERESY 219

CHAPTER XVIII
 LORD CHANCELLOR 239

CHAPTER XIX
 TYNDALE 255

CHAPTER XX
 RESIGNATION 263

CHAPTER XXI
 THE APOLOGYE................................. 275

CHAPTER XXII
 THE NUN OF KENT 293

CHAPTER XXIII
 THE OATH 313

CHAPTER XXIV
 IN THE TOWER 321

CHAPTER XXV
  THE INTERROGATIONS................................. 337

CHAPTER XXVI
  'WHILE HE WAS A PRISONER'....................... 355

CHAPTER XXVII
  THE TRIAL... 371

CHAPTER XXVIII
  'THE FIELD IS WON'................................... 385

CHAPTER XXIX
  FROM MARTYRDOM TO CANONIZATION.............. 397

BIBLIOGRAPHY... 407

APPENDIX
  GENEALOGICAL TABLE................................. 419

Preface

ANYONE who now writes about Saint Thomas More must acknowledge, as I do, indebtedness to those who have done so much to increase our knowledge of him and his times during the past fifty years or more. At the head of such a list of benefactors must be put the name of Father Thomas E. Bridgett (1829-99). He was baptised a member of the Church of England; while he was a student at St. John's College, Cambridge, a study of the life of Saint John Fisher, the faithful servant of the foundress of that College, led him to consider the claims of the Catholic Church. This 'made me refuse the oath of royal supremacy then required for a degree, and thus obliged me to leave Cambridge in 1850, and seek reconciliation with the Catholic Church.' He entered the order of the Congregation of the Most Holy Redeemer, and was ordained priest in 1856. For some years he laboured in Ireland, and there founded the Confraternity of the Holy Family for men. He returned to London in 1871, and from that date devoted his talents to the writing of books based on his wide learning and careful research. His biographies of Saint John Fisher (1888) and of Saint Thomas More (1891) were the most influential of his writings.

Father Bridgett took full advantage of the publication of the *Letters and Papers of the Reign of Henry VIII*; he wrote, 'with these great volumes as my help and guide, I had already become pretty familiar with all that bears on the life of More when composing my life of his fellow-martyr Blessed John Fisher; but I have gone through all the volumes a second time, and sought out the originals in the Record Office or British Museum wherever there seemed to remain anything to be cleared up.' This work he did thoroughly and with scrupulous accuracy as any one can testify who has gone over the same ground. The result was a notable book that stood four-square against all attacks.

The book now bears marks of the period in which it was

written; the passage of time has robbed some of the controversial parts of their original force, and this was in large measure the result of Father Bridgett's effective advocacy. It must be remembered that the first four volumes of Froude's *History* (1856) strongly reinforced the extreme Protestant interpretation of early Tudor history, and his picture of More as a 'merciless bigot' who 'fed the stake with heretics' was accepted by many thousands of readers as the truth. Another book also influenced opinion. Frederic Seebohm's most persuasively written *Oxford Reformers of 1498* was published in 1867. Even the title was specious, and Father Bridgett considered 'the whole book to be fantastic and misleading, built up from conjectures and misunderstandings and by false deductions.'[1] In his own biography, therefore, he did valiant work in combating the erroneous ideas that Froude and Seebohm had helped to establish.

Father Bridgett had some notable allies in his struggle to get the history of the days of Fisher and More in true perspective. The names of non-Catholics such as Dr. James Gairdner and Canon R. W. Dixon come to mind. Their work was followed by the historical studies of H. A. L. Fisher, and above all, of A. F. Pollard and his school. Later, a group of scholars devoted themselves to the study of the biographical sources of the life of More and to his English writings; their achievement is recorded in the Early English Text Society's editions of the lives by Roper, Harpsfield, and Ro. Ba., and in the fine and stimulating biography written by Professor R. W. Chambers (1935) in which he put most emphasis on the literary and political aspects of More's life. His chief partners were Dr. Elsie V. Hitchcock and Professor A. W. Reed.

Amongst Catholics should first be mentioned Mgr. P. E. Hallett, who, in addition to editing new editions of some of the

---

[1] It is difficult to know what influence these books now have, but both were reprinted in Everyman's Library, and so presumably had a public.

works, made the first translation into English of the life contained in Thomas Stapleton's *Tres Thomae*, published in Latin at Douai three hundred and forty years earlier. The ambitious project of a reprint of all More's English Works, based on Rastell's edition of 1557, was begun in 1931 under the editorship of W. E. Campbell. The decision to combine this with a facsimile of the Rastell edition was unfortunate; it increased the cost and deterred the general reader who had no wish for the Black Letter section of each volume; no one reads Black Letter for fun! War interrupted this project.

Mention may also be made of the Thomas More Society which was formed by members of the Bench and the Bar in 1928. Its purpose was 'to study and discuss intellectual problems touching law and legislation.' The published proceedings are not, therefore, all directly concerned with Sir Thomas More, but they include a number of important contributions dealing with his life and ideas. In particular may be mentioned R. W. Chambers's *Place of St. Thomas More in English Literature and History* (published separately, 1937), and

W. Reed's 'Young More,' in the volume *Under God and the Law* (1949).

The year 1947 saw the completion of two projects of importance to students of More. The eleventh and final volume of the Allen edition of the *Epistles of Erasmus* was published, and in the same year appeared the long-awaited *Correspondence of Sir Thomas More*, edited by Elizabeth Frances Rogers. This volume does not include the correspondence with Erasmus but references are given to the relevant volumes of the Allen edition. These volumes did not contain hitherto unknown letters, but previously it had been necessary to consult many volumes in order to read the full correspondence, and some of these were to be seen only in the greater libraries. Now it is possible to study the whole correspondence in chronological order; this in itself reveals some points that would otherwise evade notice.

My purpose in writing this new biography has been to gather together the results of these many inquiries and studies. I have emphasized the religious rather than the literary or political significance of Saint Thomas More's life. In doing so, I am following the example of Father Bridgett, and I have also adopted his method of generous quotation. He gave as his reason for this the fact that More's works (apart from Robinson's translation of *Utopia*) were not easily accessible; while it is true that some of the works have since been printed, some are now out of print, and others are expensive, or published in editions intended for the scholar. I have also followed Father Bridgett's practice of modernizing the spelling; Tudor spelling has its interest for specialists, but it is an obstacle to comfortable reading. I have added [in square brackets] modern equivalents of archaic words and expressions.

More than forty years have passed since my interest in Sir Thomas More was first roused by reading the chapter on him in Sir Sidney Lee's *Great Englishmen of the Sixteenth Century* (1904). Lee was baffled by what he regarded as the great paradox of More's life: here was an enlightened scholar dying for 'what seems, in the dry light of reason, to be superstition.' Yet this contradiction, as he regarded it, did not prevent Lee from conveying to his young reader a deep admiration for Sir Thomas More. From that time I have read all I could find in print by, or about, More, and I trust that in these pages I have shown that there was indeed no paradox to be resolved; his faith in 'Christ's Catholic known Church,' as he liked to call it, is the key to his life and death and glory.

I hope that my references in the notes and in the bibliography adequately express my obligations, but in the course of many years one gathers impressions whose origins can no longer be traced. The bibliography of More's own writings is, I believe, within the limits I have set myself, more comprehensive than any other now in print. F. and M. P. Sullivan, Rockhurst College,

Kansas, U.S.A., prepared (1946) a 'preliminary check list of material by and about Saint Thomas More.' This *Moreana* is not generally available, so I am all the more grateful for the gift of a copy. They hope to publish later a revised edition; this should be a valuable contribution to the study of Saint Thomas More and his works.

Acknowledgement is due to the executors of the late F. M. Nichols for permission to quote from his translation of the *Epistles of Erasmus*, and to Messrs. Basil Blackwell for permission to quote from G. C. Richards' translation of *Utopia*.

E. E. R.

Chapter I

The Household of Sir Thomas More

IN the late summer of 1526, Hans Holbein left Basle for Antwerp with a letter of introduction from Erasmus to Peter Gilles, the Chief Secretary of that city. The scholar wrote: 'Here the arts are coldly treated; he makes for England (Angliam) in the hope of collecting some gold angels (Angelatos).'[1] So Peter Gilles sent Holbein on to his friend Sir Thomas More who had recently moved into his new house in Chelsea. Here he welcomed the young artist who brought with him the commendations of two such friends. This was a fortunate meeting for the outcome was a series of incomparable studies and portraits that gives us the best picture we have of a Tudor family.

Sir Thomas More wrote to Erasmus in December. 'Your painter, my dearest Erasmus, is a wonderful artist; but I fear he will not find England the rich and fertile field he had hoped; however, lest he find it quite barren, I will do what I can.'[2] He commissioned Holbein to paint the family portraits. Only one has survived as Holbein left it; fortunately, this is the portrait of More himself.[3] A painting of Lady Alice More[4] may be substantially Holbein's work, but it lacks his final touches; a portrait of

---

[1] *Allen*, VI, 1740.

[2] *Ibid.* 1770.

[3] Frick Collection, New York.

[4] In possession of Lord Methuen.

Margaret Roper[5] is probably a copy of an original by Holbein.

Eight drawings[6] in the Windsor Collection were studies either for the separate paintings or for the large family group with its life-size figures. A sketch for this is now at Basle and was brought to Erasmus by Holbein on his return home in the Summer of 1528. A year passed before Erasmus wrote to Margaret Roper:

> I cannot find words to express the joy I felt when the painter Holbein gave me the picture of your whole family which is so completely successful that I should scarcely be able to see you better if I were with you. I often hope that at least once before my last day I may look upon that most dear society to which I owe a great part of whatever little fortune or glory I possess, and to none could I be more willingly indebted. The painter's skill has given me no small part of my desire. I recognize you all, but no one better than yourself. I seem to behold through all your beautiful household a soul shining forth still more beautiful. I felicitate you all on that family happiness, but most of all your excellent father.[7]

Holbein's own painting of the group has disappeared, but copies were made by inferior artists. The best is now at Nostell Priory; this was painted in 1530 by Rowland Locky and has come down from the Roper family. Some experts believe that Holbein left this painting unfinished and that Locky completed it, but though the composition is Holbein's, the work is too laboured and stiff to have owed much to his brush.

A study of the sketch and of the painting will set the scene for this biography of the central figure.

---

[5] In possession of Lord Sackville.

[6] For the sake of clearness, the following terms will here be used: 'drawing', for studies of separate persons at Windsor; 'sketch', for the Basle sketch of the group; 'painting' for the Locky and other versions of the family group now at Nostell Priory.

[7] *Allen*, VIII, 2212.

The sketch gives a better idea of the furniture of the hall or room than the painting. Locky draped the pieces in dull coverings quite unlike the tapestries and other cloths that Holbein loved to paint in detail. In the right-hand corner at the back is an interior porch with a fleur-de-lis cresting; on the left, against the wall, is a buffet; the back is of linen-fold or wavy woodwork and the canopy repeats the fleur-de-lis cresting of the porch. Some plate and a vase of flowers are on the buffet. The painting adds a lute and a viol in accordance with a note written by Holbein on the sketch against a viol hanging on the wall: *Klafikordi und ander seyte spill uf dem bank*—clavichord and other instruments on the shelf. There are three books on the buffet in the painting; one is marked '*Consolatione*,' the *De consolatione* of Boethius. In front of a plain green wall-hanging in the painting is a weight-driven chamber clock[8] suspended from the ceiling which is of wood with moulded beams. On the right is a window with clear diamond glazing, and on the ledge, more plate, a candlestick and two books. The sketch suggests that the floor was covered with rushes, but the painting shows some kind of cloth covering.

Two aspects of the sketch must impress the most casual observer. The room and its furnishings show that More's house at Chelsea was designed in a style that was new fashioned; only forty years had passed since the Battle of Bosworth, yet here is a domestic interior that, at first glance, might be described as Elizabethan. The second impression is that the family was cultured; the musical instruments and the books (there are a dozen in the sketch) indicate this, but the attitudes and expressions of the members of the group are sufficient in

---

[8] This is in the possession of the Waterton family, the best-known member of which was Charles Waterton, the naturalist. He was the grandson of Anne More, a direct descendant through Cresacre More (1572-1649) of Sir Thomas More. See Thomas Raworth's article, 'St. Thomas More's Clock' in *The Month*, June 1952. It is difficult to say how much of the original clock has survived; the dial is certainly mid-seventeenth century.

themselves to mark a family where intellectual pursuits were congenial.

The sketch is a more lively representation of the More family than the painting. A critic has written: 'The brilliant characterization in the drawing of each individual is, even today, among the most outstanding achievements of Holbein's art.'[9] A small reproduction cannot bring out the finish of the drawing; every line is firm and unhesitating.

In the centre of the group is Sir Thomas More. There are two drawings of him at Windsor; one of these, marked in a contemporary hand 'Sier Thomas Mooer,' was made for this group; the second, and more frequently reproduced, was later inscribed 'Tho: Moor Ld Chancelour,' and was for the separate portrait. They can be distinguished by the fashion of the hair; in the sketch this is swept back, while in the portrait the ends curl forward. Sir Thomas is wearing the ordinary cap and furred robe of the period, and carries a muff[10] on his left arm; he wears the livery collar of SS and portcullis with the rose pendant of Lancaster; he was not yet Lord Chancellor.

The portrait can be supplemented by a description written by Erasmus eight years earlier.

> In build and stature he is not what would be described as tall, but he is not noticeably short; and there is such proportion in all his limbs that it never occurs to one to wish him in any way different. His skin is bright and clear, and so, too, his face, which is neither pale nor ruddy, except for a faint glow which shines over it all. His hair is auburn, tinged with black, or, if you like, black tinged with auburn; his beard thin, his eyes blue-grey, but with spots of different colour—a

---

[9] Paul Ganz (Phaidon 'Holbein,' 1950).

[10] I am aware that the experts state that the muff did not come into use until the end of the sixteenth century, but as they cannot suggest any other name for the object on More's left arm, I must call it a muff.

kind which is thought to show a very happy temperament, and is much liked in England, though our countrymen prefer black. No eyes, they say, are more free from blemish. His nature may be read in his face, always pleasant and friendly and cheerful, with a readiness to smile: indeed its inclination is towards merriment rather than to grave dignity, though very far removed from silly buffoonery.[11]

The reference to More's thin beard (*barba rarior*) may seem surprising as the drawings give the impression of a clean-shaven face. A close examination of the portrait reveals a stubble as if, like some countrymen today, he shaved, or was shaved, only once a week.[12]

Holbein's portrait does not give the impression that More was 'always pleasant and friendly and cheerful.' A stranger to his life and character might be excused if he thought this the portrait of a stern man of powerful intellect. Perhaps Holbein was unable to depict lighter moods, for in the whole range of his portraits there is not one really cheerful face; his own self-portrait, with its rather sullen expression, may be the measure of his limitation. The grimness of the period was doubtless reflected in the faces of men whose fortunes were precarious; but in 1527 the clouds were still distant.

It is fortunate that a brief note has been written against each figure in the sketch. The writer was Nicolaus Kratzer (1487-1550)[13], Astronomer to Henry VIII, who taught astronomy in the More household. Holbein's fine portrait of him, painted in 1528, is

---

[11] To Ulrich von Hutten, 23rd July, 1519. *Allen*, IV, 999. Allen's translation.

[12] In 1550 a rule was made at Lincoln's Inn that no member should 'wear a beard above a fortnight's growth.' *Allen* (IV, p. 1n) suggests that More had a beard but shaved it off before Holbein painted the portrait. I think my explanation is more reasonable as it complies with the shaving habits of the time.

[13] This has, I think, been convincingly argued by Otto Pächt in *Burlington Magazine*, 1944, p. 138.

now in the Louvre. If only we knew whether the sketch was made in 1526 or in 1527, problems of dates of birth would be solved. More's own portrait has the date 1527 on the edge of the table; in the sketch is the note 'Thomas Morus, anno 50.' The round number, 50, has tempted some writers to suggest that the painting was a gift in celebration of More's fiftieth birthday, but Holbein's first visit to England was fortuitous, and More's letter to Erasmus, already quoted, implies that Holbein was employed on the obviously immediate commission.

The first figure on the left in the sketch is inscribed, *Elizebeta Dancia Thomae*[14] *Mori filia anno* 21. She was the second of Thomas More's daughters and married William Daunce, 29th September, 1525. In the sketch she is shown as pregnant; she carries a book under her arm which, in the painting, is labelled around the edge *Epistolica Senecae*. Next to her stands Margaret Gigs; the inscription reads, *Margareta Giga Clementis uxor Thomæ Mori filiabus condiscipula et cognata anno* 22. She was brought up with the More children, and, it has been suggested,[15] was the daughter of the foster-mother of Margaret More (Roper) who was born in the same year as the other Margaret. She married John Clement before 1526.

In the painting, the positions of these two figures have been interchanged; Margaret Gigs is depicted in a simpler headdress[16] than the one she has in the sketch. The drawing (incorrectly labelled by a later hand 'Mother Jak') shows her wearing the plain head-dress of the painting and in a similar attitude. This indicates

---

[14] On the sketch the -æ is written -e as was usual in Vulgar Latin.

[15] *Roper*, p. 128.

[16] The same head-dress is seen in the beautiful picture of 'Lady with Squirrel and Starling.' (Ganz, in Phaidon 'Holbein', persists in calling the bird a magpie). How much one wishes this were a portrait of Margaret Gigs! There seems no firm reason, outside the critics' imaginations, for saying that the Lady 'belonged to the More circle.' This lovely picture was discovered in 1925.

that the change was Holbein's and that the separate drawings were made after the sketch. The change is not an improvement in the composition; in the sketch Margaret Gigs is bending down towards Sir John More and is pointing to an open book she is holding: the total effect is more intimate than that made by the two rather stiff figures in the painting. Perhaps it was felt desirable to bring the daughter, Elizabeth, more closely into the family circle than she was placed in the sketch.

The next figure is that of Sir John More; the inscription reads, *Johannes Morus pater anno* 76. He is sitting on a bench or settle with his son. His red judge's robe makes a conspicuous splash of colour. He also has a muff on his left arm.

Standing at the back, between Sir John and Sir Thomas, is the diminutive figure of Anne Cresacre, a ward of Thomas More. She is described as, *Anna Grisacria Johannes Mori sponsa anno 15.* She married John More in 1529. He is standing at his father's side: *Johannes Morus Thomæ filius anno* 19. He is bareheaded and holds an open book in his hand. Holbein noted on the drawing, '*lipfarb brun*'—brown complexion.

Next to John More is Henry Patenson, Thomas More's jester or domestic fool: *Henricus Patensonus Thomæ Mori morio anno* 40. He later entered the service of the Lord Mayor of London.

More's two daughters, Margaret and Cecily, are in the foreground of the sketch. The inscriptions read, *Cecilia Herona Thomae Mori filia anno* 20, and, *Margareta Ropera Thomae Mori filia anno* 22. Cecily has what may be a rosary in her left hand, but this is not seen in the painting. She has a book in her lap. Cecily was married to Giles Heron on the same day that her sister Elizabeth married William Daunce, 29th September, 1525. Margaret More married William Roper on 2nd July, 1521. In the painting she is shown with a copy of Seneca's *Œdipus* in her lap.

In the sketch, Lady Alice More is on the extreme right; she is kneeling at a prie-dieu on which is a book of devotion; a pet monkey is clawing at her skirt. The inscription reads, *Alicia*

Thomæ Mori uxor anno 57. At the edge is a note in Holbein's hand, '*dise soli sitzen*'—and she is accordingly shown seated in the painting.

Some of the changes in the painting have already been noted; an additional figure is that of John Harris, More's clerk, who married Dorothy Colley, one of Margaret Roper's maids. He stands in the porch. The inscription reads, *Johannes Heresius Thomæ famulus anno 27.*

When Locky painted the group in 1530, he retained the inscriptions of the 1526-7 sketch; this led to confusion in dating the years of birth of the members of the family; it was assumed that, as More was there stated to be in his fiftieth year, he reached that age in 1530. The same misunderstanding was continued when in 1593, Thomas More, grandson of Sir Thomas, had a new group painted to include himself and his wife with two of their sons, Thomas and Cresacre. Of the original group, Sir Thomas with his father and children are retained with Anne Cresacre; a portrait of her as an old lady looks down at her from the wall. A number of coats of arms have been added; over two of these is the legend, 'Christiano Catholico More.'[17]

Cresacre More, the youngest of thirteen children, inherited his father's estates; his eldest brother, who is in the family group, died before his father, and two other brothers became priests. Cresacre wrote a biography of his great-grandfather; this was first published in Paris in 1626. The book does not add substantially to the records of Roper and Stapleton; these remain the primary sources of our knowledge of Sir Thomas More and his family.

---

[17] This composite picture of five generations is now in the National Portrait Gallery.

Chapter II

Boyhood and Youth

THE uncertainty of dates created by the sketch and the painting is increased by an ambiguous record left by Sir John More of the births of his children. His notes are written in a manuscript of Geoffrey of Monmouth's History of the Kings of Britain now at Trinity College, Cambridge.[1] Five of the entries are precise. Joan was born 11th March, 1474/5; Agatha, 31st January, 1478/9; John, 6th June, 1480; Edward, 3rd September, 1481; Elizabeth, 22nd September, 1482. Perversely the date of greatest importance, that of the birth of the second child, Thomas, is confusing.

In translation it reads,

> Memo. That on the Friday next after the Feast of the Purification of the Blessed Virgin Mary, *namely the seventh day of February*, between the second and third hours of the morning, was born Thomas More, son of John More, Gentleman, in the 17th year of the reign of King Edward IV after the Conquest of England.

The seventeenth year of Edward IV ran from 4th March, 1477 to 3rd March, 1478, so the 7th February would fall in 1478, but that day was a Saturday and not a Friday. The 7th February in the previous year, 1477, did fall on a Friday. Father Bridgett favoured 1478, as 'by a natural confusion it has been set down as Friday,

---

[1] MS. O.2.21.

since the birth took place after midnight.'[2] Chambers preferred 1477 until he examined the original entries; he then found that the phrase (italicized above) mentioning the seventh day of February was a later addition; he therefore came to agree with Father Bridgett's choice of 1478.[3]

Sir John More was born about 1451. It has long been thought probable that his father was a John More who was butler in Lincoln's Inn in 1464. Recent researches[4] throw doubt on this identification; a William More, citizen and baker of London, who died in 1467, has stronger claims. He married Jane Joye, *née* Leicester, whose mother and grandfather are mentioned in Sir John More's will; the grandfather was John Leicester, a Chancery clerk in the reign of Henry VI. A further link with this John Leicester may be found in a deed, dated 1455, referring to an estate in North Mimms, Herts; Sir John owned an estate known as Gobions[5] between North Mimms and Hatfield, and it was there that his son Thomas wrote the first part of *Utopia*.

John More was trained at Lincoln's Inn and became a serjeant-at-law in 1503, and a judge in the Court of Common Pleas about 1517; a few years later, probably in 1520, he was transferred to the King's Bench. It is not known when he was knighted. He was granted as arms, *Argent a chevron engrailed between three moorcocks sable crested gules.* He, or perhaps his father, may have rendered service to Edward IV, for when Sir

---

[2] A similar difficulty arises as to the days of the birth and death of Erasmus. He was born during the night, and died after midnight. See *Allen*, I, p. 578.

[3] For a discussion of the problem, see *Harpsfield,* pp. 298-303; *Roper,* p. 105; *Chambers,* pp. 48-9. Chambers' argument does not settle the problem, as the later addition might have been a deliberate correction.

[4] See the article by Margaret Hasings, 'Sir Thomas More's Ancestry,' *Times Literary Supplement,* 12th September, 1952. Also Professor A. W. Reed's lecture on 'Young More' in *Under God and the Law* (1949).

[5] Later called 'Gubbins,' and now seems to be part of Brookman's Park.

John came to make his will in 1526/7 (at the time that Holbein drew his portrait), he provided for Masses to be said for a period of seven years 'for my soul, all my Wives' souls and the souls of my Father and Mother, King Edward the Fourth ...' This provision was made more than forty years after the death of Edward IV, and argues a strong loyalty to his memory. The will does not mention Henry VII.

'All my Wives' souls' refers to his four marriages. His first wife was Agnes Granger, the mother of his six children. The family record begins with the entry, in translation,

> Memo. That on Sunday in the Vigil of St. Mark the Evangelist, in the fourteenth year of the reign of King Edward IV after the Conquest of England, John More, Gentleman, was married to Agnes, daughter of Thomas Granger, in the parish of St. Giles without Cripplegate,[6] London.

This gives us the date 24th April, 1474.

Thomas Granger became Sheriff of London in November 1503, and there is a glimpse of him in Stow's Chronicles[7] when he dined with the newly appointed serjeants-at-law, amongst them being his son-in-law. Nothing is known of the personality of Agnes Granger.

Sir John married four times. The names of his wives, after the first, were: Johanna Marshall, the widow of a wealthy mercer who died in 1498; Elizabeth Bowes, widow of another wealthy mercer who died in 1505; and, lastly, another widow, Alice Clerke, who survived Sir John. She lived on his small estate of Gobions; after her son-in-law's execution the estate was sequestrated. More makes one reference to her in *The Apology* in describing his worldly estate; he mentioned that while she lived,

---

[6] The Church was burnt down in 1545; the new one escaped the Great Fire but not the Great Blitz.

[7] Ed. of 1580, p. 876.

'whose life and good health I pray God keep and continue,' his income was modest.[8]

This tale of London citizens, lawyers and sheriffs indicates the social group to which the Mores belonged, and bears out Sir Thomas's description, 'not illustrious but honourable.'[9] Sir John's experience of marriage gives point to two sayings of his recorded by his son.

> I have heard my father merrily say every man is at the choice of his wife, that you should put your hand into a blind bag full of snakes and eels together, seven snakes for one eel, you would I ween reckon it a perilous choice to take up one at adventure though you had made your special prayer to speed well.[10]

> I would that we were all in case with our own faults, as my father saith that we be with our wives. For when he heareth folk blame wives, and say that there be so many of them shrews: he saith that they defame them falsely. For he saith plainly that there is but one shrewd wife in the world: but he saith indeed that every man weeneth he hath her; and that that one is his own.[11]

These *obiter dicta* are indications of the character of Sir John More and are in accord with the astute old judge of Holbein's drawing. Thomas More's estimate of his father is given in the Epitaph.

> His father, John More, knight, appointed by his king to the order of judges called the King's Bench, was a man courteous, affable, innocent, gentle, merciful, just, and uncorrupted.[12]

---

[8] *Apologye*, p. 51.

[9] Epitaph on Tomb (Chelsea); see below p. 273.

[10] *E.W.*, p. 165; II, p. 107.

[11] *E.W.*, p. 233; II, p. 229.

[12] '*Homo civilis, suavis, innocens, mitis, misericors, aequus et integer.*' Harpsfield, p. 280.

To this should be added Roper's account of the bearing of son to father; the passage refers to the period when Sir Thomas was Lord Chancellor.

> Whensoever he passed through Westminster Hall to his place in the Chancery by the Court of the King's Bench, if his father, one of the judges thereof, had been sat ere he came, he would go into the same Court and there reverently kneeling down in the sight of them all, duly ask his father's blessing. And if it fortuned that his father and he at readings in Lincoln's Inn, met together, as they sometimes did, notwithstanding his high office, he would offer in argument the pre-eminence to his father, though he, for his office sake, would refuse to take it.[13]

We are so accustomed to linking the names of Henry VIII and Sir Thomas More that it is well to recall that More was the senior by more than twelve years; he was born about two years after Caxton had set up his printing press in Westminster, and was five or six years old at the death of Edward IV. He retained one vivid memory of that event, and set it down in his *History of King Richard the Third*.

> Howbeit, this have I by credible information learned, that the self night in which King Edward died, one Mistlebrook long ere morning came in great haste to the house of one Pottier, dwelling in Red Cross Street without Cripplegate; and when he was with hasty rapping quickly let in, he showed unto Pottier that King Edward was departed. 'By my troth, man,' quoth Pottier, 'then will my master the Duke of Gloucester be king.'[14]

So far the English version, but the Latin adds that More

---

[13] Roper, p. 43.

[14] *E.W.*, pp. 37-8; I, p. 402.

himself heard Pottier's remark reported to his father while there was still no hint of treachery.

The London in which this sharp-eared boy grew up was a city of some 50,000 inhabitants living within the boundaries of the walls guarded by its seven gates. It was the London that William Dunbar lauded in 1501.

> Strong be thy walls that about thee stand;
> Wise be the people that within thee dwell;
> Fresh is thy river with his lusty strand;
> Blithe be thy churches, well sounding be thy bells;
> Rich be thy merchants in substance that excels. ...
> Thy famous Mayor, by princely governance,
> With sword of justice thee ruleth prudently.
> No Lord of Paris, Venice or Florence
> In dignity or honour goeth to him nigh.
> He is exemplar, lode-star, and guide;
> Principal patron and rose original.
> Above all Mayors as master most worthy:
> London, thou art the flower of Cities all.

It was a city of churches, fine buildings, gardens and orchards. There were over twenty religious houses each with its cultivated enclosure; there were the churchyards of more than ninety parishes. The town houses of lords and merchants had their gardens and many of the small houses had their plots. There is little left to help the imagination in recreating that vanished city; here and there, hidden behind buildings, a tree or a tiny yard with a patch of green hints at former pleasances; of these few vestiges, the Garden Court of the Bank of England, for instance, is all that remains of the churchyard of St. Christopher-le-Stocks. There was, of course, the other side of the scene; the poor and the vagrant were crowded in tenements or lived in huts on waste land or outside the walls.

London was a pageant to stimulate a boy. A saunter down

Cheapside, or along the river wharves, must have been an unfailing delight. Almost every day there would be some church function or procession, or some civic occasion to add dignity and colour to a busy merchant city. The Mayor and Aldermen, the Masters and Wardens of the Livery Companies and other officials had many opportunities to display their robes of Office. There was the coming and going of kings and princes, all seeking the favour of the city and the loan of its wealth. Foreign princes and nobles had to be welcomed in full state with pageants in their honour. St. Paul's dominated the city, while on the east stood the Tower, a royal palace and an ill-omened prison. It was amidst such scenes that Thomas More grew from boyhood to youth.

There is little to record of his childhood. One passage in *A Dialogue of Comfort* may be a personal memory, though it is hazardous to make the suggestion in quoting from a dramatic form of composition. If it is a record of fact, it is hardly complimentary to his mother; it at least gives us a homely glimpse of a schoolboy of those times.

> And in such wise deal they with him as the mother doth sometime with her child, which, when the little boy will not rise in time for her, but lie still a-bed and slug, and when he is up weepeth because he hath lain so long, fearing to be beaten at school for his late coming thither; she telleth him then that it is but early days, and he shall come time enough, and biddeth him go, good son, I warrant thee, I have sent to thy master myself, take thy bread and butter with thee, thou shalt not be beaten at all. And thus (so she may send him merry forth at the door, that he weepeth not in her sight at home) she studieth not much upon the matter, though he be taken tardy and beaten when he cometh to school.[15]

He went to the school attached to St. Anthony's Hospital in

---

[15] *Dialogue of Comfort*, p. 182.

Threadneedle Street.[16] This was probably the best school in the City. John Stow, writing of a period forty years later than More's schooldays, recalled the annual disputations between the scholars of the London schools on the Eve of St. Bartholomew in the churchyard of the Priory of St. Bartholomew. St. Anthony's he says, 'commonly presented the best scholars, and had the prize in those days.'[17] In his *Annals* he states that in 1555 the prizes were three silver pens, and the first was won by a St. Anthony's boy. Amongst the old boys of the school he mentions two Lords Chancellor, Sir Thomas More and Dr. Nicholas Heath, and an Archbishop of Canterbury, Dr. John Whitgift.

The master of the school in More's time was Nicholas Holt, a scholar of good reputation. The main subject was Latin both written and spoken, and the art of arguing (logic and rhetoric) found a place and prepared the pupils for those academic disputations that were a recognized part of their training. It is not known how long Thomas More was at this school.

His father arranged for the boy to enter the household of Archbishop (later Cardinal) Morton at Lambeth. Here he would continue his formal learning under the chaplain or tutor while gaining experience of the manners and conduct of a gentleman. Roper records that,

> though he was young of years, yet would he at Christmastide suddenly sometimes step in among the players, and never studying for the matter, make a part of his own there presently among them, which made the lookers on more sport than all the players beside. In whose wit and towardness the Cardinal much delighting, would often say of him unto the nobles that divers times dined with him: 'This child here waiting at table, whosoever shall live to see it, will prove a

---

[16] North side of Threadneedle St., opposite Finch Lane.

[17] *Stow*, I, p. 74.

marvellous man.'[18]

Henry Medwall may have been a member of the Archbishop's household at this period; he was later the Cardinal's chaplain. A play by him, Fulgens and Lucrece,[19] has survived in a unique copy of an edition printed by John Rastell (More's brother-in-law); two youths are represented as stepping out from the audience to improvise parts in the play. They are distinguished from other characters by being called A and B.

> B. Now have I spied a meet office for me
> For I will be of counsel, an I may.
> With yonder man—
> A.   Peace, let be!
> By God, thou wilt destroy the play.
> B. Destroy the play, quotha? nay, nay,
> The play began never till now.

The tradition of More's powers of improvisation is preserved in *The Booke of Sir Thomas More*[20] (c. 1600) where he fills in the gap caused by the absence of a player in an Interlude called *The Marriage of Wit and Wisdom*. This bent for dramatic expression is an important element in his genius.

He paid his tribute to Morton in *Utopia*. He there makes Raphael Hythlodaye recount a discussion at the Cardinal's table on the subject of the right punishment of thieves. In introducing his account, Hythlodaye said.

> During that time I was much indebted to the Right Reverend Father, Cardinal John Morton, Archbishop of

---

[18] *Roper*, p. 5.

[19] Contained in *Five Pre-Shakespearean Comedies* (World's Classics). The quotation is from Part I, lines 360-6.

[20] Contained in *The Shakespeare Apocrypha* (1908).

Canterbury, and at that time also Lord Chancellor of England, a man, Master Peter (for Master More knows about him, and needs no information from me) who deserved respect as much as for his wisdom and virtue as for his authority. He was of middle stature and showed no sign of his advanced age; his countenance inspired respect rather than fear; in discourse he was agreeable, though serious and dignified. By rough address he sometimes made trial of those who made suit to him, but in a harmless way, to see what ability in answering and presence of mind a man possessed, which virtue, provided it did not amount to impudence, gave him pleasure as akin to his own disposition, and excited his admiration as suited to those holding public office. His speech was polished and to the point. His knowledge was profound, his ability incomparable, and his memory wonderfully retentive; for by learning and practice he improved his natural qualities. The King placed much confidence in his advice, and when I was there, the state seemed to depend upon him. For in early youth he had been taken straight from school to court, had spent his whole life in important public affairs, and had had many vicissitudes of fortune, so that by many and great dangers he had acquired his sagacity, which, when thus learned, is not easily forgotten.[21]

At the end of this recital. More added his own comment.

'To be sure, Raphael,' said I, 'you have given me great pleasure; for what you have said has been both wise and witty. Besides, while listening to you I felt not only as if I were at home in my native country, but as if I had gone back to the days of my youth, being pleasantly reminded of the Cardinal in whose household I was brought up as a lad. And since you are so devoted to his memory you cannot think how

---

[21] *Utopia*, pp. 8-9; pp. 21-2.

much more attached I feel to you on that account, attached as I was to you already.[22]

It is not surprising that this shrewd and humorous elderly statesman had a considerable influence over the boy of fourteen who had been committed to his guidance. In spite of the great part played by Morton in the reign of Henry VII, he remains a shadowy figure. The term 'Morton's fork' applied to an astute dilemma for the extraction of taxes, may do him injustice. He was certainly not Wolsey's precursor, for Morton had a deep concern for the Church that was not shown by the more famous Cardinal until his disgrace left him no other business. Morton was a friend of learning and used his influence on behalf of promising scholars.

It was probably in 1492 that the Archbishop sent Thomas More to Oxford; there he stayed for two years until his father decided that it was time he began his legal training. Cresacre More said that his great-grandfather was at Canterbury Hall; the site of which is occupied by Christ Church; claims have been made for the Hall of St. Mary the Virgin, but the close connexion between the Archbishop and Canterbury College makes it likely that it was to that college the boy was sent. He lived austerely as was then customary, and in after years recalled 'Oxford fare' as in the lowest degree of economical living.

As he did not spend more than two or three years at Oxford, he would no go far beyond the *trivium*, or series of three subjects, grammar, rhetoric and logic, that formed the first stage of medieval studies. The system had not yet been greatly affected by the New Learning.

Roper tells us that he was 'sufficiently instructed' in Latin and Greek. His own writings testify to a wide reading in Latin and to great skill in its use. It is, however, unlikely that during his short

---

[22] *Utopia*, p. 25; p. 39.

time at Oxford he learned more than the rudiments of Greek. William Crocyn was teaching Greek in Oxford from 1491 and More no doubt then made his acquaintance. John Colet, Thomas Linacre and William Latimer were then in Italy and so did not meet the youth whose friendship they were later to cherish. He may have known Cuthbert Tunstal who was probably at Balliol. One contemporary, and possibly a former schoolfellow at St. Anthony's, John Holt, became a Fellow of Magdalen in 1491; four years later he was appointed schoolmaster in Cardinal Morton's household; he then wrote *Lac Puerorum*, or *Mylke for Children*, for the instruction of his pupils in Latin grammar. For this book Thomas More composed introductory and closing verses in Latin elegiacs. The first are headed '*Thomas Mori adolescentuli diserti Epigramma*' and invited the pupil to push open the new English door that John Holt had provided for them as 'a first gate to grammar'; the closing verses gave a glimpse of what lay ahead for the student.

By the time John Holt's book appeared, Thomas More had left Oxford. As the eldest son it was necessary for him to begin his training in the law. There is no reason to think that Sir John disapproved of Oxford, though it has been maintained that he feared too close an application to the classic; his son had been given as sound an education as was then available; he had been to the best school in London, and had afterwards enjoyed the privilege of living in the household of a great Churchman and statesman; then came two years at Oxford. For the study of the law, London was unique, and so Thomas More came home when he was about sixteen years old.

Chapter III

The Young Lawyer

IT must have been soon after he returned home that Thomas More fell in love with a girl named Elizabeth who was two years his junior. This is recorded in one of his Latin poems entitled '*Gratulator, quod eam repererit incolumen, quam olim ferme puer amaverat.*' The date is fixed by the fact that the poem first appeared in the 1520 (Basle) edition of his Latin epigrams and not in the 1518 edition. In the poem he states that 'five long lustres' had passed since they had first met.

> Many a long year, since first we met, has roll'd:
> I then was boyish, but now am old.
> Scarce had I bid my sixteenth summer hail,
> And two in thine were wanting to the tale;
> When thy soft mien—ah mien for ever fled!
> On my tranc'd heart its guiltless influence shed....
>
> For one, who knew with what chaste warmth you burn'd,
> Had blabb'd the secret of my love return'd.
> Then the duenna and the guarded door
> Baffled the stars, and bade us meet no more.[1]

---

[1] The translation is that of Archdeacon Francis Wrangham, the friend of Wordsworth. It will be found on p. 268 of the first volume of Arthur Cayley's *Memoirs of Sir Thomas More* (1808). The Latin poems are printed at the end of the second volume which also contains Cayley's translation of *Utopia*—as colourless as the rest of the compilation.

This romance[2] had to give place to the study of the law. Roper states that after leaving Oxford,

> he was then for the study of the law of the realm put to an Inn of Chancery called New Inn, where for his time he very well prospered; and from thence was admitted to Lincoln's Inn, with very small allowance, continuing there his study until he was made and accounted a worthy utter barrister.[3]

Stow rightly saw the analogy between the Inns of Court and a University. 'There is in and about this City, a whole University, as it were, of students, practisers or pleaders with Judges of the laws of this Realm.'[4] The Inns of Court were the Middle and Inner Temples, Lincoln's Inn, and Gray's Inn. The subordinate Inns of Chancery, such as Furnivall's and New Inn, were, as Stow wrote, 'provinces, severally subjected to the Inns of Court.' His account of the training is probably as true of the period of Henry VII as of Elizabeth's.

> They frequent readings, meetings, boltings [sifting of evidence] and other learned exercises, whereby growing ripe in the knowledge of the laws, and approved withal to be of honest conversation, they are either by general consent of the Benchers, or Readers, being of the most ancient, grave, and judicial men of every Inn of Court, or by special privilege of the present reader there, selected and called to the degree of Utter Barristers, and so enabled to be common counsellors, and to practise the law, both in their chambers, and at the

---

[2] Erasmus tells us, 'When he was of age for love, he showed no aversion from women, but he destroyed no one's good name. In fact he was always rather the tempted than the tempter and found more pleasure in the intercourse of mind than of body.' *Allen*, VI, 999. Translation from Algernon Cecil's *A Portrait of Thomas More* (1937), p. 45.

[3] *Roper*, p. 5.

[4] *Stow*, I, p. 76.

Bars.⁵

This method of training in the law was peculiar to England. It has been said of the Inns of Court of that time,

> unchartered, unprivileged, unendowed, without remembered founders, these groups of lawyers formed themselves and in course of time evolved a scheme of legal education: an academic scheme of the medieval sort, oral and disputatious. ... Now it would, so I think, be difficult to conceive any scheme better suited to harden and toughen a traditional body of law than one which, while books were still uncommon, compelled every lawyer to take part in legal education and every distinguished lawyer to read public lectures.⁶

More began his studies at New Inn probably in 1494; he was admitted to Lincoln's Inn, 12th February, 1496, being 'pardoned four vacations at the instance' of his father. Richard Staverton, who married Joan More, was admitted on the same day. This is the first date in More's life that can be given with certainty, but it is not known when he was called to the Bar; it was probably in 1501. He was then appointed Reader or lecturer at Furnivall's Inn, a position he held for over three years. His later career can be traced in the Black Books of Lincoln's Inn;⁷ from these we learn that he was Pensioner and, later, Butler in 1507, and Reader in 1511 and 1515. In February 1511, he paid a fine to be excused from acting as Marshal at the Christmas festivities, and later in that year, he paid another fine to avoid serving as Treasurer, a position that had not yet its present prestige.

Something will be said later of his work as a lawyer, but here

---

⁵ *Stow*, I, p. 78.

⁶ F.W. Maitland, *English Law and the Renaissance* (1901), pp. 26-27. An account of the Inns of Court was published in 1641 with the title, *The Third Universitie of England*. The author was Sir George Buck.

⁷ For details, see *Harpsfield*, p. 307, note on 13/2-12.

it is important to see the significance of his legal studies. His training, as we have seen, was largely oral at a time when books were still uncommon, but the library[8] at Lincoln's Inn would contain copies of important manuscripts such as the *De Legibus et Consuetudinibus Angliæ* of Henry de Bracton (d. 1268), a treatise that was not printed until 1569. This exposition of the Common Law of England helped to establish the rule of law as something apart from political expediency; it declared, for instance, that 'Everyman is presumed to be a good man till the contrary is proved by lawful evidence.' How firmly that principle was implanted in More's mind was evidenced by his later reputation as a practitioner in the courts, and an echo is found in his statement to Roper, 'I assure thee on my faith, that if the parties will at my hands call for justice, then, although my father stood on the one side, and the Devil on the other, his cause being good, the Devil should have right.' Another of Bracton's maxims, 'The King is under God and the law,' was to have special significance for More himself.[9]

It had not been without a struggle that Thomas More had obeyed his father's wishes by studying the law. Had he followed his own inclination, he would have devoted himself to learning. Erasmus tells us,

> From his earliest years he followed after good learning. As a young man he took up Greek literature and philosophy —to the distress of his father, an upright man and usually of sound sense; who being himself an authority on English Law, thought fit to check those studies by cutting off all supplies, and, indeed, More was almost disowned, because he seemed

---

[8] The library contained also the works of Aristotle, Aquinas, and other philosophers and theologians.

[9] *Roper*, p. 42.

to be deserting his father's profession.[10]

Fortunately such were his intellectual powers, he was able to follow both the career of a lawyer with distinction, and that of a scholar. Erasmus brings together the names of some scholars with whom More was associated, in a letter written from Oxford to Robert Fisher, a relation of Bishop John Fisher. This was written in December 1499.

> When I hear my Colet, I seem to be listening to Plato himself. In Grocyn who does not marvel at such a perfect round of learning? What can be more acute, profound and delicate than the judgement of Linacre? What has nature ever created more gentle, more sweet, more happy than the genius of Thomas More?[11]

Another name can be added from a letter written by John Colet by More in October 1504.

> Meanwhile I pass my time with Grocyn, Linacre, and Lily; the first, as you know, is the guide of my life in your absence; the second, the guide of my studies, and the third, the dearest companion of my affairs.[12]

Erasmus, Colet, Grocyn, Linacre, Lily, More—this notable company of scholars must not be thought of as a deliberately formed group with a defined programme; nor should they be pictured as a band of young men swept away by the appeal of the new learning. In 1500 Grocyn was about fifty-four years of age, Linacre about forty, Colet was thirty-four, Lily and Erasmus about thirty-two, and More, aged twenty-two, was the youngest of them all.

This list could be extended to show how More's wide interests

---

[10] *Allen*, VI, 999.

[11] *Allen*, I, 118.

[12] *Rogers*, pp. 8-9.

linked him with many other men of learning and their patrons. John Holt has already been mentioned; his return to Lambeth in 1494 no doubt increased More's opportunities of meeting again Cardinal Morton during the last few years of his life. Then there was Cuthbert Tunstal (1474-1559) who had studied at Oxford and Cambridge and at Padua, and was to be Bishop of London and, later, Bishop of Durham and was to be an embarrassment to Queen Elizabeth. Antonio Bonvisi should be mentioned; he was a patron of scholars rather than a scholar himself; writing to him from the Tower in 1535, Thomas More said that for nearly forty years he had been 'a continual nursling of the house of Bonvisi.'[13] Another friend was William Latimer (1460?-1545) of Oxford and Padua. To these may be added Richard Pace (1482?-1536) who spent much of his life in diplomatic service and was to follow Colet as Dean of St. Paul's. So one might go on adding the names of many of the other outstanding scholars of the time. It was a remarkable company that took delight in calling Young More their friend.

Grocyn, Linacre,[14] Colet, Lily, Tunstal, Latimer and Pace had all studied in Italy and had come under the influence of those ardent scholars who devoted their lives to the recovery and study of Greek literature and philosophy, and strove to develop a Latin style more in keeping with the age of Cicero. In Italy the revived interest in the arts and the genius of its sculptors and painters were even stronger influences on culture. Some scholars and patrons were perverted to a new paganism, but the new learning had other results in England; it turned men's thoughts to theology and to a critical consideration of the state of the Church. So Colet approached the interpretation of the Scriptures in a fresh

---

[13] *Rogers*, p. 562.

[14] 'Modern English scholarship begins with Linacre and his two friends, William Grocyn and William Latimer.' Sir J. E. Sandys, *A History of Classical Scholarship*, II, p. 228.

spirit of inquiry and his Oxford lectures on St. Paul's Epistles encouraged Erasmus to perfect his knowledge of Greek. Colet himself did not at that period know Greek; he began to study it in 1516.[15] Another aspect of this new learning was a revived interest in the Fathers of the Church; Erasmus, for instance, edited the works of St. Jerome, and More studied the writings of St. Augustine (or St. Austin, to use the English form). Then, too, the study of Plato was revived; Ficino's translation into Latin (1477) was probably the basis of More's study of a philosopher who was to influence his own thought.

Desiderius Erasmus and Thomas More first met in the summer of 1499. It is not necessary here to recount the well-known facts of the unhappy and frustrated youth of Erasmus; when he reached Paris in 1492 he was free to satisfy his craving for learning; his poverty forced him to take pupils, one of whom, William Blount, Lord Mountjoy, became his patron and brought him to England. We do not know the circumstances of the first meeting of Erasmus and More. One story puts the meeting after a dinner given by the Lord Mayor. The two men, it is said, conversed for a time in Latin, and then Erasmus exclaimed, 'Either you are More or no one'; to which More replied, 'And you are either God or the Devil or my Erasmus.' The Elizabethan Play *The Booke of Sir Thomas More* includes a scene in which More plays a trick on Erasmus at his first visit by arranging for his clerk to impersonate him (a hoary stage device even at that period). Such stories and legends gathered round the name of Sir Thomas More; each may contain a grain of fact, but it is now impossible to find it.

Our first definite information about the association between the two men comes from Erasmus; it is found in a Catalogue of his writings made in 1523.

---

[15] See below, p. 145.

Thomas More, who, while I was staying in the country house of Mountjoy, had paid me a visit, took me out for a walk, for relaxation of mind, to a neighbouring village.[16] There all the king's children, except Arthur, the eldest, were being educated. When we reached the hall [Eltham] the retinues of the house and of Lord Mountjoy were assembled. In the midst stood Henry, then nine years old [just over eight], yet already with a royal bearing, that is, with a certain loftiness of mind joined with singular courtesy. At his right was Margaret, about eleven years old [just under ten], who afterwards married James, King of the Scots. Playing at his left was Mary, four years old. Edmund [d. 1500], an infant, was carried by the nurse. More with his friend Arnold, after saluting Prince Henry, presented him with some writing or other. As I was entirely taken by surprise I had nothing to offer, and I was obliged to make a promise that I would write something to show my respect. I was somewhat vexed with More for not warning me, and especially so since the prince while we were dining sent me a note challenging my pen.[17]

Prince Edmund was born in January 1499 and died about May 1500. The Arnold here mentioned was Arnold Edward a young lawyer whose father was a merchant with a house on London Bridge. He is one of the few lawyers numbered among More's intimates. This passage is of further interest since it shows that already by 1499, when he was only twenty-one or two, Thomas

---

[16] Eltham, Kent. It was here that Prince Henry, created Duke of York in 1494, was established. Thomas More may have been visiting the Ropers at Well Hall, near by. Mountjoy was probably making his home with his father-in-law, Sir William Say, near Greenwich. Amongst the company at Eltham would be John Skelton, the Prince's schoolmaster; Erasmus and Skelton wrote complimentary verses to each other. See H.L. R. Edwards, *Skelton* (1949), pp. 66-70. Mountjoy was later appointed to supervise the Prince's historical studies.

[17] *Allen*, I, p. 6.

The Young Lawyer

More had entrance to the court.

In the autumn of that year, Erasmus was at Oxford and heard Colet lecture on the Epistles of St. Paul. Writing to More on 28th October, Erasmus said,

> Jesting aside, I do beg, sweetest Thomas, that you will cure that sickness which I have contracted from the long want of you and your handwriting, by a payment with interest. ... As for you, I reckon you will not care in what fashion I write to the best-natured of men, and one who, I am persuaded, has no little love for me. Farewell, dearest More.[18]

The affectionate tone of this letter shows how closely the two men had drawn to each other in a short period; it was the beginning of a friendship that was to grow with the years.[19] Erasmus returned to Paris at the end of January 1500.

The law and the classics do not bring us to the heart of Thomas More's inner conflict during his young manhood. Roper tells us that after the period when he was Reader at Furnivall's Inn, that is from 1501, 'he gave himself to devotion and prayer in the Charterhouse of London, religiously living there, without vow, about four years.'[20] Harpsfield elaborates this bare statement.

> Surely it seemeth by some apparent conjectures that he was sometime somewhat propense [disposed] and inclined either to be a priest, or to take some monastical and solitary life; for he continued after his aforesaid reading four years and more full virtuously and religiously in great devotion and prayer with the monks of the Charterhouse of London,

---

[18] *Nichols*, I, p. 213; *Allen*, I, 114.

[19] It may be helpful to give the dates of the five later visits of Erasmus to England: 1505-1506 (London); 1509-14 (Cambridge); May, 1515; Aug. 1516; April 1517.

[20] *Roper*, p. 6. Roper's account is not precise enough for us to be sure of the order of events in More's early life.

without any manner of profession or vow, either to see and prove whether he could frame himself to that kind of life, or at least to sequester himself from all temporal and worldly exercises.[21]

The account given by Erasmus should also be noted.

> At the same time with all his strength he turned towards the religious life, by watching, fasting, prayer, and similar exercises, preparing himself for the priesthood: more wisely than the many who rush blindly into that uphill profession without first making trial of themselves. And he had almost embraced this ministry; but being unable to master the desire for a wife, he decided to be a chaste husband rather than a priest impure.[22]

To these statements may be added the comment made by More to his daughter Margaret soon after he was committed to the Tower in 1534.

> But I assure thee, on my faith, my own good daughter, if it had not been for my wife and you that be my children, whom I account the chief part of my charge, I would not have failed long ere this to have closed myself in as straight a room, and straighter too.[23]

It is difficult to determine the character of More's relations with the Carthusians; his legal work was, apparently, not interrupted, so he must have been a guest with freedom to come

---

[21] *Harpsield*, p. 17.

[22] *Allen*, IV, 999. 'Maluit igitur maritus esse castus quam sacerdos impurus.'

[23] *Roper*, p. 76. *Stapleton* (p. 9) says that More thought of becoming a Franciscan, and does not mention the Charterhouse. Cresacre More mentions both the Charterhouse and the Franciscans. More's remark to Margaret Roper in the Tower shows that his thoughts were directed towards the Carthusians or a closed Order rather than to the Friars. Chambers (p. 77) speaks of the Observant Friars of Greenwich, but the Grey Friars in Newgate Street would have been more convenient. Stapleton states that William Lily and More debated together 'the question of becoming a priest.'

and go.[24] He would be under the spiritual direction of the monastery, and would gain an insight to Carthusian life. He retained in his active career those habits of regular prayer, of mortification and of meditation that had been established at the Charterhouse. As we get involved with the details of his crowded days, we may forget that this inner life remained his source of strength and comfort, but we cannot understand Thomas More unless we remind ourselves frequently of what the world did not see.

The last sentence of the quotation from Erasmus (p. 43), 'he decided to be a chaste husband rather than a priest impure,' has been twisted by some[25] to mean that More was shocked by the immorality they assume he found amongst the monks and the secular clergy. This is to read too much into a simple statement. No breath of scandal ever touched the Charterhouse, and many of More's intimate friends were priests. Erasmus was referring to More's own spiritual problem and to nothing else. It was not an act of revulsion, but a humble acceptance of his own nature.[26]

After More was called to the Bar 'to his great commendation, he read for a good space a public lecture of St. Augustine, *De*

---

[24] There is a difficulty in accepting the chronology suggested by Roper's phrasing. The years 1500-4 are implied as the Carthusians period, but as we shall see, the years 1501-2 were exceptionally full. He was studying Greek with Grocyn and Lily, attending lectures by Linacre on Aristotle, giving his own lectures on St. Augustine, and beginning his practice as a lawyer. By 1504 he had put himself under the spiritual direction of Colet, and had become a Member of Parliament. It is difficult to fit in any prolonged stay at the Charterhouse in this programme. A more likely period seems to be the years before his meeting with Erasmus in 1499 while he was still a student at Lincoln's Inn. The objection to this is that Roper implies that marriage (c. 1505) followed soon after the Charterhouse period. It should be remembered that Roper wrote his account twenty years after the death of More, and ten years after that of Margaret Roper. It seems to me misleading to speak of More's 'seclusion' and 'long retreat' as in the Introduction to the 1951 edition of *Utopia*, in Everyman's Library.

[25] Notably by Seebohm, *Oxford Reformers*. See Bridgett's discussion in his third chapter.

[26] *Quod si non se continent, nubant: melius est enim nubere, quam uri.* 1 Cor. 7:9.

Civitate Dei, in the Church of St. Lawrence in the old Jury; whereunto there resorted Doctor Crocyn, an excellent cunning [learned] man, and all the chief learned of the City of London.'[27] Stapleton tells us that 'he did not treat this great work from the theological point of view, but from the standpoint of history and philosophy.'[28] More was greatly influenced by St. Augustine; evidence of this is that there are more references to 'St. Austin' in More's writings than to any other of the Fathers. It is therefore desirable to know something of this book which he must have studied closely before daring to expound its ideas before an audience of scholars. A book studied in this fashion in one's early twenties leaves an indelible impression.

In The City of God St. Augustine describes two cities and the relations between them; the City of God and the City of this world, Babylon. He distinguishes between the two in this passage:

> Two loves therefore have given origin to these two cities, self-love in contempt of God unto the earthly, love of God in contempt of oneself to the heavenly. The first seeks the glory of men, and the latter desires God only as the testimony of the conscience, the greatest glory. That glories in itself, and this in God. That exalts itself in self-glory: this says to God: 'My glory and the lifter up of my head.' That boasts of the ambitious conquerors led by the lust of sovereignty: in this all serve each other in charity, both the rulers in counselling and the subjects in obeying.[29]

The citizens of these two cities are mingled in this world like the wheat and the cockle (Matt, 13, 24-30). The City of God is not to be identified with the Church on earth for some are members

---

[27] *Roper*, p. 6.

[28] *Stapleton*, p. 9.

[29] Everyman edition., II, pp. 58-59. A useful guide to this difficult book will be found in *St. Augustine's City of God*, by Joseph Rickaby, S.J. (1925).

in name only; 'the reapers shall take the tares [or cockle] out of the Church which grew (until harvest) together with the good corn.'[30] The secular state is accepted by the Christian as a necessary institution ordained by God for maintaining order and justice. But what if the earthly state is unjust or tyrannous?

When Caesar demands what is his due, the Christian renders it to him, not for love of Caesar, but for love of God. Both good and bad Princes hold their power from God, who grants it to them for purposes which we cannot understand, but of which the existence cannot be questioned. When Caesar claims something that is only due to God, the Christian refuses it, not for hate of Caesar, but for love of God; here again, the earthly city has nothing to fear from the Christian, since, a peaceful citizen, he prefers to endure injustice rather than use force, and to suffer severe punishments rather than forget the divine law of charity.[31]

Inadequate as these few sentences must be as an exposition of a great theme, they will indicate the general direction of an argument that deeply influenced Thomas More.

---

[30] II, p. 282.

[31] E. Gilson. *Introduction à l'étude de Saint Augustin* (1943), p. 235.

Chapter IV

Early Verse

A TRANSLATION of a few lines from one of Thomas More's Latin poems was given in the last chapter. This poem was published in a volume of *Epigrammata*; the epigrams themselves were translations from the Greek Anthology. More and Lily vied with each other in making these Latin versions at the period, about 1501, when they were studying Greek together. In a prefatory letter to the first edition (Basle, 1518), Beatus Rhenanus wrote:

> Thomas More is in every way admirable. His compositions are most elegant, his translations most happy. How sweetly and easily flow his verses. Nothing is forced, harsh, awkward or obscure. He writes the purest and most limpid Latin. Moreover everything is welded together with so happy a wit that I never read anything with greater pleasure. The Muses must have showered upon this man all their gifts of humour, elegance and wit. Never, however, are his sallies mordant, but easy, pleasant, good-humoured and anything but bitter. He jokes, but never with malice; he laughs, but always without offence.[1]

Some original verse in Latin is included in the book. One poem has particular interest as it gives Thomas More's opinions on the qualities that are desirable in a wife; as this was written when he was thinking of marriage it may be more than an

---

[1] *Stapleton*, p. 7.

exercise in the language. There are echoes in his married life of the sentiments expressed in two of the verses.

The poem is entitled '*Ad Candidum, qualis uxor deligenda.*'

> Far from her lips' soft door
> Be noise, her silence stern;
> And hers be learning's store.
> Or hers the power to learn.
> With book she'll time beguile,
> And make true bliss her own;
> Unbuoyed by fortune's smile.
> Unbroken by her frown.[2]

In his youth More also wrote verse in English either for the pleasure of his friends or for special occasions. The results are not remarkable and none has found its way into anthologies, but it adds to our understanding of him. The poems open the 1557 volume with the heading, 'These Four Things here following, Master More wrote in his youth for his pastime.' They are: 'A merry jest how a sergeant would learn to play the friar'; nine rimes for tapestries in Sir John More's house; 'A rueful lamentation of the death of Queen Elizabeth, mother to King Henry the Eighth, wife to King Henry the Seventh, and eldest daughter to King Edward the Fourth'; and, lastly, verses for the Book of Fortune. The last two were copied by Richard Hill, a contemporary of More's, in his Commonplace book.[3]

The Merry Jest was the only one of these that was published during More's lifetime; Julian Notary printed it about 1516. It has been suggested that the poem was made for the Sergeants' Feast,

---

[2] Francis Wrangham's translation. The Latin text is given on p. 306 of Vol. II of Cayley's *Memoirs*, and the translation on p. 264 of Vol. I.

[3] Published as *Songs, Carols*, etc. (E.E.T.S. 1907). Balliol MS. 354. The entries were made during the earlier part of the reign of Henry VIII.

13th November, 1503, when John More was among the new Sergeants-at-law.[4] The theme is that every man should keep to his own trade. This is illustrated by the tale of a sergeant (not at-law, but in the office of a constable) ordered by the Mayor to arrest a bankrupt merchant who stays at home and refuses to see any callers. The sergeant disguises himself as a friar, and in this charitable guise, is allowed to offer ghostly comfort to the merchant. The friar's habit is soon thrown off and he tries to drag the merchant off to the Compter [prison]. Then follows a struggle that is described with much gusto.

> They rent and tear,
> Each other's hair,
> And clave together fast,
> Till with lugging,
> And with tugging,
> They fell down both at last.

The wife and servant join in, the first using her distaff and the second a battledore—not the bat used in a game but the beetle used for pounding the washing; they get him down, and then,

> Up they him lift,
> And with ill thrift,
> Headlong along the stair,
> Down they him threw,
> And said, 'Adieu!
> Commend us to the Mayor!'

Good knock-about stuff, written with great spirit.

---

[4] By A.W. Reed. See E.W., I, p. 15.

The lines composed for the tapestries in Sir John More's house need not detain us; they are competent to their purpose. The third Thing, the lament on the death of Queen Elizabeth (1503) deserves more consideration, for here Thomas More showed a metrical skill that makes one regret he did not develop this vein of poetry. He uses his favourite rime-royal with, occasionally, a lengthened last line. The verses are more than a conventional tribute; Queen Elizabeth was the daughter of Edward IV and More shared his father's loyalty to the memory of that king. The Queen is imagined as speaking on her death bed; she ends each stanza with the refrain, 'Lo, now here I lie.' Here are two stanzas in the original spelling.

> Was I not borne of olde worthy linage?
> Was not my mother queen my father kyng?
> Was I not a kinges fere [wife] in marriage?
> Had I not plenty of every pleasaunt thyng?
> Mercifull god this is a straunge reckenyng:
> Rychesse, honour, welth, and auncestry
> Hath me forsaken and lo now here I ly.
>
> If worship myght have kept me, I had not gone.
> If wyt myght have me saved, I neded not fere.
> If money myght have holpe, I lacked none.
> But O good God what vayleth all this gere.
> When deth is come thy mighty messangere.
> Obey we must there is no remedy,
> We had he sommoned, and lo now here I ly.

The fourth Thing was printed at some date after 1538 by Robert Wyer in a book entitled The Book of the Fair Gentlewoman... that is to say, Lady Fortune. The verses More wrote were to be printed at the beginning of the Book of Fortune. This was an elaborate fortune-telling device by which, after a throw of the dice, the player or seeker tracked down his fortune through the book.

> The rolling dice in whom your luck doth stand,
> With whose unhappy chance ye be so wroth,
> Ye know yourself came never in mine hand.
> Lo in this pond be fish and frogges both.
> Cast in your net: but be your lief or loth.
> Hold you content as fortune list assign:
> For it is your own fishing and not mine.

These Four Things do not complete the tale of More's English verse. His translation of the life of Pico della Mirandola contains poems of his own composition. This book was printed about 1510 by More's brother-in-law John Rastell, probably some five years after the completion of the manuscript. Stapleton tells us that, after having decided to live in the world, More

> determined, therefore, to put before his eyes the example of some prominent layman, on which he might model his life. He called to mind all who at that period, either at home or abroad, enjoyed the reputation of learning and piety, and finally fixed upon John Pico, Earl of Mirandola, who was renowned in the highest degree throughout the whole of Europe for his encyclopedic knowledge, and no less esteemed for his sanctity of life. More translated into English a Latin Life of Pico by his nephew, as well as his letters, and a set of twelve counsels for leading a good life, which he had composed. His purpose was not so much to bring these to the knowledge of others, though that, too, he had in view, as thoroughly to familiarize himself with them.[5]

The book consists of a translation, with some omissions, of

---

[5] *Stapleton*, p. 10.

Giovanni Francisco Pico's biography of his uncle Giovanni Pico della Mirandola (1463-94); in addition to the short life, More translated three epistles, a commentary on Psalm XV, and a prayer; the last he put into verse. He also took as themes for original poems, all in rime-royal, Pico's 'Twelve Rules,' and 'Twelve Weapons,' of 'Spiritual Battle,' and 'Twelve Properties of a Lover.' The original biography was prefaced to Pico's Works published in 1496. The book might have been brought to England by Linacre when he returned from Italy in 1499, or by some other scholar. It has been suggested[6] that More may have learned of Pico from John Skelton, the poet, who was tutor to Prince Henry at the time of the visit of More and Erasmus to Eltham; Pico had written some verses to Skelton.

More's translation opens with a dedicatory letter 'Unto his right entirely beloved sister in Christ, Joyeuce Leigh.' She was a Poor Clare of the House of the Minoresses in Aldgate, and was of the family of Leigh, or Lee, who worshipped with the Mores at St. Stephen's, Walbrook. One of her brothers, Edward, became Archbishop of York in 1531. More offered the book as a New Year gift, and explained that Pico's

> works are such that truly, good sister, I suppose of the quantity there cometh none in your hand more profitable, neither to the achieving of temperance in prosperity, nor to the purchasing of patience in adversity, nor to the despising of worldly vanity, nor to the desiring of heavenly felicity: which works I would require you gladly to receive, ne were it that they be such that for the goodly matter (howsoever they be translated) may delight and please any person that hath any mean desire and love to God, and that yourself is such one as for your virtue and fervent zeal to God cannot but joyously receive anything that meanly soundeth either to the

---

[6] By A.W. Reed. E.W., I, p. 23.

reproach of vice, commendation of virtue, or honour and laud of God—Who preserve you.

Pico[7] had studied in the leading universities of Italy before settling in Florence. To a knowledge of Greek and Latin he added Arabic and Hebrew. His inquiring mind led him to a study of the Cabbala. He wished to reconcile Plato with Aristotle, and Platonism with Christianity; this attempted syncretism produced in him a deepened faith in the Church and a striving for personal sanctity. He came under the powerful influence of Savonarola who was executed four years after Pico had been buried in the habit of a Dominican. An extract from a letter from Lorenzo de' Medici to Lanfredini dated 14th June, 1489, illustrated the characteristics of Pico that appealed to Thomas More.

> The Earl of Mirandola has taken up his residence here, and lives as devoutly as if he were a monk. He has written, and continues to write, theological works of great value; he comments on the Psalms, says the office regularly, fasts and is continent. He lives very simply and expects only the minimum of service. He seems to me a model for everyone.

Of himself, Pico wrote, 'I prefer my own room, my studies, the pleasure I get from books, and the peace of my soul, to the palaces of princes, public affairs, hunting, and the favours of the Roman Curia.'

Such a brief notice can do little more than indicate why Thomas More was fascinated by Picus; to us the Italian seems a remote historical personage, but to More he was a contemporary, living in the same religious and intellectual atmosphere; both were excited by the renascent study of the classics; both were students of Plato; both desired to give themselves completely to

---

[7] J.M. Rigg's edition of the *Life of Pico* (1890) has a useful introduction; Pater's essay in *The Renaissance* (1873) is well known. He there says that More made his translation for 'some touch of sweetness' he found in the biography—an interesting side-light on Pater! See also L. Gautier Vignal, *Pic de la Mirandole* (Paris, 1937).

the Church. Had Pico lived he might have entered the Dominican Order; More, reluctantly, had to recognize that he was called to an active life. So it was fitting that, at the time of his own decision, he thought it well to bring before his countrymen the example of this devout scholar of Italy.

This translation is the earliest specimen we have of More's English prose. Here is a typical passage.

> Of outward observances he gave no very great force: we speak not of those observances which the Church commandeth to be observed, for in those he was diligent: but we speak of those ceremonies which folk bring up, setting the very service of God aside, which is (as Christ saith) to be worshipped in spirit and in truth. But in the inward affections of the mind he cleaved to God with very fervent love and devotion. Sometimes that marvellous alacrity languished and almost fell, and after again with great strength rose up into God. In the love of Whom he so fervently burned that on a time as he walked with John Francis, his nephew, in an orchard at Ferrara, in the talking of the love of Christ, he broke out into these words, 'Nephew,' he said, 'this will I show thee, I warn thee keep it a secret; the substance that I have left, after certain books of mine finished, I intend to give out to poor folk, and fencing myself with the crucifix, barefoot walking about the world in every town and castle I purpose to preach of Christ.' Afterwards, I understand, by the especial commandment of God, he changed that purpose and appointed to profess himself in the order of Friars Preachers.

The Life of John Picus has the additional interest of containing original verses by More on subjects suggested by counsels given by Picus. It is all but impossible for true poetry to break through the restrictions of didacticism, and Thomas More's verse lacks inspiration. Here are the two stanzas on the Fourth Condition of a Lover: 'To suffer all thing, though it were death, to be with his love.' After treating the theme in its worldly meaning, More turns to consider its spiritual application.

> If love be strong, hot, mighty and fervent,
> There may no trouble, grief, or sorrow fall,
> But that the lover would be well content
> All to endure and think it eke too small.
> Though it were death, so he might therewithal
> The joyful presence of that person get
> On whom he hath his heart and love yset.
>
> Thus should of God the lover be content
> Any distress or sorrow to endure,
> Rather than to be from God absent,
> And glad to die, so that he may be sure
> By his departing hence for to procure,
> After this valley dark, the heavenly light,
> And of his love the glorious blessed sight.

Chapter V

Marriage

THE date of More's first marriage is not known, but it was not later than January 1505. The evidence for this is that Margaret, the eldest child, was nineteen years of age in October 1524 according to Richard Hyrde's preface to her translation of Erasmus's *Precatio Dominica*, a treatise on the *Pater noster*. Roper tells the story of the marriage:

> He resorted to the house of one Master Colt, a gentleman of Essex, that had oft invited him thither, having three daughters, whose honest conversation and virtuous education provoked him there specially to set his affection. And albeit his mind most served him to the second daughter, for that he thought her the fairest and best favoured, yet when he considered that it would be both great grief and some shame also to the eldest to see her younger sister in marriage preferred before her, he then of a certain pity framed his fancy towards her, and soon after married her.[1]

This may seem to us a strange wooing, but it was in keeping with the ideas of the period when passion was not regarded as the sole basis for matrimony.

The lady of his choice was Jane, the daughter of John Colt of Netherall, near Roydon, on the Hertfordshire border of Essex. Jane Colt's grandfather, Thomas Colt (d. 1471) had been Chancellor of the Exchequer to Edward IV and as such would

---

[1] *Roper*, p. 6.

have known John More; this may explain why the two families were on visiting terms. Jane Colt was one of a very large family;[2] a younger sister, Mary, married William Kemp, and their daughter became the wife of George Cavendish, the servant and biographer of Cardinal Wolsey.

Erasmus wrote of Jane More:

> He married a young girl of good family, who had been brought up with her sisters in their parents' home in the country; choosing her, yet undeveloped, that he might more readily mould her to his tastes. He had her taught literature, and trained her in every kind of music; and she was just growing into a charming life's companion for him, when she died young, leaving him with several children.[3]

We cannot now tell whether Roper's suggestion or that of Erasmus was the correct explanation of More's choice; possibly neither was true. His own feelings were never expressed save for a line in the epitaph he composed for the family tomb.

> *Chara Thomae iacet hic Ioanna Uxorcula Mori*
> Here lies Jane, the dear little wife of Thomas More.

The diminutive '*uxorcula*' suggests a tender affection; that is how he remembered her nearly twenty years after her death.[4]

There were four children: Margaret, born in 1505; Elizabeth, born in 1506; Cecily in 1507, and John, probably in 1509.

Roper says that More 'placed himself and his wife at Bucklersbury.' They may have occupied one of the houses belonging to the Hospital of St. Thomas of Acon on the estate

---

[2] For details, see *Roper*, p. 107.

[3] *Allen*, IV, 999.

[4] He also quartered the Colt arms with his own in the More Chapel of Chelsea Parish Church.

known as The Barge, though the earliest record of More leasing a house there is dated 12th December, 1513.[5] The More family lived in Bucklersbury for some twenty years. Andrea Ammonio, Latin secretary to Henry VIII, seems to have lived with them at this period.

Shortly before his marriage, Thomas More served as a burgess in Parliament for the session 25th January to 30th March, 1504. His constituency is not known; it was not London. Roper's account reads:

> Who, ere ever he had been a reader in court, was in the latter time of King Henry VII made a burgess of the parliament, wherein there were by the king demanded (as I have heard reported) about three-fifteenths for the marriage of his eldest daughter, that then should be the Scottish Queen. At the last debating whereof he made such arguments and reasons there against, that the king's demands thereby were clean overthrown. So that one of the king's Privy Chamber, named Master Tyler, being present thereat, brought word to the king out of the parliament house[6] that a beardless boy had disappointed all his purpose.[7]

This was the last Parliament of Henry's reign. The king was in need of money and asked Parliament, not for three-fifteenths

---

[5] Letters Patent, Henry VIII, 12th August, 1539, refer to the 'tenement and messuage with the appurtenances within the Barge in Bucklersbury' which had been leased to Thomas More and Alice his wife by the hospital in December 1513. For earlier history of the Barge, see J. Watney, *The Hospital of St. Thomas of Acon* (1892), pp. 263-71. *Stow* I, 118 says that in 1603 'one great house builded of stone and timber called the old Barge' was still standing but divided into tenements. The site is probably the pre-blitz Barge Yard at the southern corner of Bucklersbury and modern Walbrook. The 'brook' itself flowed by the western boundary of the Barge, but was probably already covered in by 1500.

[6] This would be the Chapter House by Westminister Abbey, one of the few places where we can picture More in his contemporary surroundings.

[7] *Roper*, p. 7. Doubt has been thrown on the reliability of Roper's story by some historians; others, of equal authority, accept it but without committing themselves to Roper's details.

as Roper says, but for two Aids, one for the marriage the previous year of his daughter Margaret to James IV of Scotland, and the second for the knighting, fifteen years earlier, of Prince Arthur who had died in 1502. Such retroactive demands were particularly obnoxious in view of the king's growing rapacity and the extortionate methods devised by Sir Richard Empson and Edmund Dudley, the latter being speaker of the 1504 Parliament. Roper may have been exaggerating when he claimed that the opposition of Thomas More resulted in the king's demands being 'clean overthrown.' His powers as an orator were considerable, but, as a new and youngish member, he could hardly alone have effected so much by his eloquence. It is unlikely that he was speaking entirely for himself; it is probable that he was the spokesman of the City merchants who had been quick to recognize his talent, and this support may explain why the king took no direct action against the young lawyer. The king's demands were not granted in full; he got £40,000, perhaps half of what he expected.

Roper says that as Thomas More 'nothing having, nothing could lose,' the king 'devised a causeless quarrel against his father keeping him in the Tower until he had made him pay to him an hundred pounds fine.'[8]

Roper stresses the danger that threatened More.

> Shortly hereupon it fortuned that this Sir Thomas More, coming in a suit to Doctor Fox, Bishop of Winchester (one of the king's Privy Council) the Bishop called him aside, and pretending great favour towards him, promised him that, if he would be ruled by him, he would not fail into the king's favour again to restore him; meaning (as it was after conjectured) to cause him thereby to confess his offence against the king, whereby his highness might with the better

---

[8] *Roper*, p. 7.

colour have occasion to revenge his displeasure against him. But when he came from the Bishop, he fell in communication with one, Master Whitford, his familiar friend, then chaplain to that Bishop, and after a Father of Syon, and showed him what the Bishop had said unto him, desiring to have his advice therein; who, for the passion of God, prayed him in no wise to follow his counsel: 'For my lord, my master,' quoth he, 'to serve the king's turn, will not stick to agree to his own father's death.' So Sir Thomas More returned to the Bishop no more. And had not the king soon after died,[9] he was determined to have gone over the sea, thinking that being in the king's indignation, he could not live in England without great danger.[10]

Richard Fox(e), Bishop of Winchester and founder of Corpus Christi College, Oxford, was the most trusted councillor of Henry VII after the death of Cardinal Morton. Erasmus recorded a story told him by Thomas More of the Bishop's astuteness or cunning in extracting money from the clergy; he argued that those well clothed must have plenty of money, while those poorly clothed must be hoarding money; so all could pay. This seems a variation of the dilemma usually ascribed to Morton; but such chicanery is more ancient than the Tudors.

Richard Whitford was a close friend of Erasmus and More; he later entered the Brigittine monastery known as Syon House, and wrote and translated a number of books of devotion; the most influential of these was his translation of *De Imitatione Christi*. In self-abasement he called himself the Wretch of Syon.

Stapleton adds another story of the danger into which More had run by his attitude in Parliament. This concerns Edmund

---

[9] This is an instance of Roper's want of precision in his account of More's life before 1520; Henry died in 1509, five years not 'soon after' this Parliament.

[10] *Roper*, p. 7.

Dudley who, with his colleague Sir Richard Empson,[11] was executed in August 1510.

> As he [Dudley] was being led out to his execution, More went up to him and said, 'Well, Mr. Dudley, in that matter of the exactions was I not right?' 'Oh, Mr. More.' he replied, 'it was by God's guidance that you did not acknowledge your fault to the king, for if you had done so you would most certainly have lost your head.'[12]

Such conversations on the way to execution seem to us somewhat indecorous, but they were matters of course in days when executions were equally matters of course. Shakespeare made good use of the custom.

More did not take refuge on the Continent immediately after the Parliament of 1504, but in 1508 he paid short visits to the Universities of Paris and Louvain. We learn this from a letter he wrote in 1515 to Martin van Dorp, the Dutch scholar. The letter was written at Bruges.

> Seven years ago I saw something of both these Academies [Paris and Louvain]. My visits were not long, but while there I took some pains to know what subjects were taught in each and what was the manner of teaching. And although I respect them both, I have not found by what I heard when I was there or by inquiry from others, any reason to prefer that my own children, for whose education I wish to do my best, should be taught in either of them rather than at Oxford or at Cambridge.[13]

A letter written to Colet towards the end of 1504 (the year of the Parliament) contains no hint that More was anxious about his

---

[11] Empson and Dudley lived in Walbrook and were thus neighbours of the Mores, Kingsford's *Supplementary Notes* to Stow, p. 13.

[12] *Stapleton*, p. 29.

[13] *Rogers*, p. 36. *Nichols*, II, p. 224.

future; he was busy with his legal work; his chief desire was that Colet would return to London and so give him spiritual guidance.[14]

Erasmus was in England again at the end of 1505 or early in 1506 until the following June; he seems to have stayed with Colet most of the time but he saw More frequently. The two friends amused themselves translating some of the dialogues of Lucian from Greek to Latin. Thomas More translated Cynicus, Philopseudes, and Necyomantia (or Menippus). He and Erasmus each translated Tyrannicida and then wrote a declamation on the theme. The problem was that in a country where a tyrannicide was rewarded by the state, a man killed a tyrant's son, and the tyrant then, for grief, committed suicide; the question was, 'Is the assassin entitled to the reward?' Both Erasmus and More argued that he was not so entitled. On 1st May, Erasmus wrote to Richard Whitford to explain what they were doing.

> For several years my dearest Richard, I have been entirely occupied with Greek literature; but lately, in order to resume my intimacy with Latin, I have begun to declaim in that language. In so doing I have yielded to the influence of Thomas More, whose eloquence, as you know, is such that he could persuade even an enemy to do whatever he pleased, while my own affection for the man is so great that, if he bade me dance a hornpipe, I should do at once just as he bade me. He is writing on the same subject,[15] and in such a way as to thresh out and sift every part of it. For I do not think, unless the vehemence of my love leads me astray, that Nature ever formed a mind more present, ready, sharp-sighted and subtle, or in a word more absolutely furnished with every kind of faculty than his. Add to this a power of expression equal to

---

[14] *Rogers*, p. 8.

[15] *I.e.*, the tyrannicide problem.

his intellect, a singular cheerfulness of character and an abundance of wit, but only of the candid sort; and you miss nothing that should be found in a perfect advocate. I have therefore not undertaken this task with any idea of either surpassing or matching such an artist, but only to break a lance as it were in this tourney of wits with the sweetest of all my friends, with whom I am always pleased to join in any employment grave or gay. I have done this all the more willingly because I very much wish this sort of exercise to be introduced into our schools, where it would be of the greatest utility.[16]

On his way to Italy in 1506, Erasmus arranged for the book to be printed by Badius in Paris with the title *Luciani Opuscula ... ab Erasmo Roterodamo et Thomas Moro*. It was reprinted at least thirteen times during More's life; Erasmus added translations of other dialogues in later editions, but More did not increase his share.[17]

What was it in these dialogues that the two friends found so congenial? Lucian is no longer a much-read author, but at that period his works had been re-discovered and he was greatly esteemed. He was a master of the satiric dialogue, and he scoffed at pretentiousness and humbug; the gods, sophists, astrologers, and quacks were butts for his mordant wit. The Utopians were later described as taking 'delight in Lucian's sprightliness and wit.'[18] Both Erasmus and More showed a similar attitude towards the charlatans of their day; with More it was a passing phase, but Erasmus never lost the Lucianic touch.

As a preface to the book, More wrote a letter to Thomas

---

[16] *Nichols*, I, p. 406; *Allen*, I, 191.

[17] See C.R. Thompson. *The Translations of Lucian by Erasmus and St. Thomas More* (New York, 1940).

[18] *Utopia*, p. 81; p. 95.

Ruthall, one of the king's secretaries. It contains an expression of his opinions at that time.

The *Necyomantia*, the name of which is not so happy as its matter, attacks in the wittiest fashion the impositions of conjurors, the empty fictions of poets, and the uncertain sparring of philosophers on every possible subject. There remains the Philopseudes, a dialogue as profitable as it is witty, which exposes and ridicules with Socratic irony the common appetite for lying; wherein it does not much disturb me to find that the author was not sure of his own immortality; sharing in this respect the error of Democritus, Lucretius, Pliny, and many others. Why indeed should I care for the opinion of a Pagan upon matters which are among the chief mysteries of the Christian faith? The dialogue at any rate teaches us, on the one hand, not to put faith in the illusions of magic, and on the other, to keep our minds clear of the superstition which creeps in under the guise of religion. We shall lead a happier life, when we are less terrified by those dismal and superstitious lies, which are often repeated with so much confidence and authority, that even St. Augustine himself, a man of the highest intelligence, with the deepest hatred of a lie, was induced by some impostor to narrate,[19] as a true event which had happened in his own time, that story about the two Spurini, one dying and the other returning to life, which, with only a change of name, had been ridiculed by Lucian in this very dialogue so many years before. No wonder then, if ruder minds are affected by the fictions of those who think they have done a lasting service to Christ, when they have invented a fable about some Saint or a tragic description of Hell, which either melts an old woman to tears, or makes her blood run cold.

---

[19] *De cura pro mortuis*, cap. Xii, 15.

There is scarcely any life of a Martyr or Virgin, in which some falsehood of this kind has not been inserted; an act of piety no doubt, considering the risk that Truth would be insufficient, unless propped up by lies! Thus they have not scrupled to stain with fiction that Religion, which was founded by Truth herself, and ought to consist of naked truth. They have failed to see that such fables are so far from aiding religion, that nothing can be more injurious to it. It is obvious, as Augustine himself has observed,[20] that where there is any scent of a lie, the authority of truth is immediately weakened and destroyed. Hence, a suspicion has more than once occurred to me, that such stories have been largely invented by crafty knaves and heretics, partly for the purpose of amusing themselves with the credulity of persons more simple than wise, and partly to diminish the authority of the true Christian histories by associating them with fictitious fables, the feigned incidents being often so near to those contained in Holy Scripture, that the allusion cannot be mistaken. Therefore while the histories commended to us by divinely inspired Scripture ought to be accepted with undoubting faith, the others, tested by the doctrine of Christ, as by the rule of Critolaus,[21] should either be received with caution or rejected, if we would avoid both empty confidence and superstitious fear.[22]

One result of this work was to increase More's liking for the dialogue which had proved so congenial in his study of Plato; he used this form in many of his later writings and evidently found the dramatic style the best suited to his genius. It is, therefore, necessary to be careful to distinguish his own opinions from

---

[20] *De Mendacio*, cap. x, 17.

[21] Head of the Peripatetic School of Rome, c. 150 B.C.

[22] *Rogers*, pp. 12-13. *Nicholas*, I, pp. 403-5.

those of assumed characters; this is not always a simple task, but failure to carry it out may lead to attributing to him ideas and beliefs that were not in fact his.

It was probably after Erasmus had left England in 1506 that Thomas More paid a visit to his sister Elizabeth at Coventry.[23] She had married John Rastell,[24] who in 1506, succeeded his father as coroner of that town. The versatility and energy of John Rastell have the true Renaissance flavour. When he left Coventry for London, in addition to being an active lawyer, he became a printer, a writer of law books, a military engineer, a deviser of pageants and plays, and a frustrated venturer to the New Found Lands; in his last years he joined in religious controversy, and died a prisoner for obstinately protesting against tithes. This vigorous and gifted man must not be left out of the More circle, he brought into it a verve and a restlessness that must have been disturbing to quiet scholars like William Lily.

It is not known how the Rastells and Mores came together; probably it was through the law. There is a record in the King's Book of Payments for 1499 that links John More, John Rastell and Thomas More as guarantors for a sum of one hundred marks.

The visit to Coventry is of interest not only as an introduction to John Rastell but for an incident described by Thomas More in a long letter, written about 1520, to an unnamed Monk. There was, More recalled, a friar of Coventry who used to preach that whoever said daily Our Lady's Psalter[25] could never be damned. The people became over-zealous in this devotion as they took it to mean that in this fashion they could secure impunity for all sins. The parish priest at length warned them that this devotion

---

[23] *Rogers*, p. 197.

[24] For the life of this extraordinary man and of his son William and his son-in-law 'merry John Heywood,' see A.W. Reed, *Early Tudor Drama* (1926). It is shocking to record that this important contribution to scholarship was remaindered!

[25] A Rosary of a hundred and fifty Hail Marys.

must not be regarded in this way; the friar warmly maintained that he was right and the parish priest wrong. The account continues:

> While this question was raging, it happened that I arrived at Coventry on a visit to my sister. I had scarcely got off my horse when the question was put even to me, whether anyone could be damned who daily recited Our Lady's Psalter. I laughed at the foolish inquiry, but was at once warned that I was doing a dangerous thing since a most holy and learned father had preached against those that did so. I dismissed the matter as no affair of mine. I was then invited to dinner; I accepted and went. In comes an old friar, dry as dust, severe and sour; a boy follows him with some books. I saw that I was in for an argument. We sat down, and, so as to lose no time, the question was at once put by our host. The friar answered just as he had preached. I said nothing; I do not like to meddle in annoying and fruitless disputes. At last they asked for my opinion. As I was obliged to speak, I told them what I thought, but briefly and with moderation. Then the friar poured out a long prepared speech which might have made two sermons. His whole argument depended on certain miracles which he read from a *Mariale* and from other books of that kind which he had brought to the table to add authority to his speech. When he had at last finished, I quietly answered that he had said nothing in his whole discourse capable of convincing those who did not admit the truth of those miracles, which they might deny without abjuring the Christian faith, and that even if they were absolutely proved, they had little to do with the question. For though you may find a king ready to pardon something in an enemy at the prayers of his mother, yet there is nowhere one so foolish as to promulgate a law encouraging the disobedience of his subjects by a promise of impunity provided they paid homage to his mother. Much was said on both sides, but I only succeeded in getting laughed at while he

was smothered in praise.... I have not related this in order to impute crime to any body of religious, since the same ground produces herbs both wholesome and poisonous; nor do I wish to find fault with the custom of those who salute Our Divine Lady, than which nothing can be more beneficial; but because some trust so much in their devotions that they draw from them boldness to sin.[26]

The marriage of Elizabeth More to John Rastell has a special importance; their second son was William Rastell whose devotion to his uncle's memory led him to collect his English works and to publish them in the folio of 1557.

Thomas More's eldest sister, Joan, married Richard Staverton (or Stafferton) who had been admitted to Lincoln's Inn at the same date as his future brother-in-law. The marriage took place at a date earlier than 26th October, 1499, for the Hustings Rolls of the City of London record a quit-claim of a messuage by

John More of London, gentleman, and Johanna his wife; Thomas More of London, gentleman, son and heir apparent of John More of London; and Richard Staverton of London, gentleman and Joan his wife, one of the daughters of John More of London. Richard Staverton became a legal official under the City of London.

Thomas More's younger sister, Agatha and his brother, Edward, probably died young; his other brother, John, is a shadowy figure. In November 1511 Ammonio told Erasmus, 'John More brought me your letter.' Shortly afterwards Erasmus asked Ammonio 'to arrange with More for giving it [a MS] to his brother to transcribe.'[27] This suggests that John More was a scribe, or perhaps secretary to his brother; there is no later reference to him.

---

[26] *Rogers*, pp. 198-9.

[27] *Allen*, I, p. 246.

King Henry VIII

Chapter VI

The Rising Lawyer

HENRY VII died in April 1509. During his reign of twenty-four years he had established law and order but in his latter years he had become increasingly despotic and extortionate, and his death brought a sense of relief. His successor, Henry VIII, was welcomed by all, not least because nearly sixty years had passed since a son had followed a father on the throne of England. But he was also welcomed for his own sake; his magnificent figure and his intellectual and social accomplishments seemed to promise a golden reign, and men turned from the grimness of the father's last years to the dawn of the son's reign as the beginning of a new era.

Thomas More wrote congratulatory verses in Latin to Henry VIII on his coronation which took place, with that of his Queen, Catherine of Aragon, on 24th June. The British Museum has what is probably the copy presented to the king; it is a beautifully illuminated manuscript on vellum. The verses show that More shared the bright hopes of the time as he compared the prospects before the realm under his brilliant young king, 'entering into the flower of his pleasant youth,'[1] with the increasing gloom of the previous decade. He did not flatter the new king's father; he allowed him the epithet '*prudentissimus*,'[2] but he criticized his avarice. Some ten years later he defended his censure of Henry

---

[1] *Cavendish*, p. 12.

[2] *Rogers*, p. 13.

VII in a letter to *Germanus Brixius*.[3]

More was by no means singular in regarding the young king as the herald of a new era of peace and learning. Indeed his language was moderate in comparison with that used by others. Here, for instance, is what Lord Mountjoy wrote to Erasmus at the end of May 1509.

> What may you not promise yourself from a prince, with whose extraordinary and almost divine character you are well acquainted, and to whom you are not only known but intimate, having received from him (as few others have) a letter traced with his own fingers? But when you know what a hero he now shows himself, how wisely he behaves, what a lover he is of justice and goodness, what affection he bears to the learned I will venture to swear that you will need no wings to make you fly to behold this new and auspicious star.[4]

Erasmus at once set out from Italy in high hopes that at last he would be assured of a competence to enable him to continue his studies without material anxieties. During his journey he conceived the idea of what was to prove one of his most popular books, *Praise of Folly*, or *Moriæ Encomium*. In a prefatory letter to More, the author explained the origin of the book.

> When of late days I was returning from Italy to England, being unwilling to waste the whole time that I had to spend on horseback to illiterate talk, I sometimes preferred either to think over some of our common studies, or to enjoy the recollection of the friends, no less amiable than learned, that I had left there. Of these, my More, you were among the first I called to mind, being wont to enjoy the remembrance of you

---

[3] *Rogers*, Letter 86.

[4] *Nichols*, I, p. 457. *Allen*, I 215. Henry does not seem to have carried his learning much beyond that acquired during his tutelage. He was not a patron of learning; the scholars found Catherine of Aragon a more reliable and informed ally.

in your absence, as I had, when you were present, enjoyed your company, than which I protest I have never met with anything more delightful in my life. Therefore, since at any rate something had to be done, and the occasion did not seem suited for serious meditation, I chose to amuse myself with the Praise of Folly. What Pallas, you will say, put that idea into your head? Well, the first thing that struck me was your surname of More, which is just as near the name of Moria or Folly, as you are far from the thing, from which by general acclamation you are remote indeed. In the next place I surmised, that this playful production of our genius would find special favour with you, disposed as you are to take pleasure in jests of this kind— jests, which, I trust, are neither ignorant nor quite insipid —and generally in society, to play the part of a sort of Democritus; although for that matter, while from the unusual clearness of your mind you differ widely from the vulgar, still such is your incredible sweetness and good nature, that you are able to be on terms of fellowship with all mankind, and are delighted at all hours to be so.[5]

Writing to Martin Dorp in 1515, Erasmus gave an account of the composition of the book.

I was staying with More after my return from Italy, when I was kept several days in the house by lumbago. My library had not yet arrived; and if it had, my illness forbade exertion in more serious studies. So, for want of employment, I began to amuse myself with the Praise of Folly, not with any intention of publishing the result, but to relieve the discomfort of sickness by this sort of distraction. I showed a specimen of the unfinished work to some friends in order to heighten the enjoyment of the ridiculous by sharing it. They

---

[5] *Nichols*, II, p. 1; *Allen*, I, 459.

were mightily pleased, and insisted on my going on. I complied, and spent some seven days upon the work; an expenditure of time, which I thought out of proportion to the importance of the subject. Afterwards the same persons who had encouraged me to write contrived to have the book taken to France and printed.[6]

The last sentence is not candid; Erasmus himself took the manuscript to Paris in April 1511 and arranged for its printing. By 1515 he was anxious to minimize his part in the affair as the book had given great offence, and was being used in a way he had certainly not intended. This was not the only occasion when Erasmus tried to evade responsibility for his indiscretions.

More and his friends were at one with Erasmus in wishing to rid the Church of the abuses that damaged its authority and influence, and as the attack in Praise of Folly was directed against persons and superstitions and not doctrine, they hoped it would draw attention to the need for reform. But ridicule is a dangerous weapon; it can arm enemies with arguments. The name of Martin Luther was still unknown in 1510, and the danger to the Church seemed to be not so much heresy as internal corruption.

In later years More recognized the unfortunate effects that may come from satirising the weaknesses of the human instruments of the Church. Thus he wrote to Erasmus in 1532:

> Your adversaries cannot be ignorant how candidly you confess that, before these pestilent heresies arose, which have since spread everywhere and upset everything, you treated certain matters in a way you would not have treated them had you been able to guess that such enemies of religion and such traitors would ever arise. You would then have put what you had to say more mildly and with more limitations. You wrote strongly then because you were indignant at seeing how some

---

[6] *Nichols*, II, p. 5.

cherished their vices as if they were virtues.⁷

About the same time More wrote in his *Confutation of Tyndale's Answer*,

> In these days in which Tyndale hath with the infection of his contagious heresies so sore poisoned malicious and new-fangled folk... in these days in which men, by their own default, misconstrue and take harm out of the very Scripture of God, until men better amend, if any man would now translate Moria into English, or some works either that I have myself written ere this, albeit there be none harm therein, folk yet being given to take harm of that which is good, I would not only my darling's⁸ books, but mine own also, help to burn them with mine own hands, rather than folk should (though through their own fault) take any harm of them, seeing that I see them likely in these days so to do.⁹

The tragedy of Erasmus was that he never realized, as More so quickly did, how disruptive his ridicule could prove when the enemies of the Church were gathering to attack. The two men did not meet again after 1520, and, though they kept in touch with each other, there was no longer that interchange of argument in conversation that both enjoyed so much. More was ten years junior to Erasmus, and there may have been a certain measure of that uncritical admiration that a young man can give to an older. The death of John Colet in 1519 meant the loss of a friend of his own age who might have persuaded Erasmus to use his great gifts in defence of the Church. As we shall see,¹⁰ More tried to provoke him to speak out against Luther, but the result was disappointing.

---

⁷ *Allen*, X 2659.

⁸ More here uses Tyndale's reference to Erasmus.

⁹ E.W., p. 422.

¹⁰ See below, p. 215.

Erasmus went his own way. The weaknesses and contradictions of his character are revealed in his letters for all to see. His love of his own comfort, his unscrupulous search for patronage, his irritability at criticism, his timidity, his equivocations, his inability to control tongue and pen when the spirit of satire possessed him—all these traits must be admitted and weighed against his devotion to learning and his services to scholarship; yet there was a fascination of personality that few could resist. John Fisher and Thomas More remained his friends to the end; he had deep admiration and affection for both, but in their days of affliction he dared not speak out on their behalf.

The rapid increase in the use of Thomas More's services in the City of London dates from the accession of Henry VIII. This may have been a coincidence; the shadow of the displeasure of Henry VII may have been sufficient to discourage the City merchants from employing the young lawyer. A 'Thomas More, gentleman' was admitted to the freedom of the Mercers' Company, 21st March, 1509; to quote the entry in the records, 'Master Thomas More, gentleman, desired to be free of this fellowship, which was granted him by the whole company to have it frank and free.'[11] The probability is that this is our Thomas More; his admission would be by patrimony as his father was a Mercer. John Colet was also a freeman of the Company by patrimony. In September of that year Thomas More was called upon to act as Latin interpreter when the Pensionary (chief magistrate) of Antwerp came to discuss some difficulties that had arisen between that city and the Merchant Adventurers. This body was a fellowship of traders, chiefly in cloth, with Flanders, and included representatives of several of the Livery Companies, but the lead was taken by the Mercers, and it was they who asked Thomas More to be their Latin speaker.

---

[11] *Acts of Count of the Mercers' Company*, ed. L. Lyall and F.D. Watney (1936), p. 320. The editors identify this Thomas More with ours.

THE RISING LAWYER 65

An account of the matters under discussion would be out of place here; the part played by More has its importance as confirming his association with the Mercers and his recognized ability as a Latin orator. One passage from the records shows the decorum of the proceedings in the Mercers' Hall; the Church mentioned is St. Thomas of Acon.

> Then was there assigned Master Governor and three Wardens of divers Companies to go down into the Church and for to bring up the said Pensionary, and so it was done, and after he was comen up and made his obeisance, Master Governor brought him to the north end of the table and caused him to sit down his face toward the South. Then Master More sitting on the South bench next the window began to declare unto him the mind and pleasure of the Company in Latin.

The Pensionary was satisfied with the answer and 'saith that and he wist to do us any pleasure he would be glad to tarry two times so long.'

> Then when he had declared as is aforesaid all in Latin, Master More did interpret the same in English to the company, and then they arose and every man went his way.[12]

This episode and More's skill as a Latinist and orator have been used to support the argument that 'it was his training in grammar and rhetoric that opened to him the career at court.'[13] This is to put too much emphasis on but one of his many gifts; a

---

[12] *Acts*, pp. 334-5.

[13] See *Thomas More, Grammarian and Orator*, by William Nelson, *P.M.L.A.*, June 1943. Mr. Nelson also argues that it was our Thomas More who in 1513 was granted a degree in grammar (Latin) at Oxford (University Archives, Register G., fol. 183). I doubt this; by that date our Thomas More, as we shall see, was a busy official and lawyer. The name More was not uncommon; another Thomas More is found in the City records, and the Mercers' *Acts* give three John Mores. At least one writer, Russel Ames, *Citizen Thomas More* (1949), pp. 34-6.

career that led to the Woolsack called for greater abilities than those of a rhetorician. As we shall see, his skill in negotiations on behalf of the City merchants probably attracted the attention of Henry VIII and of Wolsey.

In 1510 a Thomas More was chosen a burgess to represent the City of London in Parliament; he took the place of James Yarford, a Mercer, who resigned on becoming an Alderman. Roper makes no mention of this election, and some have questioned if our Thomas More was in this Parliament. A reference in Richard Hill's *Commonplace Book* to 'Young More, burgess of the parliament for London'[14] in 1510 is evidence for the identification, since Thomas More was often distinguished in this way from his father. This is mentioned in the Epitaph: while his father was alive (up to 1530), he was 'usually called young.' James Yarford and Thomas More frequently worked together in the interests of the Mercers; the other burgesses were the Recorder and two other Mercers, John Tate and John Bruges—an indication of the influence of that company at that period. The Parliament was a short one lasting just over a month; as Thomas More replaced another burgess, his service was brief. He did not represent the City again.[15] This may be explained by his appointment as Under-Sheriff on 3rd September, 1510. The custom was to elect the Recorder, an Alderman and two Liverymen; if one of the latter became an Alderman during the Parliament, he resigned to make way for another Liveryman. An appointment under the City would probably mean that such an official could not be a burgess.

More was appointed Under-Sheriff in place of Richard Brook who had been elected Recorder of the City. Acting on behalf of one of the Sheriffs, More tried cases coming to the court of the

---

[14] Balliol MS. 354, fol. 236 verso.

[15] For a list of burgesses, see Appendix B, Vol. III, of R.R. Sharpe's *London and the Kingdom* (1895).

Poultry Compter,[16] one of the two prisons of the Sheriffs; he held this position until 1518. Erasmus, writing in 1519, thought the Under-Sheriff was a more important person than in fact he was;

> In the City of London, his birthplace, he has been for some years a judge in civil cases: an office which has little work (the court only sits on Thursday mornings till dinnertime) but confers great honour. No one has disposed of more cases than he, nor shown more honesty: indeed he usually remits the fees charged to litigants, three shillings deposited by either side beforehand, a fixed sum which may not be exceeded. By such conduct he has made himself much beloved in the City.[17]

Roper tells us that by his office as Under-Sheriff 'and his learning together (as I have heard him say) he gained without grief [trouble] not so little as four hundred pounds by the year.'[18]

Earlier that year, 22nd February, 1510, he was appointed to the Commission of the Peace for Hampshire.[19] The Tudors considerably increased the duties and powers of the justices of the peace. One or two councillors were appointed to each commission. They could not attend every session, but they went frequently enough to be able to report to the Council on the efficiency of the magistrates. More's appointment would necessitate visits to Winchester and probably Southampton. The experience brought him into contact with country problems and conditions in what was then an important wool and cloth-producing county.

By his early thirties, Thomas More had developed a fully

---

[16] This fact is given in the *Repertory* (Court of Alderman) 3,221, where on his resignation he is described as 'unus Subvicecomes Civitatis in Computatore Pulletr' london ...'

[17] *Allen*, IV, 999. Allen's translation.

[18] *Roper*, p. 6.

[19] *L.P.* (Henry VIII), I, 904. He was later appointed to the Commission of Array for Hampshire. *L.P.* (Henry VIII), I, 1812.

active life. As a lawyer he was Reader in Lincoln's Inn in 1511 and 1515, and practised in the courts; he presided over one of the Sheriff's courts in London; he was a Justice of the Peace for Hampshire; the Mercers were using his services as Latin orator, and the Staplers and Fishmongers sought his advice. Here was business enough for any man. But all this we must see against the background of his personal and family life. He had a wife and four children and his devotion to them and the cheerful companionship he gave them are a well-established tradition. Then there were his many scholar friends—Grocyn, Linacre, Ammonio, Lily, and above all, John Colet who, at this period was busy making plans with the Mercers for the future maintenance of his new school, of which Lily was the first headmaster.

If a description of More's life stopped there it would lack its essential characteristic. A few sentences from Stapleton[20] will supply what is lacking.

> First, then, as regards the service of God, he lived almost the life of a monk. Every day before all other business, except sometimes his morning studies, he heard Mass... He recited each morning and evening prayers, to which he added the Seven Penitential Psalms[21] and the Litanies. Often too he said in addition the Gradual Psalms and the *Beati Immaculati*.[22]

On 19th May, 1511, Ammonio wrote to Erasmus, 'Our sweetest More and his gentle wife, who never remembers you without wishing you well, with his children and whole household, are in excellent health.' The gentle wife, his '*cara uxorcula*,' died that summer.[23]

---

[20] Pp. 66-67.

[21] Psalms 6, 31, 37, 50, 101, 129, 142 (Vulgate numbering).

[22] Psalm 118.

[23] The exact date is not known but it was between the date of this letter and the end of October 1511; see 102.

Chapter VII

RICHARD III

THOMAS MORE'S parish priest at this time was John Bouge who later withdrew to the Carthusian monastery at Epworth in Axholm, Lincolnshire. In 1535 he wrote to Dame Katherine Mann a letter of advice and comfort in those perplexing days. From this letter we learn of Thomas More's second marriage.

> Item, as for Sir Thomas More, he was my parishioner at London. I christened him two goodly children. I buried his first wife, and within a month after he came to me on a Sunday at night late and there he brought me a dispensation to be married the next Monday without any banns asking; and as I understand she is yet alive. This Mr. More was my ghostly child: in his confession to be so pure, so clean, with great study, deliberation, and devotion, I never heard many such: a gentleman of great learning, both in law, art, and divinity, having no man like him now alive of a layman. Item, a gentleman of great soberness and gravity, one chief of the King's Council. Item, a gentleman of little refection and marvellous diet.[1]

The lady was a widow, Alice Middleton; she was seven years older than Thomas More. She may have been an Arden as the arms of that family are on the monument in Chelsea Old Church. Her first husband was a merchant of London and of the Staple at

---

[1] The full text is given in *E.H.R.*, 1892, pp. 713-15.

Calais; he died in the autumn of 1509.² One of her daughters, Alice, became as much one of More's family as his own children.

The earliest contemporary reference we have to Dame Alice More—if indeed it does refer to her—comes in a letter from Ammonio to Erasmus dated 27th October, 1511.

> I have moved at last into St. Thomas's College, where I am more housed according to my ideas than I was with More. I do not see *the hooked beak of the harpy*, but there are many other things that offend me, so that I really do not know how I can still go on living in England.³

The italicized phrase was written in Greek;⁴ it has been assumed, that the harpy was Dame Alice More, but Holbein's portrait shows that her nose was far from being hooked. So perhaps Ammonio was either writing metaphorically, or was referring to some other tormentor.

Roper does not mention Dame Alice until she visited her husband in the Tower in 1535, but Harpsfield paints a rather unattractive picture.

> After the death of his first wife, he married a widow, which continued with him till he suffered; whom he full entirely loved and most lovingly used, though he had by her no children, and though she were aged, blunt and rude. And in this he shewed his great wisdom, or rather piety, and godliness: wisdom in taking that for the best, or rather making that the best, that otherwise could not be helped; his piety and godliness in cherishing her no less lovingly and tenderly than if she had been his first young wife, blessed and adorned with happy and divers issue of her body; whom in

---

² Full details given in *Roper*, p. 124.

³ *Nichols*, II, p. 31; *Allen*, I 236.

⁴ The explanation of this baffling phrase was first given by P.S. Allen; see previous reference.

very deed he rather married for the ruling and governing of his children, house and family, than for any bodily pleasure. And yet such she was, being most spareful and given to profit, he so framed and fashioned her by his dexterity that he lived a sweet and pleasant life with her, and brought her to that case that she learned to play and sing at the lute and virginals, and every day at his returning home he took a reckoning and account of the task he enjoined her touching the said exercise.[5]

Harpsfield was here making use of the letter about More that Erasmus wrote to Ulrich von Hutten in 1519 where he calls her 'a shrewd and careful mistress of a house' and goes on to describe the musical training to which she was subjected. There is an earlier reference to her by Erasmus towards the end of his visit to the Mores in August 1516; he wrote to Ammonio, 'I feel myself becoming a stale guest to More's wife.'[6] Our sympathies may well be with her, for Erasmus must have been a pernickety person to have in the house.

Two passages in *A Dialogue of Comfort* may refer to Dame Alice More.

...as a shrewd wife once told her husband that she would do when she came from shrift [confession]. Be merry, man, quoth she now, for this day I thank God was I well shriven. And I purpose now therefore to leave off all mine old shrewdness and begin even afresh... Indeed, it seemed she spake it half in sport; for that she said she would cast away all her old shrewdness, therein I trow she sported. But in that she said she would begin it all afresh, her husband found that good earnest.

---

[5] *Harpsfield*, p. 93.

[6] *Nichols*, II, p. 320. *Allen*, II, p. 451.

It maketh me think upon a good worshipful man which, when he divers times beheld his wife, what pain she took in strait binding up her hair to make her a fair large forehead, and with strait bracing in her body to make her middle small, both twain to her great pain for the pride of a little foolish praise, he said unto her: 'Forsooth, madam, if God give you not hell, He shall do you great wrong; for it must needs be your own of very right. For you buy it very dear and take very great pain therefore.'[7]

Thomas More's services to the City and the Companies steadily increased in number and variety. We find him in 1512 going with others before the King's Council to 'know their pleasure for biscuit, etc., for the king'; he was one of the representatives of the Merchant Staplers in a dispute with the Merchant Adventurers; he was the spokesman in 'the parliament house' for the Wardens of ten Companies who agreed to put themselves temporarily under the 'Rule of the Mayor'; with his father he went to discuss some matter of City government with the Duke of Buckingham and the Bishop of Norwich. In the following year, 1513, he again attended the King's Council, and later he was appointed with others to see to the care of London Bridge. A year later he received a fee of twenty shillings as the City's adviser when some foreign alum was confiscated; he was also appointed to the Commission of Sewers for the River Thames from Greenwich to Lambeth.[8]

On 3rd December, 1514, Thomas More was admitted to the Society of Advocates, or Doctors of Civil (Roman) Law, the later Doctors' Commons. It is believed that the entry in the register is in his handwriting.[9] At that time this Society was a kind of club

---

[7] *Dialogue of Comfort*, p. 248 and 291.

[8] For full references, see *Harpsfield*, pp. 312-13.

[9] A facsimile is given in *Transactions of the Royal Society of Literature*, 1879.

including Tunstal, Colet, Crocyn and Bonner amongst its members.

During the period that he was busy in these many ways, he wrote his *History of Richard III*, of which he left two versions, one in Latin and the other in English. When the authentic English text was first published in 1557 by William Rastell, he headed it with this statement:

> The History of King Richard the Third (unfinished) written by Master Thomas More then one of the Under-Sheriffs of London, about the year of Our Lord 1513. Which work hath been before this time printed in Hardyng's Chronicle and in Hall's Chronicle, but very much corrupt in many places, sometime having less and sometime having more, and altered in words and whole sentences, much varying from the copy of his own hand, by which this is printed.

That would seem to be an unquestionable statement made by a scrupulous editor writing with full authority. Yet it has been suggested that Cardinal Morton was the author of the Latin version and More the translator. This thesis is no longer tenable; it has been fully examined and found to conflict with the evidence, external and internal. It is not proposed here to go over the ground again as this would serve no purpose.[10] It is more difficult to know which version, the Latin or the English, came first; it will suffice here to give the opinion of scholars who have carefully examined the problem; neither version is an exact translation of the other; the Latin one was intended for readers on the Continent, and the English version for this country. It seems probable that More worked on both versions at the same period.[11]

William Rastell referred to the inclusion of More's *Richard III*

---

[10] R.W. Chambers in *E.W.*, I, pp. 24-53.

[11] *E.W.*, I, p. 52 and p. 194.

in the Chronicles of Hardyng and Hall; both these were extended and edited by Richard Grafton. He included a corrupt version of More's *Richard III* in his edition of Hardyng in 1543, but, as Henry VIII was still alive, he did not give the author's name; when, soon after Henry's death in 1548, he printed Hall's Chronicle, he added a note against the account of the reign of Edward V:

> This King's time with some part of Richard the III as shall appear by a note made at that place was written by Sir Thomas More.

The second note, at the end of the story of the Princes in the Tower, read,

> From the beginning of King Edward the fifth: hitherto is of Sir Thomas More's penning.

Actually More's English narrative went further and ended with the conversation between the Bishop of Ely (Morton) and Buckingham soon after the seizure of the crown by Gloucester.

Stapleton noted that More 'studied with avidity all the historical works he could find,' and suggested that the writing of *Richard III* was 'to practise his pen.' We know that Sallust was one of the authors read in the More household, and it may have been with this writer in mind that the narrative was planned.

More selected a period for which he could draw on the personal recollections of Cardinal Morton and of his own father. No doubt the old Cardinal had enjoyed talking of his past days to his young attendant, and Sir John More's devotion to the memory of Edward IV probably put an edge to his thoughts of Gloucester. There would be also many merchants and others to give Thomas More information or gossip about those times. That some things he recorded were based on gossip must be recognized, for there are statements which the modern historian cannot accept as facts in the light of more reliable evidence. Moreover it should be remembered that, in the classical manner, More put speeches into the mouths of his characters that are dramatically conceived; again, in the style of his models, he used the history of Richard III to illustrate a theme; it is a study of dissimulation and perfidy.

It was fortunate that More's history was incorporated in the compilations of the chroniclers. Political and religious feeling made it hazardous for a printer to issue it separately, but the book could exert its influence without too much attention being drawn to the author in a folio containing the work of a number of writers. Thus it early established a conception of Richard III which later scholarship has modified but has not radically altered. Shakespeare in using Holinshed's Chronicle (which included More's narrative) helped to fix this conception when he put *Richard III* on the stage.[12]

It is a loss to history and to literature that Thomas More did not complete this vivid narrative. There is nothing earlier in English with which it can be compared. The only contemporary work that suggests a parallel is *The Life and Death of Thomas Wolsey* by the George Cavendish who married Jane More's niece. But this is a biography written as a tribute to a loved master, and not a history of a reign. The chroniclers of the time were industrious compilers and editors; Edward Hall's own account of Henry VIII's reign was not published until 1542. More's *Richard III* was a pioneer work in English historical writing, and it did not suffer the eclipse that was to obscure his other writings. His main influence, therefore, as historian and as a writer of English was largely through this unfinished book.

Dr. Johnson in his 'History of the English Language' prefaced to his Dictionary, gave over eight folio pages out of twenty-seven to extracts from More;[13] three of these were taken up with an

---

[12] For some interesting notes on Shakespeare's use of More's *Richard III*, see E.M. W. Tillyard, *Shakespear's History Plays*, (1944), pp. 38-40; 209.

[13] In introducing the extracts, Dr. Johnson wrote 'it appears from Ben Jo(h)nson that his works were considered as models of pure and elegant style.' This is misleading. Johnson made no statement that could be so interpreted. In his *English Grammar* he gave a number of examples of usage from *Richard III*, but he also quoted from Ascham, Jewel, Cheke, and

extract from *Richard III*, but no less than five were given to the poems. Johnson justified this proportion on the grounds of vocabulary rather than of style. He at the same time paid tribute to the excellence of the Rastell folio.

The game of influences and sources is an easy one to play as speculation is rarely limited by firm evidence; it is impossible to assess the effects of More's style on later writers; what could be suggested of his influence could be said with equal confidence of Berner's translation of Froissart (1523). When an attempt is made to describe More's debts to previous writers of English, it must be admitted that there is little evidence on which to base an opinion. It may be that he was influenced by the vernacular writers of books of devotion, or by the books published by Caxton; but this is little more than a harmless speculation since he himself gives no information on which to base an opinion.[14]

We do know with what intensity he studied the early Fathers of the Church, and classical writers, and to them his references are frequent. Here we are on safer ground in seeing the influence of Sallust on the form of *Richard III*, and of Lucian in the spirit of the book and in its style.

The *History* is the most consistent in style of More's English

---

Foxe (of the Martyrs), amongst others.

[14] The most important discussion of this topic is R.W. Chambers, *Continuity of English Prose*, published separately (1932) and also as an introduction to *Harpsfield*. Prof. J.S. Phillimore suggested that 'whatever the language was when More found it, where he left it, there it remained until Dryden definitely civilized it. (*Dublin Review*, July 1913). Chambers quotes, without endorsing, the opinion in *Continuity*, cxlvi, n. 5. Dr. A. C. Southern in his *Elizabethan Recusant Prose* (1950) accepts Phillimore's thesis. It is not possible here to discuss in detail a proposition I find it impossible to accept. The protagonists, while rightly drawing attention to the qualities of the prose of Catholic writers who fled abroad, have not shown that the same qualities were lacking in all English authors between More and Dryden. The exuberance of much Elizabethan and Jacobean prose has obscured the fact that, *at the same time*, there was much good, direct English being written. The prose of Shakespeare (so often overlooked) will serve as one example of many. The 'Continuity of English Prose' did not suddenly break off at More's death.

writings; he did not, unfortunately, write *Utopia* in English, and his later vernacular works were of a controversial character that called for argument rather than for narrative and description; all contain passages that are memorable; there are humorous digressions, and interludes of vivid narrative, but there are also long, complicated sentences and involved passages that make hard reading. These blemishes do not occur in the *History*, but his style is rarely simple; he likes to bring together many details to form his pictures, a kind of literary pointillism, and he delights in picturesque similes and phrases. More had a quick sense of drama and his best writing was done when this sense was called into play; the turbulent reign of Richard III provided rich material on which to work. So outstanding is this characteristic, it is not idle to speculate that had he lived in Elizabethan times, he would have found his natural form of expression in the drama.[15]

There are a number of scenes in the *History* that are dramatic reconstructions based on what More had heard or on popular report. Thus it would not be difficult to transfer to the stage the scene between Cardinal Beaufort and the Queen when he tries to persuade her to let the young Duke of York leave sanctuary.[16] Then there is the farce of the blundering sermon of Dr. Shaw when he so badly mistimed his appeal to the people to declare themselves for 'King' Richard. After explaining that King Edward was never 'lawfully married unto the Queen, but was, before God, husband unto dame Elizabeth Lacy, and so his children bastards,' the preacher declared

> But the Lord Protector, that very noble Prince, that special pattern of knightly prowess, as well in all princely behaviour as in the lineaments and favour of his visage, represented the very face of the noble Duke, his father. 'This is,' quoth he, 'the

---

[15] See J. Delcourt, *Essai sur la langue de Sir Thomas More* (Montpellier, 1913).

[16] *E.W.*, I, pp. 417-22.

father's own figure, this is his own countenance, the very print of his visage, the sure undoubted image, the plain, express likeness of that noble Duke.'

Now was it before devised that in the speaking of these words the Protector should have come in among the people to the sermonward, to the end that those words, meeting with his presence, might have been taken among the hearers as though the Holy Ghost had put them in the preacher's mouth, and should have moved the people even there to cry 'King Richard! King Richard!'—that it might have been after said that he was specially chosen by God and in manner by miracle. But this device quailed, either by the Protector's negligence or the preacher's overmuch diligence. For while the Protector found by the way tarrying, lest he should prevent[17] those words, and the doctor, fearing that he should come ere his sermon could come to those words, hasted his matter thereto: he was come to them and past them and entered into other matters ere the Protector came; whom when he beheld coming, he suddenly left the matter with which he was in hand and without any deduction thereunto, out of all order, and out of all frame, began to repeat those words again: 'This is the very noble Prince, the special pattern of knightly prowess, which as well in all princely behaviour as in the lineaments and favour of his visage representeth the very face of the noble Duke of York, his father. This is the father's own figure, this is his own countenance, the very print of his visage, the sure undoubted image, the plain, express likeness of the noble Duke, whose remembrance can never die while he liveth.' While these words were in speaking the Protector, accompanied with the Duke of Buckingham, went through the people into the place where

---

[17] Anticipate.

the doctors commonly stand, in the upper storey, where he stood to hearken the sermon. But the people were so far from crying 'King Richard!' that they stood as they had been turned into stones, for wonder of this shameful sermon. After which once ended, the preacher got him home and never after durst look out for shame but keep him out of sight like an owl; and when he once asked one that had been his old friend what the people talked of him, all were it that his own conscience well showed him that they talked no good, yet when the other answered him that there was in every man's mouth spoken of him much shame, it so struck him to the heart that within a few days after he withered and consumed away.[18]

Shakespeare made good use of More's account of Buckingham's appeal to the citizens of London;[19] this was in danger of falling as flat as Dr. Shaw's attempt, but it was better stage-managed, and Richard, feigning reluctance like a newly elected Speaker, took upon him 'the royal estate, pre-eminence, and kingdom of the two noble realms, England and France.' A well-drilled claque cried, 'King Richard!' More's comment was:

> and the people departed, talking diversely of the matter, every man as his fantasy gave him... And so they said that these matters be King's games, as it were stage plays, and for the more part played upon scaffolds. And they that wise be will meddle no farther. For they that sometime step up and play with them, when they cannot play their parts, they disorder the play and do themselves no good.[20]

The character sketches in the *History* are notable. The praise of Edward IV no doubt owed much to Sir John More's loyalty to

---

[18] *E.W.*, p. 61; I, pp. 438-9.

[19] *Richard III*, III, vii.

[20] *E.W.*, p. 66; I, p. 447.

that king's memory.

He was a goodly personage and very princely to behold, of heart courageous, politic in counsel, in adversity nothing abashed, in prosperity rather joyful than proud, in peace just and merciful, in war sharp and fierce, in the field bold and hardy, and nevertheless no farther than wisdom would, adventurous. Whose wars, whoso well consider, he shall no less commend his wisdom where he avoided than his manhood where he vanquished. He was of visage lovely, of body mighty, strong and clean made; howbeit in his latter days, with over liberal diet, somewhat corpulent and burly and nevertheless not uncomely. He was of youth greatly given to fleshly wantonness, from which health of body in great prosperity and fortune, without a special grace, hardly refraineth. This fault not greatly grieved the people, for neither could any one man's pleasure stretch and extend to the displeasure of very many, and was without violence, and, over that, in his latter days lessened and well left. In which time of his latter days this realm was in quiet and prosperous estate: no fear of outward enemies, no war in hand, nor none towards but such as no man looked for; the people towards the Prince, not in a constrained fear, but in willing and loving obedience; among themselves, the commons in good peace.[21]

The sketch of Jane Shore seems to have been written from personal knowledge of the one-time royal favourite when her fortune had declined and she was in some distress. Her father had been a mercer and so was probably known to Sir John More, and the reference to her husband suggests that he was known to the Mores.

This woman was born in London, worshipfully friended, honestly brought up, and very well married, saving somewhat

---

[21] *E.W.*, p. 35; I, p. 400.

too soon, her husband an honest citizen, young and goodly and of good substance. But forasmuch as they were coupled ere she were well ripe, she not very fervently loved, for whom she never longed. Which was haply the thing that the more easily made her incline unto the King's appetite when he required her. Howbeit, the respect of his royalty, the hope of gay apparel, ease, pleasure, and other wanton wealth, was able soon to pierce a soft, tender heart. But when the King had abused her, anon her husband (as he was an honest man and one that could [knew, or, recognized] his good, not presuming to touch a King's concubine) left her up to him altogether. When the King died, the Lord Chamberlain took her, which in the King's days, albeit he was sore enamoured upon her, yet he forbore her, either for reverence or for a certain friendly faithfulness. Proper she was and fair, nothing in her body that you would have changed, but if you would have wished her somewhat higher. Thus say they that knew her in her youth, albeit some that now see her (for yet she liveth) deem her never to have been well visaged. Whose judgment seemeth me somewhat like as though men should guess the beauty of one long before departed by her scalp taken out of the charnel house: for now is she old, lean, withered, and dried up, nothing left but rivelled skin and hard bone. And yet, being even such, whoso well advise her visage might guess and devise which parts how filled would make it a fair face. Yet delighted not men so much in her beauty as in her pleasant behaviour. For a proper wit had she, and could both read well and write, merry in company, ready and quick of answer, neither mute nor full of babble, sometimes taunting without displeasure and not without disport. ... Where the King took displeasure, she would mitigate and appease his mind; where men were out of favour, she would bring them in his grace; for many that had highly offended, she obtained pardon; of great forfeitures she got men remission; and finally, in many weighty suits she stood many men in good stead, either for none or very small rewards, and those rather gay than rich: either for that she was content with the deed self well done, or for that she delighted to be sued unto and to show what she was able to do with the King, or for that wanton women and wealthy be not always covetous. I doubt not some shall think this woman too slight a thing to be written of and set among the remembrances of great matters: which they shall specially think, that haply shall esteem her only by that they now see her. But meseemeth the chance so much the more worthy to be remembered, in how much she is now in the more beggarly condition, unfriended and worn out of acquaintance, after good substance, after as great favour with the Prince, after as great suit and seeking to with all those that those days had business to speed, as many other men were in their times, which be now famous only by the infamy of their ill deeds. Her doings were not much less, albeit they be much less remembered because they were not so evil. For men use, if they have an evil turn, to write it in marble; and whoso doth us a good turn, we write it in dust: which is not worst proved by her, for at this day she beggeth of many at this day living, that at this day had begged if she had not been.[22]

The Latin version of this History ended with the 'mockish election' of the Duke of Gloucester to the throne; the English version continued to the discussion between Buckingham and the Bishop of Ely, Morton. The increasing call upon More's services by the City merchants and by the king meant that he had less time 'to practise his pen,' and so the *History of King Richard III* remains a fragment.

---

[22] *E.W.*, p. 56; I, pp. 431-2.

Chapter VIII

SIGNS OF THE TIMES

BY his early thirties, Thomas More had established himself as a sound lawyer whose advice was increasingly sought in disputes and negotiations by the merchants of the City. He had displayed in his judicial offices an impartiality and fair-mindedness that had won confidence. This growing reputation would inevitably lead to greater opportunities for public service; the City and the Court formed a small world in which a man's abilities soon became known, and the young king was ready to employ fresh talent.

Before we consider More's public career, it is desirable to indicate the problems of the period; it is impossible to do much in a few pages, but it is essential for an understanding of Thomas More's life to see him against the background of his own day, and to banish from our memories, as far as possible, our knowledge of later developments and events.

It is, for instance, important to recall that Martin Luther did not begin his open attack on the Church until 1517. During the earlier years of Henry VIII, there were local and intermittent outbreaks of heresy which were vaguely related to Lollardy, though it is better not to emphasize that term as it suggests an organization that did not exist. Devout Catholics such as John Colet and Thomas More were, at that period, far more perturbed at deficiencies and abuses within the Church itself than by occasional cases of heresy; Erasmus had voiced this, with the approval of his London friends, in *Praise of Folly*. Colet, Dean of St. Paul's, dealt with other aspects of the same subject in his sermon before Convocation in February 1512. This was at once printed, and we may be sure that More read it with great attention; the two friends may have discussed its matter beforehand. Warham, still Lord Chancellor, had invited Colet to preach the sermon and he was probably aware of the topics to be dealt with by the Dean.

Colet took as his text Romans 12:2, which reads in the English version of the sermon (possibly his own translation),[1] 'Be you not conformed to this world, but be you reformed in the newness of your understanding, that ye may prove what is the good will of God, well pleasing and perfect.' To appreciate the boldness of the preacher's exposition and application of his text, we must see before us the company to whom it was addressed—a gathering of bishops and abbots, of priors and archdeaeons, and of representatives of the secular clergy. They may have expected a smooth, comforting discourse. Some extracts will best show the nature of Colet's criticism.

> The second secular evil is carnal concupiscence. Hath not this vice so grown and waxen in the church as a flood of their lust, so that there is nothing looked for more diligently in this most busy time of the most part priests than that doth delight and please the senses? They give themselves to feasts and banqueting; they spend themselves in vain babbling; they give themselves to sports and plays; they apply themselves to hunting and hawking; they drown themselves in the delights of this world.
>
> Covetousness is the third secular evil, the which Saint John the Apostle calleth concupiscence of the eyes. Saint Paul calleth it idolatry. This abominable pestilence hath so entered in the mind of almost all priests, and so hath blinded the eyes of the mind, that we are blind to all things but only unto those

---

[1] Printed as an Appendix in J.H. Lupton, *Life of John Colet* (1887).

which seem to bring unto us some gain. For what other thing seek we nowadays in the church but fat benefices and high promotions? Yea, and in the same promotions, of what other thing do we pass upon than of our tithes and rents, that we care not how many, how chargeful, how great benefices we take, so that they be of great value? O covetousness! Saint Paul justly called thee the root of all evil. Of thee cometh this heaping of benefices upon benefices. Of thee, so great pensions assigned of many benefices resigned. Of thee, all the suing for tithes, for offerings, for mortuaries, for dilapidations, by the right and title of the church. For the which thing we strive no less than for our own life.

We are also nowadays grieved of heretics, men mad with marvellous follies. But the heresies of them are not so pestilent and pernicious unto us and the people, as the evil and wicked life of priests; the which, if we believe Saint Bernard, is a certain kind of heresy, and chief of all and most perilous.

This reformation and restoring of the church's estate must needs begin of you our fathers, and so follow in us your priests and in all the clergy. You are our heads, you are an example of living unto us. Unto you we look as unto marks of our direction. In you and in your life we desire to read, as in living books, how and after what fashion we may live. Wherefore, if you will ponder and look unto our motes, first take away the blocks out of your eyes.

Colet sent a copy of the sermon to Erasmus who was then at Cambridge where he had been lecturing in Greek for the past year. To him it must have seemed as welcome a declaration of the need for reform as it did to Thomas More. The three friends hoped that the Church would itself remedy abuses; they were far from being alone in this desire, for the evils to be overcome were deplored by the devout and learned throughout Europe. Unhappily the government of the Church was in the hands of men who were more interested in their own material prosperity than in the propagation of the faith; the Popes of the time were intent on maintaining and extending their temporal power. There is much evidence that the mass of the people were devoted to their religion, but it was an uninstructed belief; too many of the parish priests were ignorant and could neither teach nor preach. Here lies one explanation of the ease with which the country was swept by the incoming tide of anti-clericism and protestantism.

Amongst Colet's listeners was one man who could have done much to reform the Church from within. Thomas Wolsey, then Dean of Lincoln, had just become a member of the King's Council; he was two or three years older than Thomas More; within a brief time he was to wield a power that no one, below the King, dared question; but in his own person he was to demonstrate the truth of many of Colet's strictures on the clergy, and what he called reform tended to add to his own wealth or magnificence; he aggravated the discontent he could have assuaged.[2]

The anti-clericism of the time was made more evident at the end of 1514 when a city merchant, Richard Hunne, was found hanged in the Lollards' Tower, the Bishop of London's prison by St. Paul's. The controversy over this case was long and bitter.[3] Fourteen years later Thomas More dealt with it at some length in his *Dialogue Concerning Heresies*.[4]

When Hunne's infant son died in the autumn of 1514, the

---

[2] 'Foreign policy, secular administration in the chancery and star chamber, the acquisition of wealth and ostentation of power, severally occupied far more of his energy and attention than did the purification of morals, the remedy of ecclesiastical abuses, or the defence of the faith.' A.F. Pollard, *Wolsey*, p. 217.

[3] Indeed it hasn't yet died down; see A. Ogle, *The Tragedy of the Lollard's Tower* (1949). The author examines More's view of the case, and, while admitting that he was 'a perfectly honest man' dismisses some of his arguments as 'sorry fustian'. The reader who wishes to study the case should read A.F. Pollard, *Wolsey*, pp. 31-32, and follow up his references.

[4] *E.W.*, pp. 235-40; II, pp. 232-42.

parish priest claimed the child's christening robe as a mortuary;[5] the father refused on the ground that an infant could not, in law, have any property. The priest sued him in the ecclesiastical court and won the case; thereupon Hunne brought an action for *præmunire*[6] in the king's bench; he lost the case. He was charged with heresy and lodged in the Lollard's Tower. Before the charge could be dealt with he was found hanged. Was it suicide or murder? The trial for heresy went on, and the dead man was condemned and his body burned. The coroner's jury, after a long investigation, brought in a verdict of murder against the Bishop's chancellor (or vicar-general), Dr. Horsey, and two prison servants.[7] The Bishop of London, Fitzjames, begged Wolsey to intervene as a London jury, he averred, would be so tainted with heresy as to condemn Dr. Horsey out of hand. This wild accusation brought a firm remonstrance from the city aldermen. We need not follow the rest of the proceedings; the intervention of the king ensured that the charge against Horsey was not pressed, and he retired from London.

When Thomas More came to consider the case he claimed that 'so well I know it from top to toe that I suppose there be not many men that knoweth it much better.' His opinion was that Hunne was a heretic and that Horsey was not his murderer.[8]

This mystery—for such it remains—is significant because the emphasis in the popular view was on the relation between clergy and laity. Simon Fish in his Supplication for Beggars (1528)

---

[5] A customary gift formerly claimed by the incumbent of a parish from the estate of a deceased parishioner. O.E.D.

[6] The statutes of *Praemunire* (1353 and 1393) forbade appeals to Rome on any matter that properly belonged to the king's court. Hunne claimed that the ecclesiastical court before which he was brought infringed the king's jurisdiction.

[7] See *Hall*, I, pp. 129-42.

[8] A.F. Pollard thought that More's opinion was probably right. I am puzzled by one consideration; what point could there have been in Horsey conniving at Hunne's murder?

summed up that view in the sentence, 'had not Richard Hunne commenced action of præmunire against a priest, he had been yet alive, and no heretic.' His challenge to the legal authority of the Church brought him the support of all who complained of the privileges and exactions of the clergy.

Both Colet's sermon and the Hunne case were signs of the disquiet of the period; the failure of the Church to meet grievances meant that when the testing time came few were able to distinguish essentials from accidentals.

Wolsey was soon to find the occasion for his advancement. In October 1511 Henry VIII joined the holy league formed by the Pope against France. Full of the ambitious designs of youth, Henry welcomed the chance to enter European politics against England's traditional enemy. He may have had visions of repeating Henry V's victories of a hundred years earlier, and of regaining the kingdom whose name was an empty title. The war was opposed by Foxe and Warham, but they were men of the old school trained by Henry VII to prefer peace to war; his son found in Wolsey the new man who had the necessary administrative genius to organize an army and to find ships to take it across the sea. Both had much to learn, and their first lesson was a hard one. Their ally, Ferdinand of Spain, the Queen's father, cozened them and left their army to sicken and mutiny at St. Sebastian while he annexed Navarre. Henry's prestige was retrieved in 1512 by the battle of Spurs, by the capture of Thérouenne and Tournai in France, and by the battle of Flodden in Scotland.

At the end of 1511, Ammonio wrote to Erasmus that More 'either speaks to the Archbishop or sees him every day,'[9] and he may have shared Warham's opposition to war, but his national pride was roused, as we shall see, when some years later the courage of English seamen was questioned. John Colet got into

---

[9] *Nichols*, II, p. 46. *Allen*, I, p. 243.

trouble for preaching a sermon against war just before the expedition to northern France. The views of Erasmus on the foolishness of war had been expressed in his *Praise of Folly* where warring Popes were condemned; but these views did not prevent him from writing verses on the flight of the French at the battle of Spurs. Was More thinking of the 1512-14 wars when he put into the mouth of Raphael Hythlodaye the words:

> Almost all princes prefer to occupy themselves in the pursuit of war (with which I neither have nor desire any acquaintance) rather than in the honourable activities of peace, and care much more how, by hook or by crook, they may win fresh kingdoms, than to administer well what they have got.[10]

More had special opportunities for hearing about the war; Ammonio was in attendance on the king in France, and John Rastell[11] was engaged as a military engineer.

Peace was made with France in August 1514; Wolsey came off best; he was made Bishop of Tournai and was allowed to hold this office in *commendam* with the bishopric of Lincoln; shortly afterwards he became Archbishop of York. Archbishop Warham, whose longevity was embarrassing, surrendered the great seal, and by the end of 1515 Thomas Wolsey was a Cardinal and Lord Chancellor of England. Little more than three years had passed since he sat in convocation as Dean of Lincoln and listened to Colet's impassioned call to 'look up and awake from this your sleep in this forgetful world; and at the last, being well awaked, hear Paul crying unto you: *Be you not conformable unto this world.*'

---

[10] *Utopia*, p. 7; p. 20.

[11] A.W. Reed, *Early Tudor Drama*, pp. 7-9. As a reward for his services John Rastell was granted the lands of Richard Hunne with the wardship of his two daughters.

Wolsey listened to John Colet again at Westminster Abbey when the Cardinal's hat arrived from Rome. The preacher's subject was humility: *qui se exaltat humiliabitur, et qui se humiliat exaltabitur.*[12]

---

[12] It should be remembered that it was not until 1592 that the Clementine revision of the Vulgate was declared the authentic text.

Chapter IX

Embassy to Flanders

N January 1515 Thomas More was orator for the City at the reception of the new Venetian Ambassador, Sebastian Giustiniani. They do not seem to have become better known to each other until the summer of 1516 when Erasmus asked More to present a letter to the Ambassador with a copy of his edition of the Greek New Testament which had been published that March. The book went astray, and More reported in September,

> I have delivered your letter to the Venetian Ambassador, who seems to have been ready to receive with much satisfaction the New Testament, which has been intercepted by the Carmelite. For he is entirely devoted to Sacred Literature, having gone through a course of almost all the authors who write upon minute questions, to which he attributes so much importance, that even Dorpius can go no further. Our interview was conducted with set speeches in grand style—scratching each other with mutual compliments. But to say the truth, he quite charms me, for he seems a very honourable man, with a great experience of human affairs, and now most devoted to the study of things divine, and lastly (though I do not myself put it last) very much attached to you.[1]

Giustiniani later declared in a despatch to Venice, that More was 'the most linked with me in friendship of any in this kingdom.'

Between the City's welcome to the Ambassador and the

---

[1] *Nichols*, II, p. 381; *Allen*, II, 461.

publication of the Greek New Testament, Thomas More had had his first experience of serving on an embassy abroad; this was a step towards service under the King, and it was fitting that the transition from the City to the Court should have been due to the action of the merchants.

Roper's account needs some revision.

> Of whom, for his learning, wisdom, knowledge, and experience, men had such estimation that, before he came to the service of King Henry VIII, at the suit and instance of the English merchants, he was by the king's consent made twice Ambassador in certain great causes between them and the merchants of the Steelyard: whose wise and discreet dealing therein, to his high commendation, coming to the king's understanding, provoked his highness to cause Cardinal Wolsey (then Lord Chancellor) to procure him to his service.[2]

The first embassy was to Flanders in May 1515; this was for negotiations with the Hanseatic merchants whose London representatives had their quarters in the Steelyard. The second embassy was to Calais in August 1517, and was a French, and not as Roper thought, a Hanseatic matter.

More related the circumstances of the first embassy in the opening words of *Utopia*.

> It chanced that the most invincible King of England, Henry VIII, whose princely virtues are beyond compare, had recently many weighty matters in dispute with His Serene Highness Charles, King of Castile; wherefore to debate of these and reach a settlement he sent me to Flanders along with the peerless Cuthbert Tunstal.[3]

'Charles, King of Castile,' the nephew of Catherine of Aragon, was to be known later as the Emperor Charles V. Up to 1515 he

---

[2] *Roper*, p. 9.

[3] *Utopia*, p. 1; p. 13.

had, as a minor, been in the guardianship of Margaret of Savoy, the Regent of the Netherlands. He was declared of age in that year, though only fifteen years old, and assumed the government of the Netherlands; this in fact meant that his Council would direct policy, and there was reason to believe that an alliance was contemplated with Francis I, who, at the age of twenty, had just come to the throne of France. Two embassies were therefore sent to Flanders; the first was concerned with political questions, and the second, on which More served, with commercial problems. The trade treaties made by Henry VII had lapsed with his death, and the merchants in Flanders were not willing to make agreements on the same terms. The situation became so strained that the English Parliament stopped the export of wool, but this high-handed action was as detrimental to English traders as it was annoying to the Flemish. Thomas More was included in this second embassy, at the request of the City, to help with the commercial negotiations; he had already represented the City in dealings with the Hansa and was therefore known to the merchants on both sides of the table.

The other members were Cuthbert Tunstal, Sir Thomas Spinelly, John Clifford, and Richard Sampson. Spinelly was a Florentine who had been Henry VII's agent in Flanders and remained there under Henry VIII. John Clifford was governor of the English merchants in Flanders. Richard Sampson was included at Wolsey's desire to keep an eye on his master's interests in the bishopric of Tournai. It is interesting to note that Wolsey and Sampson referred to Thomas More in their letters as 'Young More.'

The negotiations were difficult and protracted; the party was in Bruges until September and then moved to Brussels, and a month later to Antwerp. The unexpected delays led to a shortage of money; Tunstal wrote to Wolsey in July and told him that 'Master More at this time as being at a low ebb desires by your

Grace to be set on float again.'[4] And the embassy wrote to the Council on the same date:

> We beseech your good lordships, that as your wisdoms perceive, that we be like here to abide, so it will like you to order that we may have money sent us. In which doing, your lordships shall bind us to owe you our poor service and our prayer.[5]

This was signed, 'By your humble bedemen Cuthbert Tunstal, Richard Sampson, Thomas More.'

However tedious the negotiations proved to be, there were compensations. The greatest of these for More was that it brought him into close association with Tunstal and with scholars in the Low Countries. Indeed, but for these delays, *Utopia* might never have been written.

Writing from London on 5th May, 1515, Erasmus told his friend Peter Gilles of Antwerp:

> The two most learned men of all England are now at Bruges, Cuthbert Tunstal, the Archbishop of Canterbury's Chancellor, and Thomas More, to whom I inscribed the *Moria*; both great friends of mine. If you should have an opportunity of offering them any civility, your services will be well bestowed.[6]

Cuthbert Tunstal was three or four years older than More; besides being learned in Greek, Hebrew, and Civil Law, he was a mathematician. He wrote, in Latin, the first book on arithmetic to be printed in England; this was published in 1522 with the title *De Arte Supputandi*, and was dedicated to More. The opening paragraph mentions one of the difficulties they had on their embassy. It calls up a picture of the two eminent scholars frowning over their sums.

---

[4] MS. Cotton Galba B., iii, 259.

[5] *Rogers*, p. 21.

[6] *Nichols*, II, p. 258.

Some years ago now, my dear More, when transactions with money-changers concerned me, and we neither of us understood enough about calculation for me to avoid the trickery I greatly suspected, I was forced to look rather more closely into methods of ready reckoning, and to apply myself again to the art of arithmetic with which as a youth I had made some acquaintance. And when I had by this means freed myself from annoyance from crafty men, I began to reflect that it would be well worth my while for the rest of my life to have the art of reckoning sufficiently at my command to be too wide awake to be tricked by any and every swindler.

The last lines of this dedicatory letter take us a few years onward, but are of interest. More had by then become Sub-Treasurer.

To whom, indeed, can this subject be more appropriate than to you since you are constantly busied with examining accounts in the king's treasury, and, next after the President [Norfolk], hold the chief post there; you who can pass the book on to your children for them to read—children whom you take care to train in liberal studies? For to them it might be most specially beneficial—if only it were worth reading —since by nothing are the abilities of young folk more invigorated than by the study of mathematics. Farewell.[7]

Peter Gilles (Aegidius), a native of Antwerp, became Chief Secretary of that City in 1510. He devoted his leisure to learning, and his circle of scholar-friends included Erasmus, Budd, Dorp, Vives and Busleiden. The last of these, who also met More during this embassy, had been educated at Louvain and Padua where he had known Tunstal; he had various preferments in the Church, and became a member of the Council at Mechlin. He was sent on a number of embassies including one to England in 1509 on

---

[7] C. Sturge, *Cuthbert Tunstal* (1938), pp. 72 and 74; Dr. Sturge's translation.

Henry VIII's accession. He died in 1517 and left his wealth to found the Collegium Trilingua at Louvain. This group of scholars must have been delighted when Erasmus stopped in Bruges in the summer of 1515 on his way from London to Basle.

Attendant on More was young John Clement who had been amongst the earliest pupils of William Lily at Colet's new school at St. Paul's. He left school with a good grounding in Latin and Greek and entered the household of Thomas More as tutor to the children. When their father left for Bruges, Margaret was ten, Elizabeth nine, Cecily eight, and John six years old. There was also, as one of the family, More's ward, Margaret Gigs who was later to marry this young tutor.

The third edition of *Utopia* contains a woodcut by Ambrosius Holbein showing Thomas More, Peter Gilles, and Raphael Hythlodaye sitting on a garden bench; John Clements is coming from the house with refreshments. The picture is idyllic and suggests Italy rather than Flanders, but it commemorates the fortuitous but enduring outcome of that embassy—*Utopia*.

One of the many stories of Thomas More may be referred to this time.

> Sir Thomas being beyond the seas in Embassage, happened to dine amongst many strangers of divers countries; and amongst other discourses of table talk, a question was moved of the diversity of their languages, each man praising his own for the best. They concluded English to be worst of all. 'Nay, soft,' said Sir Thomas, '*suum cuique pulchrum*; but yet by your leave, I must needs speak a word in defence of my language; and by good reason I will show it is nothing inferior to any of yours. And first for antiquity. We Englishmen come of the old Britons, the Britons of Brutus, he of Æneas Silvius, and he of the gods: *O chara deum soboles*. So for antiquity I may compare with the proudest. Again you know that *omne quod difficilius pulchrius*, 'every thing the harder it is, the fairer it seems.' Now let any man here speak any sentence in

his own language, and you shall hear me dialect and pronounce it as well as himself.' And so they did. And without difficulty or difference he performed his promise. 'Now I will speak but three words, and I durst jeopard a wager that none here shall pronounce it after me; "Thwaits thwackt him with a thwitle."' And no man there could pronounce it.[8]

A few months after his return home, Thomas More sent his reflections on the experience to Erasmus.

> The Archbishop [Warham] has been at last relieved of the office of Chancellor, the burden of which, as you know, he has been anxious to shake off for some years. Having secured the privacy he has long desired, he enjoys a leisure sweetened by literature, and by the recollection of important affairs well administered. The king has put in his place the Cardinal of York, who so conducts himself as to surpass the high expectation of all. After so excellent a predecessor, it is no easy matter to give, as he does, complete satisfaction.
>
> Our embassy (for you will be interested in that, as in everything else of mine) was successful, though the affair was protracted longer than I wished. For although, when I left home, I scarcely expected to be away for two months, I spent more than six in that mission. When, therefore, I saw the business concluded for which I was myself sent, and nevertheless other matters arising which seemed to be leading to further delay, I wrote at last to the Cardinal, and obtained leave to return. . . .
>
> An ambassador's position has never had any great charms for me; indeed it does not seem to be so suitable for us laymen, as for you clergy, who, either have no wives or

---

[8] *Ro. Ba*, p. 109. This is the only source of this story, and so should be accepted with some reservation.

children, or find them wherever you go. When I am away I have two households to maintain, one in England and another abroad. I received a liberal allowance from the king for the persons I took with me, but no account is taken of those whom I leave at home; and although you know what a kind husband, what an indulgent father, what a considerate master I am, yet I have never been able to induce my family to go without food during my absence. Moreover it is easy for princes to compensate the labours and expenses of clergymen by church preferment without putting themselves to any cost, while we laymen are not provided for so handsomely or so readily. Nevertheless, on my own return I had a yearly pension offered me by the king, which whether one looked to for profit or the honour of it, was not to be despised. This, however, I have hitherto refused, and shall, I think, continue to do so, because, if I took it, the place I now hold in the City, which I prefer to a higher office, would either have to be given up, or retained, much to my regret, with some offence to the citizens, who, if they had any question with the Government, as sometimes happens, about their privileges, would have less confidence in me, as a paid pensioner of the king.

However, in that embassy of mine there were some very agreeable circumstances. In the first place there was the long and constant intercourse with Tunstal, who, as he is unsurpassed in all literary accomplishments and in strictness of life and character, is at the same time a most delightful companion. Another circumstance was my acquaintance with Busleiden, who entertained me with a magnificence suitable to his noble fortune, and a kindness proportioned to the goodness of his heart. He showed me a house adorned with singular taste and provided with the choicest furniture; he showed me many monuments of antiquity of which you know I am curious, and finally his well-stored library, and a mind still better stored. ....

But in all my journey I met with nothing I liked better than the society of your host, Peter Gilles of Antwerp, a person so learned, witty and modest, and so true a friend, that I would willingly part with a good share of my fortune to purchase his company. He has sent me your Apology ... Dorpius has had his Epistle printed and prefixed to your Apology. I should have been glad to meet him, if I had had the chance. That not being the case, I paid my respects to him by letter, indeed by a Laconic note, for I had not time to write a longer one. ...

My wife sends you her greeting, and also Clement, who makes such progress both in Latin and Greek, as to give me no slight hope of his becoming some day an ornament to his country and to letters.[9]

The letters between Erasmus, Martin Dorp (Dorpius) and Thomas More retain their interest because Dorp put forward in a friendly manner criticisms of Erasmus that were being made by Dorp's colleagues at Louvain where he was professor of philosophy. He dealt first with the *Moriæ Encomium*, and secondly with the edition of the Greek New Testament that Erasmus was then preparing. Dorp objected that the *Praise of Folly* was too harsh in its satire and, by bringing ridicule on the priests and on some religious practices would do more harm than good. He urged Erasmus to write as a counterbalance a *Defence of Wisdom*. From this he passed to the projected Greek New Testament. His main contention was:

You are proposing to correct the Latin copies by the Greek. But if I show you that the Latin version has no mixture of falsehood or mistake, will you not admit that such a work is unnecessary? But this is what I claim for the Vulgate, since

---

[9] *Nichols*, II, p. 258; *Allen*, II, 388.

it is unreasonable to suppose that the Universal Church has been in error for so many generations in her use of this edition,[10] nor is it probable that so many holy Fathers have been mistaken, who in reliance upon it have defined the most arduous questions in General Councils, which it is admitted by most theologians as well as lawyers are not subject to errors in matters of faith.

Erasmus replied to this in a letter which was published[11] in August 1515 while More was at Bruges; it bore the title, *Erasmi ad Martinum Dorpium Epistola Apologetica*; this was the Apology to which More referred. Erasmus defended his *Praise of Folly* on the grounds that laughter and even ridicule will often penetrate where plain denunciation has no effect; as to his projected Greek New Testament, he pointed out that the Fathers quoted texts differing from the Vulgate, and emendation of that version had not been forbidden, nor did he fear that the correction of textual errors would endanger anyone's faith.[12]

More came to the defence of Erasmus. His 'Laconic note' in Latin ran to sixteen thousand words; when he wrote in controversy his words sometimes came too easily, resulting in a diffuseness that clouded his argument. Occasionally this stream was interrupted by a personal reminiscence told in that lively style that seems more characteristic; the modem reader, whose interest in these old disputes is at best lukewarm, welcomes these passages as they enable him to regain breath and collect his wits.

---

[10] *Nichols*, II, p. 169; *Allen*, II, 388.

[11] This publication of letters, sometimes without the writer's permission, seems strange to us; but the idea of copyright had not yet been established. Awkward situations could arise when letters or other writings were published to the confusion of the writer; Erasmus found it convenient at times to evade responsibility for his own indiscretions on these grounds.

[12] It should be remembered that it was not until 1592 that the Clementine revision of the Vulgate was declared the authentic text.

More argued that it was important to get back to the words of the Scriptures and to the writings of the Fathers and away from the logic-chopping of the later schoolmen. In illustration of this point he narrated an incident that had taken place at the table of 'an Italian merchant as learned as he was rich.' This description suggests his friend Antonio Bonvisi.

There was present at table a monk who was a theologian and a notable disputant, lately arrived from abroad, for the very purpose of airing some questions he had got up to see what kind of debaters he could find in England, and to make his name as famous in England as in his own country. At the dinner nothing was said by anyone, however well weighed and guarded, that this man did not, before it was well uttered, seek to refute with a syllogism, though the matter belonged neither to theology nor philosophy and was altogether foreign to his profession. I am wrong: his profession was to dispute. He had stated at the beginning of dinner that he was ready to take either side on any question. By degrees our host, the Italian merchant, turned the conversation to theological topics, such as usury, tithes, or confession to friars outside the penitent's parish, and the like. Whatever was said the theologian took at once the opposite view... The merchant soon perceived that the monk was not so well up in his Bible as he was ready with his syllogisms; so he began to draw his arguments from authority rather than from reason. He invented, extempore, certain quotations in favour of his own side of the question, taking one from a supposed Epistle of St. Paul, another from St. Peter, a third from the Gospel, and affecting to do this with the greatest precision, naming the chapter, but in such a way that, if a book had sixteen chapters, he would quote from the twentieth. What did our theologian do now? Hitherto he had rolled himself up in his spikes like a hedgehog. Now he has to dodge from side to side to escape these supposed texts. He managed it, however. He had no notion that the passages quoted were spurious, while, of course, he could not refuse the authority of Scripture; but, as on the one hand, it would be a base thing to own himself beaten, he had his answer ready at once. 'Yes, sir,' he said, 'your quotation is good, but I understand the text in this way,' and then made a distinction of senses, one of which might be in favour of his adversary, the other of himself; and when the merchant insisted that his was the only possible sense, the theologian swore till you would almost believe him, that the sense which he had selected was that given by Nicolas of Lyra.[13]

So More urged the need for a direct knowledge of the Bible, 'the Queen of books';[14] this was the purpose of Erasmus in going back to the Greek from which the Latin had been translated.

The combined arguments of Erasmus and More convinced Dorp, and in 1516 he acknowledged his change of attitude towards the Greek New Testament, but not towards *Praise of Folly*. This drew from More a delightful letter.

> It was not difficult for me to foresee that you would one day think otherwise than then you thought. But that you would not only become wiser, but even in a most eloquent address proclaim that you had changed, openly, sincerely and straightforwardly, this indeed went far beyond my expectation, and indeed almost beyond the hopes and desires of all, for it seemed vain to look for such transparent honesty and want of affectation. Nothing indeed is more sad than that men should form varying judgements about identical problems; but nothing is more rare than that after they have published their views, argued strongly for them and defended them against attack they then, acknowledging the truth,

---

[13] *Rogers*, p. 46. Bridgett's translation, p. 90.

[14] *Biblicae sacrosanctae litterarum omnium reginae.*

should change their course, and, as if their voyage had been in vain, sail back into port from which they came. Believe me, dear Dorp, what you have done with such great humility, it is almost impossible to demand even from those whom the world nowadays considers as most humble... But what am I to say of a further act of modesty which throws into the shade even that singular modesty which I have been praising? Although it was due to the clearness and sincerity of your mind that you saw the truth, yet you chose to ascribe it to the admonitions of others, and even to mine.[15]

More brought back with him from Flanders the manuscript of the Second Book of *Utopia* in which that ideal state is described. He wrote the First Book to set the scene and to expose some of the weaknesses of society. Merry John Heywood, who was to marry More's niece Joan Rastell, wrote,

> There famous More did his Utopia write.
> And there came Heywood's epigrams to light.

'There' was Sir John's More's country house of Gobions. The need for a quiet place in which to write is shown in a letter to Peter Gilles prefaced to *Utopia*.

> While I am constantly engaged in legal business, either pleading or hearing, or giving an award in arbitration, or deciding a matter as judge, while I am paying a friendly visit to one man or going on business to another, while I devote almost the whole day to other men's affairs, and what remains of it, to my family at home, I leave to myself, that is to writing, nothing at all. For when I have returned home, I must converse with my wife, chat with my children, and talk to my servants. All this I count as business, for it has got to be

---

[15] *Rogers*, p. 164. *Stapleton*, p. 53.

done—and it is quite necessary unless you want to be a stranger in your own home—and one must take care to be as agreeable as possible to those whom nature has provided, or chance made, or you yourself have chosen to be companions of your life, provided you do not spoil them by kindness or through indulgence make them your masters instead of your servants. In these occupations that I have named, the day, the month, the year slip away. When then can we find time to write? Nor have I yet said anything about sleep, nor even of meals, which for many take up as much time as sleep, and that takes up almost half a man's life. So I only get for myself the time I can filch from sleep and food.[16]

Amongst 'other men's affairs' was arranging for Erasmus to receive the £20 pension Warham had granted him out of the living of Aldington, Kent. Erasmus had some scruples about being a non-resident priest, but Warham persuaded him to accept. It was not always easy to get the money to Erasmus, and he got impatient of delays. In one letter explaining how the money was to be sent, More wrote, 'When you compliment me on my scholarship, I blush to think how much I am losing every day of the less than little I ever had; which cannot but be the case with one constantly engaged in legal disputations',[17] and, he could have added, in carrying out commissions for one's friends.

Erasmus came to England soon after he received that letter; he was anxious to enlist Ammonio's help in getting a dispensation from his monastic vows; he stayed with More for a week or two, and then spent ten days with Bishop John Fisher at Rochester; the Bishop had asked for his help in his Greek studies. While he was there More 'hurried down to have another look at Erasmus,

---

[16] *Utopia*, p. 123; p. 7.

[17] Nichols, II, p. 293; Allen, II, 424.

whom he seems to fear he will not see again.'[18] Perhaps More wished to make some final arrangements about the publication of *Utopia*, for the manuscript was sent on 3rd September to Erasmus who was by then in Louvain.

More's next letter, 22nd September, makes no reference to *Utopia*, but it contains an interesting piece of news. 'Colet is already working hard at Greek with some help volunteered by my Clement.'[19] Both Fisher and Colet were probably inspired to learn Greek by Erasmus's New Testament. It is rare for a former pupil of a school to instruct the founder.

In sending the Latin text of *Utopia* to Erasmus, More wrote, 'I send you Nowhere, nowhere well written.'[20] At first the title was *Nusquama*, but just before it was printed the Greek adaptation *Utopia* (not-place) was chosen. A month later Erasmus wrote from Antwerp, 'Every care shall be taken about the Island. ... Peter Gilles is simply in love with you; you are still always with us. He is wonderfully struck with your Nusquama.'[21] Another month passed and Gerard of Nijmegen, who was corrector of the press to the printer Thierry Marten of Louvain, sent to Erasmus the news that 'our Thierry has willingly and joyfully undertaken the printing of *Utopia*. ... I will take great care that Utopia shall be produced in a handsome form, so that there may be nothing to interfere with the pleasure of the reader.'[22] In the middle of December, More wrote to Erasmus, 'I now look forward every day for our Utopia with the feelings with which a mother awaits the return of her boy from foreign parts.'[23] The book was

---

[18] *Nichols*, II, p. 323; *Allen*, II, 455.

[19] *Nichols*, II, P. 393; *Allen*, II, 468.

[20] *Nichols*, II, p. 381; *Allen* II, 461.

[21] *Nichols*, II, p. 399; *Allen*, II, 487.

[22] *Nichols*, II, p. 431; *Allen*, II, 487.

[23] *Nichols*, II, p. 447; *Allen*, I, 302.

published at the end of the year; on 4th January, 1517, Lord Mountjoy wrote to Erasmus to thank him for 'the book on the Island of *Utopia*.'[24]

In spite of the promises of Gerard, neither he nor the printer did their work well; the small quarto volume was 'criblée de fautes.'[25]

The year 1516 may be described as the last of More's freedom. The King, as Roper recorded, wished More to enter his service; this is confirmed in the extract already given from More's letter to Erasmus in May 1516. His early refusal was partly due to his reluctance to breaking his association with the City. That he was not antagonistic at that time to Wolsey is clear from his letters, and Ammonio wrote to Erasmus in February of 1516 that 'More is returned home from his friends in Flanders, having fulfilled his mission with great credit. He now haunts with us the smoky chambers of the palace. No one is more punctual in carrying his morning salutation to my Lord of York.'[26] Doubtless More had to report on the embassy, but legal and City business would take him regularly to Westminster.

The pension offered by the King would presumably have meant More's appointment to the council, each member of which had an annual fee of £100 unless he occupied a more important office. This council consisted of over a hundred members who could, when needed, be assigned to small groups or committees to carry out specific functions. Both Henry VIII and his father increasingly made use of the services of lawyers and other professional men, and did not allow the council to be dominated by the great magnates. Thomas More was the kind of adviser the

---

[24] *Nichols*, II, p. 452; *Allen*, II, 508.

[25] Marie Delcourt's introduction to her edition of the Latin text, *L'Utopie* (Paris, 1936). This is the best edition.

[26] *Nichols*, II, p. 243; *Allen*, II, 389.

Tudors preferred. His skill in negotiations had been proved; he was fluent in Latin both as a writer and as an orator, and he was closely associated with the City Companies and was trusted by them.

Roper tells us of the circumstances that made the king more anxious than ever to secure More's services.

> Now happened there after this, a great ship of his that then was Pope [Leo X] to arrive at Southampton, which the king claiming for a forfeiture, the Pope's Ambassador, by suit unto his grace, obtained that he might for his master the Pope have counsel learned in the laws of this realm, and the matter in his own presence, being himself a singular [*i.e.* above the ordinary] civilian, in some public place to be openly heard and discussed. At which time there could none of our law be found so meet to be of counsel with this Ambassador as Sir Thomas More, who could report to the Ambassador in Latin all the reasons and arguments by the learned counsel on both sides alleged. Upon this the counsellors of either part, in presence of the Lord Chancellor and other the Judges, in the Star Chamber had audience accordingly. Where Sir Thomas More not only declared to the Ambassador the whole effect of all their opinions, but also, in defence of the Pope's side, argued so learnedly himself, that both was the foresaid forfeiture to the Pope restored, and himself among all the hearers, for his upright and commendable demeanour therein, so greatly renowned that for no entreaty would the king from thenceforth be induced any longer to forbear his service.[27]

Nothing more is known of this case of Rex v. Papa, but it was a strange quirk of fortune that such a matter should have helped to bring Thomas More into the service of Henry VIII.

---

[27] *Roper*, p. 9.

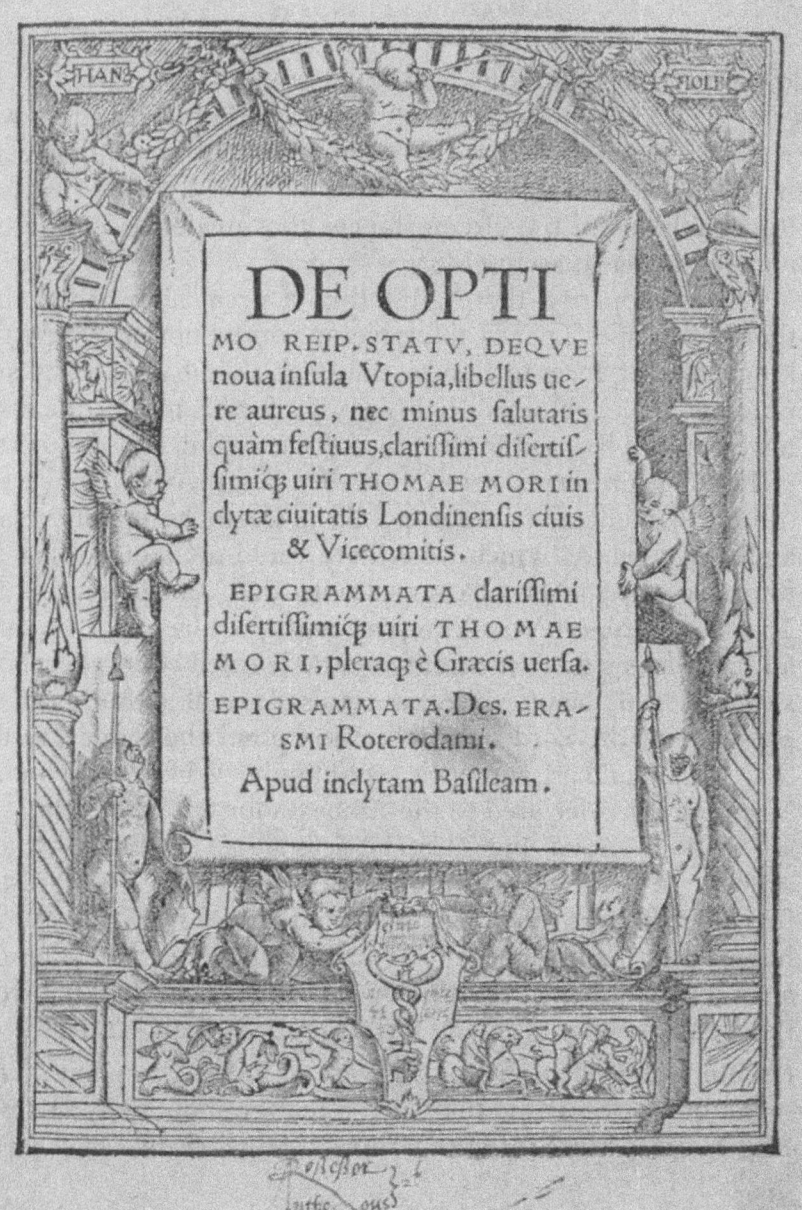

DE OPTI

MO REIP. STATV, DEQVE
noua insula Vtopia, libellus uere aureus, nec minus salutaris
quàm festiuus, clarissimi disertissimiq; uiri THOMAE MORI in-
clytæ ciuitatis Londinensis ciuis
& Vicecomitis.

EPIGRAMMATA clarissimi
disertissimiq; uiri THOMAE
MORI, pleraq; è Græcis uersa.

EPIGRAMMATA. Des. ERA-
SMI Roterodami.

Apud inclytam Basileam.

Chapter x

Utopia

IT is not difficult to picture the circumstances in which *Utopia* was conceived. The tedious delays during the drawn-out negotiations in Flanders in the summer of 1515 gave many opportunities for talk and discussion in those gatherings of scholars which were such a delight to Thomas More. For a short time they were joined by Erasmus, and his keen mind must have added zest to the arguments. Some of the meetings were in Peter Gilles' garden in Antwerp; the woodcut by Ambrosius Holbein,[1] idealized as it is, suggests a pleasant scene with the friends sitting under a tree discussing the affairs of the day, the prospects of war and peace, their own studies and the books they had been reading.

Amongst other topics, Amerigo Vespucci's account of his voyages[2] must have been considered. This would lead to talk about the new countries across the ocean, and to speculation about their methods of government. Antwerp was just the place for hearing the latest news and the most curious information from returned sailors, and it may be that one of them, whose adventures have not been recorded, had penetrated to Peru and had seen something of the Inca state where there was no private ownership of land and no money. A group of scholars would inevitably refer to Plato's *Republic*, and they may have discussed

---

[1] On p. 115.

[2] *Quattuor Americi Vesputii Navagationes*, 1507.

how his project could have been improved even without the introduction of the Christian faith. St. Augustine's *City of God* would as naturally find a place in such discussions. All this must have stimulated More to think out his own ideas of government; he rejected Plato's notion of a state organized for the benefit of a privileged aristocracy; he wanted all members of the community to benefit in a society in which the family would be the unit.

He wrote down his account of this imaginary society while he was in Flanders and no doubt discussed it with his friends. Happily he decided to write an introductory Book to provide a contrast with *Utopia* in a survey of contemporary society. So he was able to discuss the duty of princes, war and peace, crime and punishment, the greed of the rich and the sufferings of the poor.

We have seen that *Utopia* was first printed in an inaccurate text in 1516. On 1st March, 1517, Erasmus wrote to More, 'Send your revised *Utopia* here [Antwerp] as soon as you can, and we will send the copy either to Basle, or if you like to Paris.'[3] Before Erasmus could arrange for this corrected edition to be printed, another had appeared in Paris under the supervision of Thomas Lupset, a young scholar who owed his training to John Colet. This second edition was an improvement on the first but still contained many errors. More must have known that it was in preparation as it included a second letter from him to Peter Gilles. There were many delays in the printing of the third edition; in March 1518 Erasmus wrote to More, 'I have seen at last *Utopia* as it has been printed at Paris, but printed incorrectly. It is already in the press at Basle, for I had declared a cessation of friendship if they were not more expeditious in that business than they are in mine.'[4] The book was issued in that month and again at the end of the year. A German translation was published at Basle in 1524; an

---

[3] *Nichols*, II, p. 514; *Allen*, II, 543.

[4] *Nichols*, III, p. 291; *Allen*, III, 785.

Italian translation in 1548; a French translation at Paris in 1550; Ralph Robinson's English translation was published in 1551, and a Dutch translation at Antwerp in 1553.

It may seem surprising that thirty-five years passed before *Utopia* appeared in English. A translation by Thomas More himself would have been a precious book, but there is no suggestion that he ever thought of making one. His busy life after 1517 may have made such a task difficult, and in later years[5] he felt it undesirable to make any book more widely accessible to those general readers who might have misunderstood the intentions of the author when Lutheranism was becoming a menace to the unity of the Church.

Praise of Folly and *Utopia* were written when there seemed no serious threat to the Church except from its own weaknesses, but as soon as it was apparent that heresy was rapidly leading to wide-spread schism, a Catholic had to be scrupulous to avoid criticism that would increase men's doubts. 'And if anyone hurts the conscience of one of these little ones, that believe in me, he had better have been drowned in the depths of the sea, with a millstone hung about his neck.'[6]

After the execution of Thomas More in 1535, he would have been a foolhardy printer who dared to publish a translation of *Utopia*, and even in 1551 Ralph Robinson felt it necessary to apologize in his dedication to his former school-fellow, William Cecil (Burghley), because More 'could not or rather would not see the shining light of God's holy truth.'

Utopia was written in Latin because that was the common language of scholars throughout Europe, and they formed More's public. His name was on the title-page since there was no reason to conceal his authorship. It is interesting to note that when, in

---

[5] See above, p. 71.

[6] Matt. 18:6. Knox translation.

1523, Vives, at the request of Queen Catherine, drew up a scheme of study for the Princess Mary, he included *Utopia* amongst the books to be read.

The letters prefaced to the book have their own interest. They were a continuation of the custom of circulating manuscripts amongst friends with accompanying letters of recommendation. In some respects they may be thought of as an early form of reviewing long before that function became part of journalism. The letter of dedication, or the foreword by a distinguished person, may be regarded as survivals of this custom. The first (Louvain) edition of *Utopia* contained a letter from Peter Gilles to Busleiden, another with some verses from John Paludanus (a Louvain professor) to Peter Gilles, then a letter from Busleiden to Thomas More, and finally More's letter to Peter Gilles. The second (Paris) edition had in addition a long letter from Budé to Lupset, and a second letter from More to Peter Gilles. The third (Basle) edition added a letter from Erasmus to Froben, the printer. These letters were not just puffery; they were intended to explain the claims of the book to serious consideration. More himself was most anxious to know what his scholar-friends thought of this, his first bid for European fame as an author. He particularly wanted Tunstal's opinion. Unfortunately Tunstal's letter has not survived, but More wrote to him:

> ... for having so carefully read through the *Utopia*, for having undertaken so heavy a labour for friendship's sake, I owe you the deepest gratitude; and my gratitude is not less deep for your having found pleasure in the work. For this, too, I attribute to your friendship which has obviously influenced your judgement more than strict rules of criticism. However that may be, I cannot express my delight that your judgement is so favourable. For I have almost succeeded in convincing myself that you say what you think, for I know that all deceit is hateful to you, whilst you can gain no advantage by flattering me, and you love me too much to play a trick upon

me. So that if you have seen the truth without any distortion, I am overjoyed at your verdict; or if in reading you were blinded by your affection for me, I am no less delighted with your love, for vehement indeed must that love be if it can deprive a Tunstal of his judgement.[7]

More wrote to Erasmus in ecstatic vein.

Tunstal has lately sent me a letter full of the most friendly feeling; his judgement about our Republic, so frank, so complimentary, has given me more pleasure than an Attic talent! You have no idea how I jump for joy, how tall I have grown, how I hold up my head, when a vision comes before my eyes, that my Utopians have made me their perpetual sovereign. I seem already to be marching along, crowned with a diadem of wheat, conspicuous in a grey cloak, and carrying for a sceptre a few ears of corn, surrounded by a noble company of Amaurotians; and with this numerous attendance meeting the ambassadors and princes of other nations—poor creatures in comparison with us inasmuch as they pride themselves on coming out, loaded with puerile ornaments and womanish finery, bound with chains of that hateful gold, and ridiculous with purple and gems and other bubbly trifles. But I would not have either you or Tunstal form an estimate of me from the character of others, whose behaviour changes with their fortune. Even though it has pleased Heaven to raise our humility to that sublime elevation, with which no kingdom can in my judgement be compared, you shall never find me unmindful of that old familiarity which has subsisted between us while I have been in a private station; and if you take the trouble to make so small a journey as to visit me in Utopia, I will effectually provide that all the mortals who are subject to our clemency, shall show you that honour which they owe to

---

[7] *Stapleton*, p. 49; *Rogers*, p. 84.

those whom they know to be dearest to their sovereign. I was proceeding further with this most delightful dream, when the break of day dispersed the vision, deposing poor me from my sovereignty, and recalling me to prison, that is, to my legal work. Nevertheless, I console myself with the reflection that real kingdoms are not much more lasting. Farewell, dearest Erasmus.[8]

There is no dedicatory letter in *Utopia* to a patron. More was in a happier financial position than Erasmus who found it necessary, for instance, to seek the patronage of Archbishop Warham by dedicating to him the edition of Jerome. In his first letter to Peter Gilles, More solemnly followed his fantasy by saying that he and John Clement had had a dispute about the width of the River Anyder; could Peter Gilles recall what Hythlodaye said, and did he recollect in what part of the world Utopia was situated? Peter Gilles played up to his correspondent by saying in his letter to Busleiden that just when Hythlodaye was giving particulars of the position of Utopia one of the company had a fit of coughing, and so the traveller's words were lost, and now he could get no certain information about the traveller who had left the country. More had explained, probably as part of the jest, that his anxiety about the situation of Utopia was due to inquiries he had received from 'a good man and a doctor of divinity' who wanted to go as a missionary to the island. This is the origin, no doubt, of the legend, dating from Robinson's translation, that this divine was Rowland Phillips, the Vicar of Croydon; but there is no reason to think that More's manuscript was seen by anyone outside his own circle.

For more than four centuries *Utopia* has influenced men's thoughts on the nature of society and its organization. The book is so charged with ideas that varied conclusions have been

---

[8] *Nichols*, II, p. 442 (December 1516); *Allen*, II, 499.

reached by its readers. It has been regarded as a source of socialism, and Marxists have found in it, they believe, support for materialist communism. Men of less extreme views have acknowledged that *Utopia* inspired their efforts for social reform. Others have dismissed the book with impatience, and the title itself has come to mean an impracticable and visionary ideal. This view was expressed in the reign of Queen Elizabeth by Sir Thomas Smith in *De Republica Anglorum* (1583), in which he refers to utopias (the word was already in current usage) as 'feigned commonwealths, such as never was nor never shall be, vain imaginations, phantasies of philosophers to occupy the time, and to exercise their wits.' John Ruskin, in the reign of Queen Victoria, wrote, 'Thank you for getting the *Utopia* for me. What an infinitely wise—infinitely foolish—book it is! Right in all it asks—insane, in venturing to ask it, all at once—so making its own wisdom folly for evermore; and becoming perhaps the most really mischievous book ever written—except *Don Quixote.*'[9] Ruskin's own criticism of society in *Unto This Last* was condemned in its day as 'utter imbecility,' yet these two books, so unlike in many ways, inspired those working men who were the true artificers of the socialist-labour movement in this country. This fact presents an interesting paradox. Let one point of difference be considered. Hythlodaye argued that 'so sure I am that no just and even distribution of goods can be made, nor any perfect happiness be found among men, unless private property is utterly abolished.'[10] *Utopia* was a collectivist state. Ruskin held contrary views. 'I am not taking up nor countenancing one whit, the common socialist idea of division of property: division of property is its destruction.'[11] How could two books expressing

---

[9] E.T. Cood, *Life of John Ruskin*, p. 371 (July 1870).

[10] *Utopia*, p. 37; p. 15.

[11] *Unto This Last.* Note to §78.

such conflicting opinions on a crucial matter have both inspired one movement?

The resolution of this paradox will help us to understand the nature of More's book. Both he and Ruskin were intent on the question, 'How can justice and the good life be achieved in human society?' That too was the problem of Plato's *Republic*. The element common to both *Utopia* and *Unto This Last* is the moral fervour with which each writer approached his task and the zeal with which each protested against the injustices of the times—Tudor or Victorian. Ruskin surveyed a smaller field than More, but he did it with the same desire to make it possible for all, as he expressed it, 'to be holy, perfect, and pure.' The practical details of the Utopian or Ruskinian economy are not in themselves of first importance in the influence these two books have had. *Utopia* and Ruskinia cannot be reconciled but the authors were so zealous in their pursuit of justice that they inspired thousands who rejected many of the solutions proposed. This point becomes clearer if we consider the difference between the two Books of *Utopia*; had only Book Two—the account of the island and its government—been published, it would have become a literary curiosity; plain accounts of ideal states make dull reading; but the first Book is so vigorous in its criticism of early Tudor society that it carries the reader on to consider the alternative that More offers in the second Book; as the problems raised are, in varied forms, perennial, they stimulate the reader's thoughts on his own society.

A number of books[12] and essays have been written on *Utopia*; some of these ignore certain considerations that should be kept in the reader's mind if he wishes to understand the book as it was understood by More and his friends—that is, so far as a twentieth-century mind can enter the world of the sixteenth century.

---

[12] The best study is by H.W. Donner, *Introduction to Utopia* (1945).

The first consideration is that *Utopia* is a dialogue and it is sometimes as difficult to decide what More himself thought as it is to read Shakespeare's opinions from his plays. We have already noted that More's early training was in part based on the medieval method of disputation; his study of Plato and Lucian strengthened his liking for that form of argument, for the dialogue is an exchange of opinions. More's wide reading,[13] deep thinking, and practical experience of affairs, sharpened in conversation with some of the most acute thinkers of his time, all went to the writing of *Utopia*.

A second consideration to keep in mind is that Utopia is not a Christian country. More may have been thinking of St. Augustine's two cities; Utopia represents the best that can be achieved under the natural law without the grace of the Christian revelation. The implication is that if a non-Christian state could reach such a pitch of perfection, how much more blessed should be a Christian commonwealth.[14]

It is necessary to give a third warning. To apply our modern political terms, or words used by More but with modern connotations, in interpreting *Utopia*, is unhistorical and misleading. Thus a recent writer has said that 'More was a bourgeois, critical of rising capitalism and especially of declining feudalism, who hoped to reform society along bourgeois-republican lines in the immediate future.'[15] Such a statement has

---

[13] The extent of this knowledge of Latin writers is shown by Marie Delcourt in her *Utopie*; she gives a list of over a hundred rare words used by More, some of them taken from obscure authors.

[14] Seebohm in his *Oxford Reformers* missed this point. A later writer, G.G. Coulton in his *Medieval Panorama* (1938) refuses to accept More's premise. He argues (p. 677) that as Hythlodaye did not preach 'the distinctive doctrines of the Roman Church,' More must, in his heart, have approved the kind of teaching given in schools 'in the spirit of the much-abused Cowper-Temple clause,' or, as we should now say, in the spirit of the Agreed Syllabus!

[15] Russel Ames, *Citizen Thomas More* (1949), p. 18.

little relevance to More's mind; it is the result of reading into the past notions that have been formulated in a later age, and it credits him with a superhuman prevision. Other commentators have even declared that *Utopia* inspired English imperialist Realpolitik.[16] These and similar speculations tell us more about their authors than about *Utopia*.

The reader needs a lively mind to appreciate *Utopia*. More was a master of irony and satire, and his sense of fun rarely deserted him; the surface meaning may not represent his complete thought.

Erasmus made a fitting comment when he wrote to a friend, 'If you have not read More's *Utopia*, do look out for it, whenever you wish to be amused, or rather I should say, if you ever want to see the sources from which almost all the ills of the body politic arise.'[17]

With these considerations in mind we can review some of the features of *Utopia*. Other points will be more suitably noted in later chapters.

A passage from the first part, descriptive of Cardinal Morton, has already been quoted.[18] That was from Hythlodaye's account of his visit to England during which he stayed at Lambeth Palace. The conversation he reported was concerned with the condition of the people; the guests discussed, for instance, how far hanging was a deterrent to lawlessness, the dangers of a class of nobles who 'live idle themselves like drones on the labours of others' and maintain 'a huge crowd of idle followers'; they also talked of the inclosure of land for pasture by 'nobles and gentlemen and

---

[16] E.g. H. Oncken, *Die Utopia des Thomas Morus und das Macht-problem* (1922).

[17] *Nichols*, II, p. 503 (Feb. 1517); *Allen*, II, 537. It has been suggested (A.W. Reed, *Early Tudor Drama*, p. 11) that John Rastell's abortive expedition to the New Found Lands in 1517 was inspired by *Utopia*. There is no evidence of this; the fact that the voyage came after the publication of *Utopia* may have no significance. John Rastell had plenty of ideas of his own.

[18] See above, p. 31.

even holy abbots.'[19] Hythlodaye discussed how such inequalities and injustices could be avoided. His friends thought that he should serve some Prince and so work towards a realization of his ideas; but he scorned to do so since he wanted a radical change in the social order such as no Prince would tolerate, and he would not compromise his principles; it must be all or nothing. More's reply to this is important because it is in keeping with his own practice when he became the King's servant.

> 'In the private discussion of friends this philosophy of the schools is not without its charm, but in the councils of kings, where great matters are debated with great authority, there is no room for these things.' 'That is just what I meant,' said he, 'by saying there is no room for philosophy with kings.' 'Yes, there is,' said I, 'but not for the philosophy of the schools, which thinks that everything is suited to every place; but there is another philosophy, more suited to citizens, which knows its own stage, adapts itself to that, and in the play that is in hand, performs its own part, neatly and appropriately. This is what you must employ. ... Whatever play is being performed, perform it as well as you can; and do not upset it all, because you bethink you of another which has more wit. So it is in commonwealths with the deliberations of kings. Suppose wrong opinions cannot be plucked up by the root, and you cannot cure, as you would wish, vices of long standing, yet you must not on that account abandon ship of state and desert it in a storm, because you cannot control the winds. But neither must you impress upon them new and strange language, which you know will carry no weight with those of opposite conviction, but by indirect approach and covert suggestion you must endeavour and strive to the best of your power to handle all well, and what you cannot turn to

---

[19] *Utopia*, pp. 9-13; pp. 23-6.

good, you must make as little bad as you can. For it is impossible that all should be well, unless all men are good, which I do not expect for a great many years to come.'[20]

Hythlodaye went on to explain how far-reaching his solution would be, for, having seen the happiness of the Utopians amongst whom all things were held in common, he had come to the conclusion that 'no just and even distribution of goods can be made, nor any perfect happiness he found among men, unless private property is utterly abolished.'[21] This is expressed more strongly in the second book.

> So when I consider and turn over in my mind the state of all flourishing commonwealths today, so help me God, I can see nothing but a conspiracy of the rich, who are aiming at their own advantage under the name and title of the commonwealth.[22]

He considered it impracticable, and it was this scepticism that More firmly opposed this motion of common property and led Hythlodaye to give the detailed description of Utopia that forms the second part of the book.

It is better here to avoid the word 'communism'; a generation ago that term could have been applied to the Utopian economy without serious misunderstanding, but today it has acquired a special meaning that is no longer applicable to More's imagined island. The views expressed in the book by More in his own character are consistent with what is known of his real opinions. Thus on this fundamental question of property, he made his position clear in *A Dialogue of Comfort* written in the Tower in 1534. This book was in a sense his testament and the opinions expressed by Anthony were his own. Here is what he wrote on

---

[20] *Utopia*, pp. 33-4; p. 47.

[21] *Utopia*, p. 37; p. 51.

[22] *Utopia*, p. 119; p. 132.

the inequality of possessions.

But, cousin, men of substance must there be, for else shall you have more beggars pardy than there be, and no man left to relieve another. For this I think in my mind a very sure conclusion, that if all the money that is in this country were tomorrow next brought together out of every man's hand and laid all upon one heap, and then divided out unto every man alike, it would be on the morrow after worse than it was the day before.[23]

Bearing in mind, then, More's rejection of the basic principle of the Utopian economy, we can better assess the degree of approval he would give to the institutions and customs of that island. It is true that these are of his own invention, but the dramatist himself does not agree with every word spoken by his characters. More propounded a problem. 'Given a country where human reason alone ordered affairs for the general happiness, what would be the result?' His answer was—*Utopia*.

There would be no point here in reviewing all the details of the Utopian constitution and economy; More's account is clear and the reader needs no guide. There are, however, some features, which, even accepting the convention of the form of the dialogue, are so unexpected that they call for comment. Four may be instanced; these are—the marriage of priests,[24] divorce for 'intolerable offensiveness of disposition,' euthanasia for the aged, and inciting the assassination of an enemy king.[25] Not one of these is admissible by a Catholic, yet Thomas More includes them in his *Utopia*.

Perhaps we now get misled by the very word 'Utopia'; it meant no more at first than 'Not-place' and had no greater

---

[23] *Dialogue of Comfort*, p. 302.

[24] For More's views on the marriage of priests, see *A Dialogue Against Heresies*, III, ch. 13.

[25] *Utopia*, pp. 84-111; pp. 92-125.

significance than William Morris's 'Nowhere'; but it has long become a synonym for the ideal state, and we assume that everything there is More's idea of perfection and not therefore to be criticized. This was not his view; at the end of the book, writing in his own character he said, 'Many things came to my mind which seemed very absurd in the manners and laws of that people,' and again, 'though he [Hythlodaye] is a man of most undoubted learning and of great knowledge, yet I cannot agree with all that he said.'[26] This emphasizes the difficulty of deciding what More intended to be taken seriously and what he meant to be ironic or even facetious. The temptation is to dismiss as ironic or facetious those things we do not ourselves like, and that provides an easy way out of any perplexity; but there is surely a more satisfactory explanation. Let it be repeated that Utopia was a state guided by the unaided human reason; More followed this idea as far as he could, and showed us what the results might be of reason divorced from revelation. The striking fact is that his suggestions have in fact been realized. Modern society, with its indifference to revealed religion, regards a celibate priesthood as an oddity, it discusses proposals for permissive euthanasia, and it makes divorce easier and easier. It is true that political assassination is still frowned upon, but 'liquidation' connotes other horrors, and we all know the modern equivalent of the Utopians' 'placards ... set up secretly in the most prominent spots of the enemies' territory.'[27] Human reason can find convincing arguments for all these things.

One other topic calls for comment as it is linked with an aspect of More's life that has been severely criticized and misinterpreted. Sir Sidney Lee wrote, 'Nowhere indeed has the great doctrine of religious toleration been expounded with greater

---

[26] *Utopia*, pp. 121-2; p. 135.

[27] *Utopia* p. 96; p. 109.

force or fulness than in the *Utopia* ... he [More] regarded the toleration in practical life of differences on religious questions as sacrilegious.'[28] Such statements are perverse. In Utopia it was 'lawful for every man to follow what religion he chose,' but, anyone who, in trying to persuade others to adopt his beliefs, 'contended too vehemently in expressing his views, was to be punished by exile or enslavement.' One of Hythlodaye's companions was exiled 'not for despising their religion, but for stirring up strife among the people.'[29] To omit any mention of the limits set to toleration, is to give a wrong impression of the Utopian attitude. More's own practice in this matter must be discussed at length in a later chapter; here it must suffice to say that, much as he deplored and contested unorthodox opinions, his anger was particularly directed against those who disturbed the faith of others and stirred up strife. His own conduct in another field was in keeping with this principle; when he refused the oath of Supremacy, he kept quiet and would not discuss the matter with his family and friends. Even his favourite daughter Margaret did not know the grounds of his objection.

Much as one may admire some of the provisions of this imagined commonwealth, it is not, in fact, an attractive picture; the same can be said of other attempts to devise a perfect society whether by William Morris, or by H. G. Wells, or by Plato himself. They are all marked by over-regimentation and would be very dull countries in which to live. The value of these fantasies does not lie in their political viability, nor even in such attractive features as they may possess. They provoke thought on the problems of society. Plato's *Republic* stands apart in the strength of its influence on political thought, but More's *Utopia* takes a leading place in this form of writing. It is still the basis for

---

[28] *Great Englishmen of the Sixteenth Century* (1904), pp. 32-3.

[29] *Utopia*, p. 107; p. 119.

commentaries and discussions; some are written with a ponderous gravity that would have made More 'merry,' though he would also have been startled at some of the ideas fathered upon him by those who fail to appreciate his mood and purpose. This continuing study of a book written in 1515 is a tribute to the genius of its author.

Chapter XI

COUNCILLOR

HE year 1517 was a sad one for London; it saw the outbreak of lawlessness known as Ill May Day, and the plague of the sweating sickness that raged for six months.

The privileges and protection enjoyed by foreign merchants and their men were an irritant to the London populace. In times of bad trade or of poor harvests this discontent was turned on anyone who was not English. Some of the foreigners were at times overbearing and insolent, and it seems that the cavalier treatment by a Lombard of a citizen's wife brought matters to a head about Easter 1517. A Dr. Beale was persuaded to voice the grievances of the commons in a sermon, and this emboldened some agitators to organize an attack on all foreigners. Rumours that some kind of demonstration was planned for May Day reached Wolsey; the Council sent a warning to the Mayor through the Recorder and Thomas More that householders should remain indoors with their servants from the Eve of May Day until seven the next morning. Some apprentices were arrested for disobeying an order of which they may have been ignorant. At once the dreaded cry of "Prentices and Clubs!" was raised.

'Then out at every door came clubs and weapons ... then more people arose out of every quarter, and out came serving-men and water-men.' Hundreds crowded Cheapside down to St. Martin-le-Grand. 'There met with them Sir Thomas More and others, desiring them to go to their lodgings. And as they were entreating, and had almost brought them to a stay, the people of

St. Martin's threw out stones and bats [bricks], and hurt diverse honest persons that were persuading the riotous people to cease, and they bade them hold their hands, but still they threw out bricks and hot water. Then a sergeant-of-arms called Nicholas Downs, which was there with Master More, entreating them, being sore hurt, in a frenzy cried "Down with them." Then all the misruled persons ran to the doors and windows of St. Martin's, and spoiled all that they found, and cast it into the street."[1] The rioting was dying down by the time forces had been gathered for its suppression; thirteen of those imprisoned were sent to the gallows.

On 12th May, Thomas More was one of a deputation from the City to know when the Mayor and Aldermen could wait upon the King and pray his pardon for what had happened. At the audience the petitioners wore black gowns; the King told them that the Cardinal would declare his will and pleasure. Ten days later the four hundred prisoners, each in his shirt and with a halter round his neck, came before the King in Westminster Hall. They were pardoned, and the London tradition was that Queen Catherine had been responsible for this act of mercy.

Another tradition is preserved in the Elizabethan play of *The Booke of Sir Thomas More*;[2] this exists in manuscript but was not staged as the censor did not like the reference to an anti-alien riot; that kind of trouble was still a source of worry to the authorities; perhaps he also felt that while Anne Boleyn's daughter was on the throne, the less said about Sir Thomas More, the better. In this play More is represented as succeeding in his

---

[1] *Hall*, I, pp. 159-160.

[2] This play has a special interest; some scholars believe that three pages of the manuscript are in Shakespeare's handwriting; these pages include the speech made by Thomas More in pacifying the rioters. A useful survey of this attractive theory will be found in R.C. Bald's article *The Booke of Sir Thomas More and its Problems in Shakespeare Survey 2* (Cambridge 1949). He gives references to other literature on the subject.

efforts to quieten the rioters; for this he is knighted on the stage and declared to be a member of the Council; later it is declared,

> Sir Thomas More, humbly upon his knee,
> Did beg the lives of all, since on his word
> They did so gently yield. The king hath granted it,
> And made him Lord High Chancellor of England.

And one of the reprieved declared.

> More's name may live for this right noble part.
> And whensoe'er we talk of Ill May Day,
> Praise More.

Historically most of this is nonsense; its importance lies in the preservation of a Thomas More tradition in London. It was foolish of the playwrights to think they could get past the censor with such a revival of an embarrassing piece of history (however garbled) but they knew that the name of Thomas More would appeal to the people who filled the theatres.

When More came to write his Apology in 1533 he recalled that he 'was appointed among others to search out and inquire by diligent examination, in what wise and by what persons, that privy confederacy began.' It was discovered, he said, that it all began 'by the conspiracy of two young lads that were 'prentices in Cheap.' They persuaded others that hundreds of apprentices, journeymen and serving-men were in the plot; having prepared the ground they 'fled away themselves, and never came again after.'[3]

One of these two young lads made himself a nuisance in the following year to John Rastell. When his ship, 'The Barbara', put

---

[3] *Apology*, p. 177.

into Falmouth on the way, as he hoped, to the New Found Lands, the purser, John Raven, insisted on taking on board a youth named Coo,

> and because the said Rastell heard say that the said Coo should be one of the 'prentices that made the insurrection in London, he warned Raven that he should not suffer him to go with him, yet that notwithstanding he caused the said Coo to make and to pick divers quarrels to make debate among the soldiers.[4]

The expedition came to an end when the ship reached Ireland, and Coo, the stirrer-up of trouble, passes out of history.

The sweating sickness[5] broke out in London, Oxford and Cambridge in July 1517. This might be called the Tudor disease for it first appeared after the battle of Bosworth and plagued the towns at intervals for nearly a century. One of the victims in London was Ammonio, and More sent Erasmus news of his death.

> We are in greater distress and danger than ever; deaths are frequent all around us, almost everybody at Oxford, at Cambridge and here in London, having been laid up within the last few days, and very many of our best and most honoured friends being lost. Among these—I am distressed to think how it will distress you—has been our friend Andrew Ammonio, in whom both good letters and all good men have suffered a grievous loss. He thought himself protected against contagion by his temperate habit of life, and attributed it to this, that, whereas he scarcely met with any person, whose whole family had not been sick, the malady had not attacked any one of his. This boast he made to me and others not many hours before his death. For in this sweating sickness, as they call it, no one dies but on the first day. I, with my wife and

---

[4] A.W. Reed, *Early Tudor Drama*, p. 198.

[5] A military fever.

children, am as yet untouched; the rest of my family have recovered. I can assure you that there is less danger upon a field of battle than in this town. It is now, I hear, beginning to rage at Calais, when we are being forced thither ourselves to undertake a diplomatic mission—as if it were not enough to have been living in contagion here without following it elsewhere. But what is one to do? What our lot brings us must be borne; and I have composed my mind for every event. Farewell. London, in haste, the 19th day of August, 1517.[6]

The mission to Calais was concerned with trade disputes; the English mission consisted of Sir Richard Wingfield, Dr. William Knight and Thomas More. They left London in August; the negotiations proved tedious and were prolonged, partly because Wolsey used these commercial disputes as a cover for his own manoeuvres in foreign policy. It was not until December that More returned to Bucklesbury to find his family in good health. He brought back with him portraits of Erasmus and Peter Gilles painted by Quentin Metsys.[7] The first news of the project was given in a letter from Erasmus to More in May 1517, from Antwerp.

> Peter Gilles and I are being painted in one picture, which we intend to send you as a present before long. But it unluckily happened that on my return I found that Peter had been attacked by a serious illness, from which he has not even now quite recovered. I was myself fairly well, but somehow or other it occurred to my doctor to order me some pills for the purging of bile; and what he was fool enough to prescribe I was idiot enough to take. The portrait was already begun, but when I returned to the painter after taking the physic, he said it was not the same face; so the painting has been put off for

---

[6] *Nichols*, Vol. III, p. 2; *Allen*, III, 623.

[7] This artist made a fine medal of Erasmus in 1519. See Plate xv.

some days till I can look more cheerful.[8]

Shortly before leaving for Calais, More wrote,

'The picture which represents your likeness with that of our Peter is expected greedily by me. I have no patience with that illness which delays my satisfaction for so long.[9]

It was not until early September that Erasmus was able to send the diptych to More at Calais.

> I send the portraits so that we may in some way still be with you, if any chance should take us off. Peter pays half, and I half—not that we should, either of us, have been unwilling to pay the whole, but that the present may be common to us both.[10]

The portrait of Erasmus shows him as he was in his prime; the more familiar Holbein portraits were painted some years later when sickness had already made its mark. Peter Gilles is shown holding in his hand a letter from More with his handwriting skilfully imitated. This led More to write,

> My dear Peter, our Quentin has not only marvellously imitated all the objects he has depicted, but has also shown his ability to be, if he pleased, a most skilful forger, having copied the address of my letter to you in such a way that I could not write it myself so like again. Therefore, unless he wants to keep the letter for any purpose of his own, or you for any purpose of yours, please send it back to me; it will double the marvel if it is put by the side of the picture. If it has been destroyed, or if you have any use for it, I will try to copy again the imitator of my own hand.[11]

---

[8] *Nichols*, II, p. 559; *Allen*, II, 584.

[9] *Nichols*, II, p. 585; *Allen*, III, 601.

[10] *Nichols*, III, p. 41; *Allen*, 654.

[11] *Nichols*, III, p. 93; *Allen*, III, 684.

He enclosed some Latin verses with this letter. The first six lines read in translation,

> As Castor was to Pollux, so are here
> Gilles and Erasmus—each to other dear.
> More, joined to both in love, regrets that he
> Is severed from them in locality.
> To soothe his longing heart, their mental graces
> A loving scroll recalls, and I their faces.[12]

These verses were soon in circulation as was the manner of the day; such compositions were not regarded as private but as good things to be passed round to friends. More heard of one criticism and this he passed on to Erasmus.

> I am glad you liked my verses upon the picture. Tunstal praised the eleven-syllable lines more than enough; the piece in six lines moderately. A friar has ventured to find fault with the latter because I compared you to Castor and Pirithous, or Pylades and Orestes, who, like you, were friends not brothers. I could not tolerate this friar though there is some truth in what he says; so I followed up his good suggestion with a bad epigram.

> The warmest friendship to express,
> Castor, I said, loved Pollux less.
> On this a friar disputed, whether
> Friendship and brothers matched together.
> Why not? said I, can any other
> Love a man better than a brother?
> The friar laughed to hear a saying
> Such childish ignorance betraying.

---

[12] *Nichols*, III, p. 92; *Allen*, III, 684.

> Our house is large and full, said he,
> More than two hundred brothers we;
> But hang me if in all you find
> A pair of brothers of one mind.[13]

In a letter to Erasmus from Calais in October, More expressed his dislike of the kind of mission on which he was then engaged.

> I approve of your plan in not wishing to be involved in the busy trifles of princes; and you show your love for me by desiring that I may be disentangled from such matters in which you can scarcely believe how unwillingly I am engaged. Nothing indeed can be more harmful to me than my present mission. I am sent to stay at a little seaport, with a disagreeable soil and climate; and whereas at home I have naturally the greatest abhorrence of litigation, even when it brings me profit, you may imagine what annoyance it must cause one here, when it comes accompanied with loss. But my lord [Wolsey] kindly promises that the king shall reimburse the whole; when I receive it, I will let you know![14]

The ability More showed in the negotiations marked him out for further service, and it was inevitable that on his return the King should again urge More to join the Council. This time he felt unable to refuse, but it was not an easy decision to make. In a letter to Margaret Roper from the Tower in 1535, her father recalled that 'I had always from the beginning truly used myself to looking first upon God and next upon the king according to the lesson his highness taught me at my first coming to his noble service, the most virtuous lesson that ever prince taught his

---

[13] *Nichols*, III, p. 133; *Allen*, III, 706. The two portraits have long been separated. That of Erasmus is now in the Corsini Gallery, Rome, and that of Peter Gilles at Longford Castle (the Earl of Radnor). Both are reproduced in *Harpsfield*.

[14] *Nichols*, III, p. 103; *Allen*, III, 688.

servant.'[15] This suggests that Thomas More had discussed his reluctance to accept office with the King who had then set his mind at rest. To the very end of his life Sir Thomas More held the King to his word.

Roper's account is inaccurate. It reads:

> At whose first entry thereunto [the king's service] he made him master of the requests (having then no better room void) and within a month after knight, and one of his privy Council.[16]

'Master of the Requests' was a term not used in Thomas More's day; it was not until the later years of Henry VIII that it became accepted.[17] The Court referred to was at first usually spoken of as the Court of Poor Men's Causes, and dated back to the reign of Henry VII. It was then what may be called a standing committee of the Council for dealing with civil causes, while the Court of the Star Chamber dealt with criminal matters; the division was not absolute as the Star Chamber under the Lord Chancellor remained the principal court at Westminster. Wolsey decided that the Court of Poor Men's Causes should also have its permanent seat, and this was in the old White Hall;[18] the judges were members of the Council but not necessarily lawyers; Wolsey himself, it should be remembered, was not a lawyer. The surviving lists[19] of the Court of Poor Men's Causes do not include the name of Thomas More, but the lists may not be complete, or, more probably, he did not sit regularly. His attendance on the

---

[15] *Rogers*, p. 557.

[16] *Roper*, pp. 10-11.

[17] See introduction to *Select Cases in the Court of Requests*, edited for the Selden Society by I.S. Leadam (1898).

[18] Not to be confused with the later Whitehall. The White Hall was a building south of Westminster Hall. The statue of Richard I now stands on the site.

[19] See Leadam, pp. Lxxxii.

King, who was frequently on the move, would have made it impossible for him to be in the White Hall at every court. It seems that such cases were also tried wherever the King might hold his Court; when More was in attendance, he would be available for such work.

The first payment to Thomas More of a Councillor's annuity of £100 was made on 21st June, 1518, and back-dated to Michaelmas 1517.[20] It is safe to assume, therefore, that he took up his duties as a Councillor soon after his return from Calais. His father was made a judge in the Common Pleas about the same time; there may be a connexion between the two appointments.[21]

The caution with which Roper's statements should be read is again illustrated by the following quotation:

> Then died one Master Weston, the treasurer of the Exchequer, whose office after his death, the king of his own offer, without any asking, freely gave unto Sir Thomas More.[22]

Sir Richard Weston became Under-Treasurer in 1528 and lived until 1542. Thomas More succeeded Sir John Cutte who died in April 1521, and as it was usual for the Under-Treasurer to be a knight, this gives the most likely date for More's knighthood. The office was not, as Roper said, that of Treasurer, a position held by the Duke of Norfolk, but Under-Treasurer, for which the salary was £173 6s. 8d.; the first payment to Sir Thomas More dates his appointment as 2nd May, 1521.[23]

The official letters signed by Thomas More show that he was one of the Councillors in attendance on the King, and not one of

---

[20] P.R.O., C. 66, no. 637, m. 12 (patent roll); E 405, no. 202.

[21] Sir John More is first mentioned as a judge early in 1518. Was he knighted at the same time? There is no record of the date, but if it was in 1518, Roper may have confused father with son.

[22] *Roper*, p. 12.

[23] P.R.O., E. 405, no. 480.

those who remained at Westminster under the eye of the Cardinal. These letters[24] begin in July 1519 and continue for ten years; no doubt many others have disappeared. They are addressed from the King's manors or from noblemen's mansions where he had quartered himself—Woking, Easthampstead, Guildford, Abingdon, Woodstock, Hertford, Stony Stratford, Richmond and Windsor. Most of these letters are of small interest and add nothing to our knowledge of Thomas More. One of the shorter ones to Wolsey—these are in English—will serve as a specimen.

> It may like your good Grace to be advertised that I have received your Grace's letter to me directed, written the 2nd day of September, and with the same the letters congratulatory by your Grace devised in the King's name to the Duke of Venice. Which I read unto his Grace, who much commending your substantial draft and ornate device therein, hath signed and with his hearty thanks remitted the same unto your Grace again.
>
> I read also his Highness your said letters written to me which his Highness very gladly heard and in the reading said that your Grace was worthy more thanks than he could give you. And as touching the venison which he sent your Grace, he was very glad that it liked your Grace so well and would it had been much better. And thus our Lord long preserve your good Grace in honour and health.
>
> At Woking the 3rd day of September, 1523
>
> Your humble orator and must bounden bedeman
>
> Thomas More[25]

Some of the letters are long and are on more important

---

[24] They are given in *Rogers*.

[25] *Rogers*, p. 282; the letter is also there reproduced in facsimile.

matters than congratulatory epistles and gifts of venison, but the impression is that a man of Thomas More's quality was wasted in acting as an agent between the King and the Cardinal. One explanation of this close attendance on the King is given by Roper.

> And so from time to time was he by the prince advanced, continuing in his singular favour and trusty service twenty years and above. A good part whereof used the king upon holidays, when he had done his own devotions, to send for him into his traverse [closet] and there sometime in matters of Astronomy, Geometry, Divinity, and such other Faculties, and sometimes of his worldly affairs, to sit and confer with him. And other whiles would he, in the night, have him up into his leads [flat roof] there for to consider with him the diversities, courses, motions, and operations of the stars and planets. And because he was of a pleasant disposition, it pleased the king and the queen, after the Council had supped, at the time of their supper, for their pleasure, commonly to call for him to be merry with them. Whom when he perceived so much in his talk to delight, that he could not once in a month get leave to go home to his wife and children (whose company he most desired) and to be absent from the court two days together, but that he should be thither sent for again, he, much misliking this restraint of his liberty, began thereupon somewhat to dissemble his nature, and so by little and little from his former accustomed mirth to disuse himself, that he was of them from thenceforth at such seasons no more so ordinarily sent for.[26]

Erasmus commented on More's new position in a letter to Tunstal in 1518.

> I should deplore the fortune of More in being enticed into

---

[26] *Roper*, pp. 11-12.

a Court, if it were not that under such a king, and with so many learned men for companions and colleagues, it may seem not a Court but a temple of the Muses. But meanwhile there is nothing brought us from Utopia to amuse us; and he, I am quite sure, would rather have his laugh than be borne aloft on a curule chair.[27]

The first part of this quotation reminds us that the early hopes that had welcomed Henry VIII had not yet been disappointed. He was not, it is true, a liberal patron of letters, but he still liked the company of scholars and this pleasure he shared with Catherine the queen. No cloud had yet overshadowed the delight he had in her company; the Princess Mary was two years old, and, 'if it is a girl this time, by God's grace boys will follow.' One of the scholars at the Court in 1518 was Richard Pace who had become the King's chief secretary; he was a few years younger than More and had studied at Oxford and Padua. While they were at Abingdon in March 1518 Pace wrote to Wolsey that 'carding and dicing were turned into pitching arrows over the screen in the hall.'[28] He wrote again a month later to complain that

> 'Dr. Clerk and Mr. More desire your Grace to write to my Lord Steward that they may have their daily allowance of meat which has been granted them by the King. Here is such bribery that they be compelled to buy meat in the town for their servants, which is to them intolerable, and to the king's grace dishonourable.'[29]

Dr. John Clerk of Cambridge and Bologna was Wolsey's chaplain, and dean of the King's chapel; he became Bishop of Bath and Wells in 1523.

---

[27] *Nichols*, III, p. 361; *Allen*, III, 832.

[28] *L.P.*, II, 4043.

[29] *L.P.*, II, 4055.

The court moved on to Woodstock but More was kept busy at Oxford taking precautions against the spread of the plague that had broken out; infected houses had to be marked and those attending the sick had to carry white rods out of doors.[30] There is nothing surprising in such duties being undertaken by Sir Thomas More. His writings show time and time again how interested he was in questions of health and of sickness. In *Utopia*[31] the town planning and the hospital organization were in advance of Tudor practice. More had attended[32] some of the lectures of his friend Thomas Linacre, founder of the Royal Society of Physicians, and he later took a keen interest in John Clement's medical studies.[33]

Erasmus recorded two incidents of this period in a letter to a friend; no doubt he had received accounts of them from More or Pace that have not survived.

The first was that a preacher at Oxford had attacked the study of Greek. The second incident is best given in the words of the letter.

> Again, a theologian who had to preach in the presence of the King, began stupidly and impudently to attack Greek studies, and the new interpreters of scripture. Pace looked at the King to see how he took it. The King replied by a smile. When the sermon was ended the theologian was called. More was appointed to defend Greek, and the King himself was present at the discussion. After More, with much eloquence, had made a long defence, and the reply of the theologian was expected, instead of speaking he suddenly went on his knees before the King and asked pardon, affirming, however, in his

---

[30] *L.P.*, II, 4125.

[31] *Utopia*, Bk. II, chaps. 2 and 5.

[32] *Rogers*, p. 65.

[33] See Sir Arthur MacNalty's Chadwick Lecture summarized in *Nature*, 23rd Nov., 1946.

excuse, that while preaching he had felt himself inspired to say what he did against Greek. 'The spirit which inspired you,' replied the King, 'was certainly not that of Christ, but rather the spirit of folly.' Then he asked him whether he had read any of the writings of Erasmus, since the King perceived that he had been girding at me. He said that he had not. 'Then you clearly prove your folly,' said the King, 'since you condemn what you have not read.' 'Well, I have read one thing called Moria,' replied the theologian. 'May it please your Highness,' interposed Pace, 'his argument well befits that book.' Meanwhile the theologian hits on a train of reasoning to mitigate his blunder. 'I am not altogether opposed to Greek,' he says, 'since it is derived from the Hebrew.' The King, astonished at the man's folly, dismissed him, but forbade him ever again to preach at court.[34]

The outcome of these attacks on Greek was that, apparently at the King's request, More wrote a letter to the University[35] defending the study of that language; this must have been a congenial task, especially as his young friend John Clement had just been appointed by Wolsey lecturer in Greek to the University.

One passage from the letter will indicate the argument advanced by More.

> Although no one denies that a man may be saved without a knowledge of Latin and Greek or of any literature at all, yet learning, yea, even worldly learning, as he [the preacher] calls it prepares the mind for virtue. Everyone knows that the attainment of this learning is almost the only reason why students flock to Oxford. But as for rude and unlettered virtue, every honest woman can teach it to her children quite

---

[34] *Allen*, III, 948.

[35] *Rogers*, pp. 111-20.

well at home. Moreover, it must be remembered that not all who come to you, come for the study of theology. The State needs men learned in the law. A knowledge of human affairs, too, must be acquired, which is so useful even to a theologian, that without it he may perhaps sing pleasantly to himself, but will certainly not sing agreeably to the people. And this knowledge can nowhere be drawn so abundantly as from the poets, orators and historians. There are even some who make the knowledge of things natural a road to heavenly contemplation, and so pass from philosophy and the natural arts—which this man condemns under the general name of worldly literature—to theology, despoiling the women of Egypt to adorn the queen. And as regards theology itself, which alone he seems to approve, if indeed he approves even that, I do not see how he can attain it without the knowledge of languages, either Hebrew, Greek or Latin; unless, indeed, the easy-going fellow thinks that sufficient books on the subject have been written in English. Or perhaps he thinks that the whole of theology is comprised within the limits of those questions on which such as he are always disputing, for the knowledge of which I confess that little enough Latin is wanted. But to confine theology, the august queen of heaven, within such narrow limits would be not only iniquitous but impious. For does not theology also dwell in the Sacred Scriptures, and did it not thence make its way to the cells of all the ancient holy Fathers, Augustine, I mean, Jerome, Ambrose, Cyprian, Chrysostom, Cyril, Gregory and others of the same class, with whom the study of theology made its abode for more than a thousand years after the Passion of Christ before those trivial questions arose? And if any ignorant man boasts that he understands the works of those Fathers without a thorough knowledge of the language in which each wrote, he will have to boast a long time before scholars will believe him.[36]

Reginald Pole was a student at Oxford at this period and frequented the Court; he was one of the younger men who were drawn into the circle of Thomas More's friendship. The King still favoured his young kinsman and in 1521 sent him to Padua to continue his studies. A letter from More to Reginald Pole and John Clement can probably be dated in 1518.

> I thank you, my dear Clement, for being so keenly solicitous about the health of my family and myself that although absent you are careful to warn us what food to avoid. I thank you, my dear Pole, doubly for deigning to procure for me the advice of so skilful a physician, and no less for obtaining from your mother[37]—noblest and best of women, and fully worthy such a son—the remedy prescribed and for getting it made up. Not only do you willingly procure us advice, but equally evident is your willingness to obtain for us the remedy itself. I love and praise both of you for your bounty and fidelity.[38]

Another reference to Reginald Pole comes in a letter to Margaret More.

> I cannot put down on paper, indeed I can hardly express in my own mind, the deep pleasure that I received from your most charming letter, my dearest Margaret. As I read it there was with me a young man of the noblest rank and of the widest attainments in literature, one, too, who is as conspicuous for his piety as he is for learning—Reginald Pole. He thought your letter nothing short of miraculous, even

---

[36] *Stapleton*, p. 41.

[37] Margaret, daughter of the Duke of Clarence, was created Countess of Salisbury by Henry VIII in 1513; notwithstanding his declaration that she was the most saintly woman in England, he had her executed at the age of seventy-eight.

[38] *Stapleton*, p. 45. *Rogers*, p. 135.

before he understood how you were pressed for time and distracted by ill-health, whilst you managed to write so long a letter.[39]

His work as a member of the Council and his frequent absences from London, obliged Thomas More to resign his position as Under-Sheriff in July 1518. This was the end of an association with the City that was severed with considerable regret on both sides. He was, however, always happy to serve the City when he could. Thus in that year, 1518, he was orator for the Mayor and Aldermen at the City's reception of Cardinal Campeggio when he came to win support for the Pope's crusade against the Turk. The City in its turn was glad to favour applicants for office who were recommended by Thomas More.[40]

---

[39] *Stapleton*, p. 46. *Rogers*, p. 301. There are difficulties about the date of the letter, but it must have been written before 1521 when Pole left England for Italy.

[40] For details, extracted from the City Records, see *Harpsfield*, pp. 312-314.

Chapter XII

The School

THE death of John Colet at the age of fifty-three on 16th September, 1519, must have grieved Thomas More as deeply as it grieved Erasmus, who wrote, 'a death so bitter to me that the loss of no one for the last thirty years had afflicted me more. I know that it is well with him who has been taken from this wicked and troublesome world, and is enjoying the presence of his Christ, whom in his lifetime he so dearly loved.'[1] More had declared that not for generations had there been a more learned and holy man. These two citizens of London had been closely united in their spiritual lives as well as in their love of learning. Colet had hoped to withdraw from the world in his latter years and live in communion with the Carthusians at Shene. 'I am daily thinking of my retirement.' he wrote to Erasmus in 1514, 'and of my retreat with the Carthusians. My nest there is almost finished. So far as I can conjecture, you will find me there on your return dead to the world.'[2]

The year before his death he had completed the Statutes for his school of St. Paul's, and had amply endowed it from his inherited wealth. He had given deep thought to the management of the school and to the course of studies to be followed; such matters he may well have discussed with Thomas More who was himself concerned to find the best way of bringing up his own four children.

---

[1] 17th October, 1519 to Fisher.

[2] *Nichols*, II, p. 171; *Allen*, II, 315. The 'nest' was occupied by Wolsey for a brief time after his fall. *Cavendish*, p. 176.

In Utopia learning was open to all without distinction of sex; the readings and conversation at the communal meals were part of the education of all citizens. Those who showed special aptitude were allowed to devote much of their time to learning, 'and a large part of the people, men and women alike, throughout their lives, devote to learning the hours which we said were free from manual labour.'[3]

More made no distinction in his own household in the training given to girls and boys. His own four children, Margaret, Elizabeth, Cecily and John were fortunate in having his personal care and guidance in their earliest years, but from about 1515 the time he could give to them decreased as the calls upon his public service increased; this was always a matter of regret to him. His children had as companions in their studies his stepdaughter Alice Middleton and his wards Margaret Gigs and Anne Cresacre; later others were entrusted to his care just as he himself had been placed in the household of Cardinal Morton; Giles Heron, his ward, was one of these, and his nephew William Rastell must have spent many of his boyhood days in company with his cousins; young students also lived with the Mores, such as William Roper. When More's children married they continued to live with him, and their children enjoyed the same kind of education as their parents. Stapleton wrote, 'More's own four children and eleven of his grandchildren were instructed in his school during his lifetime.'[4]

A succession of tutors passed through the household; they were more than instructors of the children and grandchildren; they enjoyed the society of Thomas More and his friends and took part in those conversations and discussions in which he delighted; they were indeed members of a family in which

---

[3] *Utopia*, p. 68; p. 82.

[4] *Stapleton*, p. 100.

devotion to learning came second only to devotion to the Church.

John Clement seems to have been the first of these tutors, and the most distinguished in after life. He was, as we have seen, More's companion during the creation of Utopia. Erasmus was greatly interested in Clement's progress and sent a message to him in 1518.

> Tell Clement, who seems a most promising youth, by way of message from me, that he must abstain from study at unseasonable hours—I remember how he sticks to his book—and especially that he had better, as far as he is allowed to do so, give up writing at night. If by any chance he is obliged to write for the Cardinal's business, he should accustom himself to do so, standing. I should be sorry that this genius should be lost before its time and would rather see it saved for study, than spent upon the Cardinal's affairs.[5]

As this letter tells us, Clement entered the Cardinal's service, and was, as we have seen, appointed lecturer in Greek at Oxford. Later he studied medicine at Louvain and Siena. In 1526 he married Margaret Gigs his former pupil in Bucklesbury. About 1528 he became one of the King's physicians and was sent to attend the fallen Wolsey at Esher in his last illness.[6]

William Gonell probably followed John Clement as tutor. He had been discovered by Erasmus at Landbeach near Cambridge. He was a schoolmaster and did copying for Erasmus; he also took charge of the scholar's horse when its master was away in London. It was probably in the spring of 1518 that Thomas More wrote to Gonell about the children who had sent letters to their father at court.

> Though I prefer learning joined with virtue to all the treasures of kings, yet renown for learning, when it is not

---

[5] *Nichols*, III, p. 347; *Allen*, II, 820.

[6] *Cavendish*, p. 164.

united with a good life, is nothing else than splendid and notorious infamy: this would be specially the case in a woman. Since erudition in women is a new thing and a reproach to the sloth of men, many will gladly assail it, and impute to literature what is really the fault of nature, thinking from the vices of the learned to get their own ignorance esteemed as virtue. On the other hand, if a woman (and this I desire and hope with you as their teacher for all my daughters) to eminent virtue should add an outwork of even moderate skill in literature, I think she will have more real profit than if she had obtained the riches of Croesus and the beauty of Helen. I do not say this because of the glory that will be hers, though glory follows virtue as a shadow follows a body, but because the reward of wisdom is too solid to be lost like riches or to decay like beauty, since it depends on the intimate conscience of what is right, not on the talk of men, than which nothing is more foolish or mischievous.

The letter then urges the need

> to warn my children to avoid the precipices of pride and haughtiness, and to walk in the pleasant meadows of modesty; not to be dazzled at the sight of gold; not to lament that they do not possess what they erroneously admire in others; not to think more of themselves for gaudy trappings, nor less for the want of them; neither to deform the beauty that nature has given them by neglect, nor to try to heighten it by artifice; to put virtue in the first place, learning in the second; and in their studies to esteem most whatever may teach them piety towards God, charity to all, and Christian humility in themselves.

He advised Gonell to introduce his pupils to the works of St. Jerome and St. Augustine.

> From them they will learn in particular what end they should propose to themselves in their studies and what is the

fruit of their endeavours, namely the testimony of God and a good conscience. Thus peace and calm will abide in their hearts and they will be disturbed neither by fulsome flattery nor by the stupidity of those illiterate men who despise learning. ...

If you will teach something of this sort, in addition to their lesson in Sallust—to Margaret and Elizabeth, as being more advanced than John and Cecily—you will bind me and them still more to you. And thus you will bring about that my children, who are dear to me by nature, and still more dear by learning and virtue, will become most dear by that advance in knowledge and good conduct.[7]

The letters Thomas More wrote to his children tell us much about his wishes for their progress. Stapleton tells us that when he copied these letters (about 1588) they were 'almost worn to pieces.' We owe it to Stapleton that the text of these letters has been preserved for the originals have been lost. He does not give the years when they were written but the period 1518 to 1523 seems likely. The first to be quoted was addressed 'to Margaret, Elizabeth, and Cecily his dearest children and to Margaret Gigs whom he regards as his own child.'

I cannot express, my dearest children, the very deep pleasure your eloquent letters gave me, especially as I see that although travelling and frequently changing your abode you have not allowed your customary studies to be interfered with, but have continued your exercises in logic, rhetoric and poetry. I am now fully convinced that you love me as you should since I see that, although I am absent, yet you do with the greatest eagerness what you know gives me pleasure when I am present. When I return you shall see that I am not ungrateful for the delight your loving affection has given me.

---

[7] *Stapleton*, p. 101. *Rogers*, p. 120.

I assure you that I have no greater solace in all the vexatious business in which I am immersed than to read your letters. They prove to me the truth of the laudatory reports your kind tutor sends of your work, for if your own handwriting did not bear witness to your zealous study of literature, it might be suspected that he had been influenced by his good nature rather than by the truth. But now by what you write you support his credit, so that I am ready to believe what would otherwise be his incredible reports upon the eloquence and wit of your essays.

So I am longing to return home that I may place my pupil[8] by your side and compare his progress with yours. He is, I fear, a little lazy, but he cannot help hoping that you are not really quite so advanced as your teacher's praise would imply. Knowing how persevering you are, I have a great hope that soon you will be able to overcome your tutor himself, if not by force of argument, at any rate by never confessing yourselves beaten. Farewell, my most dear children.[9]

Margaret showed the most ability of his children and she became a learned woman. The following passage is from a letter to her.

I was delighted to receive your letter, my dearest Margaret, informing me of Shaa's[10] condition. I should have been still more delighted if you had told me of the studies you and your brother are engaged in, of your daily reading, your pleasant discussions, your essays, of the swift passage of the days made joyous by literary pursuits. For although

---

[8] Probably John More; this explains the absence of his name from the greeting. *Rogers*, p. 96, suggests that he was too young to be included in the school, and therefore proposes the year 1517, but it may equally well be assigned to a later date.

[9] *Stapleton*, p. 109; *Rogers*, p. 97.

[10] Or 'Shaw'; probably a servant as there is no prefix.

everything you write gives me pleasure, yet the most exquisite delight of all comes from reading what none but you and your brother could have written. ... I beg you, Margaret, tell me about the progress you are all making in your studies. For I assure you that, rather than allow my children to be idle and slothful, I would make a sacrifice of wealth, and bid adieu to other cares and business, to attend to my children and my family, amongst whom none is more dear to me than yourself, my beloved daughter.

The second edition of More's *Epigrammata* published in 1520 contained an epistle to his children in Latin elegiac verse. As this was not in the 1518 edition, it can be dated between those years. He composed it, he said, on horseback as he rode along muddy tracks in pouring rain, but such discomforts did not prevent him from thinking of his children. They knew how he always returned with presents for them, and how he lavished kisses on them, and had seldom used a rod—but a rod of peacock's feathers—for chastizing them.

Scitis enim quam crebra dedi oscula, verbera rara,
Flagrum pavonis non nisi cauda fuit.

Their progress in virtue and learning had increased his love for them and he begged them to continue that progress so that his present love would seem as nothing compared with what it would then become.

Another letter 'to his whole school' may have been written about 1521.

See what a compendious salutation I have found, to save both time and paper, which would otherwise have been wasted in reciting the names of each one of you, and my labour would have been to no purpose, since, though each of you is dear to me by some special title, of which I could have omitted none in a set and formal salutation, no one is dearer to me by any title than each of you by that of scholar. Your zeal for knowledge binds me to you almost more closely than the ties of blood. I rejoice that Master Drew has returned safe, for I was anxious, as you know, about him. If I did not love you so much I should be really envious of your happiness in having so many and such excellent tutors. But I think you have no longer any need of Master Nicholas since you have learnt whatever he had to teach you about astronomy. I hear you are so far advanced in that science that you can not only point out the pole-star or the dog-star, or any of the constellations, but are able also—which requires a skilful and profound astrologer—among all those heavenly bodies, to distinguish the sun from the moon! Go forward then in that new and admirable science by which you ascend to the stars. But while you gaze on them assiduously, consider that this holy time of Lent warns you, and that beautiful and holy poem of Boethius[11] keeps singing in your ears, to raise your mind also to heaven, lest the soul look downwards to the earth, after the manner of brutes, while the body looks upwards. Farewell my dearest ones.[12]

Nothing certain is known of Master Drew; he may have been the Roger Drew who became Fellow of All Souls College, Oxford, in 1512. Master Nicholas was the Nicolaus Kratzer who wrote the notes on Holbein's sketch of the More family.

The next letter may be the latest in date of those addressed to 'his whole school.'

The Bristol merchant brought me your letters the day after he left you, with which I was extremely delighted. Nothing can come from your workshop, however rude and unfinished, that will give me more pleasure than the most

---

[11] Perhaps *Boethius* (Loeb), p. 154; 'O stelliferi conditor orbis.'

[12] *Stapleton*, p. 105; *Rogers*, p. 249.

accurate thing another can write. So much does my affection for you recommend whatever you write to me. Indeed, without any recommendation, your letters are capable of pleasing by their own merits, their wit and pure Latinity. There was not one of your letters that did not please me extremely; but, to confess ingenuously what I feel, the letter of my son John pleased me best, both because it was longer than the others, and because he seems to have given it more labour and study. For he not only put out his matter well and composed in fairly polished language, but he plays with me both pleasantly and cleverly and turns my jokes on myself wittily enough. And this he does not only merrily, but with due moderation, showing that he does not forget that he is joking with his father, and that he is cautious not to give offence at the same time that he is eager to give delight.

Now I expect from each of you a letter almost every day. I will not admit excuses—John makes none—such as want of time, sudden departure of the letter-carrier, or want of something to write about. No one hinders you from writing, but, on the contrary, all are urging you to do it...

One thing, however, I admonish you, whether you write serious matters or the merest trifles, it is my wish that you write everything diligently and thoughtfully. It will be no harm, if you first write the whole in English, for then you will have much less trouble in turning it into Latin; not having to look for the matter, your mind will be intent only on the language.[13]

The first paragraph of that letter should dispose of the legend[14] that John More was dull-witted.

---

[13] *Stapleton*, p. 106; *Rogers*, p. 255.

[14] It seems to have been started in the seventeenth century; it is found in Bacon's *Apophthegms*.

Stapleton also mentions Richard Hirt as a tutor; this was Richard Hyrde who took his degree at Oxford in 1519, but from his own account, to be quoted presently, More seems to have been responsible for his 'bringing-up.' He accompanied Stephen Gardiner and Edward Foxe on their mission to the Pope in 1528; he was described by Gardiner as 'a young man learned in physic, Greek and Latin'; he died at Orvieto as the result of getting drenched in rain and flood. His association with Thomas More has a special interest. Reference has already been made to his preface to Margaret More's translation of the *Treatise on the Pater Noster* by Erasmus. In that preface he eloquently vindicated the need for the education of women. Later he translated Vives' *The Instruction of a Christian Woman*;[15] Hyrde's dedicatory epistle to Queen Catherine contains the following passage:

> Which [the translation] when I had secretly done by myself, I shewed it unto my singular good master and bringer up. Sir Thomas More, to whose judgement and correction I use to submit whatsoever I do or go about, that I set any store by: who not only for the matter itself was very glad thereof, but also that (as he then shewed me) he perceived that it should be to your noble majesty for the gracious zeal that ye bear to the virtuous education of the womankind of this realm, whereof our lord hath ordained you to be Queen, so great and special pleasure, that he had intended, his manifold business notwithstanding, to have taken the times to have translated this book himself in which he was (as he said) very glad that he was now prevented, not for eschewing of his labour, which he would have been very glad to bestow therein, but for because that the fruit thereof may now sooner come forth than he could have found the time. How be it as I answered him: It were better to bring forth dates in an

---

[15] Not published until 1540.

hundred years (for so long it is or that tree bring forth his fruit) than crabs in four years. And though he reckoned himself eased of the translating I besought him to take the labour to read it over and correct it. Which he right gladly did ... Wherefore if there be, as I well wot there is, thanks be to Master Vives the maker. If anything be well in this translation, thanks be to the labour of my good master.[16]

Thomas More and Juan Luis Vives may have met in Flanders where Vives became a professor at Louvain. He was a friend of Erasmus and it may have been at his suggestion that Vives wrote his commentary on St. Augustine's *Civitas Dei*; this would at once give him a call upon More's interest. The commentary was dedicated to Henry VIII in 1522, and in the following year Vives came to England at the Queen's invitation; she had already asked his advice on the education of the Princess Mary, and he brought with him the manuscript of his *De Institutione Feminæ Christinæ*; this he followed with his plan of studies for girls. Amongst his minor works was a declamation *Pro Noverca contra Cæcum* which was written at More's suggestion as the author related in the following passage.

> More had told the story of Quintilian's first declamation to his little boy John and to his daughters Margaret, Elizabeth and Cecily, the worthy offspring of their father. He had discoursed in such a way as to lead them all by his eloquence the more easily to the study of wisdom. He then begged me to write an answer to the declamation which he had expounded, so that the art of writing might be disclosed more openly by contradiction, and, as it were, by conflict.[17]

That is the closest view we get of Thomas More with his school.

---

[16] Foster Watson, *Vives and the Renaissance Education of Women*, (1912), p. 31.

[17] *Ibid.*, p. 17.

Another reference to Thomas More by Vives is to be found in his commentary on St. Augustine. Vives had quoted from More's translation of Lucian's *Necyomantia*.

> Thus far Lucian. We have rehearsed it in the words of Thomas More, whom to praise negligently, or as if we were otherwise employed, were grossness. His due commendations are sufficient to exceed great volumes. For what is he that can worthily limn forth his sharpness of wit, his depth of judgement, his excellence and variety of learning, his eloquence of phrase, his plausibility and integrity of manners, his judicious foresight, his exact execution, his gentle modesty and uprightness, and his unmoved loyalty, unless he will call them (as they are indeed) the patterns and lustres, each of his kind? I speak much, and many that have not known More will wonder at me; but such as have will know I speak the truth. So will such as shall either read his works, or but hear or look upon his actions.[18]

Such was Thomas More's reputation among European scholars when he was about forty-five years old.

---

[18] St. Augustine, *City of God* (Everyman ed.), II, p. 412.

Chapter XIII

'The Four Last Things'

DURING the first five years of his life as a member of the Council, Thomas More found time to write several controversial letters or pamphlets and to begin a treatise on the Four Last Things. Some were published in *Epistolæ Aliquot Eruditorum* (Antwerp, 1520) or in *Epistolæ Eruditorum Virorum* (Basle, 1520), collections of letters by scholars of the day such as Erasmus and Lupset.

Three of these letters are to Edward Lee, the brother of the Joyeuce Leigh to whom More had dedicated his Pico in 1505. Edward Lee (as he preferred to spell his name), who was to succeed Wolsey as Archbishop of York, was a scholar and a devout priest; his friendship with Thomas More was not broken by the controversy about Erasmus with which these letters are concerned. Lee had annoyed Erasmus by his criticisms of the Greek New Testament, and they waged a paper war that was not greatly to the credit of either of them. The controversy died long ago, so we need not follow in detail More's attempts to reconcile these angry scholars; he defended Erasmus but refused to break with Lee. The last letter,[1] written from court at Greenwich in 1520, ends, 'Farewell, my dearest Lee, and, if you love us, fly to us.'

Reference has already been made to Thomas More's letter-pamphlet addressed to an unknown monk; it is there that he described his visit to his sister at Coventry and his meeting with

---

[1] *Rogers*, p. 208.

an old friar. This letter also defended Erasmus, but More did not here use the friendly persuasion of his letters to Lee; he wrote in a sterner mood.

> I wonder at the unbounded leisure which you find to devote to schismatical and heretical books. Or have you so few good books that you are obliged to consume your short leisure on bad ones? If the books [of Erasmus] are good, why do you condemn them? If they are bad, why do you read them? As you gave up the care of the world when you shut yourself up in the cloister, you are not one of those to whom leave is given to read bad books for the sake of refuting them. Hence by reading what is perverse you are merely learning it. Not only do you spend good hours on bad books, but you consume much time, as it appears, in talk and gossip worse than bad books; so that I notice there is no kind of rumour or calumny which does not find its way straight to your cell. We read that formerly monks so hid themselves from the world, that they would not even read the letters sent to them by their friends, nor glance back at the Sodom they left. Now, I see, they read schismatical and heretical books, and immense volumes filled with mere trifles. Now, what they formerly dreaded to hear in the world, and fled to the cloister lest they should hear it, the cunning enemy has found a means of carrying into their very cells. Their solemn religious surroundings only serve to impose on the unwary, their leisure serves to elaborate their calumnies, their retirement from the eyes of men to prevent them from being abashed, and their closed cells to injure the reputation of those outside. Whoever enters their cells must say an 'Our Father' that the conversation may be holy. But where is the use of beginning slanderous gossip with the Lord's Prayer? If that is not taking

the Name of God in vain, what is?[2]

That passage may, by itself, give the impression that Thomas More was not a friend of the religious orders. The opposite is the truth; his belief in the sacred trust accepted by the orders was so deep-seated that he was all the more disquieted at blemishes on their conduct and reputation. In this same letter he wrote:

> I have no doubt that there is no good man to be found anywhere to whom all religious orders are not extremely dear and cherished. Not only have I ever loved them, but intensely venerated them; for I have been wont to honour the poorest person commended by his virtue, more than one who is merely ennobled by his riches or illustrious by his birth. I desire, indeed, all mortals to honour you and your orders, and to regard you with the deepest charity, for your merits deserve it; and I know that by your prayers the misery of the world itself is somewhat diminished. If the assiduous prayer of the just man is of much value, what must be the efficacy of the unwearied prayers of so many thousands? Yet, on the other hand, I would wish that you should not with a false zeal be so partial to yourselves, that if anyone ventures to touch on what regards you, you should try, by your way of relating it, to give an evil turn to what he has said well, or that what he at least intended well, you should misinterpret and pervert.[3]

He added a warning of the dangers of pharisaism.

> Everyone loves what is his own—his own farm, his own money, his own nation, his own guild or association. We prefer our own private fasts to the public fasts of the Church. If we have chosen a patron saint, we make more of him than of ten more excellent, because he is our own, and the rest of

---

[2] *Bridgett*, p. 95; *Rogers*, pp. 189-90.

[3] *Rogers*, p. 194.

the saints belong to all. Now, if anyone finds fault with this partiality he is not carping at the piety of the people, but warning them lest, under pretext of piety, impiety find an entrance. No one will blame a nation for honouring a certain saint by name for good reasons; yet it may occur to some that such partiality is carried too far when the patron saint of a hostile country is torn down and thrown out of a church into the mud.

Now, just as this kind of veneration and private ceremonial does not always turn out well with us laymen, neither does partisanship always thrive with youth who are religious. Many esteem their devotions and practices more than those of their monastery; those of their monastery more than those of their order; those of their own order more than what belongs to all religious; and those which are peculiar to religious they set more value on than the lowly, humble things which belong specially to no one, but are common to the whole Christian people—such as the plebeian virtues of faith, hope charity, the fear of God, humility, and such like. This is no new thing. It is a long time since Christ reproved the chosen race: 'Why do you transgress the commandments of God for your traditions?'

Of course, those who do so will deny it. Who is so senseless as to confess to himself that he makes more account of ceremonies than of precepts, since he knows that, unless he obeys the latter, the former are useless? Doubtless all will answer well in words if they are questioned; but by their doings they belie their words. May I be held a liar if there are not religious in certain places who observe silence so obstinately that at no price could you get them even to whisper in their corridors; but, draw them one foot outside, and they will not hesitate to storm at whoever offends them. There are some who would fear lest the devil should carry them off alive if they make any change in their dress, and who have no fear of heaping up money, or opposing and deposing their abbot. Are there not many who, if they omitted a verse of their office would think it a crime to be expiated with many tears, and who have not the least scruple to take part in calumnious gossip longer than their longest prayers? Thus they crush a gnat and swallow an elephant whole.[4]

The defence of Erasmus was a welcome task to his friend, but when he himself was attacked he wrote on his own behalf, and it was then the turn of Erasmus to try to pacify two angry men. We must go back some years to explain the occasion of this dispute. During the war of 1512, there was a small naval engagement off Brest in which an English ship, the Regent, commanded by Sir Thomas Knyvet,[5] grappled a French ship, the Cordelière; both were blown up when the magazine on the French ship was fired. Germain de Brie (Brixius), a French scholar who was Archdeacon of Albi, wrote a poem to honour the bravery of the French commander. This provoked Thomas More to write some epigrams on the poet's disparagement of the English. These verses were circulated in manuscript before they were printed in 1518 at Basle under the supervision of Erasmus. At the time More suggested that these particular epigrams 'ought to be suppressed as containing some things over bitter.' He left the final decision to Erasmus. Brie was very angry when he read these scornful verses and set to work on a reply. His friend Erasmus urged him not to publish this threatened attack; after all, he suggested, the epigrams were not personal as More did not know Brie in 1513. Such a quibble did not convince Brie, and in 1519 he published his *Antimorus*. Erasmus then tried to persuade More not to answer, but failed as a mediator, and the *Epistola ad Brixium* appeared in 1520. The subject of the dispute has no longer any significance;

---

[4] *Rogers*, pp. 195-6.

[5] Possibly a relative of Dean Colet.

the incident has interest as part of the portrait of Thomas More.

It has been well said that 'the thought is forced on us, as we read the Latin letters and dedications and controversies of the literates of the sixteenth century, that their mutual praises are somewhat boyish, and that they show themselves over sensitive of their reputation as scholars.'[6]

Sir Thomas More was concerned with a far more portentous publication at this time. Henry VIII's *Assertio Septem Sacramentorum* was printed by Pynson in 1521. This was a royal reply to Luther's *De Captivitate Babylonica* in which he rejected the teaching of the Church on the sacraments. Henry's authorship has been questioned, but he had the knowledge to plan such a book; the result is not a theological treatise, but an explanation of reasonable length[7] in language that any intelligent layman could understand. Sir Thomas More in his examination before the council in 1534 was accused of having encouraged the king to write the *Assertio* in which the authority of the Pope was maintained. In reply More said, 'I never was procurer nor councillor of his Majesty thereunto; but after it [the manuscript] was finished, by his Grace's appointment and consent of the makers of the same, only a sorter out and placer of the principal matters therein contained.'[8] What is meant by 'the makers'? The explanation may be that Henry submitted his plan, perhaps a draft, to the theologians for their criticism and they may have suggested additional arguments and references to the Fathers; the King then asked Sir Thomas More to arrange the contents and get it ready for the printer.

A copy of the book was presented to Pope Leo X in the name of the King by the Dr. John Clerk who had been at Abingdon with

---

[6] *Bridgett*, p. 188.

[7] About 50,000 words.

[8] *Roper*, p. 67.

Thomas More; as is well known, the Pope conferred on Henry the title of Defender of the Faith.[9] The book certainly betrayed no doubt as to the Papal authority.

Two quotations will show how decisively Henry accepted the primacy of the Pope.

> He [Luther] cannot deny but that all the faithful honour and acknowledge the sacred Roman See for our Mother and Supreme ... all the Churches in the Christian world have been obedient to the See of Rome.
>
> He considers not, I say, what cruel punishment he deserves, that will not obey the Chief Priest and Supreme Judge upon earth.[10]

It was such statements as these that Sir Thomas More had in mind when he told the Council in 1534 of a conversation he had had with the King.

> I said unto his Grace, 'I must put your Highness in remembrance of one thing, and that is this. The Pope, as your Grace knoweth, is a prince as you are, and in league with all other Christian princes. It may hereafter so fall out that your Grace and he may vary upon some points of the league, whereupon may grow breach of amity and war between you both. I think it best therefore that that place be amended, and his authority more slenderly touched.'
>
> 'Nay,' quoth his Grace, 'that shall it not. We are so much bounden unto the See of Rome that we cannot do too much honour to it.'
>
> Then did I further put him in remembrance of the statute of *Præmunire*, whereby a good part of the Pope's pastoral cure here was pared away.

---

[9] Confirmed to him and his successors by Parliament in 1544.

[10] *Writings of Henry VIII*, ed. Macnamara (1924), pp. 47-8. The *Assertio* is in Thomas Webster's translation printed in 1687.

To that answered his Highness, 'Whatsoever impediment be to the contrary, we will set forth that authority to the uttermost. For we received from that See our crown imperial.' Which, till his Grace with his own mouth told it me, I never heard of before.[11]

This difference of opinion turned More's thoughts to the larger question of the source of the supremacy of the Pope; was it of divine or of human origin? It may seem strange to us that such a question should have arisen, or that a man of More's intellectual eminence should not have considered it in the course of his studies of the Fathers. The events of the previous century might well excuse such doubts. The 'Babylonish Captivity,' the Great Schism, and the reigns of the Borgia and Medici Popes disturbed and confused men's minds. As an indication of the conflict of views it may be noted that the Council of Basle (1431-1438) revealed a wide variety of opinions, 'from considering the Pope divinely appointed Head of the Church, if corrigible by a General Council, to holding the Papacy to be a human and alterable invention, and from thinking that the united episcopate was the essence of a General Council to maintaining that sovereignty in the Church belonged to the whole body of the clergy.'[12]

Antonio Bonvisi told Reginald Pole of a conversation he had had with Thomas More, and the Cardinal narrated this in the course of a sermon during the reign of Mary. The subject of the primacy of the Pope had been mentioned and More expressed the opinion that the supremacy was a matter of organization and not of divine origin. Some days later he sought out Bonvisi and said, 'Whither was I falling, when I made you that answer of the primacy of the Church? I assure you, that opinion alone was enough to make me fall from the rest, for that upholdeth all.' 'He

---

[11] *Roper*, pp. 67-8.

[12] *Shorter Cambridge Medieval History* (1952), p. 971.

began,' added the Cardinal, 'to show him what he had read and studied therein, which was so fixed in his heart that for the defence of the same he willingly afterward suffered death.'[13] Unfortunately the date of that incident is not given.

A passage in a letter to Thomas Cromwell written in March 1534 is so important in its bearing on this crucial issue that it must be given in full, although it covers the same ground as More's statement to the Council shortly afterwards.

> As touching the third point, the primacy of the Pope, I nothing meddle in the matter. Truth it is, that as I told you, when you desired me to show you what I thought therein, I was myself some time not of the mind that the primacy of that See should be begun by the institution of God, until that I read in that matter those things that the King's Highness had written in his most famous book against the heresies of Martin Luther, at the first reading whereof I moved the King's Highness either to leave out that point, or else to touch it more slenderly for doubt of such things as after might happen to fall in question between his Highness and some Pope as between Princes and Popes diverse times have done. Whereunto his Highness answered me, that he would in no wise, anything minish of that matter, of which thing his Highness showed me a secret cause whereof I never anything heard before.[14] But surely after that I had read his Grace's book therein, and so many other things as I have seen by this continuance of these ten years since and more have founden to affect the substance of all the holy doctors from Saint Ignatius, disciple to St. John the Evangelist, unto our own days both Latins and Greeks so consonant and agreeing in

---

[13] Strype. *Memorials*, III, ii, pp. 491-3.

[14] Perhaps his desire for such a distinction as the title he did get. It is too early for any reference to a possible divorce as *Rogers*, p. 449 8 n. suggests.

that point, and the thing by such general councils so confirmed also, that in good faith I never neither read nor heard anything of such effect on the other side, that could ever lead me to think that my conscience were well discharged, but rather in right peril if I should follow the other side and deny the primacy to be provided by God, which if we did, yet can I nothing (as I showed you) perceive any commodity that ever could come by that denial, for that primacy is at the least wise instituted by the corps of Christendom and for a great urgent cause in avoiding of schisms and corroborate by continual succession more than the space of a thousand year at the least for there are passed almost a thousand year since the time of holy Saint Gregory.[15]

The period 'ten years since and more'[16] takes us back to about 1524. By then More had reached certainty on the origin of the primacy. He was mainly influenced, he wrote in 1523, by Bishop John Fisher, who, in addition to other arguments drawn from the Scriptures and the Fathers, told More of the decree of the Council of Florence (1439) which affirmed that to the Bishop of Rome 'in blessed Peter there was given over by Our Lord Jesus Christ full power to pasture, to rule, and to govern the whole church.'[17]

A passage from *A Dialogue Concerning Heresies* (1528) supports this view.

By this church know we the scripture; and this is the very

---

[15] *Rogers*, p. 498.

[16] This is the figure given in the final copy in More's own hand. A facsimile of this portion is reproduced in Father Philip Hughes' *The Reformation in England*, I between pp. 288 and 289. When Rastell printed the letter in *E.W.*, p. 1,426, he used an earlier draft in which the figure was 7, not 10. Some confusion has arisen by More's reference in his trial to a period of seven years, but this reference is to the possibility of a layman being Head of the Church, not to the primacy of the Pope as such. See pp. 415.

[17] In More's reply, as William Ross, to Luther's attack on King Henry's book. See Bridgett, *Fisher*, pp. 138-139.

church; and this hath begun at Christ and hath had him for their head, and saint Peter his vicar, after him, the head under him, and always since, the successors of him continually—and have had his holy faith, and his blessed sacraments, and his holy scriptures delivered, kept and conserved therein by God and his holy spirit.[18]

The same opinion is also expressed in a letter to John Bugenhagen to which reference will be made shortly.

The phrase 'ten years since and more' has been interpreted to mean he had given a decade to the study of this subject.[19] On the face of it this seems a long time for the purpose, but the statement rests on a misinterpretation of what More wrote. The passage in the letter to Cromwell may be fairly paraphrased: 'Some ten years or so ago, as a result of studying the King's book, the writings of the Fathers and of learned men of our day, I came to the conclusion that the primacy was of divine institution, and nothing I have read since has led me to change my mind.'

There is another statement in this letter that must not be passed over. 'Never thought I,' wrote More, 'the Pope above the General Council.'[20] This touches on one of the problems of the day—the relation between the Pope and a General Council. It naturally arose during the period of the Great Schism when there were rival Popes. Gerson (1363-1429) was strongly of the opinion that the authority of a General Council was superior to that of a Pope, and the Councils of Constance (1414-18) and of Basle (1431-38) adopted that view. This is not the place to discuss the Counciliar Movement, but the point may be made that More's opinion was not, for his time, as exceptional, nor as heterodox, as

---

[18] *E.W.*, p. 185; II, p. 144. For a further statement, see the extract below, p. 166, from the letter to Bugenhagen.

[19] See: *Chambers*, p. 195; *Bridgett*, p. 347.

[20] *Roggers*, p. 499.

it would be today.

We must now return to King Henry's book on the Seven Sacraments. Luther was stung to reply with a stream of invective. A King could not take notice of such an attack, and it was probably at Henry's wish that Thomas More, as has already been noted, wrote a reply under the pseudonym of Gulielmus Rosseus. Stapleton says that there was in fact a man, William Ross, who went on a pilgrimage to Rome and died in Italy; consequently people assumed he was the author of this book and did not suspect More.

It is a shock to find that More was almost Luther's match in his knowledge of the more obscure terms of abuse in the Latin language.[21] He himself felt that some kind of apology was necessary.

> I doubt not, good reader, that your fairness will pardon me that in this book you read so often what causes you shame. Nothing could have been more painful to me than to be forced to speak foul words to pure ears. But there was no help for it, unless I left Luther's scurrilous book utterly untouched, which is a thing I most earnestly desired.

If we pass over these 'foul words' we shall find much that reveals the true More. He used here a method that was to be followed in later controversies. After quoting, with scrupulous accuracy, a passage from his opponent, he gives his answer. One example will serve here.

> *Luther.* Everyone at his own risk believes truly or falsely; therefore everyone must take care for himself that he believes aright, so that common sense and the necessity of salvation prove that the judgement regarding doctrine is necessarily in the hearer. Otherwise to no purpose is it said, 'Prove all

---

[21] *Bridgett*, p. 212n., gives some specimens (in Latin) from both books. The translations here quoted are from pp. 211-17.

things, hold fast that which is good.'

More. So then, because everyone must take care to believe aright, he must have no care for Pope or councils, or church or holy fathers, or the people, or Peter or Paul, but he must himself judge boldly about everything; and because he believes at his own risk, therefore without any risk he may believe in himself against the whole world, according to that advice of the Wise Man, 'Son, rely not on thy own prudence, and be not wise in thine own eyes.'

The book ends with a vision of what might happen in Germany if Luther's teaching became generally accepted.

O illustrious Germany, can you doubt, can you doubt, when they sow such spiritual things, what kind of corporal things they will reap? ... For many of the princes see, not without pleasure, the apostacy of the clergy, gaping as they do after the possessions of the apostates, which they hope to seize as derelict. And they rejoice to see obedience withdrawn from the Sovereign Pontiff, conceiving then the hope that they may dispose it among themselves at home. On the other hand, they need not doubt, but that the people in their turn will throw off the yoke of the princes, and deprive them of their possessions. And when they shall come to do this, drunk with the blood of the princes, and exulting in the slaughter of the nobles, they will not submit even to plebeian governors; but following the dogma of Luther, and trampling the law under foot, then, at last without government and without law, without rein and without understanding, they will turn their hands against each other, and, like the earth-born brothers of old, will perish in mutual conflict. I beg of Christ that I may be a false prophet.

The conception of authority and order here expressed by More was implicit in Catholicism; it had been taken for granted in the Middle Ages; it was the threat of schism that made it necessary to warn Luther and his supporters that if they denied the spiritual authority of the Pope, they would remove the key stone of the arch that supported the order of society.

The need for this order[22] is appropriately the theme of More's speech to the rioters in *The Booke of Sir Thomas More*.

> Let me set up before your thoughts, good friends,
> One supposition, which if you will mark,
> You shall perceive how horrible the shape
> Your innovation bears; for 'tis a sin
> Which oft the apostle did forewarn us of,
> Urging obedience to authority,
> And 'twere no error if I told you all
> You were in arms 'gainst God.

The Peasants' War broke out two years after the publication of this book by William Ross. A few years later, Thomas More was engaged in another controversy, this time with John Bugenhagen, a professor at Wittenberg, who had been converted to Lutheranism by the *De Captivitate Babylonica* to which Henry VIII had replied. Bugenhagen had written a letter to 'the faithful in England.' In More's pamphlet-letter, which does not seem to have been published until 1568, he refers to the Peasants' War.

> And are you not in this matter ashamed of your great master, Luther, first the most wicked leader, and then the most villainous deserter; who after arousing, arming, and exciting the peasants to every kind of crime, when he saw that fortune threatened them with ruin, by his truculent

---

[22] This is a common theme in Elizabethan literature. The classic statement is the speech of Ulysses in *Troilus and Cressida*, I, iii; see: *The Elizabethan World Picture*, by E.M.W. Tillyard (1943). The search for a substitute for the authority of the Church is too large a subject to describe here; it would call for the study of theories ranging from the Divine Right of Kings to the Divine Right of the People.

writings, betrayed and denounced them, and gave them up to be torn to pieces by the nobles; and by his shameful flatteries tried to smother the odium that was felt against himself in the blood of the poor wretches, of whose rebellion, and slaughter he was the sole cause?[23]

This letter is important for the clear statement More there makes of his attitude towards the papacy.

I am moved to obedience to that See not only by what learned and holy men have written,[24] but by this fact especially, that we shall find that on the one hand every enemy of the Christian faith makes war on that See, and that, on the other hand, no one has ever declared himself an enemy of that See who has not also shortly after shown most evidently that he was the enemy of the Christian religion. Another thing that moves me is this that if, after Luther's manner, the vices of men are to be imputed to the offices they hold, not only the papacy will fall, but royalty, and dictatorship and consulate and every other kind of magistracy, and the people will be without rulers, without law, and without order. Should such a thing ever come to pass, as it seems indeed imminent in some parts of Germany, they will then feel to their own great loss how much better it is for men to have bad rulers than no rulers at all. Most assuredly as regards the Pope, God, who set him over His Church, knows how great an evil it would be to be without one, and I do not think it desirable that Christendom should learn it by experience. It is far more to be wished that God may raise up such Popes as befit the Christian cause and the dignity of the Apostolic office: men who, despising riches and honour, will care only for heaven, will promote piety in the

---

[23] Both passages from *Bridgett*, pp. 218-20.

[24] He is referring here especially to Saint John Fisher.

people, will bring about peace, and exercise the authority they have received from God against the 'satraps and mighty hunters of the world' excommunicating and giving over to Satan both those who invade the territories of others and those who oppress their own. With one or two such Popes the Christian world would soon perceive how much preferable it is that the papacy should be reformed than abrogated.

Thomas More was not blind to the papal scandals of the time, so his longing for 'Popes as befit the Christian cause' came from a sorrowing heart; but that in no way shook his faith in 'the authority they have received from God.'

During the period that More was busy with these pamphlet-letters, he was also composing a treatise on the text 'Remember the last things, and thou shalt not sin.'[25] He did not complete *The Four Last Things*, but dealt only with the first, Death, and even that part is unfinished; he did not treat of Judgement, Heaven, and Hell. In this grim fragment we see the Thomas More of the Holbein portrait; for here is the stern thinker with his whole mind and spirit pondering the profound mysteries of death and judgment. The early reference to the 'Dance of Death' pictured in St. Paul's is fitting; for the treatment of the subject is medieval in its stark realism.

> For those pictures express only the loathly figure of our dead bony bodies, bitten away the flesh; which, though it be ugly to behold, yet neither the light thereof, nor the sight of all the dead heads in the charnel house, nor the apparition of a very ghost, is half so grisly as the deep conceived fantasy of death in his nature, by the lively imagination graven in thine own heart. For there thou seest, not one plain grievous sight of the bare bones hanging by the sinews, but thou seest (if thou fantasy thine own death, for so art thou by this counsel

---

[25] *Ecclus.* 7:40.

advised), thou seest, I say, thyself, if thou die no worse death, yet at leastwise lying in thy bed, thy head shooting, thy back aching, thy veins beating, thine heart panting, thy throat rattling, thy flesh trembling, thy mouth gaping, thy nose sharpening, thy legs cooling, thy fingers fumbling, thy breath shortening, all thy strength fainting, thy life vanishing, and thy death drawing on.[26]

More could not use his pen for long without letting his imagination have play.

Have ye not ere this, in a sore sickness, felt it very grievous to have folk babble to you, and namely such things as ye should make answer to, when it was pain to speak? Think ye not now that it will be a great pleasure, when we lie dying, all our body in pain, all our mind in trouble, our soul in sorrow, our heart all in dread while our life walketh awayward, while our death draweth toward, while the devil is busy about us, while we lack stomach and strength to bear anyone of us so manifold heinous troubles, will it not be, as I was about to say, a pleasant thing to see before thine eyes and hear at thine ear a rabble of fleshly friends, or rather of flesh flies, skipping about thy bed and thy sick body, like ravens about thy corpse, now almost carrion, crying to thee on every side, 'What shall I have? What shall I have?' Then shall come thy children and cry for their parts; then shall come thy sweet wife, and where in thine health she spake thee not one sweet word in six weeks, now shall she call thee sweet husband and weep with much work and ask thee what shall she have; then shall thine executors ask for the keys, and ask what money is owing thee, ask what substance thou hast, and ask where thy money lieth. And while thou liest in that case, their words shall be so tedious that thou wilt wish all that they ask for upon a red

---

[26] *E.W.*, p. 77; I, p. 468.

fire, so thou mightest lie one half-hour in rest.[27]

Then the devil's ways of tempting us at death are described.

> And instead of sorrow for our sins and care of heaven, he [the devil] putteth us in mind of provision for some honourable burying—so many torches, so many tapers, so many black gowns, so many mourners laughing under black hoods, and a gay hearse, with the delight of goodly and honourable funerals: in which the foolish sick man is sometimes occupied as though he thought that he should stand in a window and see how worshipfully he shall be brought to church.[28]

So the writer turns to a consideration of the deadly sins of pride, envy, wrath, covetousness, gluttony and sloth. He uses familiar instances; vainglory, for example, is illustrated from the stage.

> If thou shouldst perceive that one were earnestly proud of the wearing of the gay golden gown, while the lorel [rogue] playeth the lord in a stage play, wouldst thou not laugh at his folly, considering that thou art very sure that when the play is done he shall go walk a knave in his old coat? Now thou thinkest thyself wise enough while thou art proud in thy player's garment, and forgettest that when thy play is done, thou shalt go forth as poor as he. Nor thou remembrest not that thy pageant may happen to be done as soon as his.[29]

One passage of this unfinished treatise refers to the judicial murder of the Duke of Buckingham in May 1521. This arbitrary act was an early example of that ruthlessness that was to become a dominant characteristic of the King. It shocked the people and

---

[27] *E.W.*, p. 78; I, p. 469.

[28] *E.W.*, p. 79; I, p. 470.

[29] *E.W.*, p. 84; I, p. 479.

they blamed Wolsey, but it was the King's act.

If it so were that thou knewest a great Duke keeping so great estate and princely port in his house that thou, being a right mean man hadst in thine heart a great envy thereat, and especially at some special day in which he keepeth for the marriage[30] of his child a great honourable court above other times; if thou being thereat, and at the sight of the royalty and honour shown him of all the country about resorting to him, while they kneel and crouch to him and at every word barehead begrace him, if thou shouldst suddenly be surely advertised, that for secret treason, lately detected to the King, he should undoubtedly be taken the morrow, his court all broken up, his goods seized, his wife put out, his children disinherited, himself cast into prison, brought forth and arraigned, the matter out of question, and he should be condemned, his coat armour reversed, his gilt spurs hewn off his heels, himself, hanged, drawn and quartered, how thinkest thou, by thy faith, amid thine envy shouldst thou not suddenly change into pity?

A manuscript containing such a note on recent events could not be passed round freely, and this fragment probably remained in the possession of Margaret Roper, and so came to her cousin, William Rastell, who printed it for the first time in 1557.

---

[30] His eldest son, Henry married a sister of Reginald Pole in 1519.

Chapter XIV

The Parliament of 1523

HOMAS MORE was present at the Field of Cloth of Gold in June 1520. That pretentious and costly occasion was a fit subject for irony, but no comment of More's has been preserved. Foreign diplomats noted that it was useless trying to get even a hint from him on state policy. Thus in 1518, Giustinian, the Venetian Ambassador, hoped to get from More some indication of English policy towards France. 'He did not open, and pretended not to know in what the difficulties consisted.' The Ambassador then complained that he was kept in the dark, to which More replied that so was everyone else.[1] He was the most discreet of councillors outside the Council; he stated his opinions there and did not hesitate to speak freely.

Stapleton records one incident.

> Soon after More's entry into the Council, Wolsey brought forward a proposal that a Supreme Constable should be created to represent the person of the King in the whole kingdom. Such a magistracy was almost unparalleled in England, but, Wolsey, whose ambition brought so much ruin on our country, doubtless hoped that he would be appointed to the new office. He strongly urged his suggestion and was meekly followed by all the nobles who formed the King's Council. No one dared to contradict or to suggest any objection until More's turn came to speak. He spoke last and in a contrary sense: but he supported his view with so many

---

[1] *Venetian Calendar*, II, p. 457.

powerful arguments that the Council wavered and declared that the matter needed fuller deliberation. The Cardinal was angry and thus addressed More: 'Are you not ashamed, Master More, being the lowest of all in place and dignity, to dissent from so many noble and prudent men? You show yourself to be a stupid and foolish councillor.' 'Thanks be to God,' replied More instantly, 'that the King's Majesty has but one fool in his Council.'[2]

Fortunately it is not necessary here to discuss Wolsey's foreign policy; still less to decide between those historians who think that he was trying to maintain a balance of power in Europe, and those who think that his real purpose was to win the Papacy for himself. Few would question that,

> throughout the whole period when he held office Wolsey was actively engaged in weaving the web of an intricate diplomatic policy, but the impression left on any critical mind is that much of the activity was illusory, and that Wolsey's schemings ultimately ended in worse than nothing.[3]

It is difficult to find the patience to follow the permutations of the shifting alliances between Henry and Francis and Charles; they tricked each other turn and turn about like a trio of card-sharpers. The Field of Cloth of Gold was an elaborate piece of deception. Two months before this meeting between Henry and Francis, the emperor Charles had visited England and had taken counsel with Henry and with his aunt Catherine. Then the King and Queen set off to meet Francis; the description of the elaborate splendour of the meeting at Guisnes fills many pages of Hall's Chronicle, and Shakespeare called it

---

[2] *Stapleton*, p. 137.

[3] C. H. Williams, *The Making of the Tudor Despotism* (1928), p. 98. See also A.F. Pollard, *Wolsey* (1929), pp. 111-64.

> The view of earthly glory: men would say,
> Till this time pomp was single, but now married
> To one above itself.[4]

From that meeting Henry went to Gravelines to further discussions with Charles, and while they feasted each other, Wolsey and the imperial councillors worked out the terms of an alliance irreconcilable with the fellowship of the Field of Cloth of Gold.

Thomas More found some relief from the tedious ceremonial in meeting for the first time such scholars as William Budé and Francis Cranevelt; above all, Erasmus was at Calais; this was probably the last time the two friends were together. Another diversion must have been the company of his brother-in-law, John Rastell, who had been commissioned to decorate the roof of the great hall erected at Guisnes.

As he played his part as an attendant councillor, More's thoughts may have turned to what he had written so ironically in *Utopia* five years earlier.

> Treaties which all other nations so often conclude, break and again renew, they never make with any nation. What is the use of a treaty, say they, as though nature did not sufficiently of herself bind one man to another, and if a man regard not her, can one suppose he will think anything of words? They are led to this opinion chiefly because in those parts of the world treaties and covenants between Princes are not observed with much good faith. In Europe, however, and especially in those parts where the faith and religion of Christ prevails, the majesty of treaties is everywhere holy and inviolable, and this arises partly through the justice and goodness of kings, and partly through their reverence and

---

[4] *Henry VIII*, I, I 15.

fear of Popes, who, as they undertake nothing themselves which they do not most conscientiously perform, so command all other rulers by all means to abide by their promises, and compel the recalcitrant by pastoral censure and severe reproof. To be sure they were right in thinking it a most disgraceful thing, that those who are specially called the faithful, should not faithfully adhere to their treaties.[5]

More shared the views of Erasmus on war, but it was not unknown in Utopia; the wars that did occur there were not for the predatory and vain-glorious motives that dominated European politics in the sixteenth century.

War, as a thing only fit for beasts, and yet not practised by any kind of beasts so constantly as by man, they regard with utter loathing, and contrary to the fashion of almost all nations they count nothing so inglorious as glory obtained in war; and so, though men and women alike constantly exercise themselves in military training, on fixed days, lest they should be unfit for war when need requires, yet they do not lightly undertake it, unless it be either to protect their own territory or drive an invading enemy out of their friends' country, or when in pity for a nation oppressed by tyranny they seek to deliver them by force of arms from the yoke and bondage of a tyrant, a course prompted merely by human sympathy.[6]

In June 1522 the Emperor again visited England. The procession of the King and the Emperor was met by the Mayor and Aldermen of London.

Where one Sir Thomas More, knight, and well learned, made to them an eloquent oration, in the praise of the two princes, and of the peace and love between them, and what comfort it was to their subjects, to see them in such amity,

---

[5] *Utopia*, p. 91; p. 105.

[6] *Utopia*, p. 94; p. 107.

The Parliament of 1523

and how that the Mayor and Citizens offered any pleasure of service that in them lay, next to their sovereign lord.[7]

For this oration the City made him a gift of money 'towards a gown of velvet.'

Charles returned to the Continent to wage war with Francis. The wisest policy for England would have been to remain neutral, and, according to an incident narrated by More to his daughter Margaret, this was the feeling of the Council.

The first fable of the rain that washed away all their wits that stood abroad when it fell, I have heard oft or this; it was a tale often told among the king's councillors by my Lord Cardinal when his Grace was Chancellor, that I cannot lightly forget it. For of truth in times past when variance began to fall between the Emperor and the French King, in such wise that they were likely, and did indeed, fall together at war, and that there were in the council here sometime sundry opinions, in which some were of the mind, that they thought it wisdom, that we should sit still and let them alone, but evermore against that way, my Lord, used this fable of those wise men, that because they would not be washed with the rain that should make all the people fools, went themselves into caves, and hid them under the ground. But when the rain had once made all the remnant fools and that they came out of their caves and would utter their wisdom, the fools agreed together, and there all to beat them. And so said his Grace that if we would be so wise that we would sit in peace while the fools fought, they would not fail after, to make peace and agree and fall at length all upon it. I will not dispute upon his Grace's council, and I trust we never made war but as reason would. But yet this fable for his part, did in his days help the king and the realm to spend many a fair penny. But that gear

---

[7] *Hall*, I, p. 250.

is past, and his Grace is gone; our Lord assoil his soul.[8]

Wolsey's view prevailed, and they all became fools! But it was decided to proceed cautiously and to keep Francis in play as long as possible. Sir Thomas More was sent to Bruges in July 1521 on a commercial mission and afterwards joined Wolsey at Calais where the Cardinal kept state 'likest a great prince.' Pace had written to Wolsey on 24 July to say that 'The king signifieth your Grace that, whereas old men do now decay greatly within this his realm, his mind is to acquaint other young men with his great affairs, and, therefore, he desireth your Grace to make Sir William Sandys and Sir Thomas More privy to all such matters as your Grace shall treat at Calais.'[9]

Once more, a Venetian Ambassador, this time to the Emperor, tried to elicit from Sir Thomas More news of the negotiations. 'During dinner we discussed the business negotiated with the Emperor, but More did not drop the slightest hint of any other treaty than that of peace between the King of France and His Imperial Majesty.'[10]

Wolsey carried on the show of friendship with Francis until the end of November although he had concluded a treaty with Charles three months earlier. Sir Thomas returned to England in October to report to the King.

A story told by Stapleton may refer to this embassy. A learned but conceited lawyer of the imperial court declared that he would solve any problem of the law of any nation. More put to him the question, 'Whether cattle taken in withernam be irrepreviable?' The challenger had to admit that the English term 'withernam'

---

[8] *Rogers*, p. 518.

[9] *S.P.*, I, p. 19.

[10] *Venetian Papers*, III, p. 302.

defeated him.[11]

The war proved a costly business, and all Wolsey's dexterity was unable to avoid additional and heavy taxation. A Parliament was inevitable, and it met on 15th April, 1523.[12] This was the first for eight years and the only one during Wolsey's chancellorship. There are no journals of the House of Commons for this period, but fortunately there is a full account in Hall's *Chronicle*.

Sir Thomas More was made Speaker; the 'election' of a Speaker was little more than the acceptance of the member already designated by the King or Council.[13] The Parliament met at Black Friars, and after the Mass of the Holy Ghost had been sung 'the king came into the Parliament Chamber and there sat down in the royal seat or throne.' Before him were the lords, spiritual and temporal, and beyond the bar, the Commons with their Speaker. There is a contemporary drawing of this scene; the original has deteriorated but a careful engraving[14] made more than two hundred years ago enables us to visualize the opening of the Parliament when Sir Thomas More, as Speaker-Elect stood with the Commons to listen to the oration made by Bishop Tunstal who spoke in place of Wolsey who, although sitting by the foot of the throne, pleaded ill-health. The subject of the speech was 'the office of a king,' and not an explanation of policy.

When the Commons presented Sir Thomas More as their Speaker,

> he according to the old usage disabled himself both in wit, learning, and discretion, to speak before the king, and brought

---

[11] *Stapleton*, p. 138. See O.E.D. for 'withernam,' but the definition will not help the layman.

[12] His constituency is not known.

[13] In the next extract from Hall, the commons are said to have chosen their Speaker, but in Roper (see below, p. 180) Wolsey says, 'When I made you speaker,' which is probably nearer the truth.

[14] Plate XVI.

in for his purpose how one Phormio desired Hannibal to come to his reading, which thereto assented, and when Hannibal was come, he began to read, *de re militare*, that is of Chivalry, when Hannibal perceived him, he called him an arrogant fool, because he would presume to teach him which was master of Chivalry, in the feats of war. So the speaker said, if he should speak before the king of learning and ordering of a commonwealth and such other like the king being so well learned and of such prudence and experience might say to him as Hannibal said to Phormio. Wherefore he desired his grace [Wolsey] that the Commons might choose another Speaker. The Cardinal answered, that the king knew his wit, learning, and discretion by long experience in his service, wherefore he thought that the Commons had chosen him as the most meetest of all, and so he did admit him.[15]

Sir Thomas then made a speech of considerable constitutional importance. Hall summarizes it in these words:

Then Sir Thomas More gave to the king his most humble thanks, and desired of him two petitions: the one, if he should be sent from the Commons to the king on message and mistake their intent, that he might with the king's pleasure resort again to the Commons for the knowledge of their true meaning; the other was, if in communication and reasoning any man in the Common House should speak more largely than of duty he ought to do, that all such offences should be pardoned, and that to be entered of record, which two petitions were granted.[16]

The first petition was customary, but the second, that freedom of speech should be allowed to each member, seems to have been a new request. Roper reports the speech in full; the following

---

[15] *Hall*, I, p. 279.

[16] *Hall*, I, p. 279.

extract gives the second petition:

> It may therefore like your most aboundant Grace, our most benign and godly King, to give to all your Commons here assembled your most gracious license and pardon, freely, without doubt of your dreadful displeasure, every man to discharge his conscience, and boldly in every thing incident among us to declare his advice; and whatsoever happen any man to say, that it may like your noble majesty of your inestimable goodness, to take all in good part.[17]

As this speech is given at such length (over a thousand words) it may probably have been copied from a record made at the time of the Parliament.[18]

It should be noted that Sir Thomas was not asking leave for the Commons to discuss anything they liked, but to express their opinions freely on matters submitted to them. The Commons had not yet gained the right to originate subjects for debate or legislation.

The only matter they had to deal with in this Parliament was taxation to meet the war expenditure, and the members certainly made full use of their freedom of speech. Wolsey's demand was for £800,000 by a tax of four shillings in the pound on lands and goods. Sir Thomas More supported this demand, according to Hall, but the Commons were not disposed to grant it.

> After long reasoning, there were certain appointed to declare the impossibility of this demand to the Cardinal which according to their commission, declared to him substantially the poverty and scarceness of the Realm. All which reasons and demonstrations, he little regarded, and then the said persons, most meekly beseeched his Grace to move the king's

---

[17] *Roper,*, p. 16.

[18] For the significance of More's speech, see J.E. Neale's essay 'The Commons' Privilege of Free Speech in Parliament' in *Tudor Studies*. (1924).

Highness to be content with a more easier sum, to which he currishly answered that he would rather have his tongue plucked out of his head with a pair of pincers than to move the king to take any less sum; with which answer they were almost dismayed, came and made report to the Common House where every day was reasoning, but little concluded. Wherefore the Cardinal came again to the Common House, and desired to be reasoned withal, to whom it was answered that the fashion of the nether House was to hear and not to reason but among themselves.[19]

According to Roper, the Cardinal began to ask each member for his opinion, and when they would not reply,

he required answer of master speaker; who first reverently upon his knees excusing the silence of the house, abashed at the presence of so noble a personage, able to amaze the wisest and best learned in a realm, and after by many probable arguments proving that for them to answer was it neither expedient nor agreeable with the ancient liberty of the house, in conclusion for himself showed that though they had all with their voices trusted him, yet except every one of them could put into his one head all their several wits, he alone in so weighty a matter was unmeet to make his Grace answer.[20]

So the debate continued, and it was not until August that at last it was proposed to offer a tax of two shillings in the pound over a period of two years, one shilling each year. Sir Thomas More persuaded them[21] to raise this to three shillings, so the final offer was three-quarters of what Wolsey had demanded.

Roper's account of this Parliament must be read with some reservations. For instance, he says that Sir Thomas More made

---

[19] Hall, I, p. 286.

[20] Roper, p. 18.

[21] Hall, I, p. 288.

The Parliament of 1523

the following speech when the Commons were informed that the Chancellor was coming to address them.

> It shall not in my mind be amiss with all his pomp to receive him, with his maces, his pillars [columns of silver], his pollaxes, his crosses, his hat, and great seal too.[22]

It is difficult to believe that More would have spoken so sarcastically to the Commons; it is the kind of remark he may have made at home in Roper's hearing.

In his account of the Parliament, Roper further says that Wolsey was angry with More because the full demand in taxation was not granted.

> And after the parliament ended, in his gallery at Whitehall in Westminster, uttered unto him his griefs saying, 'Would to God you had been at Rome, Master More, when I made you Speaker.' 'Your grace not offended, so would I too.' And to wind such quarrels out of the Cardinal's head, he began to talk of that gallery, and said, 'I like this gallery of yours, my lord, much better than your gallery at Hampton Court.'[23]

There is no independent evidence for any animosity such as this story suggests. More had, as we have seen, actually got better terms from the Commons than seemed likely, and this was a considerable achievement in their difficult mood. Indeed there is documentary evidence to show that Wolsey and More were still on good terms. On 4th August Wolsey wrote to the king:

> And, Sire, whereas it hath been accustomed that the Speakers of the Parliaments in consideration of their diligence and pains taken, have had, though the Parliament hath been right soon finished, above the £100 ordinary, a reward of £100 for the better maintenance of their household and other charges sustained in the same, I suppose. Sir, that the faithful

---

[22] *Roper*, p. 17.

[23] *Roper*, p. 19.

diligence of the said Sir Thomas More, in all your causes treated in this your late Parliament, as well for your subsidy, right honourably passed, as otherwise considered, no man could better deserve the same than he hath done. ... I am the rather moved to put your Highness in remembrance thereof, because he is not the most ready to speak and solicit his own cause.[24]

More acknowledged Wolsey's good offices in this matter in a letter from the court at Easthampstead (26th August).

Furthermore it may like your good Grace to understand that at the contemplation of your Grace's letters, the King's Highness is graciously content that beside the £100 for my fee for the office of Speaker of his Parliament, to be taken at the receipt of his Exchequer, I shall have one other hundred pounds out of his coffers by the hands of the Treasurer of his Chamber, whereof in most humble wise I beseech your good Grace that as your gracious favor hath obtained it for me so it may like the same to write to Mr. Wyatt that he may deliver it to such as I shall send for it, whereby I and all mine, as the manifold goodness of your Grace hath already bound us, shall daily more and more bounden to pray for your Grace, whom our Lord long preserve in honour and health.[25]

Roper has a story[26] that Wolsey, in his annoyance, proposed sending Sir Thomas More on an embassy to Spain in the hope that it would 'send him to his grave.' This too must be suspected as unfounded. The recurring attacks of sweating sickness and of other fevers made the chances of a fatal sickness in England as great as in Spain. Moreover the embassy was an important matter, and it was led by Bishop Tunstal; it is true that his

---

[24] *L.P.* III, 3267.

[25] *Rogers*, p. 278.

[26] *Roper*, p. 19.

companion, Sir Richard Wingfield, died in Spain, but there is no reason to see anything sinister in that misfortune.

Sir Richard had been Chancellor of the Duchy of Lancaster and High Steward of the University of Cambridge; Sir Thomas More was appointed to both positions in 1525. In the previous year he had been made High Steward of the University of Oxford,[27] and no one was more fitted by his learning and his distinction to enjoy this association with both Universities.

---

[27] See *Rogers*, Letters 131, 132, 134.

THOMAS MORE'S HOUSE, CHELSEA

Chapter XV

Chelsea

SOME would claim, not without reason, that Sir Thomas More was the greatest of all Londoners. He was born in the City, and his home was in the heart of it for nearly fifty years. We have seen how he regretted that his service with the king made it necessary for him to sever his official connexion with the City, and how, when opportunity occurred, he gladly answered any appeal from the Mayor and Aldermen. His influence remained considerable. There is a pleasant unofficial air about his relationship; thus in 1529 when he was Chancellor of the Duchy of Lancaster, he went in person to recommend his servant Walter Smith (author of *Twelve Merry Jests of one called Edith*) for the office of Sword Bearer.[1] Anyone else holding such a high position in the State might have been content to send a letter. When Sir Thomas became Lord Chancellor later in that same year, the Mayor and Aldermen sent him a tun of good wine, and, at the same time a hogshead to his aged father who was, indeed, nearing the end of his life.[2]

The greater part of More's married life was spent at the Old Barge;[3] it was there that his children grew up. When he left it, his

---

[1] *Repertory*, 8, 39.

[2] He died in 1530 at the age of seventy-seven.

[3] If ever the city of London thinks of commemorating its famous citizen, it could not do better than place a tablet on whatever building is constructed on the blitzed site of the Old Barge. A stained-glass window to Sir Thomas More in the Church of St. Laurence Jewry, where he delivered his lectures on St. Augustine's *City of God*, was destroyed in December

pupil John Clement became the tenant, and it was while paying a visit to the Clements that Sir Thomas More received the fateful summons to appear before the Commissioners at Lambeth in 1534.

Yet, in spite of this long and close connexion with the City, the name of Sir Thomas More is popularly associated with Chelsea where he lived for the last ten years of his life.[4]

His service to the king brought him not only salaries, allowances and fees but gifts of land; these included manors in Oxfordshire and Kent. There were other sources of income. In 1526 he had a license to export woollen cloth,[5] and in 1527 he had a pension of 150 crowns from the French king.[6] Then there were wardships such as those of Anne Cresacre and Giles Heron; in 1527 he became the guardian and trustee of a John Moreton who had become insane.[7] With such an increasing income it was natural for More to purchase houses and land for they provided the most secure investment—secure, that is, until the enmity of the king was incurred. In June 1523 Sir Thomas More bought Crosby Hall in Bishopsgate, but he does not seem to have occupied it, for in January 1524 he sold the lease to his friend Antonio Bonvisi who lived there until 1549 by which time

---

1940.

[4] Perhaps Ane Manning's deservedly popular *Household of Sir Thomas More* (1851) helped to emphasize the Chelsea association. The 'olde tyme' spelling is now a deterrent, but the book is a pleasing recreation of the past. She was in error in bringing Erasmus to Chelsea, but Froude made the same mistake, with less excuse, in his *Life and Letters to Erasmus* (1894. Erasmus' last visit to England was in 1517 while the Mores were still at the Old Barge.)

[5] *L.P.*, IV 2248.

[6] *L.P.*, IV, 3619. It was the accepted practice of the time for such pensions to be given when treaties were made; thus at the Peace of London (1518), Wolsey and nine other Councillors received pensions. The 1527 pensions were for the Treaty of Amiens. Such pensions were only paid as long as the alliance lasted, and even then, not regularly.

[7] R.O. Pat. C. 66/649; *Rogers*, p. 375.

England had become too Protestant for his peace of conscience.[8]

More began to buy land in Chelsea in 1524, and the family was settled there by the time of Holbein's visit in the autumn of 1526. The site of the main house was across the present Beaufort Street. There is no drawing of the exterior as it was in More's time. Holbein's sketch of the interior of the hall suggests the type of building then being erected by well-to-do merchants.

A few references give all the information there is about the house. Roper records a conversation between Sir Thomas and Dame Alice in the Tower in which she said, "And seeing you have at Chelsea a right fair house, your library, your books, your gallery, your garden, your orchard, and all other necessaries about you, where you might in the company of your wife, your children, and household be merry, I muse what a God's name you mean here still thus fondly to tarry."[9] Roper makes an important addition to this picture.

> And because he was desirous for godly purposes sometime to be solitary, and sequester himself from worldly company, a good distance from his mansion house builded he a place called the New Building, wherein there was a chapel, a library and a gallery; in which, as his use was upon other days to occupy himself in prayer and study together, so on the Friday there usually continued he from morning till evening, spending his time only in devout prayers and spiritual exercises.[10]

This New Building may be the one referred to in one of John

---

[8] See P. Norman, *Crosby Place* (1908), p. 21.

[9] *Roper*, p. 82.

[10] *Roper*, p. 25. The mansion had a sucession of owners after More's death; it was later known as Buckingham House, and Beaufort House: it was pulled down by Sir Hans Sloane in 1740. It is said that the west wall of the Moravian Burial Ground, at the angle of Milman's Street and King's Road was part of the wall of More's estate. The present Church of the Most Holy Redeemer and St. Thomas More is on the site of his property.

Aubrey's anecdotes about More.

> His country house was at Chelsea in Middlesex, where Sir John Danvers [d. 1655] built his house. The chimney piece of marble in Sir John's chamber was the chimney piece of Sir Thomas More's chamber, as Sir John himself told me. Where the gate is now, adorned with two noble pyramids, there stood anciently a gate-house, which was flat on the top, leaded, from whence is a most pleasant prospect of the Thames, and the fields beyond. On this place the Lord Chancellor More was wont to recreate himself and contemplate. It happened one time that a Tom of Bedlam came up to him, and had a mind to have thrown him from the battlements, saying, 'Leap, Tom, leap!' The Chancellor was in his gown, and besides ancient, and not able to struggle with such a strong fellow. My lord had a little dog with him; said he, 'Let us first throw the dog down and see what sport that will be.' So the dog was thrown over. 'This is a very fine sport,' said my lord, 'let us fetch him up and try once more.' While the madman was going down, my lord fastened the door, and called for help, but ever after kept the door shut.[11]

That is the kind of anecdote about Sir Thomas More that can be accepted or rejected according to the reader's own humor; it is given here for the sake of the reference to the gate-house which may have been the New Building. Danvers House was pulled down in 1696 and Danvers Street made over the site. We may conclude that the main house was opposite the end of the present Battersea Bridge, and the New Building 'a good distance away' was near the present Danvers Street with the garden between the two buildings. More's account of the gardens in *Utopia* suggests that his own garden would be a delight to him.[12] The Ropers

---

[11] John Aubrey, *Brief Lives*, etc. (ed A. Powell, 1949), p. 315.

[12] *Utopia*, p. 47; p. 61.

occupied this New Building at the time of More's death: it was then known as Butclose.[13]

Some of those strange pets may have lived in that garden who were the successors of those noted by Erasmus at the Old Barge; monkeys, foxes, ferrets, weasels, as well as many birds. We have already seen the monkey in Holbein's sketch. The house too would be full of those 'strange objects' and curiosities that, as Erasmus tells us, Sir Thomas liked to collect.

Another glimpse of More's Chelsea estate is given in a letter dated 3rd September, 1529, to his wife, and written from the court at Woodstock. News had reached him that a fire had destroyed his barns and those of his neighbours.

> Mistress Alice, in my most hearty wise I recommend me to you.
>
> And whereas I am informed by my son Heron of the loss of our barns and our neighbours also with all the corn that was therein, albeit (saving God's pleasure) it were great pity of so much good corn lost, yet since it hath liked Him to send us such a chance, we must and are bounden not only to be content but also to be glad of his visitation. He sent us all that we have lost and since He hath by such a chance taken it away again His pleasure he fulfilled. Let us never grudge thereat but take in good worth and hearty thanks Him as well for adversity as for prosperity and peradventure we have more cause to thank Him for our loss than for our winning, for His wisdom better seeth what is good for us than we do ourselves. Therefore I pray you be of good cheer and take all the household with you to church and there thank God both for that He hath given us and for that He hath taken from us and for that He hath left us, which if it please Him He can increase when He will and if it please Him to leave us yet less,

---

[13] Randal Davies, *Chelsea Old Church* (1904), pg. 106.

at His pleasure be it.

I pray you make some good search what my poor neighbours have lost and bid them take no thought therefore, for and I should not leave myself a spoon there shall no poor neighbour of mine bear no loss by any chance happened in my house. I pray you be with my children and your household merry in God and devise somewhat with your friends what way were best to take for provision to be made for corn for our household and for seed this year coming, if ye think it good that we keep the ground still in our hands, and whether ye think it good that we so shall do or not, yet I think it were not best suddenly this to leave it all up and to put away our folk off our farm, till we have somewhat advised us thereon, howbeit if we have more now than ye shall need and which can get them other masters ye may then discharge us of them but I would not that any man were suddenly sent away he wot not whither. At my coming hither I perceived none other but I should tarry still with the King's Grace but now I shall, I think, by cause of this chance get leave this week to come home and see you, and then shall we further devise together upon all things what order shall be best to take.

And thus as heartily fare you well with all our children as ye can wish; at Woodstock the 3rd day of September by the hand of

Your loving husband,
Thomas More Kg.[14]

Though More's house has disappeared, one building closely associated with his Chelsea days has survived—the More Chapel in the south aisle of the Old Church was happily not destroyed

---

[14] *Rogers*, p. 422.

when the church itself was bombed in 1941.[15] The epitaph panel (restored several times) was broken into four pieces, but the piers of the arch with the capitals designed by Holbein were not damaged. Sir Thomas More built the chapel in 1528 and composed the epitaph after he had resigned the chancellorship.

Stapleton tells us:

> In his parish church in the village of Chelsea he also built a chapel and furnished it abundantly with all things necessary for Divine Worship and with all suitable ornament and decoration. He was ever very liberal in gifts of this nature, bestowing much gold and silver plate upon his church. He used to say: 'The good give, the wicked take away.' He was accustomed to put on a surplice and chant the responses with his priest in the parish church, even when he was Lord Chancellor. Once the Duke of Norfolk came upon him when he was so employed and warned him that the King would certainly be displeased at such a proceeding as too lowly, and as unbefitting the high position he held.[16] He replied, 'It cannot be displeasing to my lord the King that I pay homage to my King's Lord.' Often he used to serve Mass for the priest, taking the place of the clerk. Sometimes in the parochial processions he would carry the Cross before the priest. Far from refusing or being ashamed to perform the duty of a common clerk or verger, he took the greatest delight therein. ... This he did regularly except when he was Lord Chancellor. ... Although for some years he was the busiest of men, yet once he had gone into church he never allowed in that sacred place any single word of worldly affairs to be uttered. As often as he entered upon any new office, or undertook any

---

[15] Blessed John Larke was nominated to be the Parish priest by Sir Thomas More. He suffered at Tyburn on 7th March, 1544.

[16] Roper reports Norfolk's words as "God body, God body, my Lord Chancellor, a parish clerck, a parish clerck! You dishonour the King and his office." (P. 51).

business of difficulty, he used to fortify himself with Holy Communion. Sometimes he used to go on pilgrimages to shrines distant as much as seven miles[17] from his home, and always on foot, a thing which even the labouring classes will scarcely do.[18]

To Sir Thomas More the religious and spiritual life of his household was the first consideration. Deep as was his love of learning, that was subordinated to the main purpose—growth in spiritual wisdom. Roper's testimony was based on his experience of living in that family.

> As Sir Thomas More's custom was daily, if he were at home, besides his private prayers with his children to say the seven Psalms, litany and suffrages following, so was his guise nightly, before he went to bed, with his wife, children and household to go to his chapel, and there upon his knees ordinarily to say certain Psalms and Collects with them.[19]

Stapleton has recorded the custom followed at meals.

> At table a passage of Sacred Scripture was read with the commentaries of Nicholas of Lyra or some other ancient writer. One of his daughters would be the reader. The passage from Scripture was intoned in the ecclesiastical or monastic fashion, and was ended with the words 'and do thou, O Lord, have mercy on us,' as in religious houses. The reading was continued until a sign was given, and then More would ask one of the company how this or that passage should be understood. Thereupon an intimate friendly conversation would take place. But if, as often happened, some learned guest were present, a more formal discussion of the passage read would be held. Afterwards More in his inimitable way

---

[17] Such as Our Lady of Willesden.

[18] *Stapleton*, p. 97.

[19] *Roper*, p. 25. The Psalms would be the Penitential Psalms.

would suggest some lighter topic, and all would be highly amused. Henry Patenson, More's fool, would now join in the conversation.[20]

Some further particulars are given by Stapleton.

> Now we will describe the care he exercised in regard to his servants. He would never allow them to waste their time in sloth or improper pastimes, as happens only too often in the houses of the English nobility where there is kept, according to the custom of the nation, a large crowd of idle and gossiping retainers. Some of these, therefore, whose office it was to accompany him abroad he placed in charge of his garden, which he divided into sections—for it was large—assigning to each his share. Some he made to sing, others to play the organ; he allowed no one, not even if he were of noble rank, to play at dice or cards.
>
> On Sundays and feast days no one was allowed to be absent from the services of the Church, and More insisted that all should be there at the very beginning of the service. On the greater feasts, Christmas and Easter, he made all rise at night and assist at the whole of the office.
>
> Every year on Good Friday he called together the whole of his family into what was called the New Building and there he would have the whole of our Lord's Passion read to them, generally by John Harris.[21]

Such a discipline as this, almost monastic in its character, might have proved irksome but for the deep sincerity of the master of the household. All witnesses bear out the truth of Erasmus's statement,

> More is a man of true piety, which he practises with regularity, yet without a trace of superstition. At definite

---

[20] *Stapleton*, p. 97.

[21] *Stapleton*, pp. 95-6.

hours he addresses his prayers to God, not in set phrases but with words that come straight from the heart. When he talks with his friends about the world to come, you can see that he is speaking in all sincerity and with good hope.[22]

Yet this deep religious life was combined with a cheerfulness that had something boyish, even puckish, in its expression. This side of his nature gave rise to many stories of More's wit and of his love of horse-play; not all these tales can be accepted as well-founded, but they are tributes to a characteristic that impressed his contemporaries and became part of his legend.

An unusual glimpse of the household is given in Walter Smith's *Widow Edyth*;[23] his appointment as City Sword Bearer in 1529 has already been noted. He had been More's personal servant for some years. His poem about 'this lying widow, false and crafty' must have been composed with the knowledge, and probably the help, of Sir Thomas More and his family. It was printed in 1525 by John Rastell, and we can be sure that it would not have been published had there been anything in it offensive to the Mores. The occasional coarseness, as we regard it now, was in keeping with the times and is less objectionable than the sly allusiveness of our modern manner. We must not here retell the story of all the 'Twelve Merry Jests of one called Edyth,' but the whole poem is in the same temper as More's early verses on 'How a Sergeant would learn to play the Friar'; indeed it is difficult to resist the conjecture that he had a share in Walter Smith's production. The Tenth Jest brings the widow to Chelsea.

> And when she saw her time, on an holy day,
> She walked to a thorp [village] called Battersea;
> And, on the next day after, she took a wherry.

---

[22] Letter to von Hutten, 23rd July 1019; *Allen*, IV, 999.

[23] Printed in Vol. III of W.C. Hazlitt's *Shakespeare Jest-Books* (1864).

> And over Thames she was rowed full merry.
> At Chelsea was her arrival,
> Where she had best cheer of all.
> In the house of Sir Thomas More.

There three young serving men became rivals for her hand, for she had given the impression that she had property. Walter Smith was one of the dupes. The other two are named.

> One of them had to name Thomas Croxton,
> And servant he was to Master Alington.
> Which had to name Thomas Arthur,
> And servant he was to Master Roper.

There was much boisterous merry-making.

> And in her chamber, the next night following,
> There was the revel and the gossiping;
> The general bumming, as Margaret Gigs said;
> Everybody laughed, and was well a-paid.

The widow Edyth was, no doubt, a myth, but she tells us something of the lighter side of the More household.

More's thoughtfulness extended beyond his household; the letter to Dame Alice that has been quoted shows how his neighbours found in him a friend. His charity is described by Stapleton.

> To his charity towards his neighbour, his constant generous almsgiving bears witness. He used personally to go into dark courts and visit the families of the poor, helping them not with small gifts but with two, three, or four pieces of gold, as their need required. Afterwards, when his dignity as Chancellor forbade him to act thus, he used to send some of his household who would dispense his gifts faithfully to

needy families, and especially to the sick and aged. This task was often laid upon Margaret Gigs, the wife of John Clement, whom More had brought up with his daughters. The chief festivals of the year were his favourite times for sending such gifts. Very often he invited his poorer neighbours to his table, receiving them graciously and familiarly. The rich were rarely invited, the nobility hardly ever. Moreover in his parish, Chelsea, he hired a house in which he placed many who were infirm, poor, or old, priding for them at his own expense. In her father's absence, Margaret Roper took charge of these. One poor widow, named Paula, who had spent all her money in litigation, he took into his own family and supported. Whenever he undertook the causes of widows and orphans, his services were always given gratuitously.[24]

The letter to Dame Alice refers to 'my son Heron.' This was Giles Heron, his ward, who had married Cecily More on 29th September, 1525, on the same day that William Daunce married Elizabeth More. Their sister Margaret had married William Roper on 2nd July, 1521. Their half-sister, Alice, married Giles Alington before 1524. John More married Anne Cresacre in 1529. It seems that they continued to live with Sir Thomas More and Dame Alice in what was a patriarchal household. Roper and Alington, as we have seen, are mentioned in the *Widow Edyth* as living in the Chelsea house. John Clement and Margaret Gigs were married in 1526, but they lived at the Old Barge after the Mores had left.

Amongst other young people who frequented the Chelsea house was John Heywood 'the mad merry wit.' who married More's niece Joan Rastell about 1523; his appointment as one of the king's servants in 1519 may have been due to More; he is described in the accounts as 'Singer' and as 'Player of the Virginals.' His brother Richard would also visit Chelsea for he

---

[24] *Stapleton*, p. 72.

and William Roper were partners. Then there was More's nephew William Rastell, who about 1527 began to take a prominent part in his father's printing business, and in 1529 set up his own press in Fleet Street, and from that time published his uncle's controversial works; this must have meant much going to and from Chelsea.

Of the three sons-in-law, William Roper is the most important, not only as the author of the foundation biography, but as the husband of Margaret More. He was the son of John Roper of Well Hall, Eltham, a close friend of Sir John More with whom he was frequently associated in legal work. His son William was born in 1498.[25] He came to live in the More household at the Barge about 1518 when he was a student at Lincoln's Inn; in 1524 he was appointed Prothonotary and a year later was called to the Bar.[26]

Margaret Roper was the favourite of her father, not that he treated her with special indulgence, but, as can be seen from their letters, there was an unusual intimacy of spirit, and her quickness of intelligence was an additional bond. She was a classical scholar of a standing unique amongst the women of her day. Erasmus adopted an emendation she suggested in an epistle of Cyprian, and, as we have seen, she translated the *Precatio dominica* of Erasmus; when her father was writing *The Four Last Things* she composed a treatise on the same subject of which he had a high opinion; this has not survived.

Extracts have already been given from some of the letters Thomas More wrote to his children and to Margaret. Further quotations from his early letters to her tell us more of father and daughter than any descriptive account could do.

The first letter is on a familiar theme.

---

[25] But see note in 'List of Illustrations' on Plate XVII.

[26] See pp. xxix-xlvii of Hitchcock's *Roper* for the best account of him.

You ask, my dear Margaret, for money, with too much bashfulness and timidity, since you are asking from a father who is eager to give, and since you have written to me a letter such that I would not only repay each line of it with a golden philippine, as Alexander did the verses of Cherilos, but, if my means were as great as my desire, I would reward each syllable with two gold ounces. As it is, I send only what you have asked, but would have added more, only that as I am eager to give, so am I desirous to be asked and coaxed by my daughter, especially by you, whom virtue and learning have made so dear to my soul. So the sooner you ask for more, the more you will be sure of pleasing your father. Good-bye, my dearest child.[27]

That letter can probably be dated in 1518; the next contains a reference to William Roper and was probably written soon after his marriage to Margaret in 1521.

There was no reason, my most sweet child, why you should have put off writing for a day, because in your great self-distrust you feared lest your letter should be such that I could not read it without distaste. Even had it not been perfect, yet the honour of your sex would have gained you pardon from any, while to a father even a blemish will seem beautiful in the face of a child...

You tell me that Nicholas [Kratzer] who is fond of you and so learned in astronomy, has begun again with you the system of the heavenly bodies; I am grateful to him, and I congratulate you on your good fortune; for in the space of one month, with only a slight labour, you will thus learn thoroughly these sublime wonders of the Eternal Workman, which so many men of illustrious and almost superhuman intellect have only discovered with hot toil and study, or

---

[27] *Stapleton*, p. 111; *Rogers*, p. 134.

rather with cold shiverings and nightly vigils in the open air in the course of many ages.

I am therefore delighted to read that you have made up your mind to give yourself diligently to philosophy, and to make up by your earnestness in future for what you have lost in the past by neglect. My darling Margaret, I indeed have never found you idling, and your unusual learning in almost every kind of literature shows that you have been making active progress. So I take your words as an example of the great modesty that makes you prefer to accuse yourself falsely of sloth, rather than to boast of your diligence, unless your meaning is that you will give yourself so earnestly to study, that your past industry will seem like indolence by comparison. If this is your meaning nothing could be more delightful to me, or more fortunate, my sweetest daughter, for you.

Though I earnestly hope that you will devote the rest of your life to medical science and sacred literature so that you may be well furnished for the whole scope of human life, which is to have a healthy soul in a healthy body, and I know that you have already laid the foundations of these studies, and there will be always opportunity to continue the building; yet I am of opinion that you may with great advantage give some years of your yet flourishing youth to humane letters and liberal studies.

It would be a delight, my dear Margaret, to me to converse long with you on these matters: but I have just been interrupted and called away by the servants who have brought in supper. I must have regard to others, else to sup is not so sweet as to talk with you. Farewell my dearest child, and salute for me my most gentle son, your husband. I am extremely glad that he is following the same course of study as yourself. I am ever wont to persuade you to yield in everything to your husband; now, on the contrary, I give you full leave to strive to get before him in the knowledge of the celestial system. Farewell again. Salute your whole company, but especially your tutor.[28]

The last of this group of letters was written just before the birth of the Ropers' first child. They had five children, two sons and three daughters, but as the dates of their births are not known, we cannot say if the first was a boy or a girl.

> Something I once said to you in joke came back to my mind, and I realized how true it was. It was to the effect that you were to be pitied, because the incredulity of men would rob you of the praise you so richly deserved for your laborious vigils, as they would never believe, when they read what you had written, that you had not often availed yourself of another's help: whereas of all writers you least deserved to be thus suspected. Even when a tiny child you could never endure to be decked out in another's finery. But, my sweetest Margaret, you are all the more deserving of praise on that account. Although you cannot hope for an adequate reward for your labour, yet nevertheless you continue to unite to your singular love of virtue the pursuit of literature and art. Content with the approbation of your conscience, in your modesty you do not seek for the praise of the public, nor value it over much even if you receive it, but because of the great love you bear us, you regard us, your husband and myself, as a sufficiently large circle of readers for all that you write.
>
> In your letter you speak of your approaching confinement. We pray most earnestly that all may go happily and successfully with you. May God and our Blessed Lady grant you happily and safely a little one like to his mother in everything except sex. Yet let it by all means be a girl, if only

---

[28] *Stapleton*, pp. 117-19.

she will make up for the inferiority of her sex by her zeal to imitate her mother's virtue and learning. Such a girl I should prefer to three boys. Good-bye, my dearest child.[29]

It was a happy chance that preserved these letters and the later ones, for Stapleton's use. Dorothy Colley, who had been Margaret Roper's maid, allowed him to copy them.

The lack of individual letters from Sir Thomas More to his other children deprives us of knowledge of them that would be precious.

---

[29] *Stapleton*, pp. 114-15.

Chapter XVI

Chancellor of the Duchy of Lancaster

THE Chancellor of the Duchy of Lancaster in Tudor times had a special association with the King. Since 1399 the extensive Lancaster estates[1] had provided a substantial part of the royal income; the Duchy was administered as a distinct unit and in the Court of Duchy Chamber, the Chancellor exercised executive and judicial powers second only to those of the central administration. His appointment to this important position increased the amount of business Sir Thomas More had with the King himself. This association was further emphasized when the King issued ordinances for the reorganization of his household in 1526.[2] There was to be a council of twenty members of whom the Chancellor of the Duchy was one; ten of them were to be in regular attendance; of these, the Bishop of Bath (Dr. John Clerk), the Secretary (Dr. William Knight), Sir Thomas More and the Dean of the Chapel, were specially named; at least two of these had to be 'always present except the King's Grace give license to any of them to the contrary.' They were to be in the council chamber morning and afternoon, 'there to be in readiness not only in case the King's pleasure shall be to commune and cofer with them upon any cause or matter, but also for hearing and direction of poor men's complaints and matters of justice.' These regulations

---

[1] A map of the widely scattered lands of the Duchy is given in *Chamber's Encyclopedia* (1950), VIII, p. 321. The title remains but the functions have become formal.

[2] Known as the odrinances of Elthan. *L.P.* iv.i.860.

to ensure 'the King's Highness shall always be furnished of an honourable presence of councillors' are an indication that Henry VIII was beginning to find the ever-growing influence of Wolsey somewhat irksome, for it was round the Cardinal that the councillors had gathered. At the age of thirty-five the King's glorious youth was over and he was becoming more concerned with policy, and not least with the problem of the succession to the throne; his only child was the Princess Mary. Wolsey had taught the King much, and he was to profit from the instruction.

Two incidents that may be dated about 1525 show the regard Henry had for the More family. A casual reference in a letter[3] tells us of the first. Henry's natural son by Elizabeth Blount was created Duke of Richmond in 1525 when he was six years old. His tutor, John Palsgrave, wrote to Sir Thomas More about the boy's studies, and asked for More's support 'to move the King's Grace that the said my Lord of Richmond may be brought up in learning.' It is interesting to note that Palsgrave said that he had already consulted William Gonell. The last sentence of the letter reads, 'When your daughters disputed in philosophy afore the King's Grace I would it had been my fortune to be present.'

The second incident is narrated by Roper; this not only shows the regard Henry had for Sir Thomas More, but the shrewdness with which More judged Henry.

> And for the pleasure he [Henry] took in his company, would his Grace suddenly sometimes come home to his house at Chelsea, to be merry with him; and after dinner, in a fair garden of his, walked with him by the space of an hour, holding his arm about his neck. As soon as his Grace was gone, I, rejoicing thereat, told Sir Thomas More how happy he was, whom the King had so familiarly entertained, as I never had seen him do to any other except Cardinal Wolsey, whom

---

[3] *Rogers*, p. 403. The date there suggested is 1529, but an earlier date seems to meet the facts.

I saw his Grace once walk with, arm in arm. 'I thank Our Lord son,' quoth he, 'I find his Grace my very good lord indeed, and I believe he doth as singularly favour me as any subject within this realm. Howbeit, son Roper, I may tell thee I have no cause to be proud thereof, for if my head could win him a castle in France (for then there was war between us) it should not fail to go.'[4]

The war in France was interrupted by the astonishing news that the French had been utterly defeated at the battle of Pavia (24th February, 1525) and that Francis had become the prisoner of the Emperor Charles. Negotiations for peace between England and France were opened by Louise of Savoy who had become Regent of France during her son's imprisonment. A commission[5] dated 28th August, 1525, from the More[6] empowered certain of the councillors to conclude a treaty. Sir Thomas More was the last named of these; he was still called Sub-Treasurer, an office he resigned later that year. The Treaty of the More, as it was known, was signed two days later. 'England, indeed, gained nothing save peace without honour.' This anti-imperial policy was unpopular and during the following years discontent increased. The landed and merchant classes found the burden of taxation a growing strain, all the more intolerable in that no man could see how England gained anything from the wars. The cutting off of trade was a more serious hardship for it meant a loss of income at a time when Wolsey's demands seemed boundless. The export of wool and cloth to the Low Countries was as important then as that of industrial products in the nineteenth century. The hardship affected all classes and found expression in popular ballads against Wolsey.

---

[4] *Roper*, p. 20.

[5] *Rogers*, p. 318.

[6] Wolsey's palace; near Rickmansworth, Herts; Moor Park preserves the name.

> By thee out of service many are constrained
> And course of merchandise thou hast restrained
> Wherefore men sigh and sob.

The same feeling is expressed in Act I, Scene 2 of *Henry VIII*: Norfolk says,

> ... upon these taxations
> The clothiers all, not able to maintain
> The many to them 'longing, have put off
> The spinsters, carders, fullers, weavers.

Wolsey, however, was playing too desperate a game to be influenced by rising discontents, or by the objections made by Norfolk, Tunstal, and other councillors. The Emperor's victories in Italy, the sacking of Rome, and the imprisonment of the Pope, served to increase Wolsey's eagerness for a French alliance against the Emperor. So in July 1527 he set out with a train of nine hundred to meet the French king at Amiens. Francis, who had been released the previous year, was only too anxious, in spite of solemn undertakings given to Charles, to form an alliance against his late jailor. Cavendish has left us a rapturous account of the Cardinal's progress 'having all his accustomed and glorious furniture carried before him.'[7]

Sir Thomas More was there as one of the councillors to treat with the French. As the many weeks dragged along, he must have thought wistfully of his many scholar-friends in the Low Countries; perhaps they managed to meet.

War was declared against the Emperor in January 1528, but there was little the English could do to help the French. English merchants in Spain and Flanders were arrested, but a truce

---

[7] *Cavendish*, p. 64.

limited to Flanders allowed some trade to reopen. The following year saw the collapse of all Wolsey's elaborate schemes; the French were again defeated; the Pope and the Emperor were reconciled, and Francis was compelled by circumstances to treat with Charles. They had both tricked Henry before, so why not again? Bishop Tunstal, Dr. William Knight and Sir Thomas More were sent to Cambrai for the negotiations; they were old colleagues in such affairs; with them was John Hacket, English Ambassador to Margaret of Savoy. Wolsey would have liked to have led the embassy himself, but he had to remain in London, for on 31st May the trial of Henry VIII's marriage suit had opened at Blackfriars before Cardinal Campeggio, and it was still on when Tunstal and his colleagues left London on 1st July.

There was little they could do to modify the political terms of the treaty; Henry was insistent that someone, either Charles or Francis, should recoup him for his expenditure and loans; this obligation was put on Francis by Charles, but the accounts between the three monarchs were by this time so confused that it was a simple matter to evade responsibility. The English envoys did, however, achieve one considerable gain; a commercial agreement was made so that full trade with Flanders and Spain could be re-established. This part of their work would appeal to Sir Thomas More whose experience of similar negotiations in the past must have been valuable. Hall noted that the peace 'was solemnly proclaimed by Heralds with trumpets of the City of London, which Proclamation much rejoiced the English merchants repairing into Spain, Flanders, Brabant, Zeeland and other the Emperor's dominions, for during the wars the merchants were evil handled on both parties which caused them to be desirous of peace.'[8]

Peace lasted for fourteen years and might indeed have begun

---

[8] *Hall*, II, p. 160.

fourteen years earlier so pointless had been England's intervention in European affairs. Sir Thomas More's own feeling about the Peace of Cambrai is expressed in his epitaph.

> Meantime he was chosen Speaker of the Commons and appointed ambassador to various courts; last of all to Cambrai, being associated with Cuthbert Tunstal, the chief of that embassy, then bishop of London and since of Durham, a man than whom the world can scarcely boast one more learned, wiser, or better. There he had the pleasure to see and to negotiate the renewal of the leagues between the chief princes of Christendom and the restoration to the world of long wished-for peace, which peace may Heaven confirm and long preserve.

This period of peace was due not so much to Henry's change of attitude towards European politics as to his preoccupation with other great matters; there was first his determination to free himself from his marriage with Catherine of Aragon, and, secondly, there was the growing tension between Church and State as the result of the spread of anti-clerical and heretical teaching.

Roper records how the King first approached Sir Thomas More for an opinion on the marriage question. According to Roper, the scruple that was to trouble the King's adaptable conscience was suggested to him by the Bishop of Lincoln at Wolsey's instigation; 'it was not lawful for him to marry his brother's wife.'

> Which the King, not sorry to hear of, opened it first to Sir Thomas More, whose counsel he required therein, showing him certain places of scripture[9] that somewhat seemed to serve his appetite; which, when he had perused, and

---

[9] *Lev.* 20:21. 'He who marrieth his brother's wife doth an unlawful thing. ... They shall be without children.' Henry seems to have interepreted 'children' as meaning 'sons.'

thereupon, as one that had never professed the study of divinity, himself excused to be unmeet many ways to meddle with such matters; the King, not satisfied with this answer, so sore still pressed upon him therefore, that in conclusion he condescended to his Grace's motion. And further, forasmuch as the case was of such importance as needed great advisement and deliberation, he besought his Grace of sufficient respite advisedly to consider of it. Wherewith the King, well contented, said unto him that Tunstal and Clerk, Bishops of Durham and Bath, with other learned of his Privy Council, should also be dealers therein.

So Sir Thomas More departing, conferred those places of scripture with expositions of divers of the old holy doctors, and at his coming to the court, in talking with his Grace of the aforesaid matter, he said, 'To be plain with your Grace, neither my Lord of Durham, nor my Lord of Bath, though I know both to be wise, virtuous, learned and honourable prelates, nor myself, with the rest of your Council, being all your Grace's own servants, for your manifold benefits daily bestowed on us so most bounden to you, be, in my judgement, meet Councillors for your Grace herein. But if your Grace mind to understand the truth, such councillors may you have devised as neither for respect of their own wordly commodity, nor for fear of your princely authority, will be inclined to deceive you.' To whom he named then St. Jerome, St. Austin, and divers other old holy doctors, both Greeks, and Latins, and moreover showed him what authorities he had gathered out of them; which, although the King (as disagreeable with his desire) did not very well like of, yet were they by Sir Thomas More, who in all his communication with the King in that matter had always most discreetly behaved himself, so wisely-tempered, that he both presently took them in good part, and oftimes had thereof conference with him again.[10]

In a letter to Thomas Cromwell, 5th March, 1534, More said that the king first broached the matter to him 'upon a time at my coming from beyond the sea.'[11] This would apply to his return from France after the negotiations at Amiens in 1527.

When Tunstal and More set out for Cambrai in 1529 they were both greatly concerned with the spread of heresy in England, and while they were abroad they asked Stephen Vaughan to send them information about English heretics in the Low Countries where he was an agent of Henry. In the previous year More had written his *Dialogue Concerning Heresies*[12] which was published in June 1529 by his brother-in-law John Rastell. This book was the first fruits of the task laid upon him by Tunstal as Bishop of London. He gave More license to read[13] the books of the 'Wycliffian and Lutheran' heretics so that they could be refuted. 'I send you,' wrote the Bishop, 'their mad incantations in our tongue and as well some of Luther's books whence these monstrous ideas have sprung.' He was well aware that More was the most learned layman of the day who had devoted much of his reading and thought to the works of the Fathers. There were refutations of these heretical books in Latin written by theologians; Tunstal saw that the immediate need was for similar work to be done for the layman in his own language. Part of the commission[14] (7th March, 1528) reads:

> Because, you, most dear brother, are able to emulate Demosthenes in our vernacular tongue no less than in Latin,

---

[10] *Roper*, p. 31.

[11] *Rogers*, p. 493.

[12] The title has been changed in the reprint of the E.W. to *Dialogue Concerning Tyndale*.

[13] This was necessary in view of such Papal Bulls as '*Inter sollicitudines*' (Leo X, 1515), and '*Consueverunt*' (Clement VII, 1524).

[14] *Rogers*, p. 386.

and are wont to be an ardent defender of Catholic truth whenever you hear it attacked, you cannot spend your leisure hours—if you can steal any from your official duties—better than in composing in our own language such books as may show to simple and unlearned men the cunning malice of the heretics, and fortify them against those impious subverters of the Church... For it is of great help towards victory to know thoroughly the plans of the enemy, what they hold and whither they tend; for if you go about to refute what they protest that they do not hold, you lose your pains. Engage therefore courageously in this holy work, by which you will benefit the Church of God, make for yourself an immortal name, and win eternal glory in heaven. We adjure you in God's name so to do and to aid the Church of God by your championship.'

Stapleton paid tribute to More's competence in theology.

I have come to the conclusion in reading through his works, that he paid special attention to the study of dogmatic theology. For when he speaks of grace, free will, merit, faith, charity and other virtues, original sin and even predestination, he is so guarded and exact in his statements that a professional theologian could scarcely speak more accurately. That he had carefully read St. Thomas [Aquinas] is proved by a story told by John Harris, his secretary. Once a pamphlet recently printed by a heretic was brought to More's notice while he was travelling by water from his home at Chelsea to London. When he had read a little he pointed out with his finger some passages to Harris. 'The arguments.' said he, 'which this villain has set forth are the objections which St. Thomas puts to himself in such and such a question and article of the Secunda Secundae, but the rogue keeps back the good Doctor's solutions.'[15]

Stapleton adds the detail that Thomas More wrote all his controversial books 'by his own hand, as he was unwilling to rely on the industry of another.' *The Dialogue Concerning Heresies* contains nearly two hundred thousand words, and it must have needed many hours of thought as well as of writing at a time when Sir Thomas More was well occupied with state and legal matters.

That year, 1528, was also one of personal anxiety. The sweating sickness raged throughout that summer and Margaret Roper was taken dangerously ill. Her husband tells the story.

> To whom, for his notable virtue and godliness, God showed as it seemed a manifest miraculous token of his special favour towards him, at such a time as my wife, as many other that year were, was sick of the sweating sickness; who, lying in so great extremity of that disease as by no invention or devices that physicians in such cases commonly use (of whom she had divers both expert, wise and well-learned, then continually attendant about her) she could be kept from sleep, so that physicians and all other there despaired of her recovery, and gave her over. Her father, as he that most entirely tendered [loved] her, being in no small heaviness for her, by prayer at God's hand sought to get her remedy. Whereupon going up, after his usual manner, into his aforesaid New Building, there in his chapel, upon his knees, with tears, most devoutly sought almighty God that it would like his goodness, unto whom nothing was impossible, if it were his blessed will, at his mediation to vouchsafe graciously to hear his humble petition. Where incontinent came into his mind that a clyster should be the only way to help her. Which, when he told the physicians, they by and by confessed

---

[15] *Stapleton*, p. 38.

that, if there were any hope of health, that was the very best help indeed, much marvelling of themselves that they had not before remembered it.

Then was it immediately ministered unto her sleeping, which she could by no means have been brought unto waking. And albeit after that she was thereby thoroughly wakened, God's marks, an evident undoubted token of death, plainly appeared upon her, yet she, contrary to all expectations, was, as it was thought, by her father's fervent prayers miraculously recovered, and at length again to perfect health restored. Whom, if it had pleased God at that time to have taken to his mercy, her father said he would never have meddled with worldly matters after.[16]

---

[16] *Roper*, p. 28. Stapleton's account (p. 70) was derived from Margaret Roper's maid. According to him, More thought of the clyster first and prayed while the doctor, who 'thought it would do no harm,' applied this remedy.

WILLIAM TYNDALE

Chapter XVII

Heresy

ONE of the difficulties in trying to understand a past period is the effort needed to forget the changes in thought that have taken place between that period and our own. It is impossible to wipe out of the mind completely the knowledge of what happened in the intervening centuries, or to obliterate the influence of the society in which we have grown up; we cannot, indeed, see things in exactly the same way as they appeared to our grandparents, or, still less, to our more remote ancestors. We must, however, make the attempt to reach an approximate appreciation of the point of view of our ancestors if we are to understand, even imperfectly, how they behaved, or why they acted as they did. This task is particularly difficult in trying to enter the mind and share the spirit of a Catholic at the beginning of the sixteenth century. Four centuries of Protestantism lie between us.

One fact is fundamental; there was then One Church, and not even the early Reformers could imagine a divided Church, still less a large number of separated congregations each claiming to be the heir of the True Church. Their aim at first was to bring the whole Church to their way of thinking; they desired reform but not schism. The fact that a multiple schism came rapidly must not obscure the fact that the idea of One Church was deeply rooted and part of common culture. It was More's distinction that he so quickly saw the threat to the unity of the Church; he was conscious of the need for reform; he had himself pointed out weaknesses and abuses; he wanted Unity and Reform, and when the choice between these was forced upon him, he chose Unity.

Failure to understand this attitude towards the One Church has prevented some writers from appreciating Sir Thomas More's detestation of heresy. They acknowledge the nobility of his character, yet are bewildered and shocked because he should have chosen to describe himself in his epitaph as 'formidable to heretics.' The very word *haereticis* was omitted when the stone was re-lettered.[1] When he sent a copy of the Epitaph to Erasmus in 1533, More said that he had deliberately included the reference to heretics.[2] During the past four centuries men have come to think that 'one religion is as good as another' as they regard none of much importance; creeds are regarded as outmoded formulas. This indifferency has of recent years received a shock in the political world; militant and materialist communism is recognized as a menace to the kind of civilization that has developed during the Christian centuries. Beliefs and ideas do seem to matter, and some States have found it necessary to safeguard their security against these disruptive doctrines. So it comes about that in the middle of the twentieth century we can better understand the attitude of the Church towards heresy than was possible during the nineteenth century.

St. Thomas Aquinas defined heresy as 'a species of infidelity in men, who, having professed the faith of Christ, corrupt its dogmas.' The heretic, while he may profess to be a Christian, selects those parts of the Church's teaching with which he agrees, and rejects the rest. The believer accepts the faith as expounded by the Church as revealed truth enshrined in tradition and the scriptures. His difficulties and problems do not in themselves constitute heresy, but he will consult those who have been appointed as his guides in matters of faith and will accept their

---

[1] This was done in 1644; it was not a suitable time for talking about heretics!

[2] *Hoc ambitiose feci.* Allen, x, 2831.

authority.

Sir Thomas More gave this advice to those who were troubled in this way.

> Let him by my poor counsel pray God inspire himself to believe and follow the thing that may be His high pleasure, and let him thereupon appoint with himself to live well, and forthwith to begin well, get himself a good ghostly [spiritual] father, and shrive him of his sins and then concerning the question, ask advice and counsel of those whom himself thinketh between God and his new-cleansed conscience, for learning and virtue most likely, without any partial [biased] learning, indifferently to tell him truth.[3]

The heretic becomes dangerous to the unity of the Church when he tries to persuade others to support his opinions against the warnings of the Church. Four centuries ago that was more apparent than it is today when there are so many long-established sects; the conception of One Church to which all Christians owe allegiance is now an ideal for which many sigh, but in More's day it was an accepted fact, and the thought of schism was as dreadful as we should regard treachery and betrayal of one's country. On this More had no doubt

> ... who so be so deeply grounded in malice, to the harm of his own soul and other men's too, and so set upon the sowing of seditious heresies, that no good means that men may use unto him, can pull that malicious folly out of his poisoned proud obstinate heart, I would rather be content that he were gone in time, than over long to tarry to the destruction of other.[4]

But, it may be asked, what of *Utopia*? More's views had not changed. It will be remembered that the Utopians were not

---

[3] *Apologye*, p. 193.

[4] *Apologye*, p. 190.

Christians; they were gradually passing from the worship of various gods to a belief in one God and in the immortality of man. Each was allowed to follow the religion of his choice and could try to persuade others to adopt his beliefs provided he used no violence or abuse. If anyone became over-zealous in propaganda and became factious, they exiled him. Such a policy, in More's opinion, was wise in a country that had not yet had the blessing of revealed truth, but it could not be followed where there existed the sure and steadfast authority of 'Christ's Catholic known church.' Those guilty of stirring up strife within that Church must first be reasoned with in all charity and every means sought to persuade them to amend their opinions and submit themselves to the authority of the Church. Should all these efforts fail, and the heretic be contumacious, then the utmost severity must be used. Those who defy the authority of the Church are likely to defy the authority of the State.[5]

When Thomas More was a young man, heresy was not a serious menace. The Lollards retained some local centres such as in East Anglia and on the Chilterns; it is, however, misleading to emphasize the name 'Lollard' as this suggests a more organized and continuous movement than in fact existed. The terms 'Known Men' or the 'Christian Brethren' were used to denote those who, in secret, studied the translated Bible and interpreted it by the light of their unaided reason. There was no means of knowing the numbers of these Brethren, but they prepared the ground for the attack on the Church. We have already noted how anti-clericism spread during this period; this was a second influence but it was not, in itself, a doctrinal revolt. Then came

---

[5] I think Chambers is misleading when he says, 'More's hatred of heresy has its root, not in religious bigotry, but in the fear of sedition, tumult and civil war characteristic of sixteenth-century statesmen' (p. 282). The root was his religious faith and his belief in One Church; when he accused heretics of sedition, he was thinking of sedition within the Church. He saw that this might well lead to sedition within the State, but that, obnoxious as it was, came second in his mind.

the effect of Luther's rebellion against the Papacy; his writings, and those of his associates, were brought into England along the trade routes from Germany and the Low Countries, and some of the City merchants, such as Richard Hunne, promoted the distribution of such books and pamphlets. Then there was a group of scholars at Cambridge who were attracted by the new doctrines; in the twenties of the century they met for discussions at the White Horse Tavern which gained the nickname of 'Little Germany.'

Even More's household was not free from these influences. Harpsfield records that at the time of his marriage (1521) William Roper was 'a marvellous zealous protestant' and was prepared to carry his enthusiasm to great lengths; it even led him, for a time, to dislike his father-in-law. Roper was impressed by Luther's *Babylonish Captivity* and *The Liberty of a Christian Man*, both published in 1520. He frequented the company 'of his own sect, of the Steelyard, and other merchants,' and with some of them was brought before Wolsey; all, except Roper, had to recant at St. Paul's Cross, but Roper,

> for love borne by the Cardinal to Sir Thomas More, his father-in-law, was with a friendly warning discharged; and, albeit he had married the eldest daughter of Sir Thomas More, whom then of all the world he did, during that time, most abhor, though he was a man of most mildness and notable patience.
>
> Now these easy, short pleasant and licentious lessons did cast him into so sweet a sleep as he was loath to wake from it. And those lessons he did so well like as he soon after gave over his fasting, praying, his Primer and all his other prayers, and got him to a Lutheran Bible, wherein upon the holy days, instead of his prayers, he spent his whole time, thinking it for him sufficient to get only thereby knowledge to be able among ignorant persons to babble and talk, as he thought, like a great doctor.

And so after he continued in his heresies, until upon a time, Sir Thomas More privately talked in his garden with his daughter Margaret, and amongst other his sayings said: 'Meg, I have borne a long time with thy husband; I have reasoned and argued with him in those points of religion, and still given to him my poor fatherly counsel; but I perceive none of all this able to call him home; and, therefore, Meg, I will no longer argue nor dispute with him, but will clean give him over, and get me another while to God and pray for him.' And soon after, as he verily believed, through the mercy of God, at the devout prayer of Sir Thomas More, he perceived his own ignorance, oversight [error], malice and folly, and turned him again to the Catholic faith, wherein, God be thanked, he hath hitherto continued.[6]

Roper himself does not record his lapse, but Harpsfield must have been sure of his information, probably derived from Roper, before including such an account in a book dedicated to 'the right worshipful Master William Roper.' It must have been soon after his return to the faith of his fathers, that Roper had a significant conversation with Sir Thomas More.

It fortuned before the matter of the said matrimony [of Henry] brought in question, when I, in talk with Sir Thomas More, of a certain joy commended unto him the happy estate of this Realm, that had so Catholic a prince that no heretic durst show his face, so virtuous and learned a clergy, so grave and sound a nobility, and so loving obedient subjects, all in one faith agreeing together. 'Truth it is indeed, son Roper,' quoth he, and in commending all degrees and estates of the same went far beyond me. 'And yet, son Roper, I pray God,' said he, 'that some of us, as high as we seem to sit upon the mountains, treading heretics under our feet like ants, live not

---

[6] *Harpsfield*, pp. 86-8.

the day that we gladly would wish to be at a league and composition with them, to let them have their churches quietly to themselves, so that they would be content to let us have ours quietly to ourselves.' After that I had told him many considerations why he had no cause so to say: 'Well.' said he, 'I pray God, son Roper, some of us live not till that day,' showing me no reason why he should put any doubt therein. To whom I said, 'By my troth, sir, it is very desperately spoken.' That vile term, I cry God mercy, did I give him. Who, by these words perceiving me in a fume, said merrily unto me, 'Well, well, son Roper, it shall not be so, it shall not be so.' Whom in sixteen years and more, being in the house conversant with him, I could never perceive as much as once in a fume.[7]

More appreciated the course of future events with greater insight than was shown in Roper's optimism which was not in keeping even with his own experience of the spreading of Lutheranism.

Such action as the Church was able to take did not substantially affect the increase in heresy. Wolsey had been present when confiscated books had been burned in St. Paul's Churchyard in May 1521; Bishop John Fisher had then preached against 'the pernicious doctrine of Martin Luther.' It seems probable that Sir Thomas More was present;[8] Richard Pace translated the sermon into Latin. Heretics were brought before the Bishops, and More mentions that he was present at some of these examinations. Most of the heretics were persuaded to recant and do penance. The position did not, however, become really serious until the unorganized groups found a spokesman in William Tyndale.

---

[7] *Roper*, pp. 34-6.

[8] *Confutation*, E.W., p. 410, and below p. 244.

In 1523 he sought to become one of Tunstal's chaplains, but the Bishop already had four and could not afford a fifth. There is no evidence that Tyndale discussed with the Bishop the project of an English translation of the New Testament, but Tyndale never forgave Tunstal and later called him 'a ducking hypocrite made to dissemble.' Tyndale left England in 1524 and never returned, but from abroad he poured into the country his translations and controversial writings. His clear style and his ability to keep within readable length in controversy gave his writings an influence that a more verbose author would have lacked. It was by these books and pamphlets that he became the rallying point for the English protestants.

His translation of the New Testament was on sale in London early in 1526. Tunstal ordered all copies to be confiscated and those collected were burned. Archbishop Warham tried to buy up the edition, but this had little effect. When Tunstal and More stopped in Antwerp on their return from Cambrai, the Bishop bought as many copies of the New Testament as he could, but the money provided funds for further editions.

We have seen how Tunstal decided that counter-propaganda was necessary and how in 1528 he authorized Sir Thomas More to refute the new doctrines. Both of them had tried to persuade Erasmus to write more vigorously against Luther. The scholar's *Essay on Free Will* (1524) had been a study of the problem of Free Will as shown in the scriptures. It was not a violent attack on Luther but a considered discussion of a fundamental question. It struck at the despairing doctrine of predestination that was one of the tenets of the new teaching. Luther was quick to answer with his *De Servo Arbitrio* in which he bitterly attacked Erasmus himself. The great scholar was sensitive to such treatment and in the first part of *Hyperaspistes* (1526) he defended himself against such insults. Thomas More wrote to urge him to write the promised second part of this work and to speak out more strongly against Luther's teaching. The letter was written from Chelsea in

December 1526; at the end it announced the arrival of Holbein. More did not hesitate to chide his old friend with a lack of courage. He had heard, he wrote, that the delay in the promised second part of *Hyperaspistes* was due to fear.

> O my dearest Erasmus, God forbid that, after all your Herculean labours and your dangers, after all the toils and vigils to benefit the world, in which you have spent the best years of your life, you should begin now so miserably to love these sick souls, that rather than be defeated in controversy, you keep silence... You have answered his [Luther's] calumnies against yourself, and transfixed him with your pen; there now remains only to treat the passages of Holy Scripture; and since in the thousand copies of your first part you have promised the world, as by so many bonds, that you would diligently execute that second part, you cannot refuse to pursue the cause of God after having successfully achieved your own, or to perform what you have publicly promised, especially since you can do it so easily.[9]

Erasmus published the second part of *Hyperaspistes* in 1527, and perhaps as the result of More's letter, he made a more outspoken attack on Luther's teaching on the relationship between God and Man. That was the last book Erasmus wrote in direct refutation of Luther.

Thomas More's aim in carrying out Tunstal's wishes was to appeal to the lettered but unlearned public that had proved so susceptible to the teachings of the Lutherans. The *Dialogue Concerning Heresies* (1529) was not a learned theological treatise; he would indeed have denied that he had the knowledge for such a task; he produced instead a readable argument put in his favourite form of a discussion. He supposed that a friend had sent him a young man (the Messenger) who wished to discuss some of

---

[9] *Allen*, VI, 1770.

the notions that were being spread about concerning the Church and its teaching. The frequent use of 'quoth he' and 'quoth I' led Tyndale to refer to the *Dialogue* as 'Quoth I, and quoth he, and quoth your friend.' The setting is not unlike that of *Utopia*.

> Nay, quoth he, it were better ye dine first. My lady will, I wene, be angry with me that I keep you so long therefrom. For I hold it now well toward twelve. And yet more angry would she wax with me if I should make you sit and muse at your meat—as ye would, I wot well, muse on the matter, if we wist what it were.
>
> If I were, quoth I, like my wife, I should muse thereon now and eat no meat for longing to know. But come on then and let us dine first and ye shall tell after.
>
> After dinner, we walked in the garden, and there shortly sitting in an arbour began to go forth in our matter.[10]

This *Dialogue* went into a second edition in 1530, and More was then able to add passages referring to Tyndale's Answer to the first edition. The full title indicates the scope of the book: 'Wherein be treated divers matters, as of the veneration of and worship of images and relics, praying to saints and going on pilgrimage, with many other things touching the pestilent sect of Luther and Tyndale, by the one begun in Saxony, and by the other laboured to be brought into England.'

It is not proposed here to attempt a summary of this book nor of any of More's controversial writings; the arguments he puts forward are orthodox; he supports them by frequent references to the Gospels and to the Epistles of St. Paul, and to the writings of the early Fathers, especially to his beloved St. Austin. It will give a better idea of his method if we see how he dealt with a specific topic.

One subject comes up again and again in this Dialogue: the

---

[10] *E.W.*, p. 177; II, pp. 128-129.

Bible, its authority, its interpretation, its translation and dissemination. First he emphasized the fact that the Church was instituted before the Gospels were written, and it was the Church that decided the canon of the scriptures.

And therefore sayeth holy Saint Austin, 'I should not believe the Gospel, but if it were for the Church.' And he sayeth good reason. For were it not for the spirit of God keeping the truth thereof in his church, who could be sure which were the very gospels? There were many that wrote that gospel. And yet hath the church, by secret instruction of God, rejected the remnant and chosen out these four for the sure undoubted true.

That is, quoth he, sure so.

This is, quoth I, so sure so, that Luther himself is driven of necessity to grant this, or else he perceiveth that there were none hold nor surety in scripture itself, if the church might be suffered by God to be deceived in that point, and to take for holy scripture that writing that indeed were not. And therefore he confesseth that this must needs be a sure infallible ground that God had given this gift unto his church, that his church can always discern the word of God from the word of men.

In good faith, quoth he, that must needs be so, or else all would fail.

Quoth I, then ye that would believe the church in no thing, nor give sure credence to the tradition of the church but if it were proved by scripture, now see it proved to you that ye could not believe the scripture but if it were proved to be scripture by the judgement and tradition of the church.

No, quoth he, but when I have learned once of the church that it is holy scripture and the word of God, then I believe it better than I believe all the church. I might by a light person sometime know a much more substantial man. And yet when I know him, I will believe him much better than him by whom

I know him, if they varied in a tale and were contrary.

Good reason, quoth I. But the church biddeth you not to believe the contrary of that the scripture sayeth. But he telleth you that in such places as ye would better believe the scripture than the church, there ye understand not the scripture. For whatsoever words it speaketh, yet it meaneth not the contrary of that the church teacheth you. And the church cannot be deceived in any such weighty point.

Whereby shall I know, quoth he?

Why be we at that point yet, quoth I? Have we so soon forgotten the perpetual assistance of the Trinity in his church, and the prayer of Christ to keep the faith of his church from failing, and the Holy Ghost sent of purpose to keep in the church the remembrance of Christ's words and to lead them into all truth?[11]

More was fearful of the private interpretations that the unlearned would read into the Bible; he saw the dangers of a 'pot parliament' in which the inexperienced readers argued amongst themselves. 'For it is a thing that requireth good help, and long time, and an whole mind given greatly thereto.'[12] The reading of the Gospel stories was one thing, but the reading of the Epistle to the Romans another. More put the emphasis on the Gospels and the Epistles in accordance with Catholic practice.[13] The first lesson at Mass is usually from one of the Epistles, and rarely from

---

[11] *E.W.*, p. 175; III, pp. 124-5.

[12] *E.W.*, p. 242; II, p. 245.

[13] 'There had been numerous partial translations of the scriptures in England, right back into Anglo-Saxon times. ... But these had been made for didactic purposes for unlearned clergy or in the instruction of lay people: and they had been limited to those parts of scripture useful for such ends, the gospels, the epistles, the psalms. ... There was, altogether, quite a good deal of biblical translation. It occurred to no one, however, to translate the whole Bible for pastoral purposes: why should it?' M. Deanesley. *The Significance of the Lollard Bible* (1951), pp. 4-5.

the Old Testament. The Psalms have always held an important place in the liturgy. The second lesson at Mass is invariably from one of the Gospels. One unforeseen result of the dissemination of the Bible in English was the increased and even unbalanced emphasis put upon the Old Testament; this led to strange applications and interpretations by extreme Protestants and Puritans.

The Messenger asked More why Tyndale's New Testament had been burned.

> It is, quoth I, to me a great marvel that any good Christian man having any drop of wit in his head, would anything marvel or complain of the burning of that book, if he know the matter. Which whoso calleth the New Testament calleth it by a wrong name, except they will call it Tyndale's Testament or Luther's Testament. For so had Tyndale, after Luther's counsel, corrupted and changed it from the good and wholesome doctrine of Christ to the devilish heresies of their own, that it was clean a contrary thing.
>
> That were marvel, quoth your friend, that it should be so clean contrary. For to some that read it, it seemed very like.
>
> It is, quoth I, nevertheless contrary; and yet the more perilous. For like as to a silver groat as a false copper groat is, never the less contrary though it be quick silvered all over; but so much the more false in how much it is counterfeited the more like to the truth; so was the translation so much the more contrary, in how much it was craftily devised like; so much the more perilous, in how much it was to folk unlearned more hard to be discerned. Why, quoth your friend, what faults were there in it?
>
> To tell you all that, quoth I, were in a manner to rehearse you all the whole book wherein there was founden and noted wrong and falsely translated above a thousand texts by tale.
>
> I would, quoth he, fain hear some one.
>
> He that should, quoth I, study for that, should study where

to find water in the sea. But I will show you for example two or three such as everyone of the three is more than thrice three in one.

That were, quoth he, very strange except ye mean more by weight, for one can be but one in number.

Surely, quoth I, as weighty be they as any lightly can be. But I mean that everyone of them is more than thrice three in number.

That were, quoth he, somewhat like a riddle.

This riddle, quoth I, will soon be read. For he hath mistranslated three words of great weight and every one of them is, as I suppose, more than thrice three times repeated and rehearsed in the book.

Ah that may well be, quoth he, but that was not well done. But I pray you, what words be they?

The one is, quoth I, this word, priests. The other the Church. The third Charity. For priests whereso he speaketh of the priests of Christ's Church, he never calleth them Priests but always seniors. The Church he calleth alway the congregation, and Charity he calleth love. Now do these names in our English tongue neither express the things be meant by them, and also there appeareth, the circumstances well considered, that he had a mischievous mind in the change.[14]

More then developed this criticism in greater detail. This led the Messenger to say,

But surely the thing that maketh in this matter the clergy most suspect, and wherein, as it seemeth, it would be full hard to excuse them is this, that they not only damn Tyndale's translation (wherein there is good cause) but over that do damn all other, and as though a layman were no Christian

---

[14] *E.W.*, pp. 220-1; II, pp. 206-7.

man, will suffer no layman have any at all. But when they find any in his keeping, they lay heresy to him therefore. And thereupon they burn up the book, and sometime the good men withal, alleging for the defence of their doing a law of their own making and constitution provincial, whereby they have prohibited that any man shall have any upon pain of heresy.[15]

More had no difficulty in showing that the constitution referred to, that of Archbishop Arundel in 1408, was misunderstood; it enacted that only translations that had been approved by the Bishops were permissible. He was quite definite on the subject.

And therefore, as I say forsooth, I can in no wise agree with you that it were meet for men unlearned to be busy with chamming[16] of holy scripture, but to have it chammed[17] unto them. For that is the preacher's part, and theirs that after long study are admitted to read and expound it. And to this extent weigh all the words, as far as I perceive, of all holy doctors that anything have written in this matter. But never meant they, as I suppose, the forbidding of the Bible to be read in any vulgar tongue. Nor I never yet heard any reason laid why it were not convenient to have the Bible translated into the English tongue. ...

There is no treatise of scripture so hard but that a good virtuous man, or woman either, shall somewhat find therein that shall delight and increase their devotion. Besides this that every preaching shall be the more pleasant and fruitful unto them when they have in their mind the place of scripture that they shall there hear expounded. For though it be, as it is

---

[15] *E.W.*, p. 214; II, pp. 213-14.

[16] Chewing over.

[17] Pre-digested as it were.

indeed, great wisdom for a preacher to use discretion in his preaching, and to have a respect unto the qualities and capacities of his audience, yet letteth that nothing but that the whole audience may without harm have read and have ready the scripture in mind that he shall in his preaching declare and expound. For no doubt is there but that God and his Holy Spirit hath so prudently tempered their speech through the whole corps of scripture that every man may take good thereby and no man harm but he that will in the study thereof lean proudly to the folly of his own wit.[18]

That last phrase 'lean proudly to the folly of his own wit' is the clue to More's though on this subject; one of the charges he made against the Lutherans and Tyndalists was that in their pride they relied too much on their own wits and not enough on the centuries of study and meditation that preceded them.

The *Dialogue* ends with a prayer that God may

send these seditious sects the grace to cease, and the favourers of those factions to amend, and us the grace that stopping our ears from the false enchantments of all these heretics, we may, by the very faith of Christ's Catholic Church, so walk with charity in the way of good works in this wretched world, that we may be partners of the heavenly bliss, which the blood of God's own son hath brought us unto.

And this prayer, quoth I, serving us for grace let us now sit down to dinner, which we did. And after dinner departed he home toward you, and I to the court.

No sooner was this work finished than Thomas More turned his attention to a short pamphlet *A supplication for the Beggars* which was probably written by Simon Fish and published in 1529. The reputed author was known as a colporteur of Tyndale's New Testament. This slanderous diatribe against the clergy is said to

---

[18] *E.W.*, p.243; II, p. 247.

have found a sympathetic reader in Henry VIII.[19] The beggars claim that they cannot get alms for their support because the clergy take most of the wealth of the country for themselves. Then follows a series of wild statements about the extortionate demands of these 'wolves'; as an example he calculated that the friars alone gathered in £43,333 6s. 8d. a year! Even the commissioners who paved the way for the dissolution, found that most of the friaries were so poor they could not pay the visitation fee. The attack made by Fish on the wealth of the clergy would have been justified if directed at such pluralists as Wolsey; the parish priests were poor men. So the author went on to refer to the Hunne case, the celebacy of the clergy, their vice and dissipation, prayers for souls in purgatory, the withholding of the New Testament in English, the statute of mortmain, and so on. His solution was to take away the property of the clergy and make them labour for their living. Into a dozen pages he compressed the most bitter of the irresponsible accusations made against the clergy. Such a hotchpotch of abuse could not be answered briefly, and Sir Thomas More needed ten times the space that Fish used.

The Supplication of Souls imagines the souls in purgatory pleading that they should not be deprived of the prayers of the living. More dealt with the charges made by Fish, such as the ill-living of the clergy, the dissemination of Tyndale's New Testament, and the Hunne case. He saw, however, that at the root of this abuse lay opposition not so much to the clergy as to the faith and authority of the Church; he therefore devoted much space to an exposition of the doctrine of Purgatory. He lightened his discussion with the humorous and imaginative expression that was typical of him. Thus he tells a story of 'a lewd gallant and a friar.'

---

[19] According to Foxe's story of Simon Fish in *Acts and Monuments*. The *Supplication for the Beggars* was reprinted by the E.E.T.S., 1871.

Whom when the gallant saw going barefoot in a great frost and snow, he asked him why he did take such pain. And he answered that it was very little pain if a man would remember hell. 'Yea, friar,' quoth the gallant, 'but what an there be none hell, then art thou a great fool.' 'Yea, master,' quoth the friar, 'but what an there be hell, then is your mastership a much more fool.'[20]

More maintained the fiction of writing as if he represented the souls in purgatory, and from this imagined viewpoint he was able to make his reader more aware of the relationship between the living and the dead. So the souls speak of the evil angels who punish them.

> And yet the despiteful sights that our evil angels bring us to behold abroad, so far augmenteth our torment, that we would wish to be drowned in the darkness that is here, rather than see the sights that they show us there. For they convey us into our own houses, and there double is our pain, with spite sometimes of the self-same thing, which while we lived was half our heaven to behold. There show they us our substance and our bags stuffed with gold, which, when we see, we set much less by them than would an old man that found a bag of cherry stones which he had laid up when he was a child. What a sorrow hath it been to some of us when the devils hath in despiteful mockage cast in our teeth our old love borne to our money, and then showed us our executors as busily rifling and ransacking our homes as though they were men of war that had taken a town by force.[21]

Or they see their wives 'waxen wanton and forgetting us their old husbands. . . .'

Yet we hear sometimes our wives pray for us warmly; for

---

[20] *E.W.*, p. 329.

[21] *E.W.*, p. 336.

in chiding with her second husband, to spite him withal, 'God have mercy.' saith she, 'on my first husband's soul, for he was a wise and honest man, far unlike you.' And then marvel we much when we hear them say so well of us, for they were ever wont to tell us far otherwise.[22]

There is true pathos in the last words of the *Supplication*.

If any point of your old favour, any piece of your old love, any kindness of kindred, any care of acquaintance, any favour of old friendship, any spark of charity, any tender point of pity, any regard of nature, any respect of Christendom, be left in your hearts, let never the malice of a few fond fellows, a few pestilent persons borne towards priesthood, religion, and your Christian faith, rase out of your hearts the care of your kindred, all force of your old friends, and all remembrance of all Christian souls. Remember our thirst while ye sit and drink; our hunger while ye be feasting; our restless watch while ye be sleeping; our sore and grievous pain while ye be playing; our hot burning fire while ye be in pleasure and sporting; so mote God make your offspring after remember you; so God keep you hence, or not here, but bring you shortly to that bliss, to which for our lord's love help you to bring us, and we shall set hand to help you thither to us.[23]

It was probably soon after Sir Thomas More had written those lines that he was called to yet greater service in the State.

---

[22] *Ibid.*

[23] *E.W.*, p. 339.

Chapter XVIII

Lord Chancellor

DURING the absence of Sir Thomas More at Cambrai in July and August 1529, 'the king's matter' had reached a crisis. On 23rd July Cardinal Campeggio prorogued the Court for the period of the Roman vacation; most men must have realized that this in effect meant that it would not sit again. This belief was confirmed when the Pope advoked the case to Rome. The feeling of many was expressed by the Duke of Suffolk: 'It was never merry in England whilst we had Cardinals among us.'[1] Campeggio had achieved the Pope's purpose—to put off a decision as long as possible.

Wolsey had failed the king. During the next three months the Cardinal's future was uncertain; his enemies, gathering for the attack, were alarmed when he had a long audience with the king; one would like to think that Henry's hesitations were due to gratitude for the services Wolsey had rendered him, but the end came on 19th October when the Lord Chancellor had to deliver up the Great Seal. Hall recorded that,

> The twenty and three day of October, the King came to his manor of Greenwich, and there much consulted with his Council for a meet man to be his Chancellor, so that in no wise he were no man of the Spirituality, and so after long debate the King resoluted himself upon Sir Thomas More, Knight, a man well learned in the tongues, and also in the

---

[1] Compare the Duke of Norfolk's statement that he 'had never read the scriptures, nor never would, and it was a merry England before this new learning came up.' L.P., xvi, 101.

Common Law, whose wit was fine, and full of imaginations, by reason whereof he was much given to mocking, which was to his gravity a great blemish.[2]

Roper stated that the king appointed More 'the rather to move him to incline to his side.'[3] In the fragment of William Rastell's biography of his uncle, both reasons are given for the choice of a layman as Lord Chancellor.

> After the death of Cardinal Wolsey, the King, not determining to have any of the spirituality to be Lord Chancellor, offered it to Sir Thomas More, who refusing it, the King was angry with him and caused him to accept it, and laboured to have him persuaded on his side in the matter of his divorce, and because he could not be persuaded, he hated.[4]

The combination of Cardinal-Archbishop-Chancellor had put too much power into the hands of one subject and had made it more difficult for that separation of State from Church that was necessary if Henry's plans were to be carried out; he intended to be in control of both State and Church, but to keep each in its own sphere of policy and influence.

It would have been surprising if More had welcomed such advancement; in spite of the king's promise that his conscience should not be troubled, More knew how unscrupulous the king could be in gaining his own ends;[5] sooner or later a clash was bound to come on the marriage question.

---

[2] *Hall*, II, p. 158.

[3] *Roper*, p. 39. More was not, as is sometimes said, the first layman to be Lord Chancellor; there were six such Chancellors between 1341 and 1455; their periods of office were usually brief.

[4] *Harpsfield*, p. 222. Rastell is in error, as More's appointment preceded the Cardinal's death by a year.

[5] Such also was Wolsey's experience as recorded by Cavendish. 'Rather than he [Henry] will either miss or want any part of his will or appetite, he will put the loss of one half of his realm in danger' (p. 245).

Lord Chancellor

The appointment was generally welcomed. Eustache Chapuys, the Imperial Ambassador, reported that 'everyone is delighted at his promotion, because he is an upright and learned man and a good servant of the Queen.'[6]

A few days after his appointment, Sir Thomas More wrote a short letter to Erasmus '*ex rusculo nostro.*' He did not say that he had become Lord Chancellor, but alluded to further state employment he was to undertake, and added, 'you who are wont to consider affairs cautiously and shrewdly will, no doubt, pity my lot.'[7]

It is unfortunate that only this and two other letters from More to Erasmus have survived for this last period, and there is only one from Erasmus. Other letters may have perished, but there is no reason to think that the friendship between the two men had cooled. It became increasingly dangerous for them to write with complete freedom; one was the servant of Henry VIII and the other of the Emperor. The link between them was maintained by more personal means. Nearly every year Erasmus used to send one of his secretaries on a tour of the Low Countries and England and these envoys visited his friends and gathered their news and their opinions for their master's benefit.[8] More was glad to receive them at Chelsea as his guests and it was in this way, for instance, that Erasmus learned so much of the life in that country retreat. On one point he was misinformed. Writing to John Faber at the end of 1532, Erasmus stated that Wolsey had suggested More as his successor. It is most unlikely that Wolsey's opinion was asked. He may have made some comment after the appointment as that given in Henry VIII.

Cromwell. Sir Thomas More is chosen Lord Chancellor in

---

[6] *L.P.,* IV, 6026.

[7] *Allen,* VIII, 2228.

[8] De Vocth, *Acta Thomae Mori* (1947), pp. 77-8.

your place.

Wolsey. That's somewhat sudden: But he's a learned man.[9]

Erasmus was possibly correct when he added that 'while he was living the Cardinal was affable enough to More, though in fact he feared rather than loved him.' Wolsey was not fond of men who had the ear of the king.

More's installation took place in the Chancery Court, which was then in the south-west corner of Westminster Hall. Roper's account reads like that of an eye-witness, and perhaps other members of the new Chancellor's household were amongst 'the people there assembled.'

> Who, between the Dukes of Norfolk and Suffolk, being brought through Westminster Hall to his place in the Chancery, the Duke of Norfolk, in audience of all the people there assembled, showed that he was from the King himself straightly charged, by special commission, there openly, in the presence of them all, to make declaration how much all England was beholding to Sir Thomas More for his good service, and how worthy he was to have the highest room in the realm, and how dearly his Grace loved and trusted him, for which, said the duke, he had great cause to rejoice. Whereunto Sir Thomas More, among many other his humble and wise sayings not now in my memory, answered, that although he had good cause to take comfort of his Highness's singular favour towards him, that he had, far above his deserts, so highly commended him, to whom therefore he acknowledged himself most deeply bounden, yet, nevertheless, he must for his own part needs confess that in all things by his Grace alleged he had done no more than was his duty, and further disabled himself as unmeet for that room, wherein, considering how wise and honourable a

---

[9] III, ii.

prelate had lately taken so great a fall, he had, he said, thereof no cause to rejoice. And as they had before on the King's behalf, charged him uprightly to minister indifferent justice to the people, without corruption or affection, so did he likewise charge them again that if they saw him, at any time, in anything, digress from any part of his duty in that honourable office, even as they would discharge their own duty and fidelity to God and the King, so should they not fail to disclose it to his Grace, who otherwise might have just occasion to lay his fault wholly to their charge.

Parliament was summoned to meet on 3rd November; it was not dissolved until April (Good Friday) 1536, and has become known as the Reformation Parliament. It met at Blackfriars, but as the plague broke out in London, it moved to Westminster.[10] Sir Thomas More as Lord Chancellor presided over the deliberations in the Lords, but as a commoner he had no vote. The picture of the opening of the 1523 Parliament probably sets the scene for the Parliament of 1529. Instead of Tunstal at the King's right hand, stood Sir Thomas More; the aged Warham, now nearing his eightieth year, would be seated where the Cardinal had sat; amongst the judges would be Sir John More.

The Lord Chancellor delivered the King's speech, which, in those days, was not a pronouncement of government policy, but an expression of the King's opinions. The authenticity of Hall's report has been questioned, but it is largely confirmed by a brief account sent by Chapuys to Charles V. The attack on Wolsey, who was still alive, seems unworthy of his successor, but our modern code of manners towards fallen opponents would have

---

[10] This proved a decisive move as Parliament has met at Westminster since 1529. This Parliament marked an advance in the prestige and influence of the Commons not only because Henry made greater use of them, but because its length, seven years, meant the development of a corporate feeling unknown in the rarely summoned and brief Parliaments of the past.

seemed finical and even hypocritical in Tudor times. Opponents in controversy did not spare each other in abuse, and, regret it as we may, More gave blow for blow. This speech may not have expressed his full opinion of Wolsey whose early career he had warmly commended; there can be less doubt that it expressed the vindictiveness of the King. Hall's report reads:

> ... the King with all the Lords of the Parliament, and Commons which were summoned to appear at that day came into the Parliament chamber, where the King sat in his throne or seat royal, and Sir Thomas More his Chancellor standing on the right hand of the King behind the bar, made an eloquent oration, declaring that like as a good shepherd which not only keepeth and tendeth well his sheep, but also foreseeth and provideth for all things which either may be hurtful or noisesome to his flock, or may preserve and defend the same against all perils that may chance to come, so the King, which was the shepherd, ruler and governor of his realm, vigilantly foreseeing things to come, considered how divers laws before this time were made now by long continuance of time and mutation of things, very insufficient and unperfect, and also by frail condition of man, divers new enormities were sprung up amongst the people for which no law was yet made to reform the same, which was the very cause why the King had summoned his high court of Parliament, and he resembled the King to a shepherd, or herdman, for this cause, for if a prince be compared to his riches, he is but a rich man, if a prince be compared to his honour, he is but an honourable man, but compare him to the multitude of his people and the number of his flock, then he is a ruler, a governor of might and puissance, so that his people maketh him a prince, as of the multitude of sheep, cometh the name of shepherd; and as you see that amongst a great flock of sheep some be rotten and faulty which the good shepherd sendeth from the good sheep, so the great wether which is of

late fallen as you all know, so crafty, so scabbedly, yea and so untruly juggled with the King that all men must needs guess and think that he thought in himself, that they had no wit to perceive his crafty doing, or else that he presumed that the King would not see nor know his fraudulent juggling and attempts; but he was deceived, for his Grace's sight was so quick and penetrable, that he saw him, yea and saw through him, both within and without, so that all thing to him was open, and according to his desert he hath had a gentle correction, which small punishment the King will not to be an example to other offenders, but clearly declareth that whosoever hereafter shall make like attempt to commit like offence, shall not escape with like punishment, and because you of the Common House be a gross multitude and cannot speak all at one time, therefore the King's pleasure is that you shall resort to the nether house and there among yourselves according to the old and ancient custom to choose an able person to be your common mouth and speaker, and after your election so made to advertise his Grace thereof, which will declare to you his pleasure what day he will have him present in this place.[11]

The Commons chose (or accepted) Thomas Audley as Speaker; he was 'a submissive instrument in the hands of Henry VIII and 'a man of low moral tone.'[12] Amongst the members were a number of More's relatives and connexions: his brother-in-law, John Rastell, sat for a Cornish borough; his three sons-in-law, William Roper, Giles Heron, and William Daunce were elected, the first for Bramber, and the other two for Thetford; Sir Giles Alington, husband of More's stepdaughter, sat for

---

[11] The Parliament Chamber was the Upper Frater of the Priory; the Commons met in a lower (nether) chamber. This seems the origin of the terms 'Upper' and 'Lower' House.

[12] D.N.B.

Cambridgeshire.

Historians are not agreed as to how far this House of Commons was packed by supporters of the King.[13] All the Tudor Parliaments contained some members who were, in effect, nominated by the Crown or by powerful nobles, but there were always others who were not complaisant servants. In this Parliament, for instance, as late as 1532, one member named Temse openly urged that the King should take back his true wife Catherine. Hall stated that 'the most part of the Commons were the king's servants;'[14] as a supporter of the king's policy he would hardly have said that without reason. Rastell overstated his case in writing,

> The king summoned a Parliament, and chose for knights and burgesses not only heretics, but also such as he and his Council were persuaded to malign the clergy and their wealth, and namely divers of his own councillors and household servants and their servants.[15]

There is a phrase in Sir Thomas More's speech at his trial that has been interpreted as a reflection on the composition of this Parliament. 'And for one Council or Parliament of yours (God knoweth what manner of one) I have all the Councils made these thousand years.' The words, 'God knoweth what manner of one,' may be a comment on the work carried out by the Parliament rather than a censure of its composition, a subject on which he may not have held exceptional opinions. He would be unaware of the significance of Henry's policy in using the Commons rather than the Lords (with an ecclesiastical majority) for the furtherance of his plans. After 1532 the skilled management of

---

[13] On this topic, see J.E. Neale, *The Elizabethan House of Commons* (1949), pp. 282-4; also J.D. Mackie, *The Earlier Tudors* (1952), pp. 349-50.

[14] *Hall*, II, p. 169.

[15] *Harpsfield*, p. 222.

Thomas Cromwell ensured that the original 1529 membership of the Commons was increasingly strengthened as an instrument of the King's will; new constituencies were created, and where changes became necessary by death or resignation, Cromwell saw to it that safe men were elected.[16] But to whatever degree the membership was influenced by the King, it must be recognized that the anticlerical legislation had popular opinion behind it.

Sir Thomas More had far less influence on affairs than Wolsey had exercised. There are no records of the discussions within the Council, so it cannot be known to what lengths he may have gone in opposing some, and modifying other, proposals.

On one matter he hoped that his position was recognized; he stood apart from all discussion on the king's marriage, but his silence was a constant irritant to the king.

The first occasion on which the matter was discussed between them has already been noted. Roper records two later discussions, and Harpsfield three. A careful comparison of these accounts with More's letter to Cromwell in 1534 suggests that they, in fact, refer to two occasions, the first on More's return from Amiens in the autumn of 1527, and the second soon after his appointment as Chancellor.[17] More's own account of this second discussion must be given at length as it provides the clue to much that was to follow.

> And after my coming home [from Cambrai] his Highness of his only goodness (as far unworthy as I was thereto) made me, as you well know, his Chancellor of this realm, soon after

---

[16] Thus in January 1534 there were forty vacancies to be filled.

[17] The four occasions were: (1) *Roper*, p. 31; *Harpsfield*, p. 44; (2) *Harpsfield*, p. 47; (3) *Roper*, p. 37; *Harpsfield*, p. 48; (4) *Roper*, p. 49; *Harpsfield*, p. 49. Harpsfield has, I think, made two occasions out of the first. Roper's reference to Stokesley in the third account, 'whom he had then preferred to the Bishop of London,' places this consultation after July 1530 when Stokesley was consecrated and nine months after More became Chancellor. This suggests the third and fourth occasions were in fact the one described by More as coming soon after his appointment. Stapleton follows More's account.

which time his Grace moved me again yet eftsoons to look and consider his great matter, and well and indifferently to ponder such things as I should find therein. And if it so were that thereupon it should hap me to see such things as should persuade me to that part, he would gladly use me among other of his councillors in that matter, and nevertheless he graciously declared unto me that he would in no wise that I should other thing do or say therein, than upon that that I should perceive mine own conscience should serve me, and that I should first look to God and after God unto him, which most gracious words was the first lesson also that ever his Grace gave me at my first coming into his noble service. This motion was to me very comfortable and much I longed beside any thing that myself either had seen, or by further search should hap to find for the one part or the other, yet specially to have some conference in the matter with some such of his Grace's learned Council as most for his part had laboured and most have found in the matter.

Whereupon his Highness assigned unto me the now most reverend fathers Archbishops of Canterbury and York with Mr. Doctor Fox now his Grace's Almoner, and Dr. Nicholas the Italian friar,[18] whereupon I not only sought and read, and as far forth as my poor wit and learning served me, well weighed and considered every such thing as I could find myself, or read in any other man's labour that I could get, which anything had written therein, but had also diligent conference with his Grace's councillors aforesaid, whose honour and worship I no thing mistrust in this point, but that they both have and will report unto his Highness that they never found obstinate manner or fashion in me, but a mind as

---

[18] Cranmer, Edward Lee, Edward Fox and Nicholas de Burgo: the last was Reader in Divinity at Oxford (D.N.B.). With Stokesley and Fox, he edited the opinions of the French and Italian Universities on the divorce; this book was translated into English by Cranmer.

toward and as conformable as reason could in a matter disputable require.

Whereupon the King's Highness being further advertised both by them and myself of my poor opinion in the matter (wherein to have been able and meet to do him service I would as I then showed his Highness have been more glad than of all such worldly commodities as I either then had or ever should come to) his Highness graciously taking in good part my good mind in that behalf used of his blessed disposition in the prosecuting of his great matter only those (of whom his Grace had good number) whose conscience his Grace perceived well and fully persuaded upon that part, and as well as myself as any other to whom his Highness thought the thing to seem otherwise, he used in his other business, abiding (of his abundant goodness) never the less gracious lord unto any man, nor never was willing to put any man to ruffle or trouble his conscience.

After this did I never no thing more therein, nor never any word wrote I therein to the impairing of his Grace's part neither before nor after, nor any man else by my procurement, but settling my mind in quiet to serve his Grace in other things I would not so much as look or wittingly let lie by me any book of the other part.[19]

The care with which More kept apart from discussions on the divorce is shown in his relations with Chapuys, the Imperial Ambassador who was a warm supporter of Catherine. More not only asked Chapuys not to visit him, but refused to receive a letter from the Emperor. Such a letter, he said, he must in duty show to the King, and any suggestion that he was in communication with the Queen's nephew 'might deprive him of the liberty he had always used in speaking boldly to King Henry

---

[19] *Rogers*, pp. 495-6.

in those matters which concerned Charles and Queen Catherine of Arragon.'[20]

The 'other things' in which Sir Thomas More served the King included his judicial work as Chancellor, and in this he must have found his chief satisfaction. His achievement is not recorded in leading judgements but in the tradition he established of even-handed and speedy justice. In this he contributed to the strengthening of public confidence in the law and its administration; that confidence was to be shaken from time to time, but those who, like Sir Thomas More, helped to keep the ideal of justice alive in men's minds, deserved well of the state, and in this lies not the least of his claims to be honoured.

Roper's testimony on this matter has special value as he himself was a lawyer and doubtless he frequently discussed legal questions and cases with his father-in-law as men of the same profession love to do.

> While he was Lord Chancellor, being at leisure (as seldom he was) one of his sons-in-law on a time said merrily unto him, 'When Cardinal Wolsey was Lord Chancellor, not only divers of his privy chamber but such also as were his doorkeepers gat great gain.' And since he had married one of his daughters, and gave still attendance upon him, he thought he might of reason look for some; where he indeed, because he was so ready himself to hear every man, poor and rich, and kept no doors shut from them, could find none, which was to him a great discourage. And whereas else, some for friendship, some for kindred, and some for profit, would gladly have had his furtherance in bringing them to his presence, if he should now take anything of them, he knew he said, he should do them great wrong for that they might do as much for themselves as he could do for them, which

---

[20] *L.P.*, v, 171.

condition, although he thought in Sir Thomas More very commendable, yet to him, he said, being his son, he found it nothing profitable. When he had told him this tale, 'You say well, son.' quoth he. 'I do not mislike that you are of conscience so scrupulous, but many other ways be there, son, that I may both do your self good and pleasure your friend also. For sometime may I by my word stand your friend in stead, and sometime may I by my letter help him; or if he have a cause depending before me, at your request I may hear him before another. Or if his cause be not all the best, yet may I move the parties to fall to some reasonable end by arbitrament. Howbeit, this one thing, son, I assure thee on my faith, that if the parties will at my hands call for justice, then, all were it my father stood on the one side, and the devil on the other, his cause being good, the devil should have right.' So offered he his son, as he thought, he said, as much favour as he could require.[21]

This probably refers to William Daunce as the next incident names Giles Heron.

And that he would for no respect digress from justice well appeared by a plain example of another of his sons-in-law called Master Heron. For when he, having a matter before him in Chancery and presuming too much of his favour, would by him in no wise be persuaded to agree to any indifferent order, then made he in conclusion a flat decree against him.[22]

Roper gives some further details of the Chancellor's ways.

This Lord Chancellor used commonly every afternoon to sit in his open hall [at Chelsea] to the intent that if any persons had any suit unto him, they might the more boldly come to his presence, and there open their complaints before him;

---

[21] *Roper*, p. 40.

[22] *Roper*, p. 42.

whose manner was also to read every bill himself ere he would award any subpoena; which bearing matter sufficient worthy a subpoena would he set his hand unto, or else cancel it.'[23]

Roper also records how the Chancellor reconciled the judges to his methods of mitigating the rigour of the law and lessening its delays.

Stapleton gives the following evidence of Sir Thomas More's efficiency in overcoming unnecessary delays.

> That tribunal [the Chancery] is so overburdened with lawsuits that it scarcely ever happens but there are numberless cases waiting for decision. Indeed when More took Office some cases were still pending which had been introduced twenty years before. But so efficiently and successfully did he carry out his duties that on one occasion—it never happened before or after—having taken his seat and settled a case, he called for the next, to be met with the answer that there was no case outstanding. 'Thanks be to God,' said More, 'that for once this busy tribunal is at rest.' Rising with joy, he ordered the fact to be inscribed in the registers of the Chancery, where it may yet be read.[24]

The charge of being influenced in his judgements by gifts from the litigants was inevitably brought against Sir Thomas More—inevitably, because the practice was so usual that any malcontent could be fairly sure that such a charge would stick; but Chancellor More did not follow the custom of the time. Roper gives three instances.

The first refers to John Parnell against whom Geoffrey and Richard Vaughan brought a suit for withholding goods to which they were entitled. The case had begun in Wolsey's time, and

---

[23] *Roper*, p. 43.

[24] *Stapleton*, p. 27.

finally came before More who decided against Parnell.

This Parnell to his Highness most grievously complained that Sir Thomas More, for making the same decree, had of the same Vaughan (unable for the gout to travel abroad himself) by the hands of his wife taken a fair great gilt cup for a bribe. Who, thereupon, by the King's appointment, being called before the whole Council, where that matter was heinously laid to his charge, forthwith confessed that forasmuch as that cup was, long after the foresaid decree, brought him for a New Year's gift, he, upon her importunate pressing upon him therefore, of courtesy refused not to receive it.

Then the Lord of Wiltshire [father of Anne Boleyn] (for hatred of his religion preferer of this suit) with much rejoicing said unto the lords, 'Lo, did I not tell you, my lords, that you should find this matter true?' Whereupon Sir Thomas More desired their lordships that as they had courteously heard him tell the one part of his tale, so they would vouchsafe of their honours indifferently to hear the other. After which obtained, he further declared unto them that, albeit he had, indeed, with much work, received that cup, yet immediately thereupon he caused his butler to fill it with wine, and of the cup drank to her, and that when he had so done and she pledged him, then as freely as her husband had given it to him, even so freely gave he the same unto her again, to give unto her husband for his New Year's gift, which, at his instant request, though much against her will, at length yet she was fain to receive, as herself, and certain other there presently before them deposed. Thus was the great mountain turned scant to a little molehill.[25]

The second and third incidents also concerned New Year's gifts. The third was the following:

---

[25] *Roper*, p. 61.

And one Master Gresham likewise, having at the same time a cause depending in the Chancery before him, sent him for a New Year's gift a fair gilted cup, the fashion whereof he very well liking, caused one of his own (though not in his fantasy of so good a fashion yet better in value) to be brought him out of his chamber, which he willed the messenger in recompense to deliver to his master, and under other condition would he in no wise receive it.[26]

There are a number of other anecdotes told of More's impartiality and humanity as a judge; not all can be accepted in the form in which they survive, but however far they may deviate from fact, they testify to the reputation he established in popular tradition.

---

[26] *Roper*, p. 63.

Chapter XIX

Tyndale

THE busy life of a Lord Chancellor could not have left Sir Thomas More much leisure, yet he found time to continue his task of refuting heresy. His *Dialogue Concerning Heresies*, published in June 1529 had called a reply from William Tyndale which was published in July 1531 with the title *An Answer unto Sir Thomas More's Dialogue*. The sub-title reads: 'Wherein he [Tyndale] declareth what the church is, and giveth a reason of certain words in the translation of the New Testament. After that he answereth particularly unto every chapter which seemeth to have any appearance of truth through all his four books.'

More must have set to work at once to deal with Tyndale's *Answer*, for the first part of his *Confutation of Tyndale's Answer* was published in the spring of 1532; this contained three books; a second part, of five books, appeared in 1533. Both were printed by William Rastell. When the work was included in the English Works of 1557, part of a ninth book was included though this broke off with the words, 'These things hath (I say) . . .' followed by a note, 'There can no more be found of this ix book written by Sir Thomas More.' Five hundred folio pages of black letter in double column are a deterrent to the modern reader, and his first impression is of the contrast between the lengths to which the two controversialists wrote. Tyndale's book contains some ninety thousand words; More's reply is nearly ten times that length. This prolixity must have limited the effect of the book; a shorter book would have had a wider circulation and the discipline thus imposed on the author would have made the arguments more pointed. There are, of course, passages that capture attention but these become rarer as the pages are turned. It may have been that the cares of state and the strain of reconciling conflicting loyalties made concentration of mind all but impossible. It is certainly true that when the tension was over, and, as he put it, the field was won, More regained his natural ease of style and cheerfulness of spirit.

The most readable part of the *Confutation* is the 'Preface to the Christian Reader.' More there dealt with a number of erroneous and heretical opinions concerning, for instance, the nature of the Church, the relation between faith and good works, prayers to the saints, and the Blessed Sacrament. A digression on 'the devil's stinking martyr,' Thomas Hitton, is not to our modern taste, and is, unhappily, but one result of the increasing exasperation that finds expression in this book. He again stated clearly his attitude towards heresy which he likened to a carbuncle.

> Towards the help whereof, if it haply be incurable, then to the clean cutting out that part for infection of the remnant am I by mine office by virtue of mine oath, and every officer of justice through the realm for his rate, right especially bounden, not in reason only and good congruence, but also by plain ordinance and statute.[1]

He ends the Preface with some good counsel.

> For surely the very best way were neither to read this [book] nor theirs, but rather the people unlearned to occupy themselves beside their other business in prayer, good meditation, and reading of such English books as most may nourish and increase devotion. Of which kind is Bonaventure of the life of Christ, Gerson of the following of Christ, and the

---

[1] *E.W.*, p. 351.

devout contemplative book *Scala Perfectionis* with such other like, than in learning what may well be answered unto heretics.²

The three books he mentioned may not be recognized by the authors and titles given. 'Bonaventure of the life of Christ' was the *Speculum vitæ Christi*. This was printed by Caxton in 1486 and wrongly ascribed to St. Bonaventura; it was written by a Carthusian, Prior Nicholas Love; it was frequently reprinted. Jean le Charlier de Gerson (1363-1429) was believed at that time to be the author of *De Imitatione Christi*; the first English translation was printed by Wynkyn de Worde in 1502; this was by Atkinson and gave the first three books; it was later (c. 1530) superseded by the complete translation by More's friend Richard Whitford and in this form it was beloved of many generations of Catholics. Walter Hilton's *Scala Perfectionis* was widely known in manuscript for many years before it was printed by Wynkyn de Worde in 1494.

It is of interest that More should have selected these three books as devotional reading for 'people unlearned'; they were frequently reprinted during his lifetime and bear witness to the piety of those who could read or of their listeners. He longed for them to continue to give their thoughts to such writings rather than puzzle their wits with controversy.

He reassured those who were not content to ignore the arguments of the day, by saying,

> Yet have I not so slightly seen unto mine own [book] nor shoffled it up so hastily, nor let it so pass unlooked over by better men and better learned also than myself, but that I trust in God it may among the better stand yet in some good stead.³

Beginning with Tyndale's Preface, More dealt with the

---

² *E.W.*, p. 356.

³ *E.W.*, p. 357.

Answer chapter by chapter and almost paragraph by paragraph. He quotes three-quarters of Tyndale's book with scrupulous accuracy. As an example of the method one of the shorter exchanges may be given. This deals with the use of 'love' and 'charity.'

Tyndale

Finally, I say not, charity God, or charity your neighbour, but, love God, and love your neighbour.[4]

More

This is a pretty point of juggling, by which he would make the reader look aside that himself might play a false cast the while, and men should see wherein the question standeth. For he maketh as though I reproved that he hath this word love in his translation in any place at all, where I neither so said, nor so thought. But the fault I found, as in my dialogue I said plainly enough, was that he rather chose to use this word love, than his word charity, in such places as he might well have used his word charity, and where the Latin text was charitas and where this holy word charity was more proper for the matter than this indifferent word love. This was the fault that I found. And therefore whereof serveth this trifling between the noun and the verb. I let him not say, love thy neighbour, nor I bid him not say charity thy neighbour, nor good affection thy neighbour, nor good mind thy neighbour, nor more than drink thy neighbour. And yet as he may say there, give thy neighbour drink, so may he if it please him, say, bear thy neighbour good mind, bear thy neighbour charity.[5]

The argument is occasionally eased by an imaginative passage that recalls a more light-hearted More. He is discussing the

---

[4] *Tyndale's Works*, III, p. 21 (Parker Society, 1850).

[5] *E.W.*, p. 434.

relation between the tradition of the Church and the Gospels as against the Protestant position that all truth is to be found in the New Testament. In his *Obedience of a Christian Man* (1527-8) Tyndale had referred to Origen as 'the greatest of heretics.'[6]

But divers things were by God to them [the Apostles] and by them to other taught by mouth, and by tradition from hand to hand delivered, and from age to age hitherto continued in Christ's Church. And that I say truth in this point, I have divers good and honest witnesses to bring forth when time requireth. Saint Austin, Saint Jerome, Saint Ciprian, Saint Chrysostom and a great many more, which have also testified for my part in this matter more than a thousand year ago. Yet have I another ancient sad father also, one that they call Origen. And when I desired him to take the pain to come and bear witness with me in this matter, he seemed at first very content. But, when I told him that he should meet with Tyndale, he blessed himself and shrank back and said, he had liever go some other way many a mile than once meddle with him. For I shall tell you, sir, quoth he, before this time a right honourable man very cunning and yet more virtuous, the good Bishop of Rochester, in a great audience brought me in for a witness against Luther and Tyndale even in this same matter, about the time of the burning of Tyndale's evil translated Testament.[7] But Tyndale as soon as he heard of my name, without any respect of honesty fell in a rage with me and all to rated me, and called stark heretic and that the starkest that ever was. This tale Origen told me and swore by Saint Simkin that he was never so said unto of such a lewd fellow since he was first born of his mother, and therefore he would never meddle with Tyndale more. Now indeed to say

---

[6] *Tyndale's Works*, I, p. 220.

[7] Sermon against Luther, 1521. *English Works of John Fisher* (E.E.T.S.), pp. 320, 333.

the truth it was not well done of Tyndale to leave reasoning and fall a scolding, chiding and brawling, as it were a bawdy beggar of Billyter Lane.[8] Fie, for shame, he should have favoured and forborne him somewhat and it had been but for his age. For Origen is now thirteen hundred year old or thereabout, and this was not much about seven year since.[9]

The book increases in dryness as More plods his way across the dreary waste-land of controversy. At the Eighth Book (page 735) he left Tyndale to deal with a tract, *What the Church Is*, by Doctor Robert Barnes, one of the most unhappy of the reformers; he fled abroad in 1528 from imprisonment as a heretic although he had publicly recanted; in 1531 he was in England under a safe-conduct from the King or Cromwell; More was of the opinion that Barnes had forfeited this safe-conduct by continuing to advocate heretical opinions. 'But let him go this once, for God shall find his time full well.'[10] After enjoying the passing favour of Henry and of Cromwell, Barnes was discarded when he had served their purposes. He took part in the condemnation of John Lambert in 1538 who was burned as a heretic; Barnes shared the same fate two years later a day or so after the execution of Thomas Cromwell. In the argument against Barnes, More covered familiar ground and there would be no point in following him here. One passage has, however, a special interest as it refers to Henry Patenson, More's fool.

> They that thus tell us, put me in mind of a tale that they tell of Mr. Henry Patenson, a man of known wisdom in London and almost everywhere else; which when he waited once on

---

[8] Billiter Street, south out of Leadenhall Street. It was the street of the bell-founders. Perhaps alliteration here decided its choice as no other explanation is known.

[9] *E.W.*, p. 410.

[10] *E.W.*, p. 343.

his master in the Emperor's court at Bruges,[11] and was there soon perceived upon the sight for a man of special wit by himself and unlike the common sort, they caught a sport in angering of him, and out of divers corners hurled at him such things as angered him and hurt him not. Thereupon he gathered up good stones, not gunstones but as hard as they, and those he put apace into his bosom, and then stood him up upon a bench, and made a proclamation aloud, that every man might hear him: in which he commanded every man upon their own perils to depart, except only those that hurled at him, to the intent that he might know them and hurl at them again, and hurt none other body but his enemies: for whosoever tarried after his proclamation made, he would take him for one of the hurlers or else for one of their counsellors, and then have at their heads, whosoever they were that would abide. Now was his proclamation in English, and the company that heard him were such as understood none, but stood still and gaped upon him and laughed at him. And by and by one hurled at him again. And anon as he saw that: 'Whoresons.' quoth he, 'ye stand still everyone, I ween, and not one of you will remove a foot for all my proclamation, and thereby I see well ye be hurlers or of counsel with the hurlers, all the whole meinie of you, and therefore have at you again.' And with the word he hurled a great stone out at adventure among them, he neither wist nor rought [recked] at whom, but lighted upon a Burgundian's head and brake his pate that the blood ran about his ears. And Master Henry bade him stand to his harms hardily, for why would he not beware then and get him thence betime, when he gave him before so fair courteous warning?

---

[11] More was in Bruges in 1521.

By the time the second volume of the Confutation was in print, Sir Thomas More was no longer Lord Chancellor. Tyndale did not reply to the book; within a year its author was in the Tower.

Chapter XX

Resignation

SOON after Parliament met in November 1529, the Commons began to discuss some of the complaints against the clergy. Three Bills were introduced; the first was to regulate fees for probate, and the second, with a glance-back to Richard Hunne, to limit the payment for mortuaries; the third dealt with pluralities of livings and non-residence. None of these directly affected the faith of the Church. Each dealt with a recognized grievance. Their significance lies in the fact that the secular power was invading a province that, hitherto, had been under the control of the ecclesiastical authorities. Convocation could, and indeed should, have dealt with such matters, but it acted too leisurely to meet the rising feeling of the populace. At that time, under the guidance of the aged Warham, it was considering the best way of improving the training and qualifications of priests; this was a fundamental need on which both More and Erasmus had placed considerable stress, but it was not the kind of problem that would excite popular opinion.

There is no record of Sir Thomas More's opinions on these three Bills; he shared the desire to remedy abuses, but he could not have approved the intervention of the secular power. As he listened to the debate in the Lords, his sympathies were probably with the opinion voiced by his friend Bishop John Fisher.

What strange words be here uttered, not to be heard of any Christian ears, and unworthy to be spoken in the hearing of Christian princes; for they say that bishops and their associates, abbots, priests, and other of the clergy are vicious, ravenous, insatiable, idle, cruel and so forth. What, are all of this sort? Or is there any of these abuses that the clergy seek not to extirpate and destroy? ... But, my lords, beware of yourselves and your country; nay, beware of the liberty of our mother the Church. Luther, one of the most cruel enemies to the faith that ever was, is at hand, and the common people study for novelties, and with good will hear what can be said in favour of heresy. What success is there to be hoped for in these attempts other than such as our neighbours have already tasted, whose harms may be a good warning to us? Remember with yourselves what these sects and divisions have wrought among the Bohemians and Germans, who, besides an innumerable number of mischiefs fallen among them, have almost lost their ancient and catholic faith; and what by the snares of John Huss, and after him Martin Luther, whom they reverence like a prophet, they have almost excluded themselves from the unity of Christ's Holy Church. These men now among us seem to reprove the life and doings of the clergy, but after such a sort as they endeavour to bring them into contempt and hatred of the laity, and so finding fault with other men's manners whom they have no authority to correct, omit and forget their own, which is far worse and much more out of order than the other. But if the truth were known, ye shall find that they rather hunger and thirst after the riches and possessions of the clergy than after amendment of their faults and abuses. ... Wherefore I will tell you, my lords, plainly, what I think; except you resist manfully by your authority this violent heap of mischief offered by the Commons, ye shall shortly see all obedience withdrawn, first from the clergy, and after yourselves, whereupon will ensue the utter ruin and danger of the Christian faith; and in place of it, that which is likely to follow, the most wicked and tyrannical government of the Turk; for ye shall find that all these mischiefs among them ariseth through lack of faith.[1]

The sequel may be given in the words of this early biographer of the Bishop.

> But when the Commons heard of these words spoken against them, they straightway conceived such displeasure against my lord of Rochester, that by the mouth of Master Audley, their Speaker, they made a grievous complaint to the King of his words, saying that it was a great discredit to them all to be thus charged that they lacked faith, which in effect was all one to say they were heretics and infidels, and therefore desired the King that they might have some remedy against him. The King, therefore, to satisfy them, called my lord of Rochester before him, and demanded why he spake in that sort. And he answered again that, being in Council, he spake his mind in defence and right of the Church, whom he saw daily injured and oppressed among the common people, whose office was not to deal with her, and therefore said he thought himself in conscience bound to defend her all that he might. The King nevertheless willed him to use his words temperately. And so the matter ended much to the discontent of Master Audley and divers others of the Common House.[2]

There was a curious oscillation in Henry's policy at this period; some of his acts seemed directed against the Church, while others were directed against heretics. The three Bills which became law early in this Parliament encouraged the Reformers to hope that he was moving towards them; there was an increase in the sale of Tyndale's New Testament and of Lutheran books and tracts. But such hopes were disappointed early in 1530. Tyndale's translations were again burned in St. Paul's Churchyard, and a royal proclamation required all magistrates and other officials to

---

[1] *The Life of Fisher* (E.E.T.S.), p. 69.

[2] *The Life of Fisher* (E.E.T.S.), p. 70.

take an oath that they would 'give their whole power and diligence' to suppress heresy.

Meanwhile the King's Matter was unresolved and Henry was seeking for new means to achieve his desire. The opinions of foreign Universities were sought and bought. In January 1530 the King sent an embassy to the Pope; it was an unpropitious moment as the Pope was crowning Charles as Emperor, and the tactless choice of the Earl of Wilshire, Anne Boleyn's father, as leader of the embassy, did not increase its chances. Then the peers and prelates were persuaded to send a memorial to the Pope asking him to grant Henry's wishes. Neither Sir Thomas More nor Bishop John Fisher signed the petition, and they thereby incurred the King's displeasure; Chapuys reported that for a time it seemed as if the Great Seal would be taken from Sir Thomas More, but he was not to have such an acceptable release from a burden that was becoming increasingly irksome.[3]

Only a few weeks after the death of Wolsey in November 1530, the clergy as a body were accused in the King's Bench of having violated the statutes of provisors and *præmunire* in recognizing the Cardinal's authority as *legatus a latere*, a dignity that had been granted him at Henry's insistency. Many were to find how easy it was to 'fall into the compass of a *præmunire*' now that Henry had discovered, or been told of, this unexpected means of extorting both submission and money. It was a perversion of justice to apply these fourteenth-century statutes collectively to men who had acted in good faith and with the knowledge of the king. The clergy of the northern province under Tunstal held out a little longer than their brethren in the south under the aged Warham, but both provinces taxed themselves heavily, and as a condition of pardon were forced to declare that Henry VIII, *defensor fidei*, was Supreme Head of the Church of

---

[3] *Span. Cal.*, pp. 599, 727, 762.

England. Warham gained one concession, the saving clause 'as far as the Law of Christ allows,' but that was dropped without notice from the Supremacy Act of 1534.

Chapuys reported to the Emperor that Sir Thomas More was so distressed at the implications of this strange title that he wanted to resign the Chancellorship.

Public opinion was still with Catherine of Aragon, and the King decided to put his case again before Parliament for the information of the members. On 30th March, 1531, Sir Brian Tuke, the clerk of Parliament, delivered a message to the Lords from the King. Once more Henry explained how troubled he was in conscience as to the validity of his marriage; then the opinions so far received from the Universities were read to the lords. Bishop Fisher was ill at the time, and both Warham and Tunstal were absent. Two bishops, Bath and St. Asaph's, spoke strongly in favour of Catherine, as did the Earl of Shrewsbury. When More was asked for his opinion, he stated that his views were known to the King; that in itself told his listeners how he stood.[4] The same message was then delivered to the Commons, but, this time, according to Hall's account, the Chancellor opened the proceedings.

> The Lord Chancellor said, you of this worshipful House I am sure be not so ignorant but you know well that the King our sovereign lord hath married his brother's wife, for she was both wedded and bedded with his brother Prince Arthur, and therefore you may surely say that he hath married his brother's wife, if this marriage be good or no, many clerks do doubt. Wherefore the King, like a virtuous prince, willing to be satisfied in his conscience, and also for the surety of his realm, hath with great deliberation consulted with great clerks, and hath sent my Lord of London here present

---

[4] *Span. Cal.*, IV, ii, pp. 84-5.

[Stokesley] to the chief Universities of all Christendom to know their opinion and judgement in that behalf. And although that the Universities of Cambridge and Oxford had been sufficient to discuss the cause, yet because they be in his realm and to avoid all suspicion of partiality he sent into the realm of France, Italy the Pope's dominions and Venetians to know their judgement in that behalf, which have concluded, written and sealed their determinations according as you shall hear read. Then Sir Brian Tuke took out of a box twelve writings sealed, and read them word by word... Then the Chancellor said, 'Now you of this Common House may report to your countries what you have seen and heard and then all men shall openly perceive that the King had not attempted this matter of will or pleasure, as some strangers report, but only for the discharge of his conscience and surety of the succession of his realm. This is the cause of our repair hither to you, and now we will depart.[5]

Roper's account reads,

All which matters, at the King's request, not showing of what mind himself was therein, he opened to the lower House of the Parliament. Nevertheless, doubting lest further attempts after should follow, which, contrary to his conscience, by reason of his office, he was likely to be put unto, he made suit unto the Duke of Norfolk, his singular dear friend, to be a mean to the King that he might, with his Grace's favour, be discharged of that chargeable room of the Chancellorship, wherein, for certain infirmities of his body, he pretended himself unable any longer to serve.[6]

The reference to physical infirmities was not a diplomatic excuse. Writing to Erasmus a year later, More told him that 'a

---

[5] *Hall*, II, pp. 185-94.

[6] *Roper*, p. 51.

disorder of I know not what nature has attacked my chest ... For when it had plagued me without abatement for some months the physicians whom I consulted gave their opinion that the long continuance of it was dangerous.'[7]

The King was, however, unwilling to let him go; while the issue of the divorce suit was undecided, it was useful to have as his Chancellor a man whose known integrity would quieten opponents with the hope that wiser counsel might yet be taken. Four months later Henry saw Catherine for the last time and left her without saying good-bye.

In March 1532 the Commons presented to the King a Petition or Supplication setting out their grievances against the clergy; this was a summary of the complaints that had become almost commonplace, but it is interesting to note that the four existing drafts of the Supplication contain many corrections and alterations in the handwriting of Thomas Cromwell whose influence was now becoming dominant. The Commons do not seem to have regarded it as a matter of urgency, for, at the time of presenting the final document, they begged the King to consider the 'pain, charge and cost his humble subjects of the nether House had sustained' and to discharge them. Henry shrewdly pointed out that, having started such a hare, they could not give up the chase; 'therefore if you will have profit of your complaint, you must tarry the time.' The Supplication was submitted to Convocation; the reply was a spirited defence by the Bishops, which the King handed to the Speaker with the comment, 'We think their answer will smally please you, for it seemeth to us very slender; you be a great sort of wise men, I doubt not but you will look circumspectly on the matter, and we will be indifferent between you.' He went on to object to Temse's speech in the house on his separation from Catherine, and once more told them

---

[7] *Allen*, x, 2659; 14th June, 1532.

how sorely he had been 'vexed in conscience.'[8]

While Convocation was discussing the Supplication, Parliament was occupied with a Bill to abolish the payment of Annates to Rome. Surprisingly this aroused some opposition in the Commons, an indication of the bewilderment that clouded men's minds at that period when no one knew the King's intentions. The application of the Act was postponed and Henry could thus use it as a threat to the Pope.

Hall records the last appearance of the Chancellor before the Commons.

> When the Parliament was begun again after Easter, there came down to the Common House the Lord Chancellor, the Dukes of Norfolk and Suffolk, the Earls of Arundel, Oxford, Northumberland, Rutland, Wiltshire and Sussex, and after they were set, the Lord Chancellor declared how the King was advertised by his Council and in especial by the Duke of Norfolk, how on the Marches between England and Scotland was very little habitation on the English side, but on the Scottish side was great habitation, and the Scots dwelled even just on the Border, by reason whereof they invaded England divers times, and did to the King's subjects great hurt and displeasure: wherefore the King intended to make dwelling houses there, and also to make divers piles and stops to let the Scottish men from their invasions, to the great commodity of all his people there dwelling, which things could not be done without great cost; wherefore considering the King's good intent, they said, that the Lords thought it convenient to grant to the King some reasonable aid toward his charges, and prayed the Commons to consult on the same, and then he and all the Lords departed. After their departure, the Commons considering the King's good intent, lovingly granted him a

---

[8] *Hall*, II, pp. 203, 209.

fifteenth toward his charges, but this grant was not enacted at this Session because that suddenly began a pestilence in Westminster, wherefore the Parliament was prorogued till the next year.[9]

The King got his money but there seems to be no further information about this early instance of a housing scheme.

The negotiations on the Supplication resulted in a number of demands being made on Convocation; their effect was to cripple the powers of that body, but Henry was still not content. On 11th May, 1532, he announced a great discovery, all the more astonishing in that he was now in the twenty-third year of his reign. Hall recorded the incident.

> The King sent for the Speaker again and twelve of the Common House, having with him eight lords, and said to them, 'Well beloved subjects, we thought that the clergy of our realm had been our subjects wholly, but now we have well perceived that they be but half our subjects, yea, and scarce our subjects: for all the Prelates at their consecration make an oath to the Pope clean contrary to the oath that they make to us, so that they seem to be his subjects and not ours; the copy of both the oaths I deliver here to you to invent some order, that we be not thus deluded of our spiritual subjects.[10]

Meanwhile yet another matter was agitating Convocation. The King had expressed his opinion that the Bishops should no longer have the power to seize heretics, 'saying it is not their duty to meddle with bodies and they are only doctors of the soul.' Chapuys reported that 'The Chancellor and the bishops oppose him. The King is very angry, especially with the Chancellor and the Bishop of Winchester [Gardiner], and is determined to carry

---

[9] By Foxe, and by *Rogers*, p. 439.

[10] *Hall*, II, p. 210.

the matter.'[11] Convocation at length gave up the struggle and agreed to all the demands made; so the clergy submitted on 15 May, 1532.

On the following day, Henry at last allowed Sir Thomas More to resign. Roper tells us how they parted.

> Then, at a time convenient, by his Highness's appointment, repaired he to his Grace, to yield up unto him the Great Seal. Which, as his Grace, with thanks and praise for his worthy service in that office, courteously at his hands received, so pleased it his Highness further to say unto him, that for the service that he before had done him, in any suit which he should after have unto him, that either should concern his honour (for that word it liked his Highness to use unto him) or that should appertain unto his profit, he should find his Highness good and gracious lord unto him.[12]

However great the sense of relief may have been, More must have given up his office with a heavy heart. During the two and a half years of his Chancellorship, he had seen the ancient authority of the Church in his own country undermined and destroyed; he had seen the King separated from the Queen and the stage set for the last act of that tragedy. It was true that the faith itself had not so far been touched by Act of Parliament, and something had been done to strengthen the enforcement of the laws against heretics, but now even this gain had been taken away by the King's attack on the powers of the bishops to apprehend heretics. More had, as in duty bound, served the State, and had, as he wrote in *Utopia*, striven 'to handle all well, and what you cannot turn to good, you must make as little bad as you can.' The lesson he had learned by bitter experience he tried to pass on to the coming man, Thomas Cromwell, an unapt pupil.

---

[11] *Rogers*, p. 447. More is referring to *John*, vi, vv, 41-68. See below, p. 271.

[12] *E.W.*, p. 255.

Now upon his resignation of his office, came Master Thomas Cromwell, then in the King's high favour, to Chelsea to him, with a message from the King; wherein, when they had thoroughly communed together: 'Master Cromwell,' quoth he, 'you are now entered into the service of a most noble, wise and liberal prince. If you will follow my poor advice, you shall, in your counsel giving unto his Grace, ever tell him what he ought to do, but never what he is able to do. So shall you show yourself a true faithful servant and a right worthy councillor. For if a lion knew his own strength, hard were it for any man to rule him.'[13]

---

[13] *Roper*, p. 57.

Chapter XXI

The Apologye

WHEN he gave up the Great Seal, Sir Thomas More lost the greater part of his income. As Lord Chancellor he had £142 15s. a year and an additional £200 as a judge of the Star Chamber Court; his perquisites included £64 a year for twelve tuns of wine, and £16 for wax. It is not known how much he received in fees but it was probably less than the £2,000 a year that Wolsey enjoyed. The lands he possessed brought in about £60 a year. His salary as a Councillor was continued until Easter 1534 when the King stopped it.[1] He had not feathered his own nest, and to men of the Cromwell type he must have seemed a foolish person. He faced the situation with his accustomed good humour. Roper tells us of a family council at which he was present.

> After he had thus given over the Chancellorship, and placed all his gentlemen and yeomen with bishops and noble men, and his eight watermen with the Lord Audley, that in the same office succeeded him, to whom also he gave his great barge, then, calling us all that were his children unto him, and asking our advice how we might now, in this decay of his ability (by the surrender of his office so impaired that he could not, as he was wont, and gladly would, bear out the whole charges of them all himself) from thenceforth be able to

---

[1] *L.P.*, IV, 6079; *P.R.O.* E405, nos. 104, 202. It would be misleading to suggest any monetary equivalent for today; the whole manner of life in Tudor times was so different from our own that a real comparison is impossible.

live and continue together, as he wished we should; when he saw us silent, and in that case not ready to show our opinions to him, 'Then will I,' said he, 'show my poor mind to you. I have been brought up,' quoth he, 'at Oxford, at an Inn of Chancery, at Lincoln's Inn, and also in the King's Court, and so forth from the lowest degree to the highest, and yet have I in yearly revenues at this present left me little above an hundred pounds by the year, so that now must we hereafter, if we like to live together, be contented to become contributaries together. But, by my counsel, it shall not be best for us to fall to the lowest fare first; we will not therefore descend to Oxford fare, nor to the fare of New Inn, but we will begin with Lincoln's Inn diet, where many right worshipful and of good years do live full well; which, if we find not ourselves the first year able to maintain, then will we next year go one step down to New Inn fare, wherewith many an honest man is well contented. If that exceed our ability too, then will we the next year after descend to Oxford fare, where many grave, learned, and ancient fathers be continually conversant; which, if our power stretch not to maintain neither, then may we yet, with bags and wallets, go a-begging together and hoping that for pity some good folk will give us their charity, at every man's door to sing Salve Regina, and so still keep company and be merry together.[2]

The good humour of that advice may obscure the light it throws on Thomas More's deep desire to keep his family together in misfortune as well as in more prosperous days. It will be noted that William Roper includes himself amongst those 'that were his children,' for so they all thought of themselves, his son and daughters, his sons-in-law, and all the grandchildren. Nor were they parted until Henry VIII came to hate the man he had once so

---

[2] *Roper*, p. 52.

loved.

Roper tells us that 'after his debts paid, he had not, I know, his chain excepted, in gold and silver left him the worth of one hundred pounds.'[3]

The loss of high rank and the deference due to it, did not trouble Thomas More, but it may have been resented, and perhaps not fully understood, by Dame Alice. He made the matter clear to her in his own fashion.

> And whereas upon holidays during his High Chancellorship one of his gentlemen, when service at the church was done, ordinarily used to come to my lady his wife's pew, and say unto her, 'Madam, my lord is gone,' the next holiday after the surrender of his office and the departure of his gentlemen, he came unto his lady his wife's pew himself, and making a low curtsy, said unto her, 'Madam, my lord is gone.'[4]

Had it not been for his household responsibilities, More would have welcomed his release without qualification. Some years earlier he had sent a copy of *Utopia* to Warham with a letter congratulating the Archbishop on his resignation of the Chancellorship.

> I ever judged your paternity happy in the way you exercised your office of Chancellor, but I esteem you much happier now that you have laid it down and entered on that most desirable leisure, in which you can live for yourself and God. Such leisure, in my opinion, is not only more pleasant than the labour you have forsaken, but more honourable than all your honours.[5]

---

[3] *Roper*, p. 55.

[4] *Roper*, p. 55.

[5] *Rogers*, p. 86. Probably early 1517.

Warham was not to have that 'desirable leisure,' for the cares of the Church increased with the years; on the last months of a long life he protested against the usurpation of the authority of the Church by Parliament and dared to remind Henry VIII of the outcome of the struggle between Henry II and St. Thomas of Canterbury. Death came to the Archbishop two months after the resignation of Sir Thomas More.[6]

He expressed the same sentiments about his own resignation in a letter to Erasmus in June.

> From the time I was a boy I have longed, dear Desiderius, that what I rejoice in you having always enjoyed I myself might some day enjoy too—namely, that being free from public business, I might have some time to devote to God and myself; that, by the grace of a great and good God, and by the favour of an indulgent prince, I have at last obtained.[7]

He goes on to lament the fact that his health has suffered and that this will rob his leisure of some of its ease.

It was not only ill-health and family cares that prevented More from enjoying the full fruits of his retirement. His duty, for such he regarded it, of combating heresy remained. It has been noted that he wrote the second part of his *Confutation* after his resignation; at the end of 1532 he wrote *A Letter ... impugning the erroneous writing of John Frith against the Blessed Sacrament of the Altar.*[8] Frith, then about thirty years old, was a prisoner in the Tower on a charge of heresy. He had gone abroad in 1528 and had associated with the German Reformers. It was while he was in England on a private visit that he was arrested, not, as has been

---

[6] *'Sat est viatici'* he said on his death-bed, when they told him he had only £30 in ready money. There is need for a full biography of William Warham.

[7] *Allen*, x, 2659.

[8] *Rogers*, pp. 440-64.

The Apologye

said,[9] by More's instructions; Frith was not in England while More was Lord Chancellor, but arrived two months after the resignation. He wrote a pamphlet on the Holy Eucharist putting forward the views that are now set out in the twenty-eighth of the Articles of Religion of the Church of England. Three copies of this pamphlet in manuscript (it does not seem to have been published) came into More's hands;[10] one was obtained from Frith by a pretended sympathizer. More's answer took the form of a letter which he sent to various friends of Frith; he decided to print it when he found that these heretical opinions were widely spread.

The Blessed Sacrament meant so much to Thomas More that any tampering with the teaching of the Church on the Eucharist hurt him more deeply than attacks on any other dogma. Yet the tone of this letter is not harsh; it may be that More hoped that 'this young man,' as he called Frith, was still open to conviction of his error. One passage will show the style of the argument. Frith maintained that an allegorical and not literal meaning should be given to the words, 'This is my body,' and, 'This is my blood.' To this More replied:

> And over this, the very circumstances of the places in the Gospel in which our Saviour speaketh of that sacrament, may make open the difference of his speech in this matter and of all those other, and that as he spake all those but in allegory, so spake he this plainly meaning that he spake of his very body and his very blood besides all allegories. For neither when our Lord said he was a very vine, nor when he said he was the door, there was none that heard him that anything

---

[9] *Allen*, x, 2659.

[10] J.F. Mozley in his biography of Tyndale (1937) makes this ingenuous comment on the manner in which More is supposed, but not known, to have obtained Frith's letter. 'More's use of underground methods springs from his one fatal mistake of regarding Lutehrans as worse than the world, the flesh and the devil,' p. 247n.

marvelled thereof. And why? For because they perceived well that he meant not that he was a material vine indeed, nor a material door neither. But when he said that his flesh was very meat, and his blood was very drink, and that they should not be saved but if they did eat his flesh and drink his blood, then were they all in such wonder thereof that they could not abide. And wherefore? But because they perceived well by his words and his manner of circumstances used in the speaking of them, that Christ spake of his very flesh and his very blood indeed. For else the strangeness of the words would have made them to have taken it as well for an allegory, as either his words of the vine or of the door. And then would they have no more marvelled at the one than they did at the other. But now whereas at the vine and the door they marvelled nothing, yet at the eating of his flesh and drinking of his blood, they so sore marvelled, and were so sore moved, and thought the matter so hard, and the wonder so great, that they asked how could that be, and went almost all their way, whereby we may well see that he spake these words in such wise as the hearers perceived that he meant it not in a parable nor an allegory, but spake of his very flesh and his very blood indeed.[11]

More had intended[12] to write a reply to Frith's *Disputation of Purgatory*, but his brother-in-law, John Rastell, whose *Book of Purgatory* (1530) had evoked Frith's treatise, took up the controversy; it is said that Frith converted Rastell to his views.

The year of the Petition or Supplication of the Commons saw the publication of *A Treatise concerning the Division between the*

---

[11] Rogers, p. 447. More is referring to *John*, vi, vv. 41-68. See below, p. 271.

[12] *E.W.*, p. 255.

Spirituality and the Temporality.[13] This was published anonymously but it seems certain that the author was a lawyer, Christopher Saint-Germain, who wrote as a Catholic but in such a Laodicean spirit that his sincerity was doubted. The similarities between his book and the Petition of the Commons suggests that it was in fact state propaganda.

The book was the occasion of the writing of *The Apologye* (1533). In it More refers to Saint-Germain as 'The Pacifier,' and to his book as 'The Book of Division.' In a later work More explained that

> mine Apology is an answer and a defence not only for my former books, wherein the new brethren[14] began to find certain faults, but over that in the selfsame part wherein I touch the 'Book of Division' it is an answer and a defence for many good, worshipful folk against the malicious slander and obloquy so generally set forth with so many some-says in that seditious book. The selfsame piece is also an answer and a defence of the very good, old, and long-approved laws both of this realm and of the whole corpse of Christendom; which laws this Pacifier in his 'Book of Division.' to the encouraging of heretics and peril of the Catholic faith, with warm words and cold reasons oppugneth.[15]

The argument ranges over the familiar ground of anti-clericism; while admitting there were abuses. More set out to defend the clergy from these scurrilous attacks. One or two matters that affect More himself call for notice. The charge was

---

[13] Printed by Thomas Berthelet, 1532. Reprinted as an Appendix to the E.E.T.S. edition of *The Apologye.*

[14] For an account of the names such as 'the known man,' 'the brethren,' etc., applied to the early protestants and reformers, see E.G. Rupp, *The English Protestant Tradition* (1949); also above p. 211.

[15] *E.W.*, p. 931.

made against him that he defended the clergy for self-interest; Tyndale had said that More's covetousness had led him to take up his pen.[16]

> And for as all the lands and fees that I have in all England, beside such lands and fees as I have of the gift of the King's most noble Grace is not at this day nor shall be while my mother-in-law liveth (whose life and good health I pray God keep and continue) worth yearly to my living the sum of full fifty pounds. And thereof have I some by my wife, and some by my father (whose soul our Lord assoil) and some have I also purchased myself and some fees have I of some temporal men. And then may every man well guess, that I have no very great part of my living by the clergy, to make me very partial to them. ... I have not had one groat granted me since I first wrote, or went about to write my Dialogue, and that was, ye wot well, the first work that I wrote in these matters.[17]

He then refers to an incident best told in Roper's words.

> And considering that for all his prince's favour he was no rich man, nor in yearly revenues advanced as his worthyness deserved, therefore at a Convocation among themselves [the bishops] and other of the clergy, they agreed together and concluded upon a sum of four or five thousand pounds, at the least, to my remembrance, for his pains to recompense him. To the payment whereof every Bishop, Abbot, and the rest of the clergy were, after the rate of their abilities, liberal contributors, hoping this portion should be to his contentation.
>
> Whereupon Tunstal, Bishop of Durham, Clerk, Bishop of Bath, and, as far as I can call to mind, Veysey,[18] Bishop of

---

[16] 'Covetousness blinded the eyes of that gleering fox.'

[17] *Apologye*, p. 51.

[18] John Veysey (1465?-1554); deprived under Edward VI.

Exeter, repaired unto him, declaring how thankfully for his travails, to their discharge, in God's cause bestowed, they reckoned themselves bounden to consider him; and that albeit they could not, according to his deserts, so worthily as they gladly would, requite him therefore, but must reserve that only to the goodness of God, yet for a small part of recompence, in respect of his estate so unequal to his worthiness, in the name of their whole Convocation, they presented unto him that sum which they desired him to take in good part. Who, forsaking it, said, that like as it was no small comfort unto him that so wise and learned men so well accepted his simple doings, for which he never intended to receive reward but at the hands of God only, to whom alone was the thanks thereof chiefly to be ascribed, so gave he most humble thanks to their honours all for their so bountiful and friendly consideration.

When they, for all their importunate pressing upon him, that few would have went [thought] he could have refused it, could by no means make him to take it, then besought they him to be content that they might bestow it upon his wife and children. 'Not so, my lords,' quoth he, 'I have liever see it all cast into the Thames, then I, or any of mine, should have thereof the worth of one penny. For though your offer, my lords, be indeed very friendly and honourable, yet set I so much by my pleasure and so little by my profit, that I would not, in good faith, for so much and much more too, have lost the rest of so many nights' sleep as was spent upon the same. And yet wish would I, for all that, upon condition that all heresies were suppressed, that all my books were burned and my labour utterly lost.'

Thus departing were they fain to restore unto every man

his own again.[19]

This incident cannot be dated with certainty, but it would seem likely that it would not be before he had finished his *Confutation*, and after his resignation from the Chancellorship. His friends would have realized that he was considerably reduced in circumstances and may have had that in their minds as well as their appreciation of the labour he had given to his task of combating heresy.

One passage in the *Apologye* may be linked with More's personal life.

> Then preacheth this Pacifier yet farther, that the clergy should wear hair. He is surely somewhat sore if he bind them all thereto, but among them I think that many do already and some whole religion [religious] doth. But yet saith this Pacifier that it doth not appear that they do so. Ah, well said! But now if all the lack stand in that point, that such holiness is hid, so that men may not see it, it shall be from henceforth well done for them, and so they will do if they be wise, upon this advertisement and preaching of this good Pacifier, come out of their cloisters every man into the market place, and there kneel down in the kennel and make their prayers in the open streets, and wear their hair shirts in sight upon their cowls and then shall it appear and men shall see it. And surely for their shirts of hair in this way were there none hypocrisy and yet were there also good policy, for then should it not prick them.[20]

The following passage in Roper's account is well known.

> And albeit outwardly he appeared honourable like one of his calling, yet inwardly he no such vanities esteeming, secretly next his body wear a shirt of hair; which my sister

---

[19] *Roper*, p. 46.

[20] *Apologye*, p. 119.

More[21] a young gentlewoman, in the summer, as he sat at supper, singly in his doublet and hose, wearing thereupon a plain shirt without ruff or collar, chancing to spy, began to laugh at it. My wife, not ignorant of his manner, perceiving the same, privily told him of it; and he, being sorry that she saw it, presently amended it.[22]

An important section of the *Apologye* deals with accusations against the clergy that they were too hasty and often unjust in their treatment of heretics. More replied that he could recall only seven[23] cases during the previous four or five years of heretics being condemned and handed over to the sheriffs for the penalty prescribed by the civil law. Only three of these were in the London diocese. He challenged the Pacifier to appear 'before the King's Grace and his Council, or in what place he list, and there prove, calling me thereto, that any one of all these had wrong.'[24]

He later took up the charge made against himself that 'while I was Chancellor, I used to examine them [heretics] with torments, causing them to be bounden to a tree in my garden, and there piteously beaten.'[25] This accusation was to be repeated, with exaggerations, up to our own day, and is still, in spite of close examination, used as a reproach. His defence must be given at length in his own words; neither the Pacifier nor anyone else has been able to shake this testimony except by the omission of significant phrases and sentences.

He first states that 'saving only their sure keeping' he never caused any heretics to be flogged except in two cases. The first

---

[21] Anne Cresacre and John More were married in 1529.

[22] *Roper*, p. 48.

[23] See James Gairdner, *The English Church in the XVIth Century*, pp. 128-34; notes on pp. 312-14, 318-23 of the *Apologye* and Chambers, *Thomas More*, pp. 274-82.

[24] *Apologye*, p. 105.

[25] *Apologye*, p. 131.

was a boy who had been taught heresy regarding the Blessed Sacrament.

Which heresy this child afterward being in service with me, began to teach another child in my house, which uttered his counsel. And upon that point perceived and known, I caused a servant of mine to stripe him like a child before my household, for amendment of himself and ensample of such other.[26]

The second case was a matter not of heresy but of indecency.

Another was one, which after that he had fallen into the frantic heresies, fell soon after into plain open frenzy besides. And albeit that he had therefore been put up in Bedlam, and afterwards by beating and correction gathered his remembrance to him, and began to come again to himself being thereupon set at liberty and walking about abroad, his old fancies began to fall again in his head. And I was from divers good holy places advertised that he used in his wandering about come into the church and there make many mad toys and trifles to the trouble of good people in the divine service and especially would he be most busy in the time of most silence while the priest was at the secrets of the Mass about the levation [elevation]. And if he spied any woman kneeling at a form if her head hung anything low in her meditations, then would he steal behind her and if he were not letted [prevented] would labour to lift up all her clothes and cast them quite over her head. Whereupon I being advertised of these pageants and being sent unto and required by very devout religious folk, to take some other order with him caused him as he came wandering by my door to be taken by the constables and bounden to a tree before the whole town, and there they striped him with rods therefore till he

---

[26] *Apologye*, p. 132.

waxed weary and somewhat lenger. ... And verily God be thanked I hear none harm of him now.

And of all that ever came in my hand for heresy, as help me God, saving as I said the sure keeping of them, and yet not so sure neither but that George Constantine could steal away; else had never any of them any stripe or stroke given them so much as a fillip on the forehead.[27]

This recollection of how one prisoner escaped led him to say something more of George Constantine; he had been very active in bringing Tyndale's New Testament[28] and other books into the country, but turned informer and gave the names of shipmasters and others who were active in this trade. More had him arrested and put in the stocks.

And some have said that when Constantine was gotten away, I was fallen for anger in a wonderful rage. But surely though I would not have suffered him go if it would have pleased him to have tarried still in the stocks, yet when he was neither so feeble for lack of meat but that he was strong enough to break the stocks, nor waxen so lame of his legs with lying but that he was light enough to leap the walls nor by any mishandling of his head or dazed in his brain but that he had wit enough when he was once out wisely to walk his way; neither was I then so heavy for the loss but that I had youth enough left me to wear it out nor so angry with any man of mine that I spake them any evil word for the matter, more than to my porter that he should see the stocks mended and locked fast that the prisoner stole not in again. And as for Constantine himself I could him in good faith good thank. For never will I for my part be so unreasonable, as to be angry

---

[27] *Apologye*, p. 132.

[28] For an account of another interview between More and Constantine, see *Hall*, II, p. 162; also *E.W.*, pp. 246-8.

with any man that riseth if he can, when he findeth himself that he sitteth not at his ease.[29]

Another case was used in accusation against More.

But now tell the brethren many marvellous lies of much cruel tormenting that heretics had in my house, so far forth that one Segar, a bookseller of Cambridge, which was in mine house about four or five days, and never had either bodily harm done him or foul words spoken him while he was in mine house, hath reported since as I hear say divers, that he was bounden to a tree in my garden, and thereto piteously beaten and yet beside that bounden about the head with a cord and wrungen that he fell down dead in a swoon. And this tale of his beating, did Tyndale tell to an old acquaintance of his own, and to a good lover of mine with one piece further yet, that while the man was in beating, I spied a little purse of his hanging at his doublet, wherein the poor man had (as he said) five mark, and that caught I quickly to me and pulled it from his doublet, and put it in my bosom, and that Segar never saw it after and therein I trow he said true, for no more did I neither nor before neither, nor I trow no more did Segar himself neither in good faith.[30]

Such tales were later incorporated in Foxe's *Acts and Monuments*, and although many of his statements have been proved 'casual and contradictory,'[31] the legend of More's cruelty became accepted. A close study of these cases shows that while Sir Thomas More was unrelenting in his pursuit of heretics, he did not go outside his proper jurisdiction, which was, in fact, no

---

[29] *Apologye*, p. 133.

[30] *Apologye*, p. 134.

[31] A.F. Pollard, *Wolsey*, pp. 211-213.

greater than that of any other magistrate.[32] He had the duty of apprehending heretics and of handing them over to the Bishop's Court. While they were in his custody he seems to have tried to urge them to submit to the Church, but there is no instance established of his having treated them with cruelty.

This libel on his friend came to the knowledge of Erasmus with the addition that More had been dismissed from the Chancellorship and that his victims were at once released from prison. Erasmus wrote to Bishop John Faber of Vienna to protest at these wild statements. A few sentences may be quoted as they throw some light on the attitude of Erasmus himself to these matters.

> But what is it that these scatterers of false tales propose? Is it to convince the sects, and favourers of sects, that a safe retreat is at hand for them in England? Why, from letters that have reached me from most trustworthy men, it appears that the king is even less tolerant of the new doctrines than the bishops and priests. There is no man of any piety who would not wish to see a reform of morals in the Church, but no one of any prudence considers it right to tolerate universal confusion.[33]

Saint-Germain did not accept More's challenge to produce his evidence, but in his reply he repeated his vague accusations against the harsh and unjust treatment of heretics by the Church. The title of the reply was *A Dialogue between two Englishmen*, whereof one was called Salem and the other *Bizance* (1533). More answered with *The Debellation*[34] *of Salem and Bizance* 'sometimes two great towns, which being under the Turk, were between

---

[32] Wolsey's greater authority was due to the fact that he was Archbishop and Legate as well as Chancellor.

[33] *Allen*, x, 2750.

[34] Conquest.

Easter and Michaelmas last 1533, by a marvellous metamorphose and enchantment, turned into Englishmen, by the wonderful inventive wit and witchcraft of Sir John Somesay the pacifier, and so conveyed by him hither in a dialogue to defend his division, against Sir Thomas More knight.' In this he noted that Saint-Germain had again avoided making specific charges that could be investigated, but had merely repeated that 'some say' this or that.

> Thereto, ye wot well, he will bring forth for the plain proof of his plain truth in the matter his old three worshipful witnesses—which yet stand all unsworn—that is to wit, Somesay, and They-say, and Folk-say. And then hath he now brought forth other two ... both as witnesses and judges too; that is, the good sely soul Simkin Salem, and his right honest neighbour, Brother Bizance.[35]

The Debellation need not detain us; it is in the main a defence of the existing laws and their enforcement against heretics. His lighter mood occasionally finds expression.

> And as for the railing fashion—if I durst be bold to tell so sad a man a merry tale, I would tell him of the friar that, as he was preaching in the country, spied a poor wife of the parish whispering with her pew-fellow; and he, falling angry thereto, cried out unto her aloud, 'Hold thy babble, I bid thee, thou wife in the red hood.' Which when the housewife heard, she waxed as angry again, and suddenly she start up and cried out unto the friar again, that all the church rang thereon, 'Marry, sir, I beshrew his heart that babbleth most of us both. For I do but whisper a word with my neighbour here, and thou has babbled there all this hour.'[36]

The last of More's controversial writings was *The Answer to the first part of the poisonous book which a nameless heretic hath*

---

[35] *E.W.*, p. 963.

[36] *E.W.*, p. 948.

named the Supper of the Lord (1533). The 'nameless heretic' was almost certainly William Tyndale. This Answer has a special interest as it contains Sir Thomas More's own translation of St. John's Gospel, chapter six, verses 41-58.

The Jews murmured therefore of that that he had said, I am the living bread, that am descended from heaven. And they said, Is not this man the son of Joseph, whose father and mother we have known. How saith he therefore I am descended from heaven. Jesus therefore answered and said unto them, Murmur not among yourself. There can no man come to me, but if the father that sent me draw him, and I shall raise him again in the last day. It is written in the prophets: And they shall be all taught of God. Everyman that hath heard of the father and hath learned, cometh to me, not because any man hath seen the father, but he that is of God hath seen the father. Verily, verily, I tell you, he that believeth in me hath life everlasting. I am the bread of the life. Your fathers have eaten manna in the desert and be dead. This is the bread descending from heaven, that if any man eat thereof, he should not die. I am the living bread that am descended from the heaven. If a man eat of this bread, he shall live forever, and the bread which I shall give, is my flesh, which I shall give for the life of the world. The Jews therefore strove amongst themselves saying, How can this man give us his flesh to eat. Then said Jesus to them, Verily, verily, I say to you, but if ye eat the flesh of the son of man and drink his blood, ye shall not have life in you. He that eateth my flesh and drinketh my blood, hath life everlasting, and I shall raise him in the last day. My flesh is verily meat and my blood is verily drink. He that eateth my flesh and drinketh my blood, dwelleth in me and I in him. As the living father sent me, I also live for the father. And he that eateth me, he shall also live for me. This is the bread descended from heaven, not as your fathers have eaten manna and are dead. He that eateth this bread, shall live for ever.[37]

More expounded this Gospel in the first book of the *Answer*, and then went on to examine the teaching of the 'nameless heretic,' or 'Master Masker,' as he called him.

The concluding words of this book expressed the hope that these heretics may yet renounce their errors and return to the Church.

> From which [heresy] our Lord give them grace truly to turn in time, so that we and they together in one Catholic Church, knit unto God together in one catholic faith, faith I say, not faith alone as they do, but accompanied with good hope and with her chief sister well working charity, may so receive Christ's Blessed Sacrament here, and specially that we may so receive himself, his very blessed body, very flesh and blood, in the Blessed Sacrament, our holy blessed house, that we may here be with him incorporate so by grace, that after the short course of this transitory life, with his tender pity poured upon us in purgatory, at the prayer of good people, and intercession of holy saints, we may be with them in their holy fellowship, incorporate in Christ in his eternal glory. Amen.

When Sir Thomas More put his pen down after writing those words he had finished his controversy with heretics; it was fitting that his last printed words in a warfare that had used up thousands of words, should be a prayer of reconciliation.

---

[37] *E.W.*, p. 1043. The reader who would like to compare this with Tyndale's translation should turn to the authorized version which here follows Tyndale almost word for word.

Chapter XXII

The Nun of Kent

OON after his resignation, Sir Thomas More had a tomb erected in his parish church at Chelsea, and to it he had the body of his first wife, Jane, the mother of his children, transferred. The tomb was not erected in the chapel he had built in 1528, but was placed in the wall of the chancel on the Epistle side of the altar where he himself had so many times served the priest at Mass. It consisted of an altar tomb with a canopy; let into the wall at the back was a black marble slab on which the epitaph was inscribed.[1]

The following is a translation.

EPITAPH
ANNO 1532

Thomas More born in the City of London of no distinguished but of an honest family somewhat of a proficient in literature when, in his youth he had pleaded at the bar some years and discharged the office of under-sheriff in that city he, by the redoubted King Henry VIII (to whom alone of kings accrued the glory, before unknown, of being deservedly entitled Defender of the Faith, as indeed he proved himself by the sword as well as the pen) was called to court chosen a privy-counsellor, knighted, and made sub-treasurer, Chancellor of Lancaster, and Chancellor of

---

[1] Chelsea Old Church was hit by a bomb on 16th April, 1941; only the More Chapel escaped complete destruction. The Vicar informs me that 'the inscription panel was broken in four places but was put together and is now temporarily affixed to the wall of the Sir Thomas More Chapel. The tomb itself survived and the memorial masonry above it has been stored complete and is awaiting permanent restoration' (1952).

England in succession, by his King's great kindness.

Meantime he was chosen Speaker of the Commons and appointed ambassador to various courts; last of all to Cambrai, being associated with Cuthbert Tunstal, the chief of that embassy, then Bishop of London and since of Durham, a man than whom the world can scarcely boast one more learned, wiser, or better.

There he had the pleasure to see and to negotiate the renewal of the leagues between the chief princes of Christendom and the restoration to the world of long wished-for peace, which peace may heaven confirm and long preserve. When he had so acquitted himself in these duties and honours that neither could his good King arraign his conduct nor the peers or commons disapprove though he had been severe to thieves, murderers, and heretics.

At length his father, Sir John More, appointed by His Majesty a judge of the King's Bench, a man of courteous pleasant manners, harmless, gentle, full of compassion, just and uncorrupt, old indeed in years, yet fresh for his age in bodily strength, after living to see his son Chancellor of England, thinking he had tarried long enough on earth passed Willingly to heaven.

The son, on the death of his father, compared to whom, while he lived, he was called a young man, and indeed seemed so to himself, wanting now his best parent and beholding four children of his own and eleven grandchildren, began to fancy himself growing old. And this fancy was strengthened by the immediate succession of a disorder in his breast, a symptom as it were of approaching age. Having then tasted plentifully of this world's pursuits, the thing which he had wished for from a boy, that he might enjoy some of his last years free, and withdrawing himself by degrees from this life's business might have leisure to meditate on his future immortality, that thing at last (if God approve) by the incomparable kindness of his most indulgent King, having resigned his honours, he hath obtained.

And he hath erected this monument, having removed hither

the remains of his first wife, as a constant memorial of his ever-approaching death. That he may not have done this in vain while yet he lived, that he dread not the approach of death, but meet it cheerfully from the love of Christ, and that he find death not his extinction but the entrance of a happier existence, do thou, reader, assist him with thy pious prayers as well now while he liveth as after his decease.

> Here lies my Jane, dear wife of Thomas More,
> And here my Alice and myself would lie;
> Three girls, a boy, my Jane her partner bore,
> With rarest stepdames may my Alice vie.
> So blessed the first my youthful years with love,
> So soothes the second my maturer day.
> Each seems in vain superior worth to prove
> For each divides my heart with equal sway.
> Religion's laws had they allowed or fate
> Here braced in triple concord could we live;
> Grant grave, grant heaven that blessed united state,
> And death afford what life could never give.[2]

More explained the purpose of the epitaph in a letter to Erasmus.[3]

Some gossips here have been spreading it about that I had to resign against my will, though I pretend it was not so. So when I set up my tomb, I determined to state the matter as it is in my epitaph, that any one might refute it who could. As soon as they had taken note of it, as they could not show it to be false, they found fault with it as boastful. I preferred this to

---

[2] This is Archdeacon Wrangham's translation; it is more literal than that by William Rastell in *E.W.*, pp. 1419-20. The Latin text is given in *Haprsfeild*, pp. 279-81.

[3] *Allen*, x, 2831. The reference to the meeting of Parliament (4th February, 1533) gives the date of the letter. This is the last letter from More to Erasmus that has survived.

allowing the other rumour to gain ground, not indeed for my own sake, for I do not care very much what men say of me, provided that God approves of me; but since I had written in our own tongue some little books against some of our defenders of contentious doctrines, I considered that I ought to defend the integrity of my name; and that you may know how boastfully I have written you shall receive my epitaph, by which you will see that in my security of conscience I by no means flatter them, to prevent them from saying about me whatever they please. I have waited now till the meeting of Parliament since I exercised and resigned my office, but as yet no one has come forward to attack me. Either I have been so innocent or else so cautious, that my opponents must let me boast of one or other of these qualities.

But as regards this business, the King has spoken many times privately, and twice in public. For in words that I am ashamed to repeat, when my successor (a most illustrious man) was installed, the King, by the mouth of the Duke of Norfolk, the Lord High Treasurer of England, ordered an honourable testimony to be given that with difficulty he had yielded to my request to retire. And now contented with this, the King, out of his singular goodness to me, had the same thing repeated by my successor in his own presence, at the solemn assembly of the Peers and Commons in the speech which is made at the opening of Parliament.

The expressions More used when speaking of Henry VIII may puzzle us since we know what happened in 1534 and 1535. The epitaph speaks of 'the incomparable kindness of his most indulgent King,' and, in the last two letters to Erasmus, More wrote of 'the favour of an indulgent prince.' and, of 'his singular goodness to me.' There is no reason for thinking that he used such phrases—and others could be quoted of later date—without meaning what he said. It must be remembered that to him the office of a prince was of divine sanction and he could never speak or write of the holder of that office without due deference. This attitude—so hard for us to appreciate—makes it all the more significant that, ultimately, he felt compelled in conscience to oppose that prince outside the Council Chamber. Two comments of his on Henry have already been quoted: the first was the remark to Roper that 'if my head should win him a castle in France, it would not fail to go,' and the second was to Cromwell warning him not to tell the King 'what he is able to do.' These showed a shrewd knowledge of the character of the man who held the office of prince, but this in no way lessened the duty that he, as a subject, owed to the prince. Where he disagreed with the King's policy, he kept silence in public; his arguments were stated in the Council or to the King himself. His duty, as he saw it, was to give good counsel and to do the work with which he was concerned with the utmost integrity. He did not form a party, nor does he seem to have consulted others of like mind, such as Bishop John Fisher; he walked alone, and at the end, even his own family was not convinced of the rightness of his decision.

More's expressions of gratitude were not conventional; he had indeed received many marks of favour, not the least being his exceptional appointment as Lord Chancellor. There was, however, the stronger bond of loyalty. Even to the end, his attitude towards Henry was deeply influenced by the memory of those years of intimacy when Thomas More was the councillor the King most liked to have by his side. There is no record of a broken friendship in More's life; there is no record of an unbroken friendship in Henry's life.[4]

For some months Thomas More was able to live the retired life he so desired; he adjusted his family affairs and gave his thoughts to his controversial writings; between the time of his

---

[4] Should an exception be made of Thomas Cranmer? There seems to have been no intimacy in their relations.

resignation and Easter 1534 he wrote some two hundred thousand words against the heretics. It was, however, impossible for a man of his eminence to remain unaffected by public events, and the pace of these quickened rapidly after 1532. Whatever attitude he took up towards these radical changes was bound to affect the opinion of others even if he kept silent. His influence was considerable; he had a European reputation and Henry was rightly concerned with the attitude of the Emperor Charles, and what part Francis of France might decide to play. The knowledge that Thomas More was not actively supporting the King would be taken into account by these two monarchs. Henry would also be conscious of the strong hold More had on the loyalty of the citizens of London to one who had served them so well, and the support, or at least the acquiescence, of the City was essential to the security of the throne. The Wars of the Roses had made that fact clear.

Henry married Anne Boleyn towards the end of January 1533; this was not officially recognized until four months later, when Archbishop Cranmer, Warham's successor, declared the marriage valid. A few days earlier, on 23rd May, he had presided over a special court at Dunstable at which, in the absence of Catherine, he pronounced her marriage with Henry to be nullified.

When Thomas More heard that Henry and Anne were married, he made the prescient comment to Roper: 'God give grace, son, that these matters within a while be not confirmed with oaths.'[5]

He himself, as Roper tells us, had to make a difficult decision when Anne was to be crowned in Westminster Abbey on 1st June, 1533.

He received a letter from the Bishops of Durham, Bath,

---

[5] *Roper*, p. 57.

The Nun of Kent

and Winchester,[6] requesting him both to keep them company from the Tower to the coronation, and also to take twenty pounds that by the bearer thereof they had sent him to buy him a gown with; which he thankfully receiving, and at home still tarrying, at their next meeting said merrily unto them, 'My lords, in the letters which you lately sent me you required two things of me, the one whereof since I was so well content to grant you, the other therefore I thought I might be the bolder to deny you. And like as the one, because I took you for no beggars, and myself I knew to be no rich man, I thought I might the rather fulfil, so the other did put me in remembrance of an emperor that had ordained a law that whosoever committed a certain offence (which I now remember not) except it were a virgin should suffer the pains of death, such a reverence had he to virginity. Now so it happened that the first committer of that offence was indeed a virgin, whereof the emperor hearing was in no small perplexity, as he that by some example fain would have had that law to have been put in execution. Whereupon when his council had sat long, solemnly debating this case, suddenly arose there up one of his council, a good plain man, among them, and said, 'Why make so much ado, my lords, about so small a matter? Let her first be deflowered, and then after may she be devoured.' And so though your lordships have in the matter of the matrimony hitherto kept yourselves pure virgins, yet take good heed, my lords, that you keep your virginity still. For some there be by procuring your lordships first at the coronation to be present, and next to preach for the setting forth of it, and finally to write books to all the world in defence thereof, are desirous to deflower you; and when they have deflowered you, then will they not fail soon

---

[6] Tunstal, John Clerk and Stephen Gardiner.

after to devour you. Now my lords,' quoth he, 'it lieth not in my power but that they may devour me; but God being my good lord, I will provide that they shall never deflower me.'[7]

Many must have noticed the absence of the former Lord Chancellor who was still one of the Council. The new Queen, so quick to see a reproach, must have read it as an insult. More was to accept the Act of Succession as within the competence of Parliament; why then did he avoid the coronation? No doubt he was sick at heart at the thought of how Catherine of Aragon had been discarded, but so were many others who had enjoyed the society of that uphappy woman. As he told the Bishops, mere presence at the coronation implied approval of what had been done. But there may have been another consideration he had in mind. The coronation was a religious act taking place in the great Benedictine Abbey with the Archbishop as the chief officiant. After the anointing, Mass was said and the new Queen 'kneeled before the altar where she received of the Archbishop the Holy Sacrament.'[8] This was something more than an act of state; it was the sanctification of a union made in defiance of the Pope who had not yet pronounced his decision on the validity of the marriage between Henry and Catherine. It may have been some such view of the matter that kept Thomas More away from the coronation.

On 11th July, 1533, the Pope excommunicated Henry and declared his marriage with Anne Boleyn invalid; the enforcement of this was held in abeyance until September in the hope that Henry would yet retrace his steps. That month saw the birth of the Princess Elizabeth. On 23rd March, 1534, the Pope gave his decision on the marriage of Henry and Catherine; it was declared valid.

---

[7] *Roper*, p. 57.

[8] *Hall*, II, p. 238.

Writing to Cromwell on 5th March, 1534, before the Pope's decision was given, More referred to Anne Boleyn as 'this noble woman really anointed Queen.'[9] Was this a phrase used in a moment of human frailty? He had already been examined by the Council in the matter of the Nun of Kent, and the shadow of the Tower was very close; who dare blame him if, as his pen moved across the paper, he tried to ward off the blow with smooth words?

Parliament was kept busy during the two sessions of 1534, the first from January to March and the second during November and December. The Restraint of Appeals Act did not pass through the Commons without opposition, but this was not on religious grounds, but for commercial reasons since it was feared that the Emperor might cut off trade with Flanders. The Act forbade all appeals to Rome; the Acts of Praemunire had forbidden them without the consent of the king. 'This statute, the first definitive infringement of the constitutional relation between the English Church and Rome, is a landmark in history.'[10] Three other Acts completed the break with Rome. The Annates Act of 1531 was made absolute; no Bulls or Briefs were to be received from, or fees paid to, Rome. The second Act stopped the payment of Peter's Pence. The third Act put into legal form the concessions made by Convocation in 1532.

Formidable as these Acts were in their effects, they do not complete the story of that year's legislation. An Act of Succession was passed in March and further strengthened in November. By this the throne was assured to the heirs of Henry and Anne, and the Princess Mary was, by implication, declared a bastard. Coupled with this was the requirement that all the king's subjects must take an oath to the succession as so determined; it became

---

[9] *Rogers*, p. 497. In printing this letter in *E.W.*, William Rastell omitted this passage.

[10] H.A.L. Fisher, *History of England*, 1485-1547.

high treason to act, or write, against the marriage of the King with Anne, and to speak against it became misprision of treason. The 'whole contents and effects' of the Act had to be accepted without question.[11]

Thomas Cromwell's influence in this session of Parliament had been paramount. He had become Chancellor of the Exchequer in April 1533, and a year later was secretary to the King and Master of the Rolls. By this time, as a result of deaths and resignations and the creation of new constituencies it would be correct to call it a packed Parliament. With the passing of the Act of Succession he put all England at the King's mercy, but Henry was to show no mercy to anyone who dared to question anything he did; the Terror had begun.

Various niggling charges were at first made in what seems to have been a determined scheme to embarrass the former Lord Chancellor and so bring him to a more accommodating frame of mind. The first move was not against Sir Thomas More himself, but against his nephew William Rastell, who was called before Thomas Cromwell and charged with having printed *The Answer to the Poisonous Book*, which Cromwell declared was an attack on the recently published *Articles devised by the Whole Consent of the King's Council*;[12] this was an official justification of the King's proceedings in his marriage. Cromwell knew, of course, that *The Answer* was written by Sir Thomas More as part of his controversy with heretics. William Rastell was able to point out that, although the book was dated 1534, it was, in fact, in print by Christmas 1533 and had, therefore, been composed before the *Articles* book was available. When he repeated this to his uncle,

---

[11] It should be noted that the Act was very much more than an enactment concerning the succession. H.A.L. Fisher described it as 'a treatise on the canon law, a constitutional enactment, and a political manifesto' (*History*, p. 326).

[12] Amongst other statements it declared that the Pope was illegitimate, guilty of simony and of heresy. See *Bridgett*, p. 317.

Sir Thomas More wrote to Cromwell. The letter is dated from Chelsea, 1st February, 1534. In this he stated the facts again, and then referred to the Articles book.

> For of many things which in that book he touched, in some I know not the law,[13] and in some I know not the fact. And therefore would I never be so childish nor so play the proud arrogant fool, by whomsoever the book had been made, and to whomsoever the matter had belonged, as to presume to make an answer to the book, concerning the matter whereof I never were sufficiently learned in the laws, nor fully instructed in the facts. And then while the matter pertained unto the King's Highness, and the book professeth openly that it was made by his honourable Council, and by them put into print with his Grace's licence obtained thereunto, I verily trust in good faith that of your good mind to me, though I never wrote you word thereof, yourself with both think and say so much for me, that it were a thing unlikely that an answer should be made thereunto by me.[14]

The next attack was direct; this was the accusation, brought apparently by the new Queen's father, the Earl of Wiltshire, of having received bribes as judge and as Lord Chancellor. An account has already been given of how easily these charges were proved frivolous.[15]

A much more serious matter came up in February 1534. This concerned the relations of Bishop John Fisher, Sir Thomas More and others with Elizabeth Barton, the Nun, or Holy Maid, of Kent.

---

[13] Canon Law.

[14] *Rogers*, p. 469.

[15] See p. 313

She was a girl of humble origin of the Parish of Aldington[16] in Romney Marsh, who had fallen into trances after a serious illness. She told of visions she had had, and she made prophecies; her utterances attracted considerable attention. These early experiences were probably genuine, but it is now impossible to decide how far she was used for undesirable purposes; had she not been encouraged to venture into the quicksands of political forecasting, the subsequent tragedy may not have happened. She became a rallying figure for the widespread opposition to the King's separation from Catherine of Aragon, and made some wild prophecies of what would happen if Henry were united to Anne Boleyn. She had an audience of the King and later saw Bishop John Fisher and Sir Thomas More. Archbishop Warham had ordered an inquiry. Bishop Fisher was inclined to think favourably of her; he did not report her prophesyings to the King as she had spoken to Henry herself. Sir Thomas More was prudent in his treatment of the Nun and gave her sound advice.

Her opposition to the King's marriage with Anne made the Nun a dangerous person; Cromwell was greatly worried at the strength of the ill-feeling in the country towards Anne and of the loyalty still shown to Catherine of Aragon. He therefore decided that the condemnation of the Nun would prove a warning to others, and at the same time provide an opportunity for dragging down some of the leading men who were not enthusiastic enough in supporting the King. In October 1533 the Nun was examined by Cranmer at Cromwell's request, but, not for the last time, the Archbishop showed what Cromwell regarded as a tendency to be too lenient. At last the Nun admitted that many things she had said were 'feigned of her own imagination.' A month later she

---

[16] Of which Erasmus had been appointed Rector in 1532; he received a pension from the acting Rector, Richard Masters who was the incumbent during the affair of the Nun of Kent; he was involved in her condemnation and executed.

The Nun of Kent

and six associates made their confession[17] at St. Paul's before being sent to the tower. The names of several important persons had been mentioned during the inquiry. At first it was proposed to bring to trial those who had not reported the Nun's words to the King; this could be interpreted as misprision of treason. But judges, who were not yet completely cowed, made difficulties. It was therefore decided to proceed by Bill of Attainder, and the Nun and her associates were accused of treason and six others of misprision of treason. Amongst these were Bishop John Fisher, Sir Thomas More, and Thomas Abell who had acted so valorously in the cause of Queen Catherine.

More at once wrote to the King and to Thomas Cromwell, reminded Henry of the promise that he would be his 'good gracious lord' and begged him that 'no sinister information move your noble Grace to any more distrust of my truth and devotion toward you, than I have, or shall during my life, give the cause.'[18] The letter to Cromwell[19] gives a full account of More's relations with the Nun of Kent. The following passages are the most important.

> It is, I suppose, about eight or nine years ago since I heard of that housewife first, at which time the Bishop of Canterbury [Warham], that then was, God assoil his soul, sent unto the King's Grace a roll of paper in which were written certain words of hers, that she had, as report was then made, at sundry times spoken in her trances; whereupon it pleased the King's Grace to deliver me the roll, commanding me to look thereon and afterward show him what I thought therein. Whereunto, at another time, when his Highness asked me, I told him, that in good faith I found nothing in these words

---

[17] Sir Thomas More was present. See below, p. 371.

[18] *Rogers*, p. 489.

[19] *Rogers*, pp. 480-8.

that I could anything regard or esteem, for saving that some part fell into rhyme, and that, God wot, full rude, else for any reason, God wot, that I saw therein, a right simple woman might, in my mind, speak it of her own wit well enough, howbeit, I said, that because it was constantly reported for truth, that God wrought in her and that a miracle was showed upon her, I durst not nor would not, be bold in judging the matter. And the King's Grace, as methought, esteemed the matter as light as it after proved lewd.

He then related how about a year previously Father Richard Risby, a Franciscan, had been staying with him over-night, and spoke to him of the wonderful 'works that God wrought in her.' But when he went on to mention her references to the King,

> I said unto him that any revelation of the King's matters I would not hear of, I doubt not that the goodness of God should direct his Highness with his grace and wisdom. ... And he and I never talked any more of any such manner of matter, nor since his departing on the morrow, I never saw him after to my remembrance, till I saw him at Paul's Cross.

About Shrovetide another visitor, Father Hugh Rich of the Observant Friars of Richmond, spoke of the Nun and mentioned her 'revelations concerning the King's Grace.' More at once refused to hear anything further adding that 'since she hath been with the King's Grace herself, and told him, me thought it a thing needless to tell the matter to me or any man else.'

Father Rich seems to have been a somewhat ardent supporter of the Nun, but Thomas More gave him a warning.

> Father Rich, that she is a good virtuous woman, in good faith, I hear so many good folk so report her, that I verily think it true, and think it well likely that God worketh some good and great things by her. But yet are, you wot well, these strange tales no part of our creed, and therefore before you see them surely proved, you shall have my poor counsel not

to wed yourself so far forth to the credence of them as to report them very surely for true, lest that, if it should hap that they were afterward proved false, it might minish your estimation in your preaching, whereof might grow great loss.

He further related that on one occasion when he was visiting the house of the Brigittines at Syon, the Nun was there and he had some conversation with her at the request of the Fathers.

> We talked no word of the King's Grace or any great personage else, nor in effect, of any man or woman, but of herself, and myself, but after no long communication had for or ever we met, my time came to go home, I gave her a double ducat, and prayed her to pray for me and mine, and so departed from her and never spake with her after.

Later he felt some misgivings at reports of unwise conversations she had with her many visitors, and he wrote to her. A copy of the letter was enclosed with his to Cromwell. In it he reminded her that he had refused to discuss with her 'any matter of princes or of the realm.' He continued,

> Now, Madam, I consider well that many folk desire to speak with you, which are not all peradventure of my mind in this point, but some hap to be curious and inquisitive of things that little pertain unto their parts, and some might peradventure hap to talk of such things, as might after peradventure after turn to much harm, as I think you have heard how the late Duke of Buckingham moved with the fame of one that was reported a holy monk and had such talking with him as after was a great part of his destruction and disinheriting of his blood and great slander and infamy of religion. It sufficeth me, good Madam, to put you in remembrance of such things as I nothing doubt your wisdom and the spirit of God shall keep you from talking with any persons specially with lay persons, of any such things as pertain to princes' affairs, or the state of the realm, but only to

commune and talk with any person high and low of such manner things as may to the soul be profitable for you to show and for them to know.[20]

He told Cromwell that he was convinced after hearing the confessions at Paul's Cross that she was 'a false deceiving hypocrite,' and he had sent word of this at the time to the Charterhouse where she had been regarded with respect.

The letter was written by an *amanuensis*, and a postscript explains the reason for this.

> I pray you pardon me that I write not unto you of mine own hand, for verily I am compelled to forbear writing for a while by reason of this disease of mine, whereof the chief occasion is grown, as it is thought, by the stooping and leaning on my breast, that I have used in writing.

One aspect of this letter to Cromwell should not be overlooked. The extracts show that Thomas More had a wide association with the religious life of his day; priests came to see him, and he visited monasteries in or near London; his advice was sought and valued. Evidently he maintained his connexion with the Charterhouse.

More asked to be heard in his own defence before the Peers, but the King preferred that he should be seen by a commission of four Councillors—Cranmer, Audley, the Duke of Norfolk, and Cromwell. Before More set out from Chelsea, William Roper 'earnestly advised him to labour unto these lords for the help of his discharge out of that Parliament Bill; who answered me he would.'[21]

The most remarkable fact about this examination was that, according to Roper's account, the Nun of Kent was not mentioned. First of all Audley urged More, as an

---

[20] *Rogers*, p. 489.

[21] *Rogers*, pp. 65-71. It is an odd fact that the five men were all named Thomas.

acknowledgement of the King's favour to him, to 'add his consent' to that of Parliament, the Bishops and the Universities to the marriage proceedings. More's reply was that, as the King had allowed him liberty of judgement, and was fully aware of his opinions, he had hoped that the subject was closed. Then the lords began to threaten him with the King's extreme displeasure, specially, as More, they alleged, had incited the King to maintain the Pope's authority in his book on the Seven Sacraments. More's answer to this ridiculous charge has already been quoted.[22] Thereupon, as Roper noted, 'thus displeasantly departed they.'

More, however, was far from displeased.

Then took Sir Thomas More his boat towards his house at Chelsea, wherein by the way he was very merry, and for that was I nothing sorry, hoping that he had got himself discharged out of the Parliament Bill. When he was landed and come home, then walked we twain alone into his garden together, where I, desirous to know how he had sped, said, 'I trust, sir, that all is well because you be so merry.'

'It is so indeed, son Roper, I thank God,' quoth he.

'Are you then put out of the Parliament Bill?' said I.

'By my troth, son Roper,' quoth he, 'I never remembered it.

'Never remembered it, sir?' said I. 'A case that toucheth yourself so near, and us all for your sake. I am sorry to hear it, for I verily trusted, when I saw you so merry, that all had been well.'

Then said he, 'Wilt thou know, son Roper, why I was so merry?'

'That would I gladly, sir,' quoth I.

'In good faith, I rejoiced, son,' quoth he, 'that I had given the devil a foul fall, and that with those lords I had gone so far as

---

[22] See above, p. 161.

without great shame I could never go back again.'[23]

Had the Nun of Kent been mentioned, More would have remembered that his name was in the Bill of Attainder. The examination had demonstrated that the real intention of the King was to frighten Thomas More into acquiescence; the matter of the Nun was a mere pretext. He now knew what lay before him; the uncertainties of his position had been swept away by this plain revelation of the King's purpose. He felt renewed confidence, too, in the fact that he had been able to withstand the threats made by the Councillors. He once admitted to his daughter Margaret that he feared pain, and 'a fainter heart than thy frail father hath, thou canst not have.' This first encounter had shown that when the time came God would 'stay me with his holy Hand.'[24]

Henry was angry when this failure was reported to him. He stopped More's salary as a councillor, and expressed his intention of forcing through the Bill of Attainder even if it meant going to the Lords himself. Audley and Cromwell knew that this might wreck the Bill, for Thomas More's reputation and popularity were so high that discontent would increase if he were condemned on such slender evidence. It was with the greatest difficulty that they persuaded the King to have More's name withdrawn. The other names remained. Bishop Fisher in his absence through sickness was fined £300; Thomas Abell was sent to the Tower where he remained until his martyrdom six years later. Elizabeth Barton and five of her associates, including Fathers Risby and Rich, and Richard Masters, suffered at Tyburn.

Roper described how the news of his exemption was received by Sir Thomas More.

> Master Cromwell, meeting me in the Parliament House, willed me to tell my father that he was put out of the

---

[23] *Roper*, p. 69.

[24] *Rogers*, p. 546.

Parliament Bill. But because I had appointed to dine that day in London, I sent the message by my servant to my wife to Chelsea. Whereof when she informed her father, 'In faith, Meg,' quoth he, '*quod differtur non aufertur.*'[25]

After this, as the Duke of Norfolk and Sir Thomas More chanced to fall in familiar talk together, the Duke said unto him, 'By the Mass, Master More, it is perilous striving with princes. And therefore I would wish you somewhat to incline to the King's pleasure. For by God's body, Master More, *Indignatio principis mors est.*'[26] 'Is that all, my lord?' quoth he. 'Then in good faith is there no more difference between your Grace and me, but that I shall die today, and you tomorrow.'[27]

---

[25] 'What is put off is not laid aside.'

[26] 'The wrath of the King is death.' Warham had used the same quotation (*Proverbs* 16:14) in advising Queen Catherine.

[27] *Roper*, p. 71. More was, of course, speaking in general terms; but Norfolk was, after a lifetime of service, to experience the wrath of the King. In 1547 he and his son, Surrey, were convicted of high treason; Surrey was executed, but Norfolk escaped the block because Henry VIII died a few hours before the time of execution.

THOMAS CROMWELL

Chapter XXIII

The Oath

ON Low Sunday, 12th April, 1534, Sir Thomas More and William Roper went to hear the sermon at St. Paul's. Afterwards they walked to the Barge in Bucklersbury to see John and Margaret Clement. While they were there, a summons was served on More to appear the next day at Lambeth before the King's Commissioners and to take the oath of succession. He at once returned to Chelsea, and it must have been a comfort to him that he had been able to visit his old home again where his family had grown up, and where John Colet and Erasmus and so many other friends had gathered round him. Roper tells us of the last hours at Chelsea.

Then Sir Thomas More, as his accustomed manner was always, ere he entered into any matter of importance, as when he was first chosen of the King Privy's Council, when he was sent Ambassador, appointed Speaker of the Parliament, made Lord Chancellor, or when he took any weighty matter upon him, to go to church and be confessed, to hear Mass, and be houseled, so did he likewise in the morning early the selfsame day that he was summoned to appear before the lords at Lambeth.

And whereas he evermore used before at his departure from his wife and children, whom he tenderly loved, to have them bring him to his boat, and there to kiss them all, and bid them farewell, then would he suffer none of them forth of the gate to follow him, but pulled the wicket after him and shut them all from him, and with an heavy heart, as by his countenance it appeared, with me and our four servants there took he his boat towards Lambeth. Wherein sitting still sadly awhile, at the last he suddenly rounded me in the ear, and said, 'Son Roper, I thank our Lord the field is won.' What he meant thereby I then wist not, yet loath to seem ignorant, I answered, 'Sir, I am thereof very glad.' But as I conjectured afterwards, it was for that the love he had to God wrought in him so effectually that it conquered all his carnal affections utterly.[1]

For an account of the proceedings at Lambeth, Roper refers the reader 'to certain letters of his, sent to my wife, remaining in a great book of his works.' Only one letter[2] described the day at Lambeth; this was written from the Tower.

The Commissioners were Cranmer, Audley, Cromwell and William Benson, Abbot of Westminster.[3] More was the only layman who came before them that day and he was the first to be called in.

> I desired the sight of the oath, which they showed me under the Great Seal. Then desired I the sight of the Act of Succession, which was delivered me in a printed roll. After which read secretly by myself, and the oath considered with the Act, I showed unto them, that my purpose was not to put any fault either in the act or any man that made it, or in the oath or any man that sware it, nor to condemn the conscience of any man. But as for myself in good faith my conscience so moved me in the matter, that though I would not deny to sware to the succession, yet unto the oath that there was offered me I could not sware, without the jeoparding of my

---

[1] *Roper*, p. 73.

[2] *Rogers*, pp. 501-7, from which the following extracts are taken.

[3] He was subsequently the first and only Bishop of Westminster and later the first Dean; d. 1549.

soul to perpetual damnation.

This careful comparison between the Statute and the Oath was significant. All that the Statute required was an oath to accept the succession as laid down in the Act, but the oath went beyond this and required acceptance of the Supremacy and the repudiation of the Pope's authority. Roper records that More said to Margaret, 'I may tell thee, Meg, they that have committed me hither for refusing of this oath not agreeable with the statute, are not by their own law able to justify my imprisonment.'[4]

The Commissioners next tried to frighten him with the danger of the King's 'great indignation.' This had been attempted when he was examined in connexion with the affair of the Nun of Kent, and it showed little appreciation of his character to imagine that a second threat of that kind would be more successful. More was well aware of the risk he ran; after all, he knew Henry better than the Commissioners who had not yet stepped on to the public stage when More and the King were intimate. When this menace failed to move him,

> I was in conclusion commanded to go down into the garden, and thereupon I tarried in the old burned chamber that looketh into the garden and would not go down because of the heat.

Having taken his decision he felt no need to spend the time in debating the matter with himself, but found amusement in watching what went on around him.

> In that time saw I Master Doctor Latimer[5] come into the garden, and there walked he with divers other doctors and chaplains of my Lord of Canterbury, and very merry I saw him, for he laughed, and took one or twain about the neck so handsomely that, if they had been women, I would have

---

[4] *Roper*, p. 78.

[5] Hugh Latimer, burnt as a heretic, 1555.

weened he had been waxen wanton. After that came Master Doctor Wilson[6] forth from the lords and was with two gentlemen brought by me, and gentlemanly sent straight unto the Tower. What time my Lord of Rochester [Fisher] was called in before them, that cannot I tell. But at night I heard that he had been before them, but where he remained that night and so forth till he was sent hither [the Tower] I never heard. I heard also that Master Vicar of Croyden,[7] and all the remnant of the priests of London, that were sent for, were sworn, and that they had such favour at the Council's hand that they were not lingered nor made to dance any long attendance to their travail and cost, as suitors were sometime wont to be, but were sped apace to their great comfort, so far forth that Master Vicar of Croyden, either for gladness or for dryness, or else that it might be seen (*quod ille notus erat pontifici*) went to my Lord's buttery bar and called for drink, and drank (*valde familiariter*).

More was called in again and the Commissioners tried to impress him with the list of those who had taken the oath. They wanted to know to what parts of the oath he objected, and his reasons for doing so. As before, he refused to give the grounds of his objections.

And that if I should open and disclose the causes why, I should therewith but further exasperate his Highness, which I would in no wise do, but rather would I abide all the danger and harm that might come toward me, than give his Highness any occasion of further displeasure.

He offered, however, to set out his reasons in writing to the

---

[6] Nicholas Wilson, chaplain to the King. He took the oath in 1537, but was again in the Tower in 1540 for supporting the Pope's authority. Released, and died 1548. See below, p. 401.

[7] Rowland Phillips; he was several times under suspicion.

King if Henry on his part would undertake not to see further offence in such a statement. The Commissioners pointed out that no such declaration by the King could stand against the application of the statute.

Cranmer then argued that because More had said that he did not condemn any who took the oath, he must have some doubts on the matter, and in such a case he should obey the King as a matter of duty. This argument for a moment made More hesitate, but he replied

> that in my conscience this was one of the cases in which I was bounden that I should not obey my prince, since that whatsoever other folk thought of the matter (whose conscience and learning I would not condemn nor take upon me to judge) yet in my conscience the truth seemed on the other side.

The Abbot of Westminster then suggested that More should defer to the opinions expressed by Parliament and the Council.

> To that I answered, that if there were no more but myself on my side, and the whole Parliament on the other, I would be sore afraid to lean to my own mind only against so many. But on the other side, if it so be, that in some things for which I refuse the oath, I have (as I think I have) upon my part as great a council and a greater too, I am not then bounden to change my conscience, and conform to the council of one realm against the general Council of Christendom.

Thomas Cromwell expressed his distress at More's decision.

> For surely the King's Highness would now conceive a great suspicion against me, and think that the matter of the Nun of Canterbury was all contrived by my drift.

To this inconsequent remark More replied shortly that 'the contrary was true and well known.' The last sentence of the letter reads:

> Howbeit (as help me God) as touching the whole oath, I

never withdrew any man from it, nor never advised any to refuse it, nor never put, nor will, any scruple in any man's head, but leave every man to his own conscience. And me thinketh in good faith, that so were it good reason that every man should leave me to mine.

The Commissioners were puzzled by More's refusal to state the reasons for his refusal to take the oath, nor were they sure how best to proceed. So for a few days they committed him to the charge of the Abbot of Westminster.

Meanwhile they had put the oath to Bishop John Fisher. He had come up from Rochester a very sick man; he asked for time to study the wording of the oath. This was granted him, but when he came again before the Commissioners and they refused to modify the oath so that it referred simply to the succession, he refused to swear and was at once sent to the Tower.

Cranmer had been seeking for a way out of the difficulty. He wrote to Cromwell suggesting that both More and the Bishop should be allowed to take the simple oath to the succession but that this fact should not be published so that people would assume that they had subscribed to the whole oath like everyone else. He thought this would quieten not only the 'Princess-Dowager' (Catherine) but the Emperor as well as 'many other within this realm.' Cromwell put this suggestion to the King who instructed him to tell Cranmer that the Bishop and More must swear to the whole oath. Otherwise 'it might be taken not only as a confirmation of the Bishop of Rome's authority, but also as a reprobation of the King's second marriage.' In that sentence lies the explanation of the refusal of Bishop John Fisher and of Sir Thomas More to take the oath.

Roper was of the opinion that 'Queen Anne by her importunate clamour' stiffened the King's attitude; there is, however, no indication that Henry showed any inclination to give way; no doubt, Anne Boleyn had her share in this act of injustice, but it was not a decisive one. Henry and Cromwell were too well aware of the dangers their policy involved to heed the spur of a woman's tongue. If they could crush Fisher and More without serious trouble in the country or from outside it, then their policy would be more secure.

On 17th April, 1534, Sir Thomas More again came before the Commissioners and refused to take the oath. He was at once sent to the Tower.

> As he was going thitherward, wearing, as he commonly did, a chain of gold about his neck. Sir Richard Cromwell,[8] that had the charge of his conveyance thither, advised him to send home his chain to his wife, or to some of his children. 'Nay, sir,' quoth he, 'that I will not; for if I were taken in the field by my enemies, I would they should somewhat fare the better for me.'
>
> At whose landing Master Lieutenant[9] at the Tower gate was ready to receive him, where the porter demanded of him his upper garment. 'Master Porter,' quoth he, 'here it is,' and took off his cap, and delivered it him saying, 'I am very sorry it is no better for you.' 'No, sir,' quoth the porter, 'I must have your gown.'
>
> And so was he by Master Lieutenant conveyed to his lodging, where he called unto him John a' Wood his own servant, there appointed to attend upon him, who could neither write nor read; and sware him before the Lieutenant that if he should hear or see him, at any time, speak or write any manner of thing against the King, the Council, or the State of the Realm, he should open it to the Lieutenant, that the Lieutenant might incontinent reveal it to the Council.

---

[8] Son of Thomas Cromwell's sister who had married Morgan Williams; Richard took his uncle's name; he was not knighted until 1540. Oliver Cromwell was a direct descendant.

[9] Sir Edmund Walsingham.

That last incident shows that Thomas More realized how careful he would have to be to avoid the least excuse for his enemies to trap him into saying something that would bring him within the law; he knew that he had been committed to the Tower without legal justification.

Chapter XXIV

In the Tower

IR THOMAS MORE was in the Tower for fifteen months, and for the first twelve he was not harassed by interrogations. After a time Margaret Roper was allowed to visit him, and later Dame Alice was also given permission; the three walked in the Tower garden together. He was able to have books and facilities for writing. The following passage in *A Dialogue of Comfort* probably refers to the room or cell in which he was writing.[1] The visitor may have been Dame Alice.

> I wist a woman once that came into a prison to visit of her charity a poor prisoner there, whom she found in a chamber, to say the truth, meetly fair, and at leastwise it was strong enough; but with mats of straw the prisoner had made it so warm both under the foot and round the walls that in these things for the keeping of his health she was on his behalf glad and very well comforted. But among many other displeasures that for his sake she was sorry for, one she lamented much in her mind, that he should have the chamber door upon him by night made fast by the jailor that should shut him in. For, by my troth, quoth she, if the door should be shut upon me I would ween it would stop up my breath. At that word of hers the prisoner laughed in his mind, but he durst not laugh aloud nor say nothing to her, for somewhat indeed he stood in awe

---

[1] The tradition is that he was imprisoned in the Beauchamp Tower. Bishop Fisher was, for a time at least, in the Bell Tower.

of her and had his finding [expenses] there much part of her charity for alms; but he could not but laugh inwardly, why he wist well enough that she used on the inside to shut every night full surely her own chamber to her, both door and windows too, and used not to open them of all the long night.[2]

Dame Alice had to pay fifteen shillings a week 'board-lodgings,' as she called it, for the support of her husband and his servant. She was puzzled and impatient at his refusal to take the oath like other people. Roper reports one conversation with her husband.

At her first coming, like a simple ignorant woman, and somewhat worldly too, with this manner of salutation bluntly saluted him:

'What the good year, Master More,' quoth she. 'I marvel that you, that have been always hitherto taken for a wise man will now so play the fool to lie here in this close, filthy prison, and be content thus to be shut up amongst mice and rats, when you might be abroad at your liberty, and with the favour and good will both of the King and his Council if you would but do as all the Bishops and best learned of this realm have done. And seeing you have at Chelsea a right fair house, your library, your books, your gallery, your garden, your orchard, and all other necessaries so handsome about you, where you might in the company of me your wife, your children, and household be merry, I muse what a' God's name you mean here still thus fondly to tarry.'

After he had a while quietly heard her, with a cheerful countenance he said unto her:

'I pray thee, good Mistress Alice, tell me one thing.'

'What is that?' quoth she.

'Is not this house,' quoth he, 'as nigh heaven as my own?'

---

[2] *Dialogue of Comfort*, p. 385.

To whom she, after her accustomed homely fashion, not liking such talk, answered, 'Tilly-vally, Tilly-vally!'

'How say you, Mistress Alice,' quoth he, 'is it not so?'

'Bone Deus, bone Deus, man! Will this gear never be left?' quoth she.

'Well then, Mistress Alice, if it be so,' quoth he, 'it is very well. For I see no great cause why I should much joy either of my gay house or of anything belonging thereunto, when, if I should but seven years lie buried under the ground, and then arise and come thither again, I should not fail to find some therein that would bid me get me out of doors, and tell me it were none of mine. What cause have I then to like such an house as would so soon forget his master?'

So her persuasions moved him but little.[3]

Margaret was her father's confidante during these months of waiting. She herself was not able to share his objections to the oath; she took it with a mental reservation, but it may not have been the same oath that was tendered to More and Fisher. Thomas More had not imposed his own opinions even on his family, but that meant no loss of confidence or of affection.

The following reassuring note was sent to Margaret as soon as possible after More arrived at the Tower.

Mine own good daughter.

Our Lord be thanked, I am in good health of body and in good quiet of mind: and of worldly things I no more desire than I have. I beseech Him make you all merry in the hope of heaven. And such things as I somewhat longed to talk with you all, concerning the world to come, our Lord put them into your minds, as I trust he doth, and better too, by his Holy Spirit: who bless you and preserve you all. Written with a

---

[3] *Roper*, p. 84.

cole[4] by your tender loving father, who in his poor prayers forgetteth none of you all, nor your babes, nor your nurses, nor your good husbands nor your good husbands' shrewd[5] wives, nor your father's shrewd wife neither, nor our other friends. And thus fare you heartily well for lack of paper.

Thomas More, Knight.

Our Lord keep me continually true faithful and plain, to the contrary whereof I beseech him heartily never suffer me live. For as for long life (as I have often told thee Meg) I neither look for, nor long for, but am well content to go, if God call me hence tomorrow. And I thank our Lord I know no person living that I would had one fillip for my sake: of which mind I am more glad than of all the world beside.

Recommend me to your shrewd Will and mine other sons, and to John Harris my friend, and yourself knoweth to whom else, and to my shrewd wife above all, and God preserve you all and make and keep you his servants all.[6]

Margaret wrote a letter to her father in which she seems to have urged him to submit to the King's wishes. The letter has not survived. William Rastell, when he printed her father's reply, said that she wrote this 'though she nothing so thought to win thereby credence with Master Thomas Cromwell that she might the rather get liberty to have free resort unto her father.' She knew that all letters to prisoners were opened; her trick succeeded but not without giving her father a shock for he took it as an expression of her true opinion. So he answered:

---

[4] Presumably, a bit of charcoal. The word 'coal' was used as a verb to mean 'to write with charcoal' (O.E.D.). A letter written in such a perishable medium would be at once copied out; Cresacre More said that his grandfather (John More) inked over the lettering.

[5] 'Shrewd' is a curious term to use; was it a private, family joke?

[6] *Rogers*, p. 507. *Rogers*, following *E.W.*, puts this letter after the one describing More's reception by the Commissioners, but it was surely written first as a hurried note of comfort sent as soon as possible.

If I had not been, my dearly beloved daughter, at a firm and fast point (I trust in God's great mercy) this good great while before, your lamentable letter had not a little abashed me, surely far above all other things, of which I hear divers times not a few terrible toward me. But surely they all touched me never so near, nor were so grievous unto me, as to see you, my well-beloved child, in such vehement piteous manner labour to persuade me that thing wherein I have of pure necessity for respect unto mine own soul, so often given you so precise answer before. Wherein as touching the points of your letter, I can make none answer, for I doubt not but you well remember that the matters which move my conscience (without declaration whereof I can nothing touch the points) I have sundry times showed you that I will disclose them to no man. And therefore, daughter Margaret, I can in this thing no further, but like as you labour me again to follow your mind to desire and pray you both to leave such labour, and with my former answers to hold yourself content.[7]

Margaret replied in a letter full of affection and appreciation but prudently avoiding any withdrawal of her previous arguments. It ends:

Your own most loving obedient daughter and bedeswoman, Margaret Roper, which desireth above all worldly things to be in John a' Wood's stead to do you some service. But we live in hope that we shall shortly receive you again, I pray God heartily we may, if it be his holy will.[8]

At last she received permission to visit her father. He wrote a brief note for her to take away to show to his friends.

To all my loving friends.

For as much as being in prison I cannot tell what need I

---

[7] *Rogers*, p. 508.

[8] *Rogers*, p. 511.

may have, or what necessity I may hap to stand in, I heartily beseech you all, that if my well-beloved daughter Margaret Roper (which only of all my friends hath, by the King's gracious favour, license to resort to me) do anything desire of any of you, of such thing as I shall hap to need, that it may like you no less to regard and tender it, than if I moved it unto you and required it of you personally present myself. And I beseech you all to pray for me, and I shall pray for you.

Your faithful lover and poor bedesman.

Thomas More, Knight, prisoner.[9]

More's family and friends were doing what they could to help him. His step-daughter, Lady Alice Alington, seized the chance of a meeting with the Lord Chancellor, Audley, to ask him to 'be still good lord unto my father.' Audley said that he had indeed been so in the matter of the Nun of Kent, but the position now was different; 'he marvelled that my father is so obstinate in his own conceit, as that everybody went forth with all save only the blind Bishop and he.' Then he laughingly related two fables, one of them being Wolsey's tale of the fools and the rain. 'I was abashed of this answer,' Alice wrote to Margaret, 'and I see no better suit than to Almighty God.'[10]

When Margaret next went to the Tower she took Alice's letter with her to show her father. The discussion they had is recorded in a remarkable letter from Margaret to Alice. When William Rastell published it, he suggested that it was possibly the composition of More himself. Its form is that of a dialogue with Alice's letter as the theme; Margaret puts some of the arguments that she may have advanced in the letter that had so upset her father. The fact alone suggests that her answer to Alice was a studied piece of composition since she would not otherwise have

---

[9] *Rogers*, p. 511.

[10] *Rogers*, pp. 512-73.

repeated suggestions that she knew her father so disliked. Perhaps father and daughter as they sat together, or walked in the Tower garden, planned the letter between them as an answer to those who thought More was being foolishly obstinate; then, when she got back to Chelsea, Margaret wrote the whole discussion down in this notable letter.

She refers in the opening paragraphs[11] to his state of health and to their customary devotions when they met.

> When I had a while talked with him, first of his diseases both in his breast of old, and his reins now by reason of gravel and stone, and of the cramp also that divers nights grippeth him in his legs, and that I found by his words that they were not much increased, but continued after their manner that they did before, sometime very sore and sometime little grief, and that at that time I found him out of pain, and (as one in his case might) meetly well-minded, after our seven Psalms[12] and the Litany said, to sit and talk and be merry, beginning first with other things of the comfort of my mother, and the good order of my brother, and all my sisters, disposing themself every day more and more to set little by the world, and draw more and more to God, and that his household, his neighbours, and other good friends abroad, diligently remembered him in their prayers. ...

She then produced Alice Alington's letter and gently urged him to consider again the possibility of submitting to the King.

> With this my father smiled upon me and said, 'What, Mistress Eve (as I called you when you first came) hath my daughter Alington played the serpent with you, and with a letter set you a-work to come tempt your father again, and for the favour that you bear him labour to make him swear

---

[11] *Ibid.*, pp. 514-32, from which the following extracts are taken.

[12] The Penitential Psalms.

against his conscience, and so send him to the devil?'

He read the letter twice.

And after that he paused, and then thus he said, 'Forsooth, daughter Margaret, I find my daughter Alington such as I have ever found her, and I trust ever shall, as naturally minding me as you that are mine own. Howbeit, her take I verily for mine own too, since I have married her mother, and brought up her of a child as I have brought up you, in other things and learning both, wherein I thank God she findeth now some fruit, and bringeth her own up virtuously and well.

...

In this matter she hath used herself like herself, wisely and like a very daughter toward me, and in the end of her letter, giveth as good counsel as any man that wit hath would wish, God give me grace to follow it and God reward her for it. Now daughter Margaret, as for my lord [Audley] I not only think, but have also found it, that he is undoubtedly my singular good lord. And in mine other business concerning the silly nun, as my cause was good and clear, so was he my good lord therein, and Master Secretary [Cromwell] my good master too. For which I shall never cease to be faithful bedesman for them both and daily do I, by my troth, pray for them as I do for myself. And whensoever it should happen (which I trust in God shall never happen) that I be found other than a true man to my prince, let them never favour me neither of them both, nor of truth no more it could become them to do.

He then discussed Audley's two fables and showed that they were not applicable to his problem. The reference to 'the blind Bishop' brought this comment:

For albeit, that of very truth, I have him [Fisher] in that reverent estimation, that I reckon in this realm no one man, in wisdom, learning and long approved virtue together, meet to be matched and compared with him, yet that in this matter I was not led by him, very well and plainly appeareth, both in that I refused the oath before it was offered him, and in that also his Lordship was content to have sworn of that oath (as I perceived since by you when you moved me to the same) either somewhat more, or in some other manner than ever I minded to do. Verily, daughter, I never intend (God being my good lord) to pin my soul at another man's back, not even the best man that I know his day living; for I know not whither he may hap to carry it.

Bishop John Fisher and Sir Thomas More do not seem to have spoken to each other while they were in the Tower. More sent him presents of food, and towards the end, they exchanged some notes. Fisher was, from the beginning, kept more rigorously confined than More.

Margaret put forward the argument that since this was a Matter approved by Parliament, he should hesitate again before opposing its decisions. More elaborated the reply made to the Commissioners when they made the same point.

'Marry, Margot.' quoth my father again, 'for the part that you play, you play it not amiss. But Margaret first, as for the law of the land, though every man being born and inhabiting therein, is bounden to the keeping in every case upon some temporal pain, and in many cases upon pain of God's displeasure too, yet is there no man bounden to swear that every law is well made, nor bounden upon the pain of God's displeasure to perform any such point of the law, as were indeed unlawful. Of which manner kind, that there may such hap to be made in any part of Christendom, I suppose no man doubteth, the General Council of the whole body of Christendom evermore in that point except; which, though it may make some things better than other, and some things may grow to that point, that by another law they may need to be reformed, yet to institute any thing in such wise, to God's displeasure, as at the making might not lawfully be performed, the spirit of God that governeth his church, never hath it suffered, nor never hereafter shall, his whole Catholic Church lawfully gathered together in a General Council, as Christ hath made plain promises in Scripture.'

His detailed exposition of this aspect of his problem silenced Margaret.

When he saw me sit with this very sad, as I promise you, sister, my heart was full heavy for the peril of his person, for in faith I fear not his soul, he smiled upon me and said, 'Now, now, daughter Margaret. What now mother Eve? Where is your mind now? Sit not musing with some serpent in your breast, upon some new persuasion to offer father Adam the apple yet once again.'

'In good faith, father,' quoth I, 'I can no further go. . . . For since the example of so many wise men cannot in this matter move you, I see not what to say more, but if I should look to persuade you with the reason that Master Henry Patenson made. For he met one day one of our men, and when he asked where you were, and heard that you were in the Tower still, he waxed even angry with you and said,

'Why? What aileth him that he will not swear? Wherefore should he stick to swear? I have sworn the oath myself!' And so I can in good faith go now no further neither, after so many wise men whom you take for no example, but if I should say like Master Harry, "Why should you refuse to swear, father? For I have sworn myself."

At this he laughed and said, 'That word was like Eve too, for she offered Adam no worse fruit than she had eaten herself.' 'But yet, father,' quoth I, 'by my troth, I fear me very sore that this matter will bring you in marvellous heavy trouble. You know well that as I showed you, Master Secretary [Cromwell] sent you word as your very friend to remember that Parliament lasteth yet.'

'Margaret,' quoth my father, 'I thank him right heartily. But as I showed you then again, I left not this gear unthought on. And albeit I know well that if they would make a law to do me any harm, that law could never be lawful, but that God shall I trust keep me in that grace that concerning my duty to my prince no man shall do me hurt but if he do me wrong (and then as I told you, this is like a riddle, a case in which a man may lose his head and have no harm), and notwithstanding also that I have good hope that God shall never suffer so good and wise a prince, in such wise to requite the long service of his true faithful servant, yet since there is nothing impossible to fall, I forgot not in this matter the counsel of Christ in the Gospel, ere I should begin to build this castle for the safeguard of my own soul, I should sit and reckon what the charge would be. I counted, Margot, full surely many a restless night, while my wife slept, and weened that I slept too, what peril was possible for to fall to me, so far forth that I am sure there can come none above. And in devising, daughter, thereupon, I had a full heavy heart. And yet (I thank our Lord) for all that, I never thought to change, though the very uttermost should hap me that my fear ran upon.'

Finally he reaffirmed his trust in God.

And finally Margot, this wot I well, that without my fault he will not let me be lost. I shall therefore with good hope commit myself wholely to him. And if he suffer me for my faults to perish, yet shall I then serve for a praise of his justice. But in good faith, Meg, I trust that his tender pity shall keep my poor soul safe and make me commend his mercy. And therefore mine own good daughter, never trouble thy mind for anything that ever shall hap to me in this world. Nothing can come but that that God will.

This letter ends abruptly without any personal greeting from

Margaret to Alice; this supports the view that it was a carefully thought out reply, devised as a conversation, to those critics who could not understand More's position. It may have been used in this way by being passed from hand to hand as prudently as possible. The readers would note that More still avoided telling them exactly the grounds of his refusal.

There was a third prisoner in the Tower, Dr. Nicholas Wilson, who had been sent there, it will be recalled, just before More made his second appearance before the Commissioners. After some months of imprisonment, Wilson seems to have faltered in his resolution and it was spread about that he had taken the oath. More wrote two letters to him; the first was brief and opened with these sentences.

> Our Lord be your comfort and whereas I perceive by sundry means that you have promised to swear the oath, I beseech our Lord give you thereof good luck.[13]

This complete confidence in the sincerity of others is also shown in a report of a remark More made regarding Bishop Tunstal. One of his servants, named Burton, came to see More and Fisher. More asked Burton how his master was and whether he was likely to join them in the Tower. Burton replied that he did not know the Bishop's mind in the matter. To this More replied, 'If he do not, no force, for if he live he may do more good than to die with us.'[14]

The second letter to Dr. Wilson seems to have been in answer to one showing that his mind was still unsettled and begging for More's counsel. The reply was of some length but it did not attempt to guide Wilson; it recapitulated their discussion together at the time when the King had asked More to consult with others

---

[13] *Rogers*, p. 532.

[14] Christopher Chaytor, Tunstal's Episcopal Registrar, reported this in 1539. See Appendix XVI of C. Sturge's *Cuthbert Tunstal*. 'No force'—'no matter.'

on the matter of his marriage. More gave his reasons for refusing 'to blame or dispraise the conscience of other men. ... I find of mine own life, matters enough to think on.' In the course of the letter he mentioned that he had been so ill while a prisoner that he had expected to have given up my ghost ere this.'

Whether it was this letter or not that stiffened Dr. Wilson's resolution is not known, but he remained in the Tower and it was not until 1537 that he at last took the oath and was released. He received preferment in the church, but his subsequent career showed that he was by no means satisfied that he had taken the right course.

Toward the end of 1534, Thomas More was subjected to greater restrictions, and apparently, no visitors were allowed. The greatest deprivation was that he could no longer hear Mass as he seems previously to have done in one of the Tower Chapels, St. Peter ad Vincula or St. John's. Margaret wrote in great distress, and her father replied:

> The cause of my close keeping again did of likelihood grow of my negligent and very plain true word which you remember. And verily whereas my mind gave me (as I told you in the garden) that some such thing were likely to happen, so doth my mind always give me that some folk yet ween that I was not so poor as it appeared in the search, and that it may therefore happen, that yet eftsoons ofter than once, some new sudden searches may hap to be made in every house of ours as narrowly as is possible. Which thing, if ever it so should hap, can make but game to us that know the truth of my poverty, but if they find my wife's gay girdle and her golden beads. Howbeit I verily, believe in good faith, that the King's Grace of his benign pity will take nothing from her. I thought and yet think that I was shut up again, upon some new causeless suspicion, grown peradventure upon some secret sinister information, whereby some folk haply thought that there should be found against me some other greater

things. But I thank our Lord whensoever this conjecture hath fallen in my mind, the clearness of my conscience hath made mine heart hop for joy... Now have I heard since that some say that this obstinate manner of mine, in still refusing the oath, shall peradventure force and drive the King's Grace to make a further law for me. I cannot let [hinder] such a law to be made. But I am very sure that if I died by such a law, I should die for that point innocent afore God. And albeit, good daughter, that I think our Lord hath the hearts of kings in his hand, would never suffer of his high goodness, so gracious a Prince, and so many honourable men, and so many good men as be in the Parliament to make such an unlawful law, as that should be if it so mishapped, yet lest I note that point unthought upon, but many times more than one revolved and cast in my mind before my coming hither, both that peril and all other that might put my body in peril of death by the refusing of this oath. In devising thereupon, albeit (mine own good daughter) that I found myself (I cry God mercy) very sensual and my flesh much more shrinking from pain and from death, than methought it the part of a faithful Christian man, in such a case as my conscience gave me, that in the saving of my body should stand the loss of my soul, yet I thank our Lord, that in that conflict, the Spirit had in conclusion the mastery, and reason with help of faith finally concluded, that for to be put to death wrongfully for doing well (as I am very sure I do, in refusing to swear against mine own conscience, being such as I am not upon peril of my soul bounden to change whether my death should come without law or by colour of law) it is a case in which a man may lose his head and yet have none harm, but instead of harm inestimable good at the hand of God.[15]

---

[15] *Rogers*, pp. 540-2.

In a later letter Margaret seems to have spoken of her sense of fraility in facing their troubles. To this her father answered:

> Surely, Meg, a fainter heart than thy frail father hath, canst you not have. And yet I verily trust in the great mercy of God that he shall of his goodness so stay me with his holy hand that he shall not finally suffer me to fall wretchedly from his favour. And the like trust, dear daughter, in his high goodness I verily conceive of you.[16]

A priest, "one Master Leder," of whom nothing further is known, wrote to Sir Thomas More at the beginning of 1535; he appears to have heard that More had at last taken the oath. The final paragraph of his answer reads:

> It hath been showed me that I am reckoned wilfull and obstinate because that since my coming hither I have not written unto the King's Highness and by mine own writing made some suit unto his Grace. But in good faith I do not forbear it of any obstinacy, but rather of a lowly mind and a reverent, because that I see nothing that I could write but that I fear me sore that his Grace were likely rather to take displeasure with me for it than otherwise, while his Grace believed me not that my conscience is the cause but rather obstinate wilfulness. But surely that my let [obstruction] is but my conscience, that knoweth God to whose order I commit the whole matter. *In cuius manu corda regum sunt.* I beseech our Lord that all may prove as true faithful subjects to the King that have sworn, as I am in my mind very sure that they be, which have refused to swear.[17]

Had a rumour been deliberately spread about that Sir Thomas More had at last submitted to the King's pleasure?

---

[16] *Rogers*, p. 546.

[17] *Rogers*, p. 550.

Chapter XXV

The Interrogations

AT the end of 1534 Dame Alice More and the family appealed to the King. They had been greatly alarmed at Sir Thomas More's rapid decline in health while in the Tower; his infirmities had increased and he himself thought that he could not recover from the pain and weakness that beset him. The King, in the ruthless pursuit of his desire to make all men approve of all his actions, was concentrating his anger on two very sick men; the aged Bishop was manifestly near his end, and Sir Thomas More, suffering from some disease of the chest, and tortured with gravel and the stone, was unlikely to live long.

The appeal shows something of the strain under which the More family was living at this time.

> In lamentable wise, beseech your most noble Grace your most humble subjects and continual bedesfolk, the poor miserable wife and children of your true, poor, heavy[1] subject and bedesman, Sir Thomas More, Knight, that whereas the same Sir Thomas being your Grace's prisoner in your Tower of London by the space of eight months and above, in great continual sickness of body and heaviness of heart, during all which space notwithstanding that the same Sir Thomas More had by refusing of the oath forfeited unto your most noble Grace all his goods and chattels and the profit of all his lands, annuities and fees that as well himself as your said

---

[1] Weighed down with sorrow.

bedeswoman his wife should live by, yet your most gracious Highness of your most blessed disposition suffered your said bedeswoman, his poor wife, to retain and keep still his moveable goods and the revenues of his lands to keep her said husband and her poor household with.

So it is now, most gracious Sovereign, that now late by reason of a new Act or twain made in this last passed prorogation of your Parliament, not only the said former forfeiture, but also the inheritance of all such lands and tenements as the same Sir Thomas had of your most bountiful gift, amounting to the yearly value £66 is forfeited also. And thus (except your merciful favour be showed) your said poor bedeswoman his wife, which brought fair substance to him, which is all spent in your Grace's service, is likely to be utterly undone and his poor son, one of your said humble suppliants, standing charged and bounden for the payment of great sums of money due by the said Sir Thomas unto your Grace, standeth in danger to be cast away and undone in this world also. But over all this the said Sir Thomas himself, after his long true service to his power diligently done to your Grace, is likely to be in his age and continual sickness, for lack of comfort and good keeping, to be shortly destroyed, to the woeful heaviness and deadly discomfort of all your said sorrowful suppliants.

In consideration of the premises, for that his offence is grown not of any malice or obstinate mind, but of such a long continual and deep-rooted scruple, as passeth his power to avoid and put away, it may like your most noble Majesty of your most abundant grace to remit and pardon your most grievous displeasure to the said Sir Thomas and to have tender pity and compassion upon his long distress and great heaviness, and for the tender mercy of God to deliver him out of prison and suffer him to live the remnant of his with your said poor bedeswoman his wife and other of your poor suppliants his children, with only such entertainment of living as it shall like your most noble Majesty of your gracious alms and pity to appoint him. And this in the way of mercy and pity, and all your said poor bedesfolk I shall daily during their lives pray to God for the preservation of your most royal estate.[2]

The appeal had no effect, and the disposal of More's lands was continued. In December 1534 a corrody he held in the monastery of Glastonbury was granted to Richard Snell, a yeoman of the Crown; in the next month More's Oxfordshire manors went to Henry Norris, an adherent of Anne Boleyn, and in April her brother, Sir George Boleyn (Rochford) took possession of the manor of South in Kent;[3] both he and Norris were executed two days before the Queen in 1536.

More had attempted before his arrest to provide for his children, but these arrangements were set aside by the attainder except the provision for the Ropers; a lucky matter of dates saved their share of the property.[4]

Parliament met in November 1534 and completed the structure of Tudor despotism. The Act of Supremacy declared the King to be 'the only supreme head in earth of the Church of England'; there was no saving clause 'as far as the law of Christ allows.' The Act of Succession was strengthened by the inclusion of the oath. The Act of Treasons made it high treason after 1st February, 1535, 'maliciously to wish, will, or desire by words or writing, or by craft imagine, invent, practise, or attempt any bodily harm to be done or committed to the king's most royal person, the queen's, or their heirs apparent, or deprive them or any of them of their dignity, title or name of their royal estates, or

---

[2] *Rogers*, pp. 547-9.

[3] *L.P.*, VII, 1601; VIII, 149, 632.

[4] *Roper*, pp. 79-80.

slanderously and maliciously publish and pronounce, by express writing or words, that the king, our sovereign lord, should be heretic, schismatic, tyrant, infidel, etc.' This Act was like Browning's mythical text:

> Once you trip on it, entails
> Twenty-nine distinct damnations,
> One sure, if another fails.

The word 'maliciously' had been included after some discussion in the Commons in the hope that it would put some limit on the application of the Act; but it proved no obstacle to the Council and judges.

An Act of Attainder was passed against Bishop Fisher, Nicholas Wilson, and four others, and a separate Act against Sir Thomas More; this meant that his property was forfeited to the Crown and he was condemned to perpetual imprisonment. The Act of Treasons provided new means for ensnaring such inflexible opponents as Fisher and More; if, after 1st February, they could be persuaded to express, or even to hint, an opinion that came within the meaning of the Act, then they could be brought to trial. Cromwell, therefore, now used all his skill to get the crucial evidence; he succeeded with Fisher, but perjured testimony had to be used against More.

The first interrogation[5] in the Tower was on 30th April, 1535. More's account is in a letter written to Margaret a day or two afterwards.

> I doubt not but by reason of the Councillors resorting

---

[5] There is some difficulty about dates. The indictment (*Harpsfield*, pp. 269-276) refers to two interrogations, 7th May and 3rd June. More's letter is definite; 'the last day of April.' Roper refers to a visit from Cromwell (see below, p. 318) which may be the interrogation of 7th May. The indictment makes no reference to the one on 30th April, but this produced no useful material for the case.

hither, in this time (in which our Lord be their comfort) these fathers of the Charterhouse and Master Reynolds of Syon that be now judged to death for treason (whose matters and causes I know not) may hap to put you in trouble and fear of mind concerning me being here prisoner, specially for that it is not unlikely but that you have heard that I was brought also before the Council here myself.[6]

The Carthusians were John Houghton, Prior of the House of the Salutation, London; Augustine Webster, Prior of the House of the Visitation, Axholme, and, Robert Lawrence, Prior of Beauvale, Nottinghamshire. With them were Dr. Richard Reynolds of the Brigettine House of Syon, and John Hale, Rector of Isleworth, who had critized the morality of Henry VIII. Prior Houghton and Dr. Reynolds were well known to Sir Thomas More, and he may have known John Hale. The Carthusians had taken the oath to the succession after some misgivings in 1534 at the persuasion of Archbishop Lee of York and Bishop Stokesley of London. The matter was remote from the contemplative lives of these monks who had few contacts with the outside world. The oath of Supremacy was a different question, for this touched the Church. Prior Houghton sought an interview with Thomas Cromwell on 16th April; with him were the Priors of Beauvale and Axholme; they guilelessly asked to be excused from taking the oath. They were quickly disillusioned and within less than a fortnight they, with Richard Reynolds and John Hale, had been tried and condemned as traitors.

More continues:

> On Friday the last day of April in the afternoon, Master Lieutenant came in here unto me, and showed me that Master Secretary would speak with me. Whereupon I shifted my gown, and went out with Master Lieutenant into the gallery

---

[6] *Rogers*, pp. 550-4, from which the quotations are taken.

to him. Where I met many, some known and some unknown in the way. And in conclusion coming into the chamber where his Mastership sat with Master Attorney, Master Solicitor, Master Bedyll, and Master Doctor Tregonwell. I was offered to sit with them, which in no wise I would.

The attorney-general, Sir Christopher Hales, was one of the capable agents of Henry's policy who reaped their reward when the monasteries were dissolved. The solicitor-general, Sir Richard Rich, was a more sinister, time-serving creature. Thomas Bedyll, 'that smooth, sedate archdeacon,'[7] was clerk of the Privy Council; Dr. John Tregonwell (knighted, 1555) had been proctor for the King in the marriage proceedings, and he was to be the least unscrupulous of the monastic visitors.

Thomas Cromwell opened the interrogation.

Master Secretary showed unto me that he doubted not but that I had by such friends as hither resorted to me seen the new statutes made at the last sitting of the Parliament. Whereunto I answered: yea, verily. Howbeit, forasmuch as being here, I have no conversation with any people, I thought it little need for me to bestow much time upon them, and therefore I redelivered the book shortly and the effect of the statutes I never marked nor studied to put in remembrance. Then he asked me whether I had not read the first statute of them, of the King being Head of the Church. Whereunto I answered, yes. Then his Mastership declared unto me, that since it was now by Act of Parliament ordained that his Highness and his heirs be, and ever right have been, and perpetually should be, Supreme Head in earth of the Church of England under Christ, the King's pleasure was that those of his Council there assembled should demand mine opinion, and what my mind was therein.

---

[7] Matthew, *The Reformation and the Contemplative Life* (1934), p. 237.

It will be noted that the words 'under Christ' are used here. Did Cromwell slip them in knowing that More had not studied the Act in detail?

> Whereunto I answered that in good faith I had well trusted that the King's Highness would never have commanded any such question to be demanded of me, considering that I ever from the beginning well and truly from time to time declared my mind unto his Highness, and since that time I had said unto your Mastership, Master Secretary, also, both by mouth and by writing. And now I have in good faith discharged my mind of all such matters, and neither will dispute King's titles nor Pope's, but the King's true faithful subject I am and will be, and daily I pray for him and all his, and for you all that are of his honourable Council, and for all the realm, and otherwise than this I never intend to meddle.

Cromwell urged that the King was anxious to release More provided he would submit himself.

> Whereunto I shortly (after the inward affection of my mind) answered for a very truth, that I would never meddle in the world again, to have the world given me. And to the remnant of the matter, I answered in effect as before, showing that I had fully determined with myself neither to study nor meddle with any matter of this world, but that my whole study should be upon the passion of Christ and mine own passage out of this world.

More was then asked to withdraw for a while, and on his return Cromwell tried another argument, this time with a threat behind it. Did not More still think it his duty, though if prisoner and condemned to a life sentence, to obey the King who would follow the course of his law toward such as he shall find obstinate?' He pointed out that More's attitude made other men 'so stiff.' To this More replied:

I do nobody harm, I say no harm, I think no harm, but wish everybody good. And if this be not enough, to keep a man alive in good faith I long not to live. And I am dying already, and have since I came here, been divers times in the case that I thought to die within one hour, and I thank our Lord I was never sorry for it, but rather sorry when I saw the pang pass. And therefore my poor body is at the King's pleasure, would God my death might do him good.

A note of impatience may be traced in these answers to the repetition of the old questions; it was as if More felt weary of the whole senseless business of trying to break down his resolution to follow the way shown to him in long hours of prayer and meditation; it was as if the world and all its problems had passed beyond his awareness; all that remained was his soul and God.

So he returned to his prison chamber, 'and here am I yet in such case as I was, neither better nor worse.'

Dame Alice More wrote to Thomas Cromwell at this period begging for sympathy in her straitened conditions: 'to show your most favourable help to the comforting of my poor husband and me, in this our great heaviness, extreme age, and necessity.' There is no record of a reply.

Margaret was given permission to see her father again, and her visit was on 4th May, the day on which the three Carthusian Priors with Richard Reynolds and John Hale were drawn to Tyburn. The day was probably chosen by the authorities in the hope that the daughter might more deeply move her father by her distress when they saw the prisoners leave on their dolorous but triumphant journey. Roper recorded what Sir Thomas More said to his daughter as they watched from his window.

> He, as one longing in that journey to have accompanied them, said unto my wife then standing there besides him: 'Lo, dost thou not see, Meg, that these blessed fathers be now as cheerfully going to their deaths as bridegrooms to their marriage? Wherefore thereby mayst thou see, mine own good

daughter, what a great difference there is between such as have in effect spent all their days in a straight, hard, penitential, and painful life religiously, and such as have in the world, as thy poor father hath done, consumed all their time in pleasure and ease licentiously. For God, considering their long continued life in most sore and grievous penance, will no longer suffer them to remain here in this vale of misery and iniquity, but speedily hence taketh them to the fruition of his everlasting Deity; whereas thy silly father, Meg, that like a most wicked caitiff hath passed forth the whole course of his miserable life most sinfully, God, thinking him not worthy so soon to come to that eternal felicity, leaveth him here yet still in the world, further to be plunged and turmoiled with misery.[8]

Roper tells of a visit from Thomas Cromwell to More that seems to have been distinct from the more formal interrogations.

Within a while after, Master Secretary, coming to him in the Tower from the King, pretended much friendship towards him, and for his comfort told him that the King's Highness was his good and gracious lord, and minded not any matter wherein he should have any cause of scruple, from henceforth to trouble his conscience. As soon as Master Secretary was gone, to express what comfort he conceived of his words, he wrote with a coal, for ink then had he none, these verses following:

> Eye-flattering Fortune, look thou never so fair.
> Nor never so pleasantly begin to smile,
> As though thou wouldst my ruin all repair,
> During my life thou shalt not me beguile.
> Trust shall I God to enter in awhile

---

[8] *Roper*, p. 80.

> His haven of heaven sure and uniform.
> Ever after thy calm look I for a storm.[9]

These were not the only verses he wrote in prison. Other lines, headed 'Davy the Dicer,' are given in the works.

> Long was I, lady Luck, your serving man,
> And now have lost again all that I gat,
> Wherefore when I think on you now and then,
> And in my mind remember this and that,
> Ye may not blame me though I beshrew your cat,
> But in faith I bless you again a thousand times
> For lending me now some leisure to make rhymes.[10]

At the end of May, news reached England that the Pope had created Fisher a Cardinal. Chapuys reported to the Emperor:

> As soon as the King heard that the Bishop of Rochester had been created a Cardinal, he declared in anger several times that he would give him another hat, and send the head afterwards to Rome for the cardinal's hat. He sent immediately to the Tower those of his Council to summon again the said Bishop and Master More to swear to the King as Head of the Church, otherwise before St. John's day [St. John the Baptist, 24th June] they should be executed as traitors. But it has been impossible to gain them, either by promises or threats, and it is believed they will soon be executed. But as they are persons of unequalled reputation in this kingdom, the King, to appease the murmurs of the world, has already on Sunday last caused preachers to preach against them in most of the churches here, and this will be continued

---

[9] *Roper*, p. 81.

[10] *E.W.*, p. 1432.

next Sunday. And although there is no lawful occasion to put them to death, the King is seeking if anything can be found against them, especially if the said bishop has made suit for the hat.[11]

Chapuys wrote on 16th June; he was referring to the interrogation of 3rd June. By that date three more of the London Carthusians were in the Marshalsea and another ten were in Newgate where they were left to starve in chains. Margaret Clement (Gigs) did her utmost to succour them, but her valiant efforts were thwarted.

More had to face a more distinguished Commission of the Council: Cranmer, Archbishop of Canterbury; Audley, Lord Chancellor; Lord Suffolk, the King's brother-in-law; Lord Wiltshire, the Queen's father, and Thomas Cromwell.

In writing an account of the interrogation, More showed how clearly he saw that the intention of the questioning was to compel him to make some definite statement that would incriminate him.

> And verily to be short I perceived little difference between this time and the last, for as far as I can see the whole purpose is either to drive me to say precisely the one way, or else precisely the other.[12]

Cromwell first reviewed the previous meetings and gave, in More's opinion, a fair account of his answers.

> Whereupon he added thereunto that the King's Highness was nothing content nor satisfied with mine answer, but thought that by my demeanour I had been occasion of much grudge and harm in the realm, and that I had an obstinate mind and an evil toward him and that my duty was, being his subject, and so he had sent them now in his name upon mine

---

[11] *L.P.*, VIII, p. 876.

[12] *Rogers*, pp. 555-9, from which the following quotations are made.

allegiance to command me to make a plain and terminate answer whether I thought the statute lawful or not and that I should either knowledge and confess it lawful that his Highness should be Supreme Head of the Church of England or else to utter plainly my malignity. Whereto I answered that I had no malignity and therefore could none utter. ... For if it so were that my conscience gave me against the statutes (wherein how my mind giveth me I made no declaration) then I nothing doing nor nothing saying against the statute it were a very hard thing to compel me to say either precisely with it against my conscience to the loss of my soul, or precisely against it to the destruction of my body.

Cromwell then argued that just as More when Chancellor had examined heretics and compelled them to make precise answers concerning the Pope's authority, so the King, being by law Supreme Head, could 'compel men to answer precisely to the law here.'

I answered and said that I protested that I intended not to defend any part or stand in contention, but I said there was a difference between those two cases because that at that time as well here as elsewhere through the corps of Christendom the Pope's power was recognized for an undoubted thing which seemeth not like a thing agreed in this realm and the contrary taken for truth in other realms, whereunto Master Secretary answered that they were as well burned for denying of that, as they be beheaded for denying of this, and therefore as good reason to compel them to make precise answer to the one as to the other.

Two questions were then put to him.

The first whether I had seen the statute. The other whether I believed that it were lawful made statute or not. Whereupon I refused the oath and said further by mouth that the first I had before confessed, and to the second I would make no answer.

Which was the end of the communication and I was thereupon sent away.

More now saw that the end could not long be delayed. His thoughts turned with gratitude to his old friends and he sent messages to those with whom he could safely communicate. One such letter has survived; it was written to Antonio Bonvisi, 'his old and dear friend' of forty years. As a foreign merchant, he was not likely to incur the anger of the King; he sent More a warm gown and to him and Fisher gifts of food and wine. The letter was written in Latin but a translation was printed in the works.

> And this faithful prosperity and friendship of yours towards me (I wot not how) seemeth in a manner to counterpoise this unfortunate shipwreck of mine, and saving the indignation of my Prince, of me no less loved than feared, else as concerning all other things, doth almost more than counterpoise. For all those are to be accounted amongst the mischances of fortune. But if I should reckon the possession of so constant friendship (which no storms of adversity hath taken away, but rather hath fortified and strengthened) amongst the brittle gifts of fortune, then were I mad. For the felicity of so faithful and constant friendship in the storms of fortune (which is seldom seen) is doubtless a high and noble gift proceeding of a certain singular benignity of God. And indeed as concerning myself, I cannot otherwise take it nor reckon it, but that it was ordained by the great mercy of God that you good Master Bonvisi amongst my poor friends, such a man as you are and so great a friend, should be long afore provided, that should by your consolation, assuage and relieve a great part of these troubles and griefs of mine, which the hugeness of fortune hath hastily brought upon me. I therefore my dear friend and of all mortal men to me most dearest, do (which now only I am able to do) earnestly pray Almighty God, which hath provided you for me, that since he hath

given you such a debtor as shall never be able to pay you, that it may please him of his benignity to requite this bountifulness of yours which you every day thus plenteously pour upon me. And that for his mercy's sake he will bring us from this wretched and stormy world into his rest where shall need no letters, where no wall shall dissever us, where no porter shall keep us from talking together, but that we may have the fruition of the eternal joy with God the Father, and with his only begotten Son our Redeemer Jesus Christ, with the Holy Spirit of them both, the Holy Ghost proceeding from them both.[13]

The interrogations had failed in their purpose; the prisoner had made no statement that could be used against him. Three servants were, therefore, questioned in the hope of getting some incriminating evidence. They were—Richard Wilson, Fisher's servant; John a' Wood, More's servant; and George Gold a servant of the Lieutenant. The results were meagre.[14]

There had been some exchanges of notes and gifts between the two prisoners. Wilson 'had sent Master More's servant half a custard on Sunday last, and long since, green sauce [salad]. More, or his servant, sent him [Fisher] an image of St. John and apples and oranges after the snow that fell last winter. On New Year's Day, More sent a paper with writing, £2,000 in gold, and an image of the Epiphany.' The £2,000 'in gold' must have been one of More's bits of fun, perhaps the sum in figures, or a drawing of money bags, was on the scrap of paper. George Gold admitted carrying letters between the two prisoners but these had been burned as 'there was no better keeper than fire.' John a' Wood said that the messages between Fisher and More were about the

---

[13] *Rogers*, p. 562. Bonvisi left England in 1549; he died abroad in 1558 and was buried at Louvain.

[14] *L.P.*, VIII, 856, 858, 859.

answers each had given to the members of the Council, but this was simply information and not advice.

On 12th June the Bishop was questioned. He admitted that letters had passed between Sir Thomas More and himself, but denied that there was any question of counsel; each wanted to know how the other had fared. Two days later, Sir Thomas More was examined about these letters. He said he had wanted George Gold to show the letters to a friend (probably Gold could not read) and, if there was anything of importance in them, to report the contents to the Council, but Gold had preferred to burn them. There had been no attempt at agreed answers to the questions that would be put to them. When Fisher had suggested that the word 'maliciously' would exempt all who spoke without malice, More had warned him that the word would not be interpreted so liberally. He acknowledged writing letters to Margaret, and explained that he sent her accounts of his examinations as soon afterwards as possible as he believed she was with child and her anxiety for him might prove harmful.

Three questions were then put to him:

    1. Whether he would obey the King as Supreme Head? He can make no answer.

    2. Whether he will acknowledge the King's marriage with Queen Anne to be lawful and that with Lady Catherine invalid?

Never spoke against it; can thereunto make no answer.

    3. Where it was objected to him that by the said statute he, as one of the King's subjects, is bound to answer the said question, and recognize the King as supreme Head, like all other subjects?

He can make no answer.[15]

An even more rigorous imprisonment was enforced. Richard

---

[15] *L.P.*, VIII, 867.

Southwell[16] (knighted 1542) with an official named Palmer[17] came soon after the last interrogation to remove all books, papers and writing materials. It would seem that John a' Wood had already taken away the manuscripts that were later to be printed by William Rastell. While this was being done, Sir Richard Rich arrived and engaged Sir Thomas More in conversation. He had just been successful in trapping Bishop Fisher into making a statement that brought him within the reach of the Act, but this had been done on a false promise that the King would regard the Bishop's opinions as confidential.

Roper's record reads:

> Master Rich, pretending friendly talk with him, among other things, of a set course, said thus unto him:
>
> 'Forasmuch as it is well known, Master More, that you are a man both wise and well learned as well in the laws of the realm as otherwise, I pray you therefore, sir, let me be so bold as of good will to put unto you this case. Admit there were, sir,' quoth he, 'an Act of Parliament that all the realm should take me for king. Would not you, Master More, take me for king?'
>
> 'Yes, sir,' quoth Sir Thomas More, 'that would I.'
>
> 'I put case further,' quoth Master Rich, 'that there were an Act of Parliament that all the realm should take me for Pope. Would not you then. Master More, take me for Pope?'
>
> 'For answer, sir,' quoth Sir Thomas More, 'to your first case: the Parliament may well, Master Rich, meddle with the state of temporal princes. But to make answer to your other case, I put you this case: Suppose the Parliament would make

---

[16] See D.N.B. Holbein painted a fine portrait of Southwell, a man of easy principles who, with one brief period of imprisonment, managed to adjust himself to the changing needs of the Government. He died in Elizabeth's reign, a wealthy man.

[17] Possibly Sir John Palmer, Sheriff of Surrey; a noted dicer who won money from Henry VII, but was eventually hanged.

a law that God should not be God. Would you then, Master Rich, say that God were not God?'

'No, sir,' quoth he, 'that would I not, since no Parliament may have any such law.'

At the trial Sir Richard Rich said, on oath, that More then added the words, 'No more could Parliament make the King Supreme Head of the Church.' It would indeed have been astonishing if Thomas More, in casual conversation with a man he distrusted, had made a statement of a kind he had scrupulously avoided making ever since he had first refused to take the oath.

Stapleton recorded that after the removal of his books, More closed the shutters of his window; when he was asked why he did this, he replied, 'Now that the goods and the implements are taken away, the shop must be closed.'[18] He gave his time to prayer and meditation.

---

[18] *Stapleton*, p. 140.

Chapter XXVI

'While He Was a Prisoner'

HE last four hundred pages of Sir Thomas More's *English Works* contain the writings made 'while he was a prisoner in the Tower.' Some are incomplete, or consist of gathered fragments preserved by his children.

The most considerable of these writings is the *Dialogue of Comfort against Tribulation*; this was completed and was probably the earliest of his prison productions. It was first printed by Richard Tottel for William Rastell in 1553, the year in which Queen Mary came to the throne. It was again printed in 1573 by John Fowler in Antwerp. Here too there was a link with the More household, for John Fowler married Alice, the daughter of John Harris, More's secretary, and of Dorothy Colley, who had been Margaret Roper's maid. This family piety is easily understood; the book was, in a sense, Thomas More's testament to his children. We do not know how the manuscript was smuggled out of the Tower; the Council would certainly not have permitted such a manuscript of 150,000 words to pass out of its control. Perhaps Margaret Roper took home portions as they were written, and no doubt John a' Wood had his share in saving the precious book.

The title page explains that the Dialogue was written 'by an Hungarian in Latin, and translated out of Latin into French and out of French into English.' This curious pedigree was part of the dramatic make-believe that appealed to the author. The two speakers are the aged Anthony and his young nephew Vincent, and they discuss the danger threatening Christendom by the advance of the Turks into Hungary under Sulaiman the Magnificent. This historical setting was analogous to the advance of heresy in Europe, but the analogy is not pressed too far. In this period of danger, Vincent sought comfort of his uncle and the theme of the Dialogue is stated in the opening paragraphs.

Vincent. But now, my good uncle, the world is here waxen such, and so great perils appear to fall at hand, that methinketh the greatest comfort that a man can have is when he may see that he shall soon be gone; and we that are likely long to live here in wretchedness have need of some comfortable counsel against tribulation, to be given us by such as you be, good uncle, that have so long lived virtuously and are so learned in the law of God as very few be better in this country here, and have had of such things as we do now fear good experience and assay in yourself, as he that hath been taken prisoner in Turkey two times in your days, and now likely to depart hence ere long. But that may be your great comfort, good uncle, since you depart to God; but us here shall you leave of your kindred a sort of sorry comfortless orphans, to all whom your good help, comfort, and counsel hath long been a great stay, not as an uncle unto some and to some as one farther of kin, but as though that unto us all you had been a natural father.

Anthony. ... But whensoever God take me hence, to reckon yourselves then comfortless, as though your chief comfort stood in me, therein make you, methinketh, a reckoning very much like as though you would cast away a strong staff, and lean upon a rotten reed. For God is and must be your comfort, and not I. And He is a sure comforter that, as he said unto his disciples, never leaveth His servants in case of comfortless orphans; not even when he departed from His disciples by death, but both, as He promised, sent them a comforter, the Holy Spirit of His Father and Himself, and made them also sure that to the world's end He would ever dwell with them

Himself. And therefore if you be part of His flock and believe His promise, how can you be comfortless in any tribulation, when Christ and His Holy Spirit, and with them their inseparable Father (if you put full trust and confidence in them), be never one finger breadth of space of time from you?[1]

This is not a controversial work but it contains much that has a bearing on the heresies of the times. Thus on good works, Anthony says:

> As for the merit of man in his good works, neither are they that deny it full agreed among themself, nor any man is there almost of them all that since they began to write hath not somewhat changed and varied from himself. And far the more part are thus far agreed with us, that like as we grant them that no good work is aught worth to heavenward without faith, and that no good work of man is rewardable in heaven of its own nature, but through the mere goodness of God that lust to set so high a price upon so poor a thing, and that this price God setteth through Christ's passion, and for that also that they be His own works with us (for good works to Godward worketh no man without God work with him); and, as we grant them also that no man may be proud of his works for his own unperfect working, and for that in all that man may do he can do God no good, but is a servant unprofitable and doth but his bare duty; as we, I say, grant unto them these things, so this one thing or twain do they grant us again, that men are bound to work good works if they have time and power, and that whoso worketh in true faith most, shall be most rewarded.[2]

---

[1] *Dialogue of Comfort*, p. 143.

[2] *Dialogue of Comfort*, pg. 175.

It will be noticed that More was here hoping for a better understanding with the Reformers. Earlier in the same chapter he wrote, 'in some communications had of late together, hath appeared good likelihood of some agreement to grow together in one accord of faith.' There is no information to explain what is here meant by 'some communication'; the reference may not be to specific discussions but part of the drama of the dialogue. His attitude towards heresy was not modified, but he may have felt that, faced with the imminent disruption of 'the corps of Christianity,' even the heretics would draw back.

This passage is a fair sample of the somewhat involved style in which More wrote in expounding ideas or in setting out an argument. His pen moved with greater ease when he was writing narrative, or was recording conversation where there was a quick give and take between the speakers. The following extracts from this dialogue illustrates his unlaboured style.

> And many fond fools are there that when they lie sick will meddle with no physic in no manner wise, nor send his water to no cunning man, but send his cap or his hose to a wise woman, otherwise called a witch. Then sendeth she word again that she hath spied in his hose where, when he took no heed, he was taken with a sprite between two doors as he went in the twilight. But the sprite would not let him feel it in five days after, and it hath all the while festered in his body, and it is the grief that paineth him so sore, but let him go to no leechcraft, nor any manner physic, other than good meat and strong drink, for syrups would souse him up. But he shall have five leaves of valerian that she enchanted with a charm, and gathered with her left hand. Let him lay those five leaves to his right thumb, not bind it fast to, but let it hang loose thereat by a green thread; he shall never need to change it, look it fall not away, but let it hang till he be whole and he shall need no more. In such wise witches, and in such mad medicines have there many fools more faith a great deal than

in God.³

There are a number of indirect references to his family, one or two of these have already been quoted; the following passage refers to Margaret Clement (Gigs) who shared her husband's skill in medicine. The extract will also serve as a good specimen of More's skill in dialogue.

Anthony has just mentioned 'a strange case which my body felt once in great a fever.'

Vincent. What strange case was that, uncle?

Anthony. Forsooth, cousin, even in this same bed, it is now more than fifteen year ago, I lay in a tertian and had passed, I trow, three or four fits. But after fell there on me one fit out of course, so strange and marvellous, that I would in good faith have thought it impossible. For I suddenly felt myself verily both hot and cold throughout all my body, not in some part the one and in some part the other, for that had been, you wot well, no very strange thing to feel the head hot while the hands were cold, but the selfsame parts, I say so God save my soul, I sensibly felt and right painfully too all in one instant both hot and cold at once.

Vincent. By my faith, uncle, this was a wonderful thing, and such as I never heard happen any man else in my day, and few men are there of whose mouths I could have believed it.

Anthony. Courtesy, cousin, peradventure letteth you to say that you believe it not yet of my mouth neither; and surely for fear of that you should not have heard it of me neither, had there not another thing happed me soon after, after.

Vincent. I pray you what was that, good uncle?

Anthony. Forsooth, cousin, this I asked a physician or

---

³ *Dialogue of Comfort*, pg. 197.

twain that then looked unto me, how this should be possible; and they twain told me both that it could not be so but that I was fallen into some slumber and dreamed that I felt it so.

Vincent. This hap hold I little cause you to tell that tale more boldly.

Anthony. No, cousin, that is true, lo. But then happed there another, that a young girl in this town, whom a kinsman of hers had begun to teach physic, told me that there was such a kind of fever indeed.

Vincent. By our Lady, uncle, save for the credence of you the tale would I not yet tell again upon that hap of the maid. For though I know her now for such as I durst well believe her, it might hap her well at that time to lie because she would you should take her for cunning.

Anthony. Yes, but then happed there yet another hap thereof, cousin, that a work of Galen, *De differentiis febrium*, is ready to be sold in the booksellers' shops. In which work she shewed me then the chapter where Galen saith the same.

Vincent. Marry, uncle, as you say, that hap happened well; and that maid had (as hap was) in that one point more cunning than had both your physicians besides, and hath, I ween, at this day in many points more.

Anthony. In faith so ween I too; and that is well wared on her, for she is very wise and well learned, and very virtuous too. But see now what age is. Lo, I have been so long in my tale that I have almost forgotten for what purpose I told it. Oh, now I remember me...[4]

The following tale was used in a discussion on suicide.

Anthony. There was here in Buda, in King Ladislaus's days, a good, pure, honest man's wife. This woman was so fiendish, that the devil, perceiving her nature, put her in the

---

[4] *Dialogue of Comfort*, pg. 222.

mind that she should anger her husband so sore that she might give him occasion to kill her, and then should he be hanged for her.

Vincent. This was a strange temptation indeed. What the devil should she be the better then?

Anthony. Nothing, but that it eased her shrewd stomach before to think that her husband should be hanged after. And peradventure, if you look about the world and consider it well, you shall find more such stomachs than a few. Have you never heard no furious body plainly say that to see some such man have a mischief he would with goodwill be content to lie as long in hell as God liveth in heaven?

Vincent. Forsooth, and some such have I heard of.

Anthony. This mind of his was not much less mad than hers, but rather haply the more mad of the twain. For the woman peradventure did not cast so far peril therein. But to tell you now to what good pass her charitable purpose came: As her husband (the man was a carpenter) stood hewing with his chip-axe upon a piece of timber, she began after her old guise so to revile him that the man waxed wroth at last and bade her get in, or he would lay the helm of his axe about her back, and said also that it were little sin even with that axehead to chop off that unhappy head of hers that carried such an ungracious tongue therein. At that word the devil took his time, and whetted her tongue against her teeth. And when it was well sharped she sware to him in very fierce anger: By the mass, whoreson husband, I would thou wouldst; here lieth mine head, lo (and therewith down she laid her head upon the same timber log), if thou smite it not off, I beshrew thine whoreson's heart. With that, likewise as the devil stood at her elbow, so stood (as I heard say) his good angel at his, and gave him ghostly courage, and bade him be bold and do it. And so the good man up with his chip-axe, and at a chop chopped off her head indeed. There were standing other folk by, which had a good sport to hear her chide, but little they looked for this chance till it was done ere they could let it. They said they heard her tongue babble in her head, and call Whoreson whoreson, twice after that the head was from the body. At the least wise, afterward unto the king thus they reported all, except only one, and that was a woman, and she said that she heard it not.

Vincent. Forsooth, this was a wonderful work. What came, uncle, of the man?

Anthony. The king gave him his pardon.

Vincent. Verily he might in conscience do no less.[5]

Such extracts do not go to the heart of this book; they are the lighter passages in a discussion of the relation between the soul and God. A number of chapters, for instance, expound verses in the 90th[6] Psalm, one of the Compline Psalms. Throughout the Dialogue there are memorable passages that reveal how deeply Thomas More had meditated upon the Scriptures and upon his own experience of life. A final extract is more typical of the spirit of the book; here his thoughts must have gone to that separate building of his at Chelsea where he was able to withdraw from the world and give himself to prayer and meditation.

> Let him also choose himself some secret solitary place in his own house, as far from noise and company as he conveniently can, and thither let him sometime secretly resort alone, imagining himself as one going out of the world even straight into the giving up his reckoning unto God of his sinful living. Then let him there before an altar or some pitiful image of Christ's bitter Passion (the beholding whereof may put him in remembrance of the thing, and move him to devout compassion) kneel down or fall prostrate as at the feet of

---

[5] *Dialogue of Comfort,* p. 254.

[6] Vulgate numbering; 91 according to the Hebrew.

Almighty God, verily believing Him to be there invisibly present, as without any doubt He is. There let him open his heart to God and confess his faults such as he can call to mind, and pray God of forgiveness. Let him call to remembrance the benefits that God hath given him, either in general among other men or privately to himself, and give Him humble hearty thanks therefore. There let him declare unto God the temptations of the devil, the suggestions of the flesh, the occasions of the world and of his worldly friends, much worse many times in drawing a man from God than are his most mortal enemies. Which thing our Saviour witnesseth Himself where he said: *Inimici hominis domestici eius*: The enemies of a man are they that are his own familiars. There let him lament and bewail unto God his own frailty, negligence, and sloth in resisting and withstanding of temptation, his readiness and pronity to fall thereunto. There let him lamentably beseech God of His gracious aid and help to strength his infirmity withal, both in keeping him from falling and, when he be by his own fault misfortuneth to fall, then with the helping hand of His merciful grace to lift him up and set him on his feet in the state of His grace again. And let this man not doubt but that God heareth him and granteth him gladly his boon. And so, dwelling in the faithful trust of God's help, he shall well use his prosperity and persevere in his good profitable business, and shall have therein the truth of God so compass him about with a pavis [shield] of His heavenly defence, that of the devil's arrow flying in the day of worldly wealth he shall not need to dread.[7]

The second of these prison writings was the short *Treatise to receive the Blessed Body of our Lord, sacramentally and virtually both*. Here, as in others of this group of last writings, are echoes

---

[7] *Dialogue of Comfort*, pg. 288.

of the past. The following passage recalls those happy days when the King would 'come to his house at Chelsea to be merry with him.'

> For if we will but consider, if there were a greatly worldly prince which for special favour that he bare us, would come visit us in our own house, what a business we would then make, and what a work it would be for us, to see that our house were trimmed up in every point, to the best of our possible power, and every thing so provided and ordered that he should by his honourable receiving, perceive what affection we bare him, and in what high estimation we have him, we should soon by the comparing of that worldly prince, and this heavenly prince together (between which twain is far less comparison than is between a man and a mouse) inform and teach ourself how lowly mind, how tender loving heart, how reverend humble manner, we should endeavour ourself to receive this glorious heavenly king, the king of all kings, Almighty God himself, that so lovingly doth vouchsafe to enter, not only into our house (to which the noble man Centurion knowledged himself unworthy) but his precious body into our vile wretched carcass, and his holy spirit into our simple soul.[8]

In the interrogation of 30th April, Thomas More declared that he had put aside the world and was determined 'that my whole study should be upon the passion of Christ and mine own passage out of the world.' The fruits of this study are given in the unfinished *Treatise upon the Passion of Christ*. More began to write this in English and then continued in Latin; this portion was translated into English by Mary Basset,[9] one of the daughters of

---

[8] *E.W.*, p. 1,266

[9] She helped Wm. Rastell financially in the publication of *E.W.* For an account of the Basset family, see Appendix I of the E.E.T.S. edition of Ro. Ba's *Life of Sir Thomas More*.

'WHILE HE WAS A PRISONER' 365

Margaret Roper.

The full title More gave to this work explains its intended scope.

> A treatise historical, containing the bitter passion of our saviour Christ, after the course and order of the four evangelists, with an exposition upon their words, taken for the most part out of the sayings of sundry good old holy doctors, and beginning at the first assembly of the bishops, the priests, and the seniors of the people, about the contriving of Christ's death, written the 26th chapter of St. Matthew, the 13th of St. Mark and the 22nd of St. Luke, And it endeth in the committing of his blessed body into his sepulchre, with the frustrate provision of the Jews, about the keeping thereof with the soldiers appointed thereto, written in the 27th of St. Matthew, the 15th of St. Mark, the 23rd of St. Luke and the 19th of St. John.[10]

The book begins with an account of the angels and of the creation and fall of mankind and 'the determination of the Trinity for the restoration of mankind.' Had More in mind the twelfth and thirteenth books of St. Augustine's *City of God*? Amongst the 'old holy doctors' quoted were the favourite St. Austin, and St. Jerome, St. Basil, St. Cyprian and St. Bede. This implies that the prisoner must have had with him a large number of books.

More did not altogether avoid controversial matters in this treatise; indeed that would have been impossible in a book on such a subject. He excused this in the following note:

> Now albeit (as I suppose) few men have less lust to move great questions, and put manner of dispicions [disputations] in unlearned men's mouths than I, which rather would wish every man to labour for good affections, than to long for the knowledge of less necessary learning, or delight in debating of

---

[10] *E.W.*, p. 1,270.

sundry superfluous problems, yet of some such demands as I now see many men of much less than mean learning, have oft right hot in hand, I shall not let one or twain myself here a little to touch.[11]

Each part of the treatise ends with a prayer. One may be given:

> O holy blessed Saviour Jesus Christ which willingly didst determine to die for man's sake, mollify mine hard heart, and supple it so by grace, that through tender compassion of thy bitter passion, I may be partner of thy holy redemption.

When he printed this Treatise in the works, William Rastell wrote:

> A work of truth full of good and godly lessons which he began being then a prisoner, and could not achieve and finish the same, as he that ere he could go through therewith (even when he came to the exposition of the word *Et incecerunt manus in Jesum*) was bereaved and put from his books, ink and paper, and kept more straitly then before, and soon after also was put to death himself.[12]

This Treatise is followed by 'certain devout and virtuous instructions, meditations, and prayers, made and collected by Sir Thomas More.' Thus there is a cento of verses selected from the first sixty-six Psalms. One 'Godly Meditation' might be called the sum of his life's devotions.

Give me Thy grace good Lord to set the world at nought.
To set my mind fast upon thee.
And not to hang upon the blast of men's mouths.
To be content to be solitary.
Not to long for worldly company.
Little and little utterly to cast off the world

---

[11] *E.W.*, p. 1,281.

[12] *E.W.*, pg. 1,404.

And rid my mind of all the busyness thereof.
Not to long to hear of any worldly things
But that the hearing of worldly fantasies may be to me displeasant.
Gladly to be thinking of God.
Piteously to call for his help.
To lean unto the comfort of God.
Busily to labour to love him,
To know mine own vility and wretchedness,
To humble and meeken myself under the mighty hand of God,
To bewail my sins passed.
For the purging of them, patiently to suffer adversity.
Gladly to bear my purgatory here.
To be joyful of tribulations,
To walk the narrow way that leadeth to life.
To bear the cross with Christ.
To have the last things in remembrance.
To have ever afore mine eye, my death,
A death, that is ever at hand,
To make death no stranger to me.
To foresee and consider the everlasting fire of hell.
To pray for pardon before the judge come.
To have continually in mind, the passion that Christ suffered for me.
For his benefits incessantly to give him thanks.
To buy the time again that I before have lost.
To abstain from vain confabulations.
To eschew light foolish mirth and gladness.
Recreations not necessary, to cut off.
Of worldly substance, friends, liberty, life, and all to set the loss at right nought, for the winning of Christ.
To think my most enemies my best friends.
For the brethren of Joseph could never have done him so much good with their love and favour
as they did him with their malice and hatred.
These minds are more to be desired of every man
than all the treasure of all the princes and kings,
Christian and heathen, were it gathered and

laid together all upon one heap.[13]

Copies of these prayers and meditations were circulated amongst friends of the family. One meditation that is not in the works is found in the commonplace book[14] of Robert Parkyn (d. 1570), curate of Adwick-le-Street, Doncaster. In a chronicle covering the years 1532 to 1555 he noted, 'And by cause the good Bishop of Rochester and Sir Thomas More two virtuous men and great clerks would not consent to the King that he should be Supreme Head of Holy Church, therefore they were both headed in the month of June at London.' Barnborough, to which John More and his wife Anne (Cresacre) probably retired after his father's death, is within a few miles of Adwick; this would explain how Robert Parkyn came to see the manuscripts of the prayers and meditations he copied into his book. One, of some length, is not in the works; there seems little doubt that it is, as he claimed, by Sir Thomas More. The last sentences read:

> Wherefore dear Father, when thou hast straitly commanded me thus to love thee with all my heart and thus I would right gladly, but without thy help and without thy holy spirit I cannot perform the same. I beseech thee shed upon my heart thy most holy spirit, by whose gracious presence I may be warmed, heated, and kindled with the spiritual fire of charity and with the sweet brenning love of all ghostly affections that I may fastly set my heart, soul and mind upon thee and surely trust that thou art my well beloved Father. And according to the same I may love thee with all my heart, with all my soul, with all my mind and with all my power. Amen.

---

[13] *E.W.*, p. 1,416.

[14] This meditation was published in *The Church Quarterly Review*, July-Sept. 1937, by A.G. Dickens. The MS. is now in the Bodleian Library, MS. Lat., th. D. 15.

RICHARD RICH

Chapter XXVII

The Trial

JOHN FISHER was brought to trial on 17th June, 1535. The main charge against him was his statement to Sir Richard Rich that 'the King our sovereign lord is not Supreme Head in earth of the Church of England.' This admission had been made on the promise of Rich that the answer was for the personal information of the King and would not be used in evidence. Fisher's plea that he had not spoken in malice was brushed aside by the court. He was condemned to death as a traitor, and beheaded on 22nd June. His naked body was left on the scaffold until the evening when some soldiers gave it perfunctory burial in the churchyard of All Hallows, Barking (by the Tower).

Three monks of the Charterhouse, Humphrey Middlemore, William Exmewe and Sebastian Newdigate had suffered at Tyburn a week before Saint John Fisher.

Sir Thomas More must have been kept acquainted with these sorrowful events, and it may have been hoped that these proofs of the inflexibility of the royal will would daunt him. It was not until 1st July that his trial began.

From the Tower he was taken by the river to Westminster, a two-and-a-half miles passage that so many made in hope or despair. The trial was held in the Hall in which both he and his father had administered justice. Amongst the Commissioners were the Lord Chancellor (Audley), the Dukes of Norfolk and Suffolk, Queen Anne's father and brother, and Thomas Cromwell. Even they could not have been unmoved as they saw the prisoner slowly moving up the Hall with the aid of a staff; for this enfeebled man, with his whitening hair and long beard, and his drawn features had been the King's companion and one they had counted it a privilege to know.

The indictment,[1] based on the Act of Supremacy and not on the Act of Succession, was read at the opening of the proceedings. There were four counts.

    1. That on 7th May, More had refused to give his opinion on the King's marriage and on the Supremacy;

    2. That on 12th May, he had, in a letter to Bishop Fisher said that he himself had refused to answer;

    3. That he had written to Bishop Fisher that 'the Act of Parliament is like a sword with two edges, for if a man answer one way it will confound his soul, and if he answer the other way, it will confound his body'; the fact that Fisher had used these very words proved that there was a conspiracy between them;

    4. That on 12th June, More had said to Sir Richard Rich that the King could not be made Supreme Head of the Church in England by Act of Parliament.

Each offence was said to have been done maliciously (*maliciose*), a word that was used eight times in the indictment.

The Lord Chancellor and the Duke of Norfolk made one more attempt to persuade More to submit to the King's will 'that ye shall taste of his gracious pardon.' To this More replied:

> My Lords, I do most humbly thank your honours of your great good will towards me. Howbeit, I make this my boon and petition unto God as heartily as I may, that he will vouchsafe this my good, honest and upright mind to nourish, maintain and uphold in me even to the last hour and extreme moment that ever I shall live. Concerning the matters you

---

[1] The full text is given in *Harpsfield*, pp. 269-76.

now charge and challenge me withal, the articles are so prolix and long that I fear, what for my long imprisonment, what for my long lingering disease, what for my present weakness and debility, that neither my wit, nor my memory, nor yet my voice, will serve to make so full, so effectual and sufficient answer as the weight and importance of these matters doth crave.[2]

He was then allowed to sit down while he continued his reply to the charges.

Touching the first article, wherein is purpose that I, to utter and show my malice against the King and his late marriage, have ever repined [murmured at] and resisted the same, I can say nothing but this: that of malice I never spake anything against it, and that whatsoever I have spoken in that matter, I have none otherwise spoken but according to my very mind, opinion and conscience. In the which, if I had not, for discharging of my conscience to God and my duty to my Prince, done as I have done, I might well account myself a naughty, unfaithful and disloyal subject. And for this mine error (if I may call it an error, or if I have been deceived therein) I have not got scot-free and untouched, my goods and chattels being confiscate, and myself to perpetual prison, adjudged, where I have now been shut up about fifteen months.

Whereas now farther in this article is contained that I have incurred the danger and penalty of the last Act of Parliament, made since I was imprisoned, touching the King's Supremacy and that I have as a rebel and traitor gone about to rob and spoil the king of his due title and honour. ...

---

[2] This and following extracts otherwise not identified are from *Harpsfield*, pp. 183-97. Harpsfield combined Roper's account with that given in the Paris Newsletter or in the *Expositio*, see below, pp. 376-7.

> Touching, I say, this challenge and accusation, I answer that, for this my taciturnity and silence, neither your law nor any law in the world is able justly and rightly to punish me, unless you may besides lay to my charge either some word or some fact in deed.

More had gone straight to the weak points of the indictment; the law under which he was charged had been made after he had been sent to the Tower, and, secondly, no law could make a crime of silence. The attorney-general (Sir Christopher Hales) could not let this pass; some answer must be made to what was a legal argument of some force. He therefore objected that silence itself could be a kind of treason, since a good subject would actively in speech support the law.

More replied:

> Truly, if the rule and maxim of the civil law be good, allowable and sufficient, that *Qui tacet, consentire videtur* (he that holdeth his peace seemeth to consent), this my silence implieth and importeth rather a ratification and confirmation than any condemnation of your statute. For as for that you said, that every good subject is obliged to answer and confess, ye must understand that, in things touching conscience, every true and good subject is more bound to have respect to his said conscience and to his soul than to any other thing in all the world beside; namely, when his conscience is such sort as mine is, that is to say, where the person giveth no occasion of slander, of tumult and sedition against his Prince, as it is with me; for I assure you that I have not hitherto to this hour disclosed and opened my conscience and mind to any person living in all the world.

All the records show the truth of this last statement; even in his letters to Margaret he refused to state his reasons for declining the oath.

In answer to the second article. More expressed his regret at

The Trial 375

the burning of the letters between Fisher and himself as their production in court would have cleared both of them of the charge of plotting; his advice to Fisher had been to do what he thought was right.

> And other answer upon the charge of my soul made I none. These are the tenours of my letters upon which ye can take no hold or handfast by your law to condemn me to death.

His description of the Act as a two-edged sword was, he pointed out, conditional and not absolute.

> Neither do I know what kind of answer the Bishop made; whose answer, if it were agreeable and correspondent to mine, that happed by reason of the correspondence and conformity of our wits, learning and study, not that any such thing was purposely concluded upon and accorded betwixt us.

So they came to the fourth article, the conversation with Sir Richard Rich. The conversation in the Tower, as reported by Roper, has already been quoted. His account of what happened at the trial itself, is, at this point, our best authority.

> And for proof to the Jury that Sir Thomas More was guilty of this treason, Master Rich was called forth to give evidence unto them upon his oath, as he did. Against whom thus sworn, Sir Thomas More began in this wise to say: 'If I were a man, my lords, that did not regard an oath, I needed not, as it is well known in this place, at this time, nor in this case to stand here as an accused person. And if this oath of yours, Master Rich, be true, then pray I that I never see God in the face; which I would not say were it otherwise, to win the whole world.'
>
> Then recited he to the court the discourse of their communication in the Tower according to the truth, and said:
>
> 'In good faith, Master Rich, I am sorryer for your perjury than for my own peril. And you shall understand that neither I, nor no man else to my knowledge, ever took you to be a

man of such credit as in any matter of importance I, or any other, would at any time vouchsafe to communicate with you. And I, as you know, of no small while have been acquainted with you and your conversation, who have known you from your youth hitherto, for we long dwelled both in one parish together, where, as yourself can tell (I am sorry you compel me so to say) you were esteemed very light of your tongue, a great dicer, and of no commendable fame. And so in your house at the Temple, where hath been your chief bringing up, were you likewise accounted.

Can it therefore seem likely unto your honourable lordships that I would, in so weighty a cause, so unadvisedly overshoot myself as to trust Master Rich, a man of me always reputed for one of so little truth, as your lordships have heard, so far above my sovereign lord the King, or any of his noble Councillors, that I would unto him utter the secrets of my conscience touching the King's Supremacy, the special point and only mark at my hands so long sought for: a thing which I never did, nor never would, after the statute thereof made, reveal either to the King's Highness himself, or to any of his honourable councillors, as it is not unknown to your honours, at sundry several times sent from his Grace's own person unto the Tower unto me for none other purpose? Can this in your judgements, my lords, seem likely to be true? And yet, if I had so done indeed, my lords, as Master Rich hath sworn, seeing it was spoken but in familiar secret talk, nothing affirming, and only in putting cases, without other displeasant circumstances, it cannot justly be taken to be spoken maliciously; and where there is no malice, there can be no offence. And over this I can never think, my lords, that so many worthy Bishops, so many honourable personages, and so many worshipful, virtuous, wise and well-learned men as at the making of that law were in the Parliament assembled, ever meant to have any man punished by death in whom there could be found no malice, taking "malitia" for "malevolentia." For if "malitia" be generally taken for "sin," no man is there then that can thereof excuse himself: *Quia si dixerimus quod peccatum non habemus, nosmetipsos seducimus, et veritas in nobis non est.* And only his word "maliciously" is in the statute material.'[3]

He added that the favours the King had shown him in the past would alone be sufficient to convince them of the folly of accusing him of malice.

Rich was not to be discredited without an attempt to set himself right. He called Richard Southwell and Master Palmer to swear to the truth of his report since they were in the room while he was speaking to More. Both, to their honour, said that they were so busy putting Sir Thomas More's books in a sack that they gave no heed to the conversation.

With this rebuttal of the key evidence, the case should have fallen to the ground. 'All which notwithstanding,' wrote Roper, 'the Jury found him guilty.'

Lord Chancellor Audley then began to give judgement, but More interrupted him with a reminder that 'when I was toward the law the manner of such case was to ask the prisoner, before judgement, why judgement should not be given against him.' This error in procedure may not have been intentional though it is possible that the King had given instructions that More was not to be allowed to speak at any length. The lapse may have been due to the emotional tension of the occasion. Although the Commissioners were obeying the King's will, they must have felt some compunction at carrying out their task. This was no ordinary prisoner before them; he was, by common consent, one of the great men of his day; there was here no clear case of treason or of contemplated treason, and perjury had to be used to

---

[3] *Roper*, p. 87.

bring him within the scope of the law. This strained atmosphere may explain Audley's lapse; it was an unspoken desire to get the shameful business over and done with.

So Thomas More at last could speak his mind. Here is Harpsfield's account of his speech.

'Seeing that I see ye are determined to condemn me (God knoweth how) I will now in discharge of my conscience speak my mind plainly and freely touching my Indictment and your Statute withal.

And forasmuch as this Indictment is grounded upon an Act of Parliament directly repugnant to the laws of God and his Holy Church, the supreme government of which, or of any part thereof, may no temporal Prince presume by any law to take upon him, as rightfully belonging to the See of Rome, a spiritual pre-eminence by the mouth of our Saviour himself, personally present upon earth, only to St. Peter and his successors, bishops of the same See, by special prerogative granted, it is therefore in law, amongst Christian men, insufficient to charge any Christian man.'

And for proof thereof, like as among divers other reasons and authorities he declared that this realm, being but one member and small part of the Church, might not make a particular law disagreeable with the general law of Christ's universal Catholic Church, no more than the City of London, being but one poor member in respect of the whole realm, might make a law against an Act of Parliament to bind the whole realm. So further showed he that it was contrary both to the laws and statutes of our own land yet unrepealed, as they might evidently perceive in Magna Charta. ... And also contrary to the sacred oath which the King's Highness himself and every other Christian Prince always with great solemnity received at their coronations, alleging moreover, that no more might this realm of England refuse obedience to the See of Rome than might the child refuse obedience to his own natural father.

This appeal to 'the general law of Christ's universal Catholic Church' was the unshakable foundation of More's position; to understand its full significance is to appreciate his resolute opposition to the Royal Supremacy, and the cause of his martyrdom.

Audley commented that it was strange that More should hold his opinion contrary to the considered opinions of the Bishops and Universities.

To this Sir Thomas More replied, saying that these seven years seriously and earnestly he had beset his studies and cogitations upon this point chiefly, among other, of the Pope's authority.

That is Harpsfield's version, but it is misleading; the authority he was using, what is called the Paris News-Letter, states that during the course of seven years' study 'I have not read in any Doctor approved of the Church that a secular [prince] can or ought to be head of the spirituality.' Thus the question here was not the Supremacy of the Pope as Harpsfield implied, but the possibility of a layman being Head of the Church; More was referring to the Supremacy assumed by Henry under the Act. Seven years takes us back to 1528 when the validity of the King's marriage had become the dominating issue. More had evidently seen even then that, if the King did not get his way, he would break from Rome and make the Church in England a separate institution. This foresight need not surprise us for other instances have been given of More's ability to follow the chain of cause and effect to a conclusion; this was one of his characteristics that impressed Roper. This reference to a seven-year period must not be confused with More's statement in a letter to Cromwell in 1534[4] that 'these ten years since and more' he had studied the

---

[4] See above, p. 213.

question of the Primacy of the Pope; he was then looking back to the publication of Henry's *Assertio septem Sacramentorum.* It was that book which had first roused More's interest in a subject he had not previously considered thoroughly. At that time, of course, there was not the least hint that the King could be 'head of the spirituality,' a notion that would have shocked the royal author himself.

Harpsfield gives the next part of the speech verbatim.

'If there were no more but myself upon my side, and the whole Parliament upon the other, I would be sore afraid to lean to mine own mind only against so many. But if the number of Bishops and Universities be so material as your lordship seemeth to take it, then see I little cause, my lord, why that thing in my conscience should make any change. For I nothing doubt but that, though not in this realm, yet in Christendom about, of these well-learned Bishops and virtuous men that are yet alive, they be not the fewer part that are of my mind therein. But if I should speak of those that are already dead, of whom many be now Saints in heaven, I am very sure it is the far greater part of them that, all the while they lived, thought in this case that way that I think now; and therefore am I not bounden, my lord, to conform my conscience to the Council of one realm against the general Council of Christendom. For of the aforesaid holy Bishops I have, for every Bishop of yours, above one hundred. And for one Council or Parliament of yours (God knoweth what manner of one) I have all the Councils made these thousand years. And for this one kingdom, I have all other Christian realms.'

The Duke of Norfolk interrupted to say, 'We now plainly perceive that ye are maliciously bent.' The remark suggests that the Duke was glad to have, at last, some statement in support of a charge that had not been established by evidence.

'Nay, nay, quoth Sir Thomas More, 'very and pure necessity

for the discharge of my conscience, enforceth me to speak so much. Wherein I call and appeal to God, whose only sight pierceth into the very depths of man's heart, to be my witness. Howbeit, it is not for this Supremacy so much that ye seek my blood, as for that I would not condescend to the marriage.'

So the speech abruptly ends in this account leaving the last sentence hanging in the air. There is, however, what may be an earlier version[5] that is harsher in tone and more relentless in argument, and may represent more accurately what More actually said.

According to this alternative version More replied to Norfolk that he was moved by his religious faith to speak plainly. The Act of Supremacy was an impious statute as it was in direct violation of the baptismal union with the one Holy, Catholic Church which no one may dissever; the Act was an invasion of the rights of the Catholic Church, one and indivisible. He went on to say that he knew this matter of the Supremacy was not in fact the cause of his condemnation; the true reason was that he had refused to consent to the King's second marriage, and he drew a comparison with the position of John the Baptist who rebuked Herod and Philip's wife, for he could see little difference between a man marrying a second wife during the lifetime of the first, and a woman leaving her husband for another man. He thus refused to approve this infamous marriage. He then made a reference to the influence of Anne Boleyn, and expressed a hope of the King's repentance.

When More had finished speaking, the Lord Chancellor hesitated to pronounce sentence at once; he asked the Lord Chief Justice, Sir John Fitzjames, 'whether this indictment were sufficient or not'; a curious question to put at the end of a trial. The answer was as curious: 'My lords all, by St. Julian (that was

---

[5] See below pp. 413-14, for discussion of *Ordo Condemnatonis Thomae Mori*.

ever his oath) I must needs confess that, if the Act of Parliament be lawful, then the indictment is good enough.' It was as if the Lord Chief Justice had doubts on the sufficiency of the indictment; perhaps More's arguments had shaken his confidence.

Sentence of death was then pronounced. The Commissioners asked Thomas More if he had anything further to say. His answer was brief.

'More have I not to say, my lords, but that like as the blessed Apostle St. Paul, as we read in the Acts of the Apostles, was present and consented to the death of St. Stephen, and kept their clothes that stoned him to death, and yet be they now both twain holy Saints in heaven, and shall continue there friends together for ever, so I verily trust, and shall therefore rightly pray, that though your lordships have now here on earth been judges to my condemnation, we may yet hereafter in heaven merrily all meet together, to our everlasting salvation. And thus I desire Almighty God to preserve and defend the King's Majesty, and send him good counsel.'

There is no record of any members of the More family being present at the trial; even if the public was admitted, which is improbable. More may have asked his own relatives to stay away. Roper states that he himself was not present, and his account of the trial was based on reports made to him by, amongst others, Sir Anthony St. Leger, Richard Heywood, and John Webbe. The first two were lawyers so may have been there in some official capacity; nothing is known of John Webbe. Richard Heywood's brother, Merry John Heywood, had married Thomas More's niece, Joan Rastell; he would therefore have a close interest in the trial, and was probably the family's chief informant of what happened.

Roper wrote down the following account of what took place after the trial.

The Trial

Now, after this arraignment, departed he from the bar to the Tower again, led by Sir William Kingston, a tall, strong, and comely knight, Constable of the Tower, and his very dear friend. Who, when he had brought him from Westminster to the Old Swanne towards the Tower, there with an heavy heart, the tears running down by his cheeks, bade him farewell. Sir Thomas More, seeing him so sorrowful, comforted him with as good words as he could, saying: 'Good Master Kingston, trouble not yourself, but be of good cheer; for I will pray for you and my good Lady your wife that we may meet in heaven together, where we shall be merry for ever and ever.'

Soon after, Sir William Kingston, talking with me of Sir Thomas More, said: 'In good faith, Master Roper, I was ashamed of myself, that, at departing from your father, I found my heart so feeble, and his so strong, that he was fain to comfort me, which should rather have comforted him.'[6]

At Tower Wharf, More's son John, with Margaret Roper and Margaret Clement, contrived to reach him through the throng. John knelt for a blessing and then father and son kissed for the last time; Margaret Clement embraced him; his muchloved daughter, Margaret, was not easily parted from him:

> As soon as she saw him, after his blessing on her knees reverently received, she hasting towards him, and, without consideration or care of herself, pressing in among the throng and company of the guard that with halberds and bills went round about him, hastily ran to him, and there openly in the sight of them all, embraced him, took him about the neck and kissed him. Who, well liking her most natural and dear daughterly affection towards him, gave her his fatherly

---

[6] For this and next extract, *Roper*, pp. 97-99.

blessing and many godly words of comfort besides. From whom after she was departed, she, not satisfied with the former sight of him and like one that had forgotten herself, being all ravished with the entire love of her dear father, having respect neither to herself, nor to the press of the people and multitude that were there about him, suddenly turned back again, ran to him as before, took him about the neck and divers times together most lovingly kissed him, and at last, with a very full heart, was fain to depart from him; the beholding whereof was to many of them that were present thereat so lamentable that it made them for very sorrow thereof to mourn and weep.

Chapter XXVIII

'The Field Is Won'

FOUR full days passed between the trial and the execution. These were spent in prayer and meditation. It does not seem that Sir Thomas More saw any member of his family during that time. He may have wished it so. Margaret sent her maid Dorothy Colley[1] to the Tower each day, and on the last visit she brought back to her mistress his hair shirt and scourge with this letter.

Our Lord bless you good daughter and your good husband and your little boy and all yours and all my children and all my godchildren and all our friends. Recommend me when you may to my good daughter Cecily, whom I beseech our Lord to comfort, and I send her my blessing and to all her children and pray her to pray for me. I send her an handkercher and God comfort my good son her husband. My good daughter Daunce hath the picture in parchment that you delivered me from my Lady Conyers,[2] her name is on the back side. Shew her that I heartily pray her that you may send it in my name again for a token from me to pray for me.

I like special well Dorothy Colley, I pray you be good unto her. I would wit whether this be she that you wrote me of. If not I pray you be good to the other, as you may in her affliction and to my good daughter Joan Allen to give her I

---

[1] *Stapleton*, p. 205.

[2] Nothing is known of Lady Conyers.

pray you some kind answer, for she sued hither to me this day to pray you be good to her.

I cumber you good Margaret much, but I would be sorry, if it should be any longer than tomorrow, for it is St. Thomas Eve[3] and the utas of Saint Peter[4] and therefore tomorrow long I to go to God, it were a day very meet and convenient for me. I never liked your manner toward me better than when you kissed me last for I love when daughterly love and dear charity hath no leisure to worldly courtesy.

Farewell my dear child and pray for me, and I shall for you and all your friends that we may merrily meet in heaven.

I thank you for your great cost.

I send now unto my good daughter Clement her algorism stone[5] and I send her and my good son and all hers God's blessing and mine.

I pray you at time convenient recommend me to my good son John More. I liked well his natural fashion. Our Lord bless him and his good wife my loving daughter, to whom I pray him be good, as he hath great cause, and that if the land of mine come to his hand, he break not my will concerning his sister Daunce. And our Lord bless Thomas and Austen and all that they shall have.[6]

There is no mention in this letter of Dame Alice More, but she may have had a separate message from her husband. His last thoughts are here turned to his children and grandchildren, but he mentions also Margaret's maids, Dorothy Colley and Joan Allen. Cecily Heron and Elizabeth Daunce received mementos as

---

[3] The body of St. Thomas of Canterbury was translated to the shrine in the Cathedral on 7th July, 1220. The shrine was destroyed in 1538 and the relics burned.

[4] Octave-day of St. Peter and St. Paul.

[5] Probably a slate on which the prisoner could write when he no longer had pen and ink.

[6] *Rogers*, p. 563.

well as blessings; John and Margaret Clement shared his blessings; he recalled with special thankfulness the farewells of John and Margaret; and last come little Thomas and Austin, the sons of John More and Anne Cresacre.

Early in the morning of 6th July, 1535, Thomas Pope,[7] an official of the Tower, and well-known to Thomas More, told him that he was to be executed within a few hours.

'Master Pope,' quoth he, 'for your good tidings I most heartily thank you. I have been always much bounden to the King's Highness for the benefits and honours that he hath still from time to time most bountifully heaped upon me; and yet more bound am I to his Grace for putting me into this place where I have had convenient time and space to have remembrance of my end. And so help me, God, most of all, Master Pope, am I bound to his Highness that it pleaseth him so shortly to rid me out of the miseries of this wretched world. And therefore will I not fail earnestly to pray for his Grace, both here and also in another world.'

'The King's pleasure is further,' quoth Master Pope, 'that at your execution you shall not use many words.'

'Master Pope,' quoth he, 'you do well to give me warning of his Grace's pleasure, for otherwise I had purposed at that time somewhat to have spoken, but of no matter wherewith his Grace, or any other, should have had cause to be offended. Nevertheless, whatsoever I intended, I am ready obediently to conform myself to his Grace's commandments. And I beseech you, good Master Pope, to be a mean unto his Highness that my daughter Margaret may be at my burial.'

'The King is content already,' quoth Master Pope, 'that your wife, children and other friends shall have liberty to be present thereat.'

---

[7] See *D.N.B.* He was also in the service of Audley; he founded Trinity College, Oxford, out of wealth that came mainly from monastic lands.

'O how much beholden then,' said Sir Thomas More, 'am I to his Grace, that unto my poor burial vouchsafe to have so gracious consideration.'[8]

This talk of the King's 'gracious consideration' and the deference shown to his 'Grace' and his 'Highness' may seem to us affected and unreal, but it was a genuine expression of an attitude of mind; it was the way men thought in those days; nor was there any irony intended; unless the sincerity of such phrases is recognized, it is impossible to understand the period, still less to understand Sir Thomas More. Whatever he did, the King remained the Prince to whom the subject owed a duty.

More decided to wear the fine gown that had been given him by Antonio Bonvisi; he thought it would please his old friend as well as the executioner whose perquisite it would be.

> ... which Master Lieutenant espying, advised him to put it off, saying that he that should have it was but a Javill [scoundrel].
>
> 'What, Master Lieutenant,' quoth he, 'shall I account him a Javill that shall do me this day so singular a benefit? Nay, I assure you, were it cloth of gold, I would account it well bestowed on him, as St. Cyprian did who gave his executioner thirty pieces of gold.' And albeit at length, through Master Lieutenant's importunate persuasion, he altered his apparel, yet after example of that holy martyr St. Cyprian, did he, of that little money that was left him, send one Angel of gold to his executioner.[9]

So he wore a coarse, grey gown belonging to John a' Wood; he carried in his hand a red cross.

The distance from the Tower to the scaffold was less than three hundred yards, yet the crowded incidents of Sir Thomas

---

[8] *Roper*, p. 100.

[9] *Roper*, p. 102.

More's progress along that way have become part of London's legend. His cheerfulness in face of death was in keeping with the spirit of his fellow citizens, and they treasured his last witty sayings. These were not, however, to the taste of one Londoner, Edward Hall, who, while professing to be shocked that a former Lord Chancellor should end his life 'with a mock,' was careful to record his words. Hall is here the primary authority; he himself was an Under-Sheriff in 1535 and his account was written many years before Roper put down his recollections, and half a century before Stapleton collected the reminiscences of Margaret Clement and Dorothy Colley. Hall may have been present in his capacity of Under-Sheriff, but, if he was not there, his position enabled him to get firsthand evidence. His narrative, therefore, deserves to be quoted in full.

> This man was also counted learned, and as you have heard before he was Lord Chancellor of England, and in that time a great persecutor of such as detested the supremacy of the Bishop of Rome, which he himself so highly favoured that he stood to it till he was brought to the scaffold on the Tower Hill where on a block his head was stricken from his shoulders and had no more harm.

This seems to be an echo of More's remark to the Commissioners that 'a man may lose his head and yet have none harm.'

> I cannot tell whether I should call him a foolish wiseman, or a wise foolish-man, for undoubtedly he beside his great learning, had a great wit, but it was so mingled with taunting and mocking, that it seemed to them that best knew him, that he thought nothing to be well spoken except he had ministered some mock in the communication, insomuch as at his coming to the Tower, one of the officers demanded his upper garment for his fee, meaning his gown and he answered he should have it, and took him his cap saying it was the uppermost garment that he had. Likewise, even going

to his death at the Tower Gate, a poor woman called unto him and besought him to declare that he had certain evidences of hers in the time that he was in office (which after he was apprehended she could not come by) and that he would entreat she might have them again, or else she was undone. He answered, 'Good woman, have patience a little while, for the King is good unto me that even within this half hour he will discharge me of all businesses, and help thee himself.' Also when he went up the stair on the scaffold, he desired one of the Sheriff's officers to give him his hand to help him up, and said, 'When I come down again, let me shift for myself as well as I can.' Also the hangman kneeled down to him asking him forgiveness for his death (as the manner is) to whom he said, 'I forgive thee, but I promise thee that thou shalt never have the honesty of the striking of my head, my neck is so short.' Also, even when he should lay down his head on the block, he having a great gray beard, striked out his beard and said to the hangman, 'I pray you let me lay my beard over the block lest ye should cut it.' Thus with a mock he ended his life.[10]

Roper's account is very brief.

Going up the scaffold, which was so weak that it was ready to fall, he said, merrily to Master Lieutenant,[11] 'I pray you, Master Lieutenant, see me safe up, and for my coming down let me shift for myself.'

Then desired he all the people thereabout to pray for him, and to bear witness with him that he should now there suffer death in and for the faith of the Holy Catholic Church. Which done, he kneeled down, and after his prayers said, turned to the executioner and with a cheerful countenance spake thus

---

[10] *Hall*, II, p. 265.

[11] Hall was probably correct in saying 'one of the Sheriff's officers.'

to him, 'Pluck up thy spirits, man, and be not afraid to do thine office; my neck is very short; take heed therefore thou strike not awry for the saving of thine honesty.'[12]

Stapleton was able to record the recollections of Margaret Clement who had been present at the execution; these included the story of the woman and her 'evidences,' or documents; two other incidents are given.

> As he was passing on his way, a certain woman offered him wine, but he refused it, saying, 'Christ in his passion was given not wine, but vinegar, to drink.' ... He was again interrupted by another woman, who perhaps felt she had a grievance or perhaps was suborned by others, and now cried out that he had done her a grave injury while he was Chancellor. 'I remember your case quite well,' he gravely replied, 'and if I had to pass sentence again, it would be just the same as before.'[13]

To these may be added Stapleton's earlier tale of the Winchester man; his was not a legal case, but that of a man beset by temptation. Perhaps he was a link with the days when More administered justice in Hampshire.

> A certain citizen of Winchester was for a long time so troubled by the gravest temptations to despair that prayer and the advice of his friends seemed of no avail. At length by a friend he was brought to see More, who, pitying the man's misery, gave him good and prudent counsel. It was not by his words, however, but by his prayers to God that More at length obtained for the man relief from his grievous temptation. The man remained free from his distress so long as More was at liberty and he had access to him. But when More was imprisoned the temptation returned with still

---

[12] *Roper*, p. 103.

[13] *Stapleton*, p. 209.

greater force than before. The unhappy man, so long as More was in the Tower, spent his days in misery without hope of cure. But when he heard that More was condemned to death he went up to London in order that, at whatever risk to himself, he might speak to him as he was going out to execution. On More's way, then, from the Tower to the scaffold he burst through the guards and cried out with a loud voice, 'Do you recognize me Sir Thomas? Help me, I beg you: for what temptation has returned to me and I cannot get rid of it.' More at once answered, 'I recognize you perfectly. Go and pray for me, and I will pray earnestly for you.' He went away, and never again in his whole life was he troubled with such temptations.'[14] On the scaffold he recited the 50th Psalm, Miserere mei.[15]

His last words according to the Paris Newsletter were that he begged them earnestly to pray for the King that he might have good counsel, protesting that he himself died the King's good servant, but God's first.[16]

After his conviction, Sir Thomas More composed this prayer:

Almighty God, have mercy on ... and on all that bear me evil will, and would me harm, and their faults and mine together, by such easy tender merciful means as thine infinite wisdom best can devise, vouchsafe to amend and redress, and make us saved souls in heaven together where we may ever live and love together with Thee and thy blessed saints, O

---

[14] *Stapleton*, pg. 71.

[15] *Stapleton*, pg. 210. Hebrew, Psalm 51.

[16] *Harpsfield*, p. 266.

glorious Trinity, for the bitter passion of our sweet Saviour Christ. Amen.[17]

The head, parboiled as was customary, was put on a stake on the tower of London Bridge, from which Fisher's head had just been removed. Margaret Roper was determined to save it, and when, a month later, she heard that it was to be thrown into the river, as Fisher's had been, she bribed the executioner, who had charge of these remains, to let her have it. She preserved it during her lifetime, and it is now in the Roper vault at St. Dunstan's, Canterbury.

The family was permitted to bury the body in the little chapel of St. Peter ad Vincula in the Tower. Stapleton's account must be given.

Margaret Roper from earliest morning had been going from church to church and distributing such generous alms to the poor that her purse was now empty. After her father's execution she hastened to the Tower to bury his body, for the Lieutenant had promised to allow this with the permission of the King, which was readily given. In her hurry she forgot to replenish her purse and found that she had no winding-sheet for the body. She was in the greatest distress and knew not what to do. Her maid Dorothy, afterwards the wife of Mr. Harris, suggested that she should get some linen from a neighbouring shop. 'How can I do that,' she answered, 'when I have no money left?' 'They will give you credit,' replied the maid. 'I am far away from home,' said Margaret, 'and no one knows me here, but yet go and try.' The maid went into a neighbouring shop and asked for as much linen as was needed: she agreed on the price. Then she put her hand into

---

[17] *E.W.*, p. 1406.

her purse as if to look for the money, intending to say that unexpectedly she found herself without money, but that if the shopkeeper would trust her she would obtain the price of the linen as quickly as possible from her mistress and bring it back. But although the maid was quite certain that she had absolutely no money, yet in her purse she found exactly the price of the linen, not one farthing more nor less than the amount she had agreed to pay. Dorothy Harris who is still living [1588] here in Douai, has told me these details again and again.

The Church of St. Peter ad Vincula had just been rebuilt by Henry VIII. There had been only one burial there before that of Thomas More. The body of John Fisher was brought to the Church from All Hallows.[18] It is said that Margaret Roper gained permission for this removal, but it is probable that the King or Cromwell wished to make an end of the visits that were being increasingly made to the Bishop's resting place. Both bodies were buried in the west end of the Church and their bones may not have been disturbed in later reconstructions.

The little church was to be the sepulchre within the next decade of other victims of Henry's tyranny; amongst them were Anne Boleyn and her brother, Thomas Cromwell, and the aged Countess of Salisbury, the mother of Reginald Pole.

It was he who paid a fine tribute to Thomas More in a dissertation he sent to the King in 1536, published later as *Pro Ecclesiasticæ Unitatis Defensione*. This was an outspoken criticism of Henry's policy and an appeal to him to repent. The King was angered; such a passage as the following was the more mortifying by its implications than if Pole had accused him plainly of judicial

---

[18] *The Grey Friar's Chronicle* (Camden Society edition, p. 38) records that the body of Bishop Fisher was 'buried in the Churchyard of Barking by the north door,' and after the execution of More, 'then was taken up the Bishop again and both of them buried within the Tower.'

murder.

O City of London, you saw led out from prison on a charge of treason the man at whose tribunal you had so lately beheld others standing for a similar crime; the man whom you had known as a boy, a youth, and whom you had marked in later life, as, amid the applause and congratulations of all, he mounted through every grade of honour, until he reached the very highest office. And because he was your own citizen and child, not without a secret sense of joy you beheld his prosperous career tending always to your own praise and honour. You saw him at last led out as a criminal from prison, in sordid dress, and grown old, not by the lapse of years, but by the squalor and sufferings of his dungeon, and for the first time you beheld his head made white by long confinement; you saw his weak and broken body leaning on a staff, and even so scarcely able to stand, and dragged along the way that led to the place of trial, or rather of certain condemnation. Could you see this spectacle with dry eyes? Or could you without tears see him return by the same road condemned to the penalty of traitors, while you knew that his fidelity towards yourself could never be shaken by bribes or threats? How, indeed, could the citizens of London be unmoved, when I see utter strangers, who never knew him and never received benefit from him, conceive such sorrow in reading the story of his trial as not to be able to restrain their tears. I myself, who have loved and venerated him, not because of private affection, but because of his virtue and integrity and benefits to my country, writing now about his death, in my exile far from England, feel the tears gush to my eyes against my will, so that, as God is my witness, they hinder my writing and blot the words that I have written."[19]

---

[19] *Pro Ecclesiasticae*, f. xciii.

Chapter XXIX

From Martyrdom to Canonization

N a Hungarian castle, proud that it never yielded to the Turk, among the portraits of the princely owners is a dark picture labelled "Thomas More." And when asked, "Who is this More?" the soldier-custodian will answer, "He was a great Englishman. The King cut his head off, but he had done nothing wrong".[1]

That plain judgement would have been made by many Englishmen at the time of the martyrdom, had they dared to open their mouths. King Henry and Thomas Cromwell were well aware of the risk they took of rousing European opinion against them when the news of the executions of Fisher and More and the Carthusians was received. But at home, too, there was a serious danger that their ruthlessness would provoke effectual opposition. So they hastened to forestall criticism.

> The magistrates at Quarter Sessions were ordered to declare to the people the treasons committed by the late Bishop of Rochester and Sir Thomas More; who thereby, and by divers secret practices, of their malicious minds intended to seminate, engender, and breed a most mischievous and seditious opinion, not only to their own confusion, but also of divers others, who lately suffered execution according to their

---

[1] P.S. Allen in the Introduction to his Selections from More's English Works (1924). Perhaps today the comrade-custodian explains that the portrait is a forerunner of Karl Marx.

demerits.²

Those who dared to express sympathy for Fisher and More were prosecuted. Thus at the end of 1539, John Beche, Abbot of St. John's, Colchester, was charged, amongst other offences, with having called them martyrs.

Criticism in England could be driven underground, but it could not be suppressed abroad. What would the Emperor and the King of France think and say? What would they do?

> Soon after whose death came intelligence thereof to the Emperor Charles. Whereupon he sent for Sir Thomas Elyot, our English Ambassador, and said unto him: 'My Lord Ambassador, we understand that the King, your master, hath put his faithful servant and grave, wise Councillor, Sir Thomas More, to death.' Whereunto Sir Thomas Elyot answered that he understood nothing thereof. 'Well.' said the Emperor, 'it is too true. And this will we say, that if we had been master of such a servant, of whose doings ourself have had these many years no small experience, we would rather have lost the best city of our dominions than have lost such a worthy Councillor.' Which matter was by the same Sir Thomas Elyot to myself, my wife, to Master Clement and his wife, to Master John Heywood and his wife, and divers others his friends accordingly reported.³

The Pope had appealed to the Emperor and to the King of France on the death of Bishop Fisher 'to execute justice on Henry when required,' but Charles and Francis were too busy watching each other to take action against England.

---

² Strype's *Memorials*, I, Ap., p. 211.

³ *Roper*, pp. 103-4. This incident raises difficulties; Elyot left the Imperial Court in 1532. Roper's list of those who heard this report is so definite that it must be assumed that there was substance in his recollection but he may have got details confused. For discussion, see *Harpsfield*, pp. 353-4.

The following instructions were sent by Cromwell in August 1535 to Sir John Wallop, the English resident at the French Court:

Touching Master More and the Bishop of Rochester, with such others as were executed here, their treasons, conspiracies and practices, secretly practised, or well within the realm as without, to move and stir dissension, and to sow sedition within the realm, intending thereby not only to the destruction of the king, but also the whole subversion of the same, being explained and declared and openly detected and so manifestly proved before them, that they could not avoid nor deny it, and they thereof lawfully convicted and condemned of high treason by the due order of the law of this realm, so that it shall and may well appear to all the world that they, having such malice rooted in their hearts against their prince and sovereign, and the total destruction of the commonweal of this realm, were well worthy, if they had had a thousand lives, to have suffered ten times a more horrible death and execution than any of them did suffer.[4]

A letter was also sent to Sir Gregory Casale, the resident at the Papal Court. After stating that Henry owed no account of his actions except to God 'with whose will they are in perfect harmony,' the letter puts forward the same reasons for the execution that had been set before Francis. In both letters, it may be noted, the King explained how lenient he had been since Fisher and More had been executed and not hanged, drawn and quartered; no reference was made to the far different treatment of 'such others as were executed here.'

We have already seen how Cardinal Pole expressed his horror at the execution in the treatise *Pro Ecclesiasticae* which he sent to Henry.

But what of Erasmus? He had been informed of the

---

[4] 23rd August. MS. Harl. 288, fol. 39-46.

imprisonment of both his old friends, but he made no public protest. Shortly after he had heard of Fisher's execution, he wrote to Bartholomew Latonus, 'It is only too true that Thomas More has long been in prison and his fortune confiscated. It is said that he too has been executed, but as yet I have no certain news. Would that he had not got himself involved in this dangerous business, and had left theology to the theologians.'[5]

Thomas Cromwell was well aware of the influence Erasmus could wield on European opinion if he defended Fisher and More and condemned their executions. But Cromwell knew his man and showed his customary astuteness in dealing with him. He sent one of his agents, Thomas Theobald, to Louvain to see Conrad Goclenius who was a regular correspondent of Erasmus. On 10th August, 1535,[6] Goclenius sent him the first definite news of the execution of More; he passed on Theobald's official explanation, but coupled with this (and here we can see the hand of Cromwell) was an assurance that the pension Erasmus drew from Aldington would be paid regularly. Erasmus wrote to his friends of his distress at the news. So to the Bishop of Cracow, Peter Tomiczki, he wrote on 31st August:

> You will learn from a letter which I enclose the fate of Thomas More and the Bishop of Rochester. They were the wisest and most saintly men that England had. In the death of More I feel as if I had died myself, but such are the tides of human things. We had but one soul between us.[7]

We need not doubt the depth of his sorrow, but the habits of a lifetime are not easily conquered by a sick, aged man; he made no public pronouncement.

His friends sent him such information as they could gather,

---

[5] 24th August. *Allen*, XI, 3048.

[6] *Allen*, XI, 3037.

[7] *Allen*, XI, 3049.

but, as one of them declared, no one dared write direct from England.[8] At the end of September, Goclenius sent an account of the trial;[9] we do not know what this was; it may have been a copy, or translation, of the Paris News Letter which had been in circulation for the past two months. In December, Damien a Goes sent him an Italian account of the trial which he had received from Cardinal Pole whom he had probably met in Padua.[10] This, again, may have been a version of the Paris News Letter.

It has been argued that Erasmus wrote the account of More's trial and death that is usually known as the *Expositio Fidelis*;[11] there seems to have been an early version of this in circulation late in July; of this he certainly was not the author as he did not know of More's execution at that date. A later version was printed that year by Froben at Basle; as Erasmus was then living with Froben, he no doubt had something to do with its preparation for the press, possibly adding fresh details to the original version. At the most his share was that of editor and not author.

Some Latin verses, *Carmen heroicum in mortem Thomae Mori*,[12] published in 1536 have been attributed to Erasmus; they express a burning indignation at the outrage of More's execution. Even if he composed these lines, he avoided putting his name to them. During the last months of his life he was intent on collecting his Aldington pension and on seeking the patronage of Cranmer. He died, aged about seventy, almost exactly a year after Thomas More.

Edward Hall in his *Triumphant Reign of Henry VIII*

---

[8] *Allen,*, XI, 3042.

[9] *Allen*, XI, 3061.

[10] *Allen*, XI, 3076.

[11] For discussion see Harpsfield, pp. 254-7; *Allen*, XI, pp. 368-78.

[12] *Harpsfield*, p. 255.

represented More as 'a great persecutor,' but like other detractors, he could not withhold some measure of admiration.

It was not until the reign of Queen Mary (1553-8) that Sir Thomas More could again be openly praised in England. Those five years saw the publication of the English Works through the piety and care of William Rastell; during those years also William Roper recorded his memories, and Nicholas Harpsfield wrote his biography of More; the death of the Queen prevented publication. During the reign of Elizabeth, the surviving members of the More household, except Roper, went into exile. They provided Thomas Stapleton with the material for his life of Sir Thomas More in his *Tres Thomæ* published at Antwerp in 1588 when the expectations of Catholics abroad, though not in England, were revived by the sailing of the Armada. Towards the end of the reign, Catholics again hoped that events might favour them. It was at this period that the unidentified Ro.Ba. wrote his biography; it is not known how widely it was circulated, but as eight manuscripts have survived, it probably had many readers. It was a coincidence that at the same time a group of playwrights drafted *The Booke of Sir Thomas More*; they could not be suspected of Catholic leanings; indeed one of them, Anthony Munday, had been placed as an informer in the English College at Rome, and later was working for Topcliffe.

Catholic hopes were again in the ascendancy with the marriage of Charles I to Henrietta Maria in 1625. The next few years saw the first publication of Roper's Life (1626), and of Cresacre More's Life (c. 1630).

One small sign of the place that Thomas More held in men's minds is a portrait medallion struck during the seventeenth century. There is a specimen in the British Museum; the work is rather crude; nothing is known of its origin or purpose. The reverse shows a cypress tree cut down, with the words *svavius olet*, a reference to the belief that a cypress smells even more sweetly after felling.

Sufficient has been said in the Preface to this book about later biographies, but there is one work that calls for comment. Anne Manning's *Household of Sir Thomas More* was published in 1851 and at once became popular; it was reprinted many times during the lifetime of the authoress, and in Everyman's Library it renewed its appeal.[13] It is no exaggeration to say that the popular conception of Sir Thomas More during the last hundred years has been considerably influenced by that imaginative reconstruction. It is an attractive picture, a little whimsical perhaps, but a sound corrective to Froude. Miss Manning evidently had access to a manuscript of Harpsfield's *Life*, for she refers to William Roper's Protestant interlude.

In the seventeenth century, John Aubrey, who was not a Catholic, wrote, 'Methinks 'tis strange that all this time he [More] is not canonized, for he merited highly of the church.'[14]

The first step on the long way to canonization may be said to have been Pope Paul III's pronouncement in letters to the Emperor and the King of France; Fisher and More and others, he wrote, had died 'for God, for the Catholic Religion, for justice and for truth.' Gregory XIII granted permission to Nicholas Circinianus in 1579 to paint frescoes depicting the English martyrs in the Church of St. Stephen in Rome and in the English Church of the Holy Trinity in Rome.

Richard Smith,[15] Bishop of Chalcedon, drew up in 1628 a list of English martyrs, and twelve years later, Pope Urban VIII granted faculties to the Archbishop of Cambrai to appoint commissioners to study the evidence concerning those martyrs who, for at least a hundred years previously, had been venerated.

---

[13] Between 1906 and 1938 this was reprinted eight times.

[14] *Brief Lives*, ed. A. Powell (1949), p. 317.

[15] Editor's note: For more about Bishop Richard Smith, and his role in drafting the work that would pave the way for canonization of many English Martyrs, see Hughes, *Rome and the Counter-Reformation in England*, also published by Mediatrix Press.

Political and other disturbances prevented this commission from carrying out its task.

It was not until 1855, when Cardinal Wiseman was Archbishop of Westminster, that the cause of the English Martyrs was again brought forward with Canon John Morris (later of the Society of Jesus) as postulator. The process of beatification and canonization is a long one as it entails an exhaustive investigation of all the records and evidence. There were other impediments at that time, and thirty years passed before Pope Leo XIII by a decree confirmed 'the honour given to the Blessed Martyrs John Cardinal Fisher, Thomas More, and others put to death in England for the Faith from the year 1535 to 1583.' The number of martyrs thus beatified was fifty-four. The decree was dated from Rome, 29th December, 1886.

The approach of the four hundredth anniversary of the martyrdom of Blessed John Fisher and of Blessed Thomas More made many hope that they would be canonized. The movement to promote their cause was remarkable for the support given, not only, as was to be expected, by the leaders and members of the Catholic Church in England, but for that given by eminent scholars and others who were not Catholics. So on 4th April, 1934, a petition bearing 170,000 signatures was presented to Pope Pius XI. Support also came for the canonization of Blessed Thomas More in a petition submitted by all the Judges and the Catholic members of the Bar of the Irish Free State. The Holy Father was deeply impressed by this strongly expressed hope, and the cause was pressed forward.

On 10th February, 1935 a Solemn Decree was promulgated stating that the martyrdom and the cause of the martyrdom of Blessed John Cardinal Fisher and Blessed Thomas More is so clearly established, that, without further signs or miracles, it is possible to proceed to the final stage of the canonization. By this special act, the pope shortened the normal process.

At a consistory on 3rd March an address of thanks to the Pope was made by Monsignor (later Cardinal) Hinsley. 'This speech was a striking one in faultless Italian. ... 'The Holy Father and the many Cardinals present were notably impressed.'

The ceremony of canonization took place on 19th May, 1935.

The Collect in the Votive Mass of Saint Thomas More reads:

> O God, who, when the blessed martyr Thomas had to choose between the allurements of the world and the pains of imprisonment and death, didst give him strength to embrace thy cross with a cheerful and resolute spirit, we pray thee grant that we too, thanks to his intercession and example, may fight manfully for faith and right, and be found worthy to make a joyful entrance into everlasting bliss.

BIBLIOGRAPHY

I. CHIEF REFERENCES

Allen. "Opus Epistolarum Des Erasmi Roterodami", ed. P. S. Allen. 11 vols. Reference to volume and number.

Apologye. "The Apologye of Syr Thomas More, Knyght", ed. A. I. Taft. (E.E.T.S. 1930).

Bridgett. "Life and Writings of Blessed Thomas More", by Revd. T. E. Bridgett. Third edition (1898).

Cavendish. "The Life and Death of Thomas Wolsey", by George Cavendish. Temple Classics Edition (1908).

Chambers. "Thomas More", by R. W. Chambers (1935).

Dialogue of Comfort, Everyman's Library edition in modern spelling (1951).

E.W. "The Works of Sir Thomas More, Knight. . . .", ed. William Rastell (1557). First reference to this edition; second reference to volume and page of reprint (1931).

Hall. "Henry VIII", ed. by Charles Whibley, 2 vols. (1904).

Harpsfield. "The Life and Death of Sir Thomas More..." ed. E. V. Hitchcock and R. W. Chambers (E.E.T.S. 1932).

L.P. "Letters and Papers of the reign of Henry VIII", ed. J. S. Brewer, etc. (1826 onwards).

Nichols. "The Epistles of Erasmus", translated by F. M. Nichols, 3 vols. (1901-18). Reference to volume and page.

Rogers. "The Correspondence of Sir Thomas More", ed. E. F. Rogers (1947). Reference to page unless stated.

Roper. "The Lyfe of Sir Thomas Moore, knighte", by William Roper, ed. E. V. Hitchcock (E.E.T.S. 1935).

Stapleton. "The Life and Illustrious Martyrdom of Sir Thomas More". Part III of "Tres Thomæ", by Thomas Stapleton, translated by Mgr. P. E. Hallett (1928).

Stow. "A Survey of London", by John Stow, ed. 2 vols. by C. L. Kingsford (1908).

Utopia. First reference to translation by G. C. Richards (1923); second reference to Everyman's Library edition of Robinson in modern spelling (1951).

II. WORKS OF SIR THOMAS MORE

(A) COLLECTED EDITIONS
  (i) English
The workes of Sir Thomas More Knyght, sometime Lorde Chauncellour of England, wrytten by him in the Englysh tonge.
Printed at London at the costes and charges of John Cawood, John Waly, and Richard Tottell. Anno. 1557.
(Edited by William Rastell, and dedicated to Queen Mary.)
Reprint. A reprint, planned to occupy seven volumes, was begun in 1931 when two volumes were published.
Edited by W. E. Campbell, etc.
Vol. I. Early poems, Pico, Richard III, Four Last Things. Vol. II. Dialogue concerning Tyndale (i.e. Dialogue concerning Heresies).
(The Introductions, etc., are valuable.)

(ii) Latin
1. *Thomas Mori . . . Lucubrationes ad innumeris mendis repurgatae. . . .*
Basil[iae] Apud Episcopium F[rates.] 1563.
(This contains the account of More sent by Erasmus to Hutten, and the Expositio Fidelis.)
2. *Thomæ Mori . . . Omnia, quae hujusque ad manus nostras pervenerunt, Latina opera. . . .*
Apud Petrum Zangrium: Lovanii, 1565. *Ioannem Bogardum: Lovanii,* 1565.
(Included Latin text of Richard III supplied by William Rastell. Apart from the imprints, these editions are identical. Both were re-issued in 1566.)
3. *Thomæ Mori . . . Opera omnia. . . .*
Sumtibus C. Genschii: Francofurti ad Moenum et Lipsice. 1689.

(This combined the Basle and Louvain editions with Stapleton's Life and some additional matter.)

(B) SEPARATE WORKS

N.B. This list contains first publications with notes on some later editions. The entries are in chronological order.

1. *Luciani Dialogi compluria opuscula longe festiuissima ab Erasmo Roterodamo et Thoma Moro interpretibus optimis in Latinorum lingua traducta hac sequentur serie.*
Ex Aedibus Ascensionis [Paris] 1506
(Six other editions, besides reprints, were published during More's lifetime; they varied in contents, the later ones containing additional matter by Erasmus.)

2. *Here is conteyned the lyfe of J. Picus Erie of Mydrandula ... With dyvers eypstles & other werkes of ye sayd J. Picus.*
(Printed by John Rastell, c. 1510; a pirated edition was also published by Wynkyn de Worde.)

3. *A mery jest how a sergeant would learne to play the frere.*
London. Julian Notary (1516?)

4. UTOPIA.
Libellus vere aureus nec minus salutaris quam festiuus de optimo reip. statu, deque noua Insula Utopia authore clarissimo viro Thoma Moro inclytae civitatis Londonensis due & vicecomiti cura M. Petri Mgidii Antuerpiensis, & arte Theodorid Martini Alustensis, Typographi almae Londaniensium Academiae nunc primum accuratissime editus.
(1516. The first edition; it contained many errors.)
Ad lectorem. Habes candide lector opusculum illud vere aureum Thomæ Mori ... de optimo republicae statu deque noua Insula Utopia. ...
(Paris, 1517. This was Lupset's edition.)
De Optimo reip. statu deque nova insula Utopia libellus uere aureus, nec minus salutaris quam festiuus, clarissimi disertissimique

uiri Thomæ Mori inclytae civitatis Londinensis duis & Vicecomitis. Epigrammata clarissimi disertissimique uiri Thomae Mori, pleraque e Greeds uersa Epigrammata. Des Erasmi Roterodami. Apud inclytam Basileam. (March 1518. This was Froben's first edition. A second edition was published in November 1518 with a title-page border by Holbein.)

L'Utopie.
Texte latin edite par Marie Delcourt.
Paris, 1936. Translations.
(This is the best Latin text.)
German, Basle, 1524.
Italian, Vinegia, 1548.
French, Paris, 1550.
English, London, 1551.

A fruteful and pleasaunt worke of the best state of a publyque weale, and of the new yle called Utopia: written in Latine by Syr Thomas More Knyght, and translated into Englyshe by Raphe Robynson Citizein and Goldsmythe of London, at the procurement, and earnest request of George Tadlowe Citizein & Haberdassher of the same Citie. Imprinted at London by Abraham Vele, dwelling in Pauls churchyarde at the synge of the Lambe. Anno. 1551. Other English translations: Burnet, 1684; Cayley, 1808; Paget, 1800; G. C. Richards, 1923.

(Robinsons translation, with the Latin text of Froben's edition, was edited by J. H. Lupton in 1895.)

5. *Thomæ Mori Epistola ad Germanum Brixium ...*
London, Richard Pynson, 1520.
(Reprinted, Rogers, pp. 212-239.)

6. *Epigrammata ... Thomæ Mori ...*
Basle, John Froben, 1518.
The Latin Epigrams of Thomas More.

Edited and translated, L. Bradner and C. A. Lynch, University of Chicago, 1953.
7. *Epistolas Aliquot Eruditorum.*
Antwerp, M. Hillen, 1520.
  (This contains More's letter to a monk and a letter to Edward Lee. Reprinted, Rogers, pp. 137-154; 165-206. *Epistolae Eruditorum Virorum*, published by Froben at Basle later in 1520, contained other letters to Lee. Reprinted, Rogers, pp. 206-212.)
8. *Eruditissimi viri G. Rossei opus elegens quo pulcherrime retegit ac refellit insanes Lutheri calumnias: quibus Anglios Galliaeque Regem Hernicum . . . scurra turpissime insectatur. Sometimes referred to as: Vindicatio Henrici VIII ... a Calumnis Luthere.*
London: Richard Pynson: 1523.
(Gulielmus Rosseus was Sir Thomas More.)
9. *The supplycacyon of Soulys. Made by syr Thomas More knyght ... Agaynst the supplycacyon of beggars.* London: William Rastell: 1529?.
10. *A dyaloge of syr Thomas More knygthe: one of the counsayll of oure soverayne lorde the kyng & chancellour of hys duchy of Lancaster. Wherein he treatyd of dyvers maters as of the veneration & worshypp of ymagys & relyques prayng to sayntys & goyng on pylgrymage. Wyth many othere thyngys touchyng the pestylent sect of Luther and Tyndale by the tone bygone in Saxony and by tother laboryd to be brought into England.*
London: John Rastell: 1529.
(William Rastell printed a revised edition in 1530-1.)
11. *The confutacyon of Tyndales answere made by syr Thomas More Knyght. . . .* London: William Rastell: 1532.
12. *The Second parte of the Confutacyon of Tyndals Answere. In whyche is also confuted the chyrche that Tyndale devyseth. And the chyrche also that frere Barns devyseth.* London: William Rastell: 1533.
13. *A Letter of syr Tho. More Knyght impugnynge the erronyouse*

wrytyng of John Fryth agaynst the Blessed Sacrament of the aultare.
London: William Rastell: 1533.
(Reprinted, Rogers, pp. 439-464.)
14. *The Debellacyon of Salem and Bizance.*
London: William Rastell: 1533.
15. *The apologye of syr T. More knyght.*
London: William Rastell: 1533.
(Reprinted for E.E.T.S., 1930, edited by A. I. Taft.)
16. *Syr Thomas Mores answere to the fyrst parte of the poysoned booke, which a nameless heretyke hath named the Super of the Lorde.*
London: William Rastell: 1534.
17. *The Boke of the fayre Gentylwoman . . . Lady Fortune.* London: Robert Wyer: after 1538.
18. *The chronicle of Jhon Hardyng. . . .*
London: Richard Grafton: 1543.
(Contains a corrupt version of Richard III. It was not published separately until 1641 when it was printed by Thomas Payne and M. Simmons, London.)
19. *A dialoge of comfort against tribulacion, made by Syr Thomas More Knyght and set foorth by the name of an Hungarian, not before this time imprinted.*
London: Richard Tottel: 1553.
(Reprinted: John Fowler at Antwerp, 1573; modem spelling, edited by Mgr. P. E. Hallett, 1937; Everyman's Library, with Utopia, 1951.)
20. *Doctissimi D. T. Mori . . . Epistola in qua . . . respondit literis Ioannis Pomerani.*
Louvain: John Fowler: 1568.
(This letter to John Bugenhagen, or Pomeranus, is reprinted, Rogers, pp. 324-365.)
21. *Epistola Thomæ Mori ad Academiam Oxon.*
Oxford: T. Huggins: 1633.

(Reprinted, Rogers, pp. 112-120.)

(C) LETTERS

Until recently it has been necessary to refer to many volumes in order to read Sir Thomas More's letters; they have now been collected in two works:
1. *The Correspondence of Sir Thomas More.*
   Edited by Elizabeth Frances Rogers (Princeton, 1947). This does not contain the correspondence with Erasmus, but references are given to,
2. *Opus Epistolarum Des. Erasmi Roterodami.*
   Edited by P. S. Allen, etc., 11 Volumes (1906-1947).

III. LIFE OF SIR THOMAS MORE
BIOGRAPHIES

(i) Early biographies
1. The *Life* by William Roper is the primary authority. It consists of recollections written down about 1556 for the use of Nicholas Harpsfield who had been chosen by Roper to write the biography of Sir Thomas More. Roper did not repeat more than was necessary of what was available in print; thus he said nothing about More's writings since Harpsfield would have these at hand, and the Rastell edition of the English Works was nearly ready.
   The result is not a carefully planned book but a unique record. It was first published, in English, in Paris, in 1626. The standard edition was published for the E.E.T.S. in 1935, and edited by Dr. Elsie V. Hitchcock.
2. In order of time, but not of importance, came Harpsfield's *Life and Death of Sir Thomas More.* Harpsfield not only had the active guidance of Roper, but he himself had spent the years 1550-1553 at Louvain in company with the Clements and the Rastells, and he must have learned much from them. The

death of Queen Mary prevented the publication of this biography; it was first printed in 1932 for the E.E.T.S. in an edition magnificently edited by Dr. Hitchcock and Professor R. W. Chambers.
3. Second in importance to Roper's Life is Thomas Stapleton's *Tres Thomæ*, the three being, St. Thomas the Apostle, St. Thomas of Canterbury, and Sir Thomas More. This was published at Douai in 1588 in Latin. Stapleton drew upon the memories of his fellow-exiles; had he not made copies of some of the documents possessed by Dorothy Colley, they would have gone unrecorded.

A French translation was published in 1849, and the first English translation of the life of Sir Thomas More, in 1928; this was made by Mgr. P. E. Hallett.
4. William Rastell wrote a biography of his uncle; this has been lost except for parts referring to Bishop John Fisher. These are reprinted in Harpsfield, pp. 221-252.

(ii) Trial and Execution
Three documents have to be considered:
   -the Paris News Letter (Harpsfield, pp. 254-266),
   -the *Expositio Fidelis* (Allen, XI, pp. 368-378),
   -the *Ordo Condemnationis* (*Acta Thomæ Mori*, Louvain, 1947)
Reference has already been made to the Paris News Letter and to the *Expositio Fidelis* (see above p. 341). The most likely claimant to be the author of the first is Philippe Dumont (Montanus), a former pupil of Erasmus, who seems to have been in Paris during the summer of 1535. There is no clue to the far more interesting question of who was responsible for sending, or taking, the account of More's trial and death to Paris so speedily after the execution. Any suggestion must be highly speculative.

A third document has now to be discussed. This was discovered by Professor Henry de Vocht of Louvain and published in 1947 in a volume entitled *Acta Thomæ Mori*. This *Ordo Condemnationis Thomæ Mori* was found with other transcripts in a volume that had belonged to Gerard Morinck, a lecturer at Louvain and a contemporary of Goclenius. Professor de Vocht suggests that it was this account, the *Ordo*, that Goclenius sent to Erasmus on 28 September 1535 (Allen, XI, 3061). The date of the document is not certain; the reference to the year 1535 ("anno illo quo perierat") was added at a later date than the transcription. Professor de Vocht's interesting speculations cannot be set out in detail here; his conclusion is that this *Ordo* is a translation of an English account (now lost) of More's trial, written by William Rastell and sent to Goclenius; that Erasmus himself wrote the first version (now lost) of the *Expositio* based on Rastell's account, and claimed, to cover himself, that it came from a correspondent in Paris; this first *Expositio* was translated into French (the Paris News Letter) and into German; later Erasmus published an enlarged edition of the *Expositio*, and it is this second version that has survived. According to this, the *Ordo* is the closest version now available of Rastell's original account. This ingenious theory raises many problems—more, indeed, than it solves. It is dependent on two lost documents and on hypotheses difficult to reconcile with known dates. To take the central assumption—that William Rastell wrote an account of the trial that reached Goclenius during September. There is no valid reason for assuming that William Rastell wrote such an account at that time, and it is very doubtful if he was at the trial; had be been there, surely either Roper or Harpsfield would have made some reference to his recollections, or to any account he may have written immediately after the trial from reports made to him by those who were present.

The interest of the *Ordo* is that it makes some points of More's replies clearer than those given in the two other accounts.

Finally it may be said that Harpsfield's account remains the most reliable; he had not only the Paris News Letter and the *Expositio* available, but also Roper's supplementary, and most important, notes.

Richard Heywood, who was at the trial, was still alive when Harpsfield was collecting his material. Moreover, as was noted earlier, Harpsfield had associated with the Clements and the Rastells during their three and a half years of exile in Louvain (1549 to 1553), and they must have talked over every detail of the trial. It must be assumed that the Paris News Letter and the *Expositio* were accepted by Roper and others of the family as correct as far as they went; what was lacking was supplied by Roper.

(iii) Later biographies

1. A biography by "Ro.Ba." (whose identity has not been established) was written about 1600, and remained in manuscript until it was published in Vol. 2 of Christopher Wordsworth's *Ecclesiastical Biography* (1810). It was separately published for the E.E.T.S. in 1950, and edited by Dr. Hitchcock, Mgr. P. E. Hallett and Professor A. W. Reed. It adds little to the three earlier biographies on which it is based; its main interest is literary.
2. About 1631 Cresacre More wrote a biography of his greatgrandfather; this was, for many years, the best known biography. Until 1828 it was ascribed to Cresacre's brother, Father Thomas More. There are a few notes on the family that give the book a special value.
3. This biography and Roper's notes were the basis of several short nineteenth-century accounts of Sir Thomas More's life, and of the biography by Sir James Mackintosh (1830).
4. The first substantial addition to knowledge of Sir Thomas More and his times, after the sixteenth century, came with the publication from 1826 of the *Letters and Papers of the Reign of*

Henry VIII, edited at first by J. S. Brewer, and later by James Gairdner. Full use of this new material was made by Father Thomas E. Bridgett in his *Life and Writings of Sir Thomas More* (1891).
See Preface to this book.
5. *Sir Thomas More and His Friends* by E. M. G. Routh (1934); a good biography that added to our knowledge of More's connexion with the City of London; it was overshadowed by the deservedly popular:
6. *Thomas More* by R. W. Chambers (1935) which emphasized the literary and political significances of More's life.
7. *A Portrait of Sir Thomas More* by Algernon Cecil (1937), an illuminating commentary rather than a plain biography.
8. *Erasmus, Tyndale and More* by W. E. Campbell (1949), a pleasantly discursive book by one of the editors of the reprint of More's English Works.

IV. GENERAL

The footnotes to this book give the titles of many books and articles about Sir Thomas More.
For the general history of the times, the reader should consult the bibliography in J. D. Mackie, *The Earlier Tudors* (Oxford History of England, 1952).
There is a useful guide to books on the Reformation in T. M. Parker, *The English Reformation to 1558* (1950). The reader is recommended to study *The Reformation in England*, Vol. I (the King's Proceedings), by Father Philip Hughes (1950).
A French scholar's estimate is given in *The Reformation in England* by G. Constant. The first volume covers the years 1509 to 1547. This English translation (by Canon R. E. Scantlebury) was published in 1934.

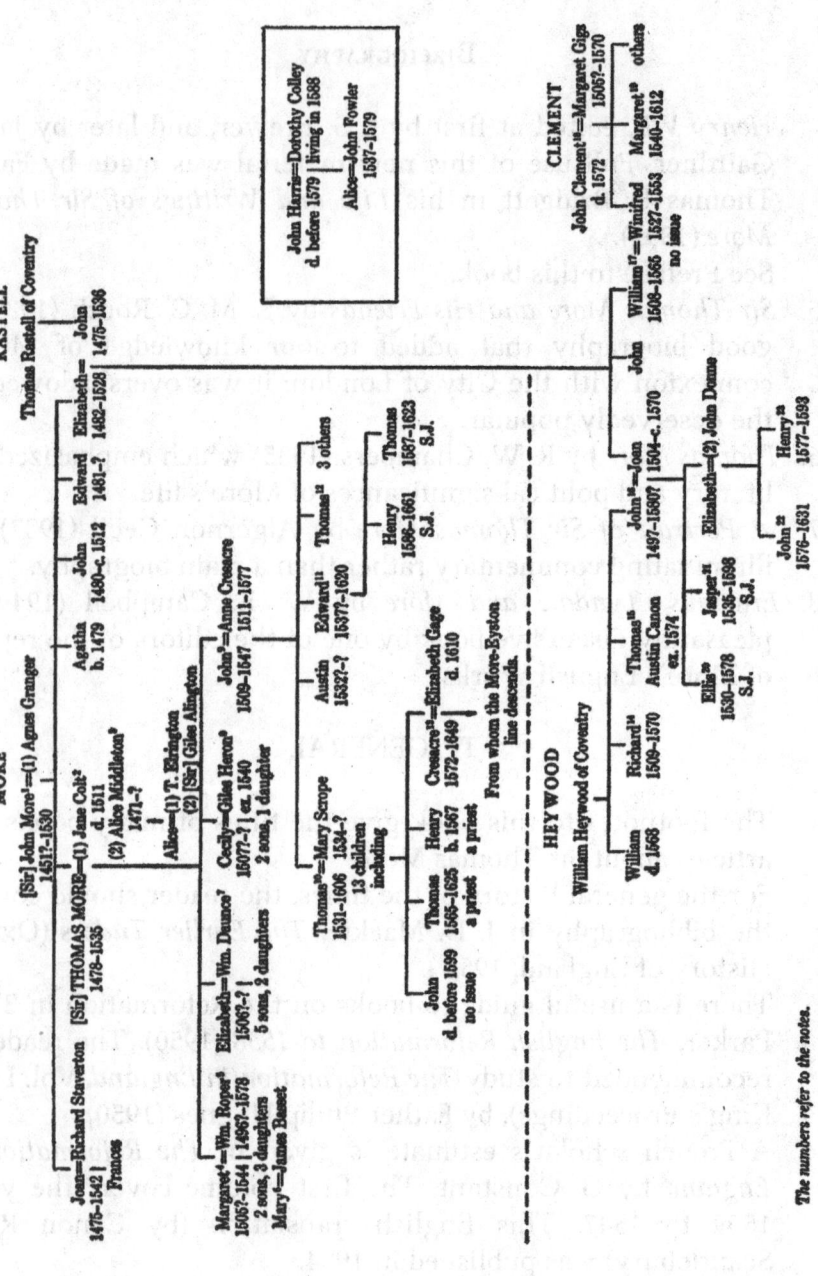

APPENDIX

GENEALOGICAL TABLE

Notes

1. His fourth wife, Alice Clerke, had to leave Gobions after the attainder of Sir Thomas More. She died in 1544.
2. Jane Colt's niece, Margery Kemp, married George Cavendish, the biographer of Wolsey.
3. Dame Alice More was granted a pension of £20 a year in 1536 and she was allowed to retain her husband's lands in Battersea. There was a dispute about this property between her and William Roper, and Sir Giles Alington brought them to agreement. See Roper, pp. xli-xlii.
4. Margaret Roper was imprisoned in the Tower after her father's death, and closely questioned about his papers, and her possession of his head. She kept both. To quote Cresacre More, "after a short imprisonment she was at last sent home to her husband." See Harpsfield, pp. 78-9. She died in 1544 and was buried in the More Tomb in Chelsea Church.
5. For the life of William Roper, see Roper, pp. xxix-xliii. He was imprisoned in 1542 for aiding a Catholic; he was summoned before the Council in 1568 "for having relieved with money certain persons who have departed out of the realm." These were no doubt Catholics who had fled the country. He gave a bond for his good behaviour. He was a prosperous lawyer, and active in local affairs in Kent. Both he and William Rastell were made freemen of Canterbury on 14th September, 1555. Evidently the authorities kept an eye on him, but he continued his generous help to Catholics. He was buried in the Roper vault at St. Dunstan's, Canterbury.
6. For Mary Basset, see Harpsfield, p. 83; also Ro. Ba. (E.E.T.S.) Ap.

I.

7. For Daunce, see note (9) below.
8. For Giles Heron, see Roper, pp. 117-122. The exact nature of the treason that brought him to Tyburn is not clear. Cromwell's memoranda show that he was concerned to get Heron convicted. There is no tradition that Heron died for conscience' sake; it may be noted, however, that of the five who were hanged with him, three were monks and one a friar.
9. John More was imprisoned after his father's death, but, to quote his grandson, Cresacre, "because they had sufficiently fleeced him before and could get little by his death, he got at last his pardon and liberty." His wife, Anne Cresacre, had inherited the Barnborough (W.R.) estate, so "he enjoyed a competent living to keep him out of a needy life." In 1543 he was involved with his brother-in-law, William Daunce, and John Heywood (who married Joan Rastell) in the attempt to establish a charge of heresy against Cranmer. How this was frustrated is dramatised by Shakespeare in Henry VIII, v. iii. John More and William Daunce were pardoned in April 1544 (L.P. Vol. XIX, i, 444). John Heywood made a public recantation at St. Paul's Cross three months later. Amongst those who suffered at Tyburn as a result of this affair were John Larke, who had been appointed parish priest at Chelsea by Sir Thomas More, and John Ireland who had been More's chaplain. See Roper, pp. 115-117.
10. Thomas More (shown in the composite group) lived at Barnborough. Gobions was restored to him by Queen Mary on condition that it was leased to the Princess Elizabeth for her life; he entered into possession on the death of Queen Elizabeth, and lived there for his last three years. He was several times imprisoned. See Harpsfieldy pp. 294-296.
11. Cresacre More had a poor opinion of his uncle Edward (p. 291), but his two sons, Henry and Thomas, were both Jesuit

priests and suffered imprisonment. See DJM.B.
12. This Thomas More became a "professed minister" (Cresacre More, p. 291).
13. Cresacre's eldest brother John (seen in the composite group) died before his father, and as the second and third sons were priests, Cresacre inherited Gobions (or More Place) and Barnborough. He had been trained at Douai, but left when he became the only son to inherit the estates. One of his daughters was Gertrude (Helen) More, O.S.B. (1606-1633), whose "Spiritual Exercises" were edited by Fr. Augustine Baker. His grandson, Basil, sold Gobions as his grandfather, Sir Basil Brook, had lost his property as an active royalist who was also a Catholic; two of Basil's sisters were imprisoned during the Popish Plot, and one, Margaret, died in prison (1679). Basil's great-grandson, Father Thomas More, S.J. (1722-1807) was the last heir male of Sir Thomas More. His younger brother, Christopher, was also a Jesuit priest. His youngest sister, Mary (1732-1807), was Prioress of the English Convent, Bruges, and played a heroic part during the Napoleonic Wars. Fr. Thomas More was provincial in England from 1769 until the suppression of the Society in 1773, when Bishop Challoner made him his vicar-general for the ex-Jesuits. It would be possible, and is tempting, to fill many pages with notes about the great company of those who can claim to be descended from Sir Thomas More. Many were secular priests, or entered one of the religious orders.
14. Richard Heywood was a law partner of William Roper. He was present at More's trial. See Roper, p. 96.
15. Thomas Heywood was an Austin Canon at St. Osyth's, Essex. He was executed in 1574 for saying Mass "in Lady Brown's house in Cow Lane," (Holbom).
16. John Heywood "the mad, merry wit," dramatist and musician, frequented More's house at Chelsea and stayed at Gobions. He fled to Louvain in July 1564 and outlived most of his

contemporaries. See A. W. Reed, Early Tudor Drama.
17. William Rastell, printer and lawyer, fled to Louvain with the Clements in December 1549; he returned in 1553 soon after his wife's death; she was buried in St. Peter's, Louvain. Under Mary he was made a judge. He edited and arranged for the printing of More's English Works (1557, London) and possibly of the Latin Works (Louvain) which appeared in 1565 the year of his death. He was buried with his wife. See A. W. Reed, Early Tudor Drama.
18. John Clement and his wife took refuge in Louvain from 1549 to 1553, and again from 1563. He died in Malines in 1572.
19. Margaret Clement was Prioress of St. Ursula's, Louvain, and founder of St. Monica's, the mother community of the present one at Newton Abbot.
20. Ellis Heywood was a Fellow of All Souls, Oxford (1548); he wrote Il Moro, an entirely fanciful account of a conversation at Sir Thomas More's house at Chelsea. He was, for a time, secretary to Cardinal Pole. He entered the Society of Jesus in 1566. Died at Louvain, 1578. See DJN.B.
21. Jasper Heywood was a page to Princess Elizabeth. Fellow of All Souls, Oxford (1558); translated three of Seneca's tragedies. Entered the Society of Jesus, 1562; succeeded Persons as Superior of English Mission. Imprisoned, 1583, and then banished. Died at Naples, 1598. See D.N.B.
22. John Donne, a poet and later appointed Dean of St. Paul's, 1621, was brought up as a Catholic but apostatized about 1600.
23. His brother Henry died in Fleetwood Prison in 1593; he was charged with harbouring a priest, William Harrington, who suffered at Tyburn in 1594.
24. John Harris fled to Louvain early in Elizabeth's reign. He taught Latin and Greek. His wife was still alive in 1588. His son-in-law, John Fowler, printed the Antwerp edition of the *Dialogue of Comfort* (1573).